MIWK PUBLISHING
CARRY ON CONFIDENTIAL

Andy Davidson is the editor of the Carry On website www.carryonline.com and a regular commentator on British television, radio and films. He is co-author of *Auton: Shock & Awe* and has also co-written *MAXIMUM POWER!* a humorous guide to the BBC TV series Blake's 7 which is available to order from www.miwk.com. His latest book, *Jaunt: An Unofficial Guide to the Tomorrow People*, is available now from Miwk Publishing.

He lives in a shed at the bottom of a garden in Surrey and bakes a mean pasty.

D1438456

ANDY DAVIDSON

CARRY ON CONFIDENTIAL

CARRY ON CONFIDENTIAL

ISBN 978-1-908630-01-8

Copyright © Miwk Publishing Ltd 2012.
This revised edition published September 2013.

First published February 2012 by Miwk Publishing Ltd.
Miwk Publishing, 12 Marbles Way, Tadworth, Surrey KT20 5LW.

The right of Andy Davidson to be identifed as the author of this work have been asserted in accordance with the Copyright, Designs and Patents Act 1988.

A CIP catalogue record for this book is available from the British Library.

Cover artwork by Jess Pillings, cover design by Robert Hammond.
Book design by Mark Frost.

Typeset in Sabon, Univers and Jack Armstrong.

Printed in Great Britain by TJ International, Padstow, Cornwall.

Paper stock used is natural, recyclable and made from wood grown in sustainable forests. The manufacturing processes conform to environmental regulations.

WWW.MIWKPUBLISHING.COM

This product was lovingly Miwk made

For Wendy, who has been subjected to more innuendo and sauce than anyone should have to endure during the writing of this book. She watched a few Carry On films with me, too.

Also, for my beautiful children, Harriet, Emily and Sam

CONTENTS

INTRODUCTION

At the heart of the Carry On films is a sense of British-ness - of the stiffest of stiff upper lips. The dinner scene at the end of Carry On Up the Khyber sums-up the series in a perfect plaster-dusted nutshell: the whole world is going to hell in a handcart but there is a little oasis of stillness that is forever silly, innocent and fun. To me, that is what these wonderful British comedies are all about. The Carry Ons are not about real life, they are about getting the most out of life and laughing at everything that gets in the way, be it a daffodil-brandishing matron or your world quite literally crumbling around your ears.

If you're a child of the 1970s and 80s, as I was, you should be forgiven for going through life believing that a little bit of sauciness never does anyone any harm. Big bouncing boobs are a fascination. Enormous, handbag-wielding battle axes and thin weedy men are funny and you stifle a titter when anyone asks you for a large one.

When I grew up, you couldn't escape the Carry On gang. There were annual Christmas specials on the telly, Sid James, Hattie Jacques, Kenneth Williams and the rest of the gang starred in TV sitcoms, children's programmes and light entertainment shows. They were on the radio and in the pages of newspapers, magazines and even in my treasured Look-In comics. There was the Carry On Laughing series and if you hadn't had your fill of the Carry On team by the time the ad breaks rolled around, there was Barbara Windsor flogging fresh cream cakes, Kenneth Williams turning the toilet blue or Hattie Jacques patting her ample bottom encouraging you to shop at Asda.

The Carry On team were everywhere.

I have been a devoted fan of the Carry Ons for as long as I can remember. I spent much of my childhood in Brighton and I've felt part of the Carry On family ever since I first saw the gang having the time of their lives on the seafront in Carry On at your Convenience and Carry On Girls.

It is an obsession that's grown over the years. In 1994, l set up a website to celebrate the Carry On team. Carry On Line existed in various forms for the next 15 years but following the death of "Mr Carry On", Peter Rogers in 2009, I reluctantly decided to close the website. But my love of these comedy classics and the people who made them wouldn't go away.

Carry On Confidential is an affectionate guide to the Carry Ons, compiled with the assistance of fans around the world, Gerald Thomas' original and mind-bogglingly comprehensive production notes, and a deeper knowledge of the films than is quite healthy in a supposedly normal human being. It's technical, nit-picky and, at times a little snide, but it's all done with a love for these wonderful films and the equally wonderful people who made them. This book is designed to be enjoyed with the films, pointing out gags, bloopers and tit-bits of useless information as you watch them.

It'll also tell you where to go if you want to find out where the films were made. It may be true that the Carry On team rarely ventured far from home, but wherever they did go, this book documents not only the precise location but also tells you how you can find it. There's a QR link for every major location which, when scanned with a smartphone, will fire up Google Maps and Sat-nav you right to the door – or the rain-soaked field. If you don't have a smartphone don't worry because I have also included the full address and postcode of every location, so you will still be able to find them.

Now for a brief word about the format - for each blooper, gaffe or, for want of a better word, nit-pick, I have included a specific time where it can be spotted. These times are based on the Special Edition DVD of the film - the kind that have been widely available since 2003 and are generally accepted as the definitive versions of each film.

The timings are specific and verified. Don't do what I did and play the DVD on a laptop - as I found out to my cost – because then the timings creep about all over the place. Use a real, honest-to-goodness DVD player or PS3. If you don't own the DVD and you're watching a Carry On via TV, video or elsewhere, the book will still point out where you should look but some of the timings might be a little out.

Now – a word of caution. Many of the places listed in this book are private businesses and residences and I urge you to respect the privacy of the owners of these locations. With that, all that remains it to say I hope you enjoy reading this book as much as I did writing it.

Andy

Oh, go on then...
Carry On!

THE CARRY ON FILMS:
CARRY ON SERGEANT

1958

Screenplay by Norman Hudis
Based on "The Bull Boys" by RF Delderfield, with additional material by John Antrobus
Music Composed & Conducted by Bruce Montgomery
Played by the Band of the Coldstream Guards

CAST   CHARACTER

William Hartnell	Sergeant Grimshaw
Bob Monkhouse	Charlie Sage
Shirley Eaton	Mary Sage
Eric Barker	Captain Potts
Dora Bryan	Norah
Bill Owen	Corporal Bill Copping
Charles Hawtrey	Peter Golightly
Kenneth Connor	Horace Strong
Kenneth Williams	James Bailey
Terence Longdon	Miles Heywood
Norman Rossington	Herbert Brown
Gerald Campion	Andy Galloway
Hattie Jacques	Captain Clark
Cyril Chamberlain	Gun Sergeant
Gordon Tanner	1st Specialist
Frank Forsyth	2nd Specialist
Basil Dignam	3rd Specialist
John Gatrell	4th Specialist
Arnold Diamond	5th Specialist
Martin Boddey	6th Specialist
Ian Whittaker	Medical Corporal
Bernard Kay	Injured Recruit
Anthony Sagar	Stores Sergeant
Alec Bregonzi	1st Storeman
Graham Stewart	2nd Storeman
Alexander Harris	3rd Storeman
Pat Feeney	4th Storeman
Edward Judd	5th Storeman
Ronald Clarke	6th Storeman
David Williams	7th Storeman
Martin Wyldeck	Mr Sage
Helen Goss	Mary's Mum
Terry Scott	Sergeant O'Brien
John Matthews	Sergeant Matthews

Edward Devereaux..Sergeant Russell
Leigh Madison ....Sheila
Recruits: Jack Smethurst, Haydn Ward, Brian Jackson, Graydon Gould, Don McCorkindale, Jeremy Dempster, Leon Eagles, Terry Dickenson, Malcolm Webster, Henry Livings, Patrick Durkin, Derek Martinus, James Villiers, Michael Hunt

CREW

Production Manager ....Frank Bevis
Art Director ....Alex Vetchinsky
Director of Photography ....Peter Hennessy
Editor..Peter Boita
Camera Operator..Alan Hume
Assistant Director ....Geoffrey Haine
Sound Editor..Seymour Logie
Sound Recordists ....Robert T MacPhee
                                                                           & Gordon K McCallum
Continuity...Joan Davis
Make-up ....Geoffrey Rodway
Hairdresser...Stella Rivers
Dress Designer ....Joan Ellacott
Casting Director...Betty White
Set Dresser ....Peter Murton
Titles ....Pentagon Films
Producer..Peter Rogers
Director...Gerald Thomas

Nat Cohen & Stuart Levy present a Peter Rogers production.
Distributed by Anglo Amalgamated Film Distributors Ltd

PRODUCTION DETAILS:

Budget: £74,000
Filming: 24th March 1958 – 2nd May 1958
Duration: 83m
Black & White
General Release: September 1958, Certificate U
TV Premiere: 1st October 1966, ITV (ABC Midlands & North)
Home Video: 1988 (VHS), 2001 (DVD)

IN A NUTSHELL:

"The biggest shower that ever reigned in the British Army!"

As retirement looms ever closer, Sergeant Grimshaw (William Hartnell) dreams of ending his Army career on a high with his last intake of recruits taking away the coveted Star Squad prize. But Grimshaw's hopes appear dashed when he meets his recruits, a group of misfits and malcontents who have anything but the right stuff.

Charlie Sage (Bob Monkhouse) received his call-up papers on his wedding day, so a life in the Army is the last thing on his mind. His fellow recruits show similar promise –

hypochondriac Horace Strong is convinced that he's suffering every disease known to medical science (and a few more besides), James Bailey (Kenneth Williams) resents the very presence of the Army and would much rather focus on the finer things in life. Pete Golightly (Charles Hawtrey) is the clumsiest recruit in this, or any other man's army; and Miles Heywood's (Terence Longdon) father is a top ranking General – he only enlisted because he is slumming it.

Faced with this set of the rawest of raw recruits, Sergeant Grimshaw resigns himself to going out with somewhat less than a bang. But what Dragon Platoon lack in the right stuff, they make up for out of sheer determination.

REVIEW:

The Carry On films get off to an unassuming start with perhaps the most traditionally comic entry in the series. Of course, at the time the team had no idea they were taking the first steps on the road to becoming a comedy legend. Carry On Sergeant was simply a low-budget, stand-alone comedy; just another in the string of movies put together by Rogers and Thomas. When Carry On Sergeant went before the cameras, there were no particular expectations other than that "The Bull Boys" (as it was originally known) should make people laugh and return a profit. Judged solely on these criteria it was a resounding success.

The template for the early days of the Carry On series doesn't really change much over the next few films. The Hudis mantra was to write comedies with which the audience could readily identify and the best way to do that was to throw characters into situations that cinema audiences would find familiar. With National Service still in effect back in 1958, a squad of raw recruits was just such a situation.

Similarly, we've all been to hospital at least once in our lives and everyone knows that if you don't know the time you should (at least back then) ask a policeman. Thus, the Carry On formula as we know and love it was set from day one. A group of misfits thrown together into a situation where they are seemingly doomed to heroic and hilarious failure, only for them to ultimately pull together and emerge covered in something resembling glory.

The characters (or caricatures) that we have come to know and love as the series goes on are embryonic in this first outing, but their foundations are there. Kenneth Williams represents the puffed up voice of rebellion, haughty and somewhat snobbish; Charles Hawtrey is the delicate, effete fool and Kenneth Connor a bumbling mess of nerves. He's a somewhat heightened "everyman" character with whom the audience can easily sympathise.

Uniquely, but unsurprisingly given the film's roots, the hero of the film is a relative straight man, in the form of Bob Monkhouse. It's all-too-easy to forget Monkhouse's presence in Carry On Sergeant as he is one of a very few characters in these films whom you could consider "normal". He keeps the story moving, moons over Shirley Eaton when the fancy takes him but other than providing an introduction to the Carry On team, he does not ultimately do much of any consequence.

The real stars of the film are those who'll go on to become the Carry On team, although whether that was the intent at the time is debatable; I would suggest not. The success of Carry On Sergeant is the serendipitous result of a talented cast of seasoned professionals, a scriptwriter who knows his onions and a director with a flair for physical comedy all coming together to create a perfect vignette of life in National Service.

Carry On Sergeant may be simply an affectionate look at a world gone by, but the quality of the talent involved before and behind the camera hints that the team is capable of something truly special. It is an unremarkable film which does a simple job and it does it well. It's easy to see why it was a success. It is not so much a touchstone for the series as a tantalising glimpse of what they might eventually become.

VIEWING NOTES:

- *Carry On Sergeant started life as "The Bull Boys", a script by RF Delderfield about ballet dancers being conscripted into National Service. Delderfield's script had done the rounds of various studios before Peter Rogers decided that with work the concept had the makings of a successful film. Rogers handed the script to staff writer Norman Hudis and the rest became Carry On history.*

- *The film went into production as "The Bull Boys" and retained the name until distributors voiced their dislike for the title. The next Rogers/Thomas comedy was already well into production with a similar cast, story and - as was agreed by all concerned - a similar chance of being a hit. The decision was taken to put a common title around both films, so that audiences could identify more readily with these new comedies.*

- *Why was "Carry On" chosen? In 1957, there had been a relatively successful film from director Val Guest called "Carry On Admiral". Peter Rogers and Stuart Levy of Anglo Amalgamated suggested the Carry On moniker because it was a common enough expression in both the military and medical professions and, not entirely coincidentally, because with a relatively successful film already out there, audiences who enjoyed Carry On Admiral were more likely to go and see more of these new Carry On films.*

- *Peter Rogers originally offered the director's chair to Val Guest, but Guest's decision to decline was followed by a general murmur around Pinewood that the film had little chance of success. Gerald Thomas, who had worked as a director for Rogers before on Time Lock, Circus Friends and The Duke Wore Jeans, agreed to direct.*

- *At the time Carry On Sergeant was made, none of the "regular" Carry On team were established as major stars of the big screen, so their names appear further down the cast list in favour of then-marquee names like Hartnell and Monkhouse.*

- *Charles Hawtrey was by far the most well-known of the Carry On regulars at this point and as a result is billed above his future team members for the first and only time. Billing would become a particular issue with Hawtrey throughout the series.*

- *Although he wouldn't re-join the Carry On team until much later, Terry Scott plays a minor role in Carry On Sergeant, as Sergeant Paddy O'Brien.*

- *On viewing the final cut, studio executives knew they had a success on their hands, but the magnitude of that success was unprecedented. Carry On Sergeant was the third highest grossing film in the UK for 1958, after Bridge over the River Kwai and Dunkirk. At the domestic box office, Carry On Sergeant on its initial run went on to take a record breaking £500,000.*

CARRY ON COCK-UPS:

Technical	34m 47s	Keep a close eye on Charles Hawtrey during the scene where the fire extinguishers go off. As the chaos worsens, his cries of dismay do not match the movement of his mouth.
Continuity	36m 56s	Take a look at the board as Eric Barker posts the training progress charts. It is clearly marked as the 29th intake. At the end of the film, as the troops are passing out, they are named as the 60th.

Technical	37m 20s	This shot of the recruits being shown how to strip a Bren gun will get another airing in a few minutes.
Continuity	37m 31s	Terence Longdon's socks do not quite look like regulation Army issue!
Continuity	37m 55s	But that little mistake is rectified in the next shot.
Continuity	41m 11s	William Hartnell throws the rifle back to Kenneth Connor after narrowly avoiding being impaled. When we see Connor catch the gun, it is pointing in the opposite direction to which it was thrown.
Technical	44m 50s	Look familiar? That is the exact same clip of a Bren gun being stripped down as was used in the earlier montage.
Continuity	52m 12s	Kenneth Williams is not standing next to Terence Longdon in the shot before Kenneth Connor grabs the rope.
Continuity	52m 17s	But he appears there long enough to jeer at Connor's performance before disappearing again in the next shot.
Technical	1h 16m 52s	It goes without saying that the band isn't actually playing the music live as the parade is filmed, but director Gerald Thomas does a great job of disguising the fact until now. At this point you can see that the band's actions aren't synched with the music.

LOCATIONS:

Time	Description	Address	Also seen in	Location Link
1m 39s	The Sages' wedding scene - exterior	St Mary & All Saints Church Windsor End Beaconsfield HP9 2JW		
3m 39s	Arrival at Heathercrest	Pinewood Studios North entrance Pinewood Road Iver Bucks SL0 0NH	Carry On Spying	
5m 23s	Heathercrest barracks	Stoughton Road Guildford Surrey GU2 9RU		

40m 15s	Bayonet training	Black Park Black Park Rd Wexham Slough Berks SL3 6DR	Carry On Cabby Carry On Cowboy Carry On Cleo Carry On Screaming! Carry On Don't Lose your Head Carry On Dick	

CARRY ON ABROAD:

Let's go, Sergeant – *Belgium*
Attention Recruits! – *Denmark*
Cheer Up! Chest Out! – *Germany*

CARRY ON COLLECTING:

• Postcard featuring UK One-Sheet poster released in 1998 by The London Postcard Company as part of their "British Classics Series 1" collection.

• Die-cast 1:60 scale army truck featuring Carry On Sergeant poster art by Lledo, 1998, as part of their "Days Gone" range. The lettering on the truck incorrectly states "Heathercroft National Service Depot".

• A Carry On first class stamp and associated collectibles (presentation pack, postcard) featuring UK Quad poster for Carry On Sergeant released in 2008 by Royal Mail.

SOUNDTRACK:

Main title theme available on "Carry On"
Various Artists, CD, Silva Screen 2005
Themes, cues and dialogue taken from the original film soundtracks

"Carry On Suite" (incorporating music from Sergeant, Teacher and Nurse) available on "The Carry On Album, Music from the Films"
Gavin Sutherland & the Prague Philharmonic Orchestra, CD, ASV 1999
Newly performed renditions of classic Carry On themes

DVD:

Carry On Sergeant
Warner Home Video, 2001
PAL, Region 2 (Europe, Middle East & Japan), Black & White

The Ultimate Carry On (Carry On Sergeant – Carry On Screaming!)
Warner Home Video, 2001
PAL, Region 2 (Europe, Middle East & Japan), Colour, Black & White

DeAgostini Carry On DVD part-work
DeAgostini/Carlton, 2003
PAL, Region 2 (Europe, Middle East & Japan), Colour, Black & White

Carry On – The Ultimate Collection
ITV Studios Home Entertainment, 2006
PAL, Region 2 (Europe, Middle East & Japan), Colour, Black & White
Special features as for individual ITV/Carlton/Optimum releases

Carry On Sergeant
Optimum Home Releasing, 2008
PAL, Region 2 (Europe, Middle East & Japan), Black & White
Main feature, Commentary track (Dora Bryan, Terence Longdon, Shirley Eaton), Stills, Trivia, Trailer

Carry On Collection Vol.1 (Sergeant / Teacher / Nurse / Constable)
Optimum Home Releasing, 2008
PAL, Region 2 (Europe, Middle East & Japan), Black & White
Special features as for individual ITV/Carlton/Optimum releases

Carry On – The Ultimate Collection
ITV Studios Home Entertainment, 2008
PAL, Region 2 (Europe, Middle East & Japan), Colour, Black & White
Special features as for individual ITV/Carlton/Optimum releases

VHS:

Carry On Sergeant
Warner Home Video, 1988
PAL, Black & White

Carry On Sergeant
Warner Home Video, 1995
PAL, Black & White

Carry On Sergeant / Carry On Cleo
Warner Home Video, 1993
PAL, Black & White, Colour

Carry On Sergeant / Carry On Cleo
Warner Home Video, 2001
PAL, Black & White, Colour

DeAgostini Carry On VHS part-work
DeAgostini/Carlton, 2003
PAL, Colour, Black & White

CARRY ON NURSE

1959

Screenplay by Norman Hudis
Based on an idea by Patrick Cargill & Jack Beale
Music Composed & Conducted by Bruce Montgomery

CAST

CHARACTER

Kenneth Connor	Bernie Bishop
Shirley Eaton	Staff Nurse Dorothy Denton
Charles Hawtrey	Humphrey Hinton
Hattie Jacques	Matron
Terence Longdon	Ted York
Bill Owen	Percy Hickson
Leslie Phillips	Jack Bell
Joan Sims	Student Nurse Stella Dawson
Susan Stephen	Nurse Georgie Axwell
Kenneth Williams	Oliver Reckitt
Wilfrid Hyde-White	The Colonel
Susan Beaumont	Frances James
Norman Rossington	Norm
Jill Ireland	Jill Thompson
Joan Hickson	Sister
Ann Firbank	Helen Lloyd
Irene Handl	Mrs Hickson
Susan Shaw	Jane Bishop
Michael Medwin	Ginger
Cyril Chamberlain	Bert Able
Brian Oulton	Henry Bray
Edward Devereaux	Alec Lawrence
Frank Forsyth	John Gray
John Matthews	Tom Mayhew
Graham Stewart	George Field
David Williams	Andrew Newman
Patrick Durkin	Jackson
June Whitfield	Meg
Marianne Stone	Mrs Alice Able
Hilda Fenemore	Rhoda Bray
Martin Boddey	Perkins
Rosalind Knight	Nurse Nightingale
Marita Stanton	Rose Harper
Leigh Madison	Miss Winn
Stephanie Schiller	New Nurse
Christine Ozanne	Fat Maid
Lucy Griffiths	Trolley Lady

John van Eyssen .... Mr Stephens
Harry Locke.. Mick
Anthony Sagar .... 1st Ambulance Driver
Fred Griffiths .... 2nd Ambulance Driver
Charles Stanley .... Porter
Shane Cordell... Attractive Nurse
Jeremy Connor.. Jeremy Bishop
John Horsley.. Anaesthetist

CREW

Production Manager .... Frank Bevis
Art Director .... Alex Vetchinsky
Director of Photography .... Reginald Wyer
Editor... John Shirley
Camera Operator... Alan Hume
Assisstant Director .... Stanley Hosgood
Sound Editor... Roger Cherrill
Sound Recordists .... Robert T MacPhee & Bill Daniels
Continuity.. Penny Daniels
Make-up .... George Blackler
Hairdresser... Pearl Orton
Dress Designer .... Joan Ellacott
Casting Director.. Betty White
Set Dresser .... Arthur Taksen
Nurses uniforms.. Courtaulds
Producer... Peter Rogers
Director.. Gerald Thomas

Nat Cohen & Stuart Levy present a Peter Rogers production.
Distributed by Anglo Amalgamated Film Distributors Ltd

PRODUCTION DETAILS:

Budget: £71,000
Filming: 3rd November 1958 - 12th December 1958
Duration: 86 min
Black & White
General Release: March 1959, Certificate U
TV Premiere: 25th March 1967, ITV (ABC Midland & North)
Home Video: 1979 (VHS/Betamax), 2001 (DVD)

IN A NUTSHELL:

"From the same stars and team that gave you the sensational comedy success "Carry On Sergeant""

Haven Hospital is having trouble living up to its name. Staff and patients alike live in fear of Matron's (Hattie Jacques) footsteps coming down the hall. The nurses in the men's ward are hardly what you would call competent and there is an extremely demanding patient in a private room who seems to think the whole place exists only for his benefit.

Journalist Ted York (Terence Longdon) is rushed to Haven Hospital with appendicitis. While he is in there York's editor commissions the journalist to write a series of articles based on hospital life. He is not short of inspiration: Boxer Bernie Bishop (Kenneth Connor), is rushed into hospital with an injured hand following another disastrous fight; Mister Hinton (Charles Hawtrey) spends his days plugged into the hospital radio, shutting out the clamour of the ward and the bookish Oliver Reckitt (Kenneth Williams) is struggling to come to terms with his feelings for his friend's sister Jill (Jill Ireland).

When newcomer Jack Bell's (Leslie Phillips) operation to remove a bunion is delayed, he shares the champagne he set aside for a romantic evening with his girlfriend with his fellow patients and between them they decide to carry out the operation themselves.

Matron will be pleased.

REVIEW:

Far more than its predecessor, Carry On Nurse is the film which kicked off the Carry On films as a series and it's easy to see why Rogers and Thomas realised, that, when making the film, they had the beginnings of something remarkable.

The premise of Carry On Nurse is nothing new. Once more, we have a group of strangers thrown together in to a situation where they have to learn to work together to overcome adversity. As in Carry On Sergeant, it is really the developing characters who grab the audience's attention.

Kenneth Williams, Charles Hawtrey, Joan Sims, Shirley Eaton, Hattie Jacques and Bill Owen work brilliantly together, sparking off each other in every scene. The situation and plot become secondary to the spectacle of the cast doing what they do best and it is there that Carry On Nurse, like so many other Carry Ons, really makes an impact.

The main characters in Nurse are essentially the same as in the previous film, their personas changing little, as most will continue to do through their Carry On careers. Williams is once more the officious know-all but he remains an immensely likeable character. Hawtrey is the idiotic child, and Connor the repressed romantic lead. Together with Hattie Jacques, Leslie Phillips and Joan Sims a core team is emerging.

Where Carry On Nurse is less successful is in the way it continually tries to tug at the viewer's heart strings. The early Carry Ons are often accused of being overly sentimental, even mawkish, and Carry On Nurse is without doubt the worst offender. There's the love story between York and Nurse Denton, the growing romance between Reckitt and Jill, Bernie Bishop's tender moment with his son at the end of the film and plenty more little tear-jerkers along the way. There is simply too much emotion coming from too many different characters. Nevertheless, Carry On Nurse remains a delightfully intimate film which, despite slipping into the odd moment of soppiness, is never too far away from a gag or a spot of sauciness.

VIEWING NOTES:

- *The continuity of the series is established from the very start as Carry On Nurse opens with a fresh arrangement of Bruce Montgomery's theme from Sergeant. The same tune, in various forms, will stay with the series until Carry On Cruising, when ill-heath caused the composer to part company with the Carry Ons.*

- Patrick Cargill and Jack Beale received a credit for their play "Ring for Catty" being the inspiration behind Nurse. Betty Box, wife of Peter Rogers and herself the producer of the phenomenally successful "Doctor" films (directed by Gerald Thomas' brother, Ralph), had seen the original play and suggested the idea of a medical Carry On. That's as far as their "inspiration" went, according to Norman Hudis, who cites his own experience when hospitalised for an appendix operation (and the fact that his wife, Rita, was a nurse) as the real inspiration for the film. Rita Hudis was, many years later, a medical advisor on the hugely popular US sitcom, M*A*S*H*.

- Terence Longdon's character is based on Hudis' own experience. Hudis remained grateful for, as he called it, the "free research" he was able to conduct when he was hospitalised with appendicitis shortly after he began work on the script.

- Ring for Catty was later adapted by Rogers and Thomas in a more complete form as the 1962 film "Twice Around the Daffodils".

- In November 1958, while Carry On Nurse was still in production, and while Carry On Sergeant was doing great business at the cinema, Peter Rogers announced to the press that the next four Carry On comedies would be Carry On Teacher, Carry On Constable, Carry On Regardless and What A Carry On. Three of those eventual films we all know and love. Sadly, however, there is no record of the plans for What a Carry On.

- Rogers also went on to announce that the "regular" Carry On team would henceforth be Kenneth Williams, Kenneth Connor, Charles Hawtrey, Hattie Jacques, Bill Owen, Terence Longdon and Joan Sims.

- Several cast members had trouble staying awake under the hot studio lights when snuggled up in their comfy hospital beds. Kenneth Connor is said to have been told off on several occasions when his snoring was picked up by the sound man. True to form, Kenneth Williams disputed claims that he fell asleep until Gerald Thomas produced photographic evidence. While he snoozed between scenes, the director had photographed him with a sign placed against his chest reading "Spare a copper guv for an ex- actor available on HP to careful users".

- Outside the Colonel's room is a sign bearing the name of the doctor who's treating him – one Dr Taksen. Arthur Taksen was the set dresser on the film.

- The daffodil gag, arguably the film's most famous scene, was dreamed up by Norman Hudis' mother in law, Ethel Good. It was originally intended to appear earlier in the film but was moved to the end, providing a comedic, rather than a romantic, climax. The originally-planned ending saw Ted York and Nurse Denton leaving the hospital to start their future together.

- Carry On Nurse was for many years the biggest grossing UK film on US soil. It received its US premiere at the Granada Theatre in downtown Dallas where cinema-goers were presented with a plastic daffodil on arrival. Thousands of the fake flowers had been specially imported from Japan to coincide with the launch.

- Carry On Nurse was the highest grossing film in the UK and the biggest UK film worldwide in 1959. By the end of the year it had reaped well over £1,000,000 at the box office. In the US alone, 1959 receipts were £357,000 within 12 months of the film's launch. By December 1961, the film had broken all records, netting £725,000 from US and Canadian sales. In Los Angeles, Carry On Nurse played for 56 consecutive weeks.

- *Anglo Amalgamated offered Peter Rogers a five-film contract based on the success of Carry On Nurse. At the same time, Gerald Thomas wisely renegotiated his contract with Peter Rogers so that he would, henceforth, take an equal share of the profits.*

- *Wilfrid Hyde-White contacted Peter Rogers in anger following the release of Carry On Nurse, humiliated about the incident with the daffodil. However, as fans will know there is nothing shown on screen of the daffodil doing anything or being anywhere it should not have been.*

- *Bernie Bishop's son, seen at the end of the film, is played by Kenneth Connor's real son, Jeremy. Jeremy Connor would go on to appear in Carry On Dick as one of the criminals seen at the beginning of the film. He also appeared in Carry On Behind as the student eating an ice cream at the start of the film; and Carry On England as "Gunner Hiscocks". There was also an un-credited walk-on part for Connor in Carry On Constable.*

- *Carry On Admiral was re-released shortly after Carry On Nurse in an attempt to boost sales, but cinema audiences were no fonder of the film the second time around.*

CARRY ON COCK-UPS:

Technical	3m 10s	There is a lack of punctuation on the signage around the hospital as witnessed by the sign on the outside of the ward – "Mens surgical ward", "Sisters room".
Continuity	5m 24s	Take a look at the newspaper Wilfrid Hyde-White is holding. He's looking at the Birmingham Card. In the following close-up, it reads "Fontwell Card." A moment later, when Harry Locke enters the room he's not holding the paper at all.
Technical	12m 06s	As the nurses pull down Kenneth Connor's shorts you can see he's wearing a garment underneath.
Continuity	21m 21s	Bill Owen puts his tobacco tin and papers on the bedside table. We then cut to a different angle they're still sitting on his chest when he lights up. The camera then cuts back to the original angle and there they are on the bedside table.
Continuity	21m 32s	The piece of paper Irene Handl's holding moves as we go from one camera angle to the next.
Continuity	34m 54s	As the nurse gives Kenneth Connor a bed bath he is positioned differently as we switch between shots.
Technical	43m 32s	Harry Locke briefly slips out of his Irish accent after Joan Sims calls him a clumsy oaf.
Trivia	1h 03m 51s	Something of an unusual Carry On debut but the feet you see here represent Bernard Bresslaw's first on-screen appearance. Bresslaw quite literally stood in for Terence Longdon, whose legs were deemed not manly enough for the shot. Bresslaw, the previous year, had a hit single with "Mad Passionate Love", the B-side of which, ironically, was "You Need Feet".

Continuity	1h 06m 18s	Leslie Phillips holds the book differently over the next few shots as we switch between camera angles.
Continuity	1h 16m 27s	The nurse tied up in bed only has her hands tied, not her feet. The lazy mare could have easily got up by herself!
Continuity	1h 17m 09s	Kenneth Williams holds the scalpel differently over the next few shots. He's also holding Leslie Phillips' foot in the close-up, whereas in the previous shot he was gripping his lower leg.

LOCATIONS:

Time	Description	Address	Also seen in	Location Link
1m 31s	Baby Show	South Lodge Pinewood Studios Iver Heath Bucks SL0 0NH	Carry On Screaming! (Dan Dan's public convenience was situated to the right of the gates).	
1m 55s	Exterior – Haven Hospital	Heatherden Hall Pinewood Studios Iver Heath Bucks SL0 0NH	Carry On up the Khyber Carry On Camping Carry On at your Convenience Carry On Again Doctor Carry On England	
34m 32s	The dashing doctor walks out into the hospital grounds	Clubhouse entrance (back of Heatherden Hall) Pinewood Studios Iver Heath Bucks SL0 0NH	Carry On up the Khyber Carry On Don't Lose your Head Carry On Camping Carry On Henry	

CARRY ON CUTTING:

- *The scene where Hickson's (Bill Owen) weights fall off and roll around the floor would have ended on a gag considered too saucy for audiences of the day. As filmed, the next line was "Nurse, please pick up Mr Hickson's balls".*

- *In a sequence cut from the final print, Nurses Dawson and Axwell return from a night out. Dawson, in an attempt to hide from Sister, manages to hide in the mortuary and gives the porter (played by Charles Stanley) the shock of his life.*

- *Ted York's operation scene was also lost to the editor's scissors. After the anaesthetist (played by John Horsley) sedates York, he drifts off into happy oblivion, where he dreams he is Nurse Axwell's Mr Right.*

CARRY ON ABROAD:

40 Degrees of Love – *Belgium*
Isn't it Wonderful, Doctor? – *Denmark*
Laughing Gas & Beautiful Girls – *Finland*
A Thermometer for the Colonel – *France*
Carry On – 41 Degrees of Love – *Germany*
Nurse does all the Work – *Greece*
40 Degrees of Love – *South America*

CARRY ON COLLECTING:

• Ring for Catty: A Play in Three Parts by Patrick Cargill & Jack Beale
  S French, 1956, ISBN: B0000CJKFB

• Postcard featuring UK Quad poster released in 1998 by The London Postcard Company as part of their "British Classics Series 3" collection.

SOUNDTRACK:

Main title theme available on "Carry On"
Various Artists, CD, Silva Screen 2005
Themes, cues and dialog taken from the original film soundtracks

"Carry On Suite" (incorporating music from Sergeant, Teacher and Nurse) available on "The Carry On Album, Music from the Films"
Gavin Sutherland & the Prague Philharmonic Orchestra, CD, ASV 1999
Newly performed renditions of classic Carry On themes

DVD:

Carry On Nurse
Warner Home Video, 2001
PAL, Region 2 (Europe, Middle East & Japan), Black & White

The Ultimate Carry On (Carry On Sergeant – Carry On Screaming!)
Warner Home Video, 2001
PAL, Region 2 (Europe, Middle East & Japan), Colour, Black & White

DeAgostini Carry On DVD partwork
DeAgostini/Carlton, 2003
PAL, Region 2 (Europe, Middle East & Japan), Colour, Black & White

Carry On – The Ultimate Collection
ITV Studios Home Entertainment, 2006
PAL, Region 2 (Europe, Middle East & Japan), Colour, Black & White
Special features as for individual ITV/Carlton/Optimum releases

Carry On Nurse
Optimum Home Releasing, 2007
PAL, Region 2 (Europe, Middle East & Japan), Black & White
Special Features: Commentary (Shirley Eaton, Terence Longdon), Stills, Trivia, Trailer

Carry On Collection Vol.1 (Sergeant / Teacher / Nurse / Constable)
Optimum Home Releasing, 2008
PAL, Region 2 (Europe, Middle East & Japan), Black & White
Special features as for individual ITV/Carlton/Optimum releases

Carry On – The Ultimate Collection
ITV Studios Home Entertainment, 2008
PAL, Region 2 (Europe, Middle East & Japan), Colour, Black & White
Special features as for individual ITV/Carlton/Optimum releases

VHS:

Carry On Nurse
EMI, 1979
PAL, Black & White

Carry On Nurse
Warner Home Video, 1988
PAL, Black & White

Carry On Cabby / Carry On Nurse
Warner Home Video, 1993
PAL, Black & White

Carry On Nurse
Warner Home Video, 1997
PAL, Black & White

Carry On Cabby / Carry On Nurse
Warner Home Video, 2001
PAL, Black & White

DeAgostini Carry On VHS partwork
DeAgostini/Carlton, 2003
PAL, Colour, Black & White

BETAMAX:

Carry On Nurse
EMI, 1979
PAL, Black & White

CARRY ON TEACHER

1959

Screenplay by Norman Hudis
Music Composed & Conducted by Bruce Montgomery

CAST   CHARACTER

Kenneth Connor	Gregory Adams
Charles Hawtrey	Michael Bean
Leslie Phillips	Alistair Grigg
Joan Sims	Sarah Allcock
Kenneth Williams	Edwin Milton
Hattie Jacques	Grace Short
Rosalind Knight	Felicity Wheeler
Cyril Chamberlain	Alf
Ted Ray	William Wakefield
Richard O'Sullivan	Robin Stevens
George Howell	Billy Haig
Roy Hines	Harry Bird
Diana Beevers	Penny Lee
Jacqueline Lewis	Pat Gordon
Carol White	Sheila Dale
Paul Cole	Atkins
Jane White	Irene
Larry Dann	Boy

CREW

Production Manager	Frank Bevis
Art Director	Lionel Couch
Director of Photography	Reginald Wyer
Editor	John Shirley
Camera Operator	Alan Hume
Assistant Director	Bert Batt
Sound Editor	Leslie Wiggins
Sound Recordists	Robert T MacPhee & Gordon K McCallum
Continuity	Tilly Day
Make-up	George Blackler
Hairdresser	Olga Angelinetta
Dress Designer	Laurell Staffell
Casting Director	Betty White
Set Dresser	Terence Morgan
Producer	Peter Rogers
Director	Gerald Thomas

Nat Cohen & Stuart Levy present a Peter Rogers production. Distributed by Anglo Amalgamated Film Distributors Ltd

PRODUCTION DETAILS:

Budget: £78,000
Filming: 15th March 1959 – 24th April 1959
Duration: 86m
Black & White
General Release: August 1959, Certificate U
TV Premiere: 24th December 1966, ITV (ABC Midland & North)
Home Video: 1988 (VHS), 2001 (DVD)

IN A NUTSHELL:

"You roared at Carry On Sergeant! Howled at Carry On Nurse! You'll be convulsed by Teacher"

William Wakefield (Ted Ray), acting head of Maudlin Street School, spots an advertisement for a brand new "super" school close to his home town and decides the time has come to move on. He needs a spotless record in order for his application to succeed and with a forthcoming inspection by the Ministry of Education (in the guise of Rosalind Knight) and child psychologist Alistair Grigg (Leslie Phillips), Wakefield turns to his staff for help to ensure everything goes according to plan.

Wakefield briefs the teaching staff (Kenneth Williams, Hattie Jacques, Kenneth Connor, Joan Sims and Charles Hawtrey) of his plans but he is overheard by pupil Robin Stevens (a young Richard O'Sullivan). While the teaching staff vow to make the inspection a success, Stevens and his fellow pupils, who have grown fond of the head, decide to sabotage the inspection in the hope that Wakefield will be forced to stay on as headmaster.

So begins an increasingly hilarious war of attrition between the teachers and pupils with each fighting for their own noble cause.

REVIEW:

Carry On Teacher follows the same basic premise as its predecessors but the additional twist of making the Carry On team the victims, rather than the instigators of chaos, gives a whole new perspective on the incompetent misfits. This kind of conflict would be used to drive a number of other Carry Ons but never quite as successfully as in Carry On Teacher.

If the central premise of a film is people being terribly nasty to each other it helps if you can engage readily with both sets of protagonists and understand just why they are behaving the way they are. Later entries like Carry On England tend to forget this important factor with less than pleasant results.

Carry On Teacher is at its heart even more of a tear-jerker than Carry On Nurse, but the emotion here isn't force fed. It emerges naturally through the course of the film until we reach the genuinely beautiful moment when the pupils reveal their plan to Wakefield. Honestly, it gets me every time.

The Carry On regulars do their usual sterling work - everyone plays their role to perfection in what is my favourite of the series to date. It is a perfectly composed film, all wrapped up neatly in just a couple of locations. The growing sense of panic as the teachers realise that the children's bad behaviour is orchestrated and escalating is brilliantly delivered and of course, funny. Properly, laugh out loud funny.

Ted Ray's headmaster is the perfect Carry On foil and it's a shame the people at ABC put their collective foot down and ended what could have been a long and happy Carry On career. Ray's character is more than a little inspired by Will Hay and that's something I would love to have seen more of as part of the team dynamic.

There is genuine warmth to the early Carry On films and it is never more evident than in Carry On Teacher. Maudlin Street School is a warren of wood-panelled corridors, tiny offices and cluttered classrooms and the studio-bound nature of the piece, together with a smaller than usual cast (of adults, at least) lends the film a unique intimacy. It's a cosy little film, made all the more so by the fact that everyone is acting with the very best of intentions, even if the means hardly justify the ends.

VIEWING NOTES:

- *Once again, the continuity of the Carry On series is bolstered by yet another arrangement of Bruce Montgomery's theme from Carry On Sergeant.*

- *Ted Ray was under contract to ABC Pictures but had not been used by them until now. Rogers and Thomas had previously cast Ray in their 1959 film, "Please Turn Over", alongside Joan Sims, Charles Hawtrey and Leslie Phillips and, following Teacher, there were plans to make him a regular member of the team. Sadly, following ABC's insistence that under contract, Ray could not appear in any more of Rogers' films, he was dropped.*

- *Bruce Montgomery's theme whenever the children go out into the playground is based on the nursery rhyme "Girls and Boys go out to Play".*

- *Typecast from a ridiculously early age, Richard O'Sullivan plays a character called Robin. Although this is O'Sullivan's sole contribution to the Carry On series, he was on Gerald Thomas' list of preferred actors to appear in Carry On England.*

- *The Daily Express of February 4 1959 ran a less than flattering story about "plump" Joan Sims entering a health farm for two weeks in order to lose weight in preparation for her role as Miss Allcock.*

- *Leslie Phillips had to work hard on his pronunciation of "Allcock" at the censor's request. For the line to remain uncut, he was told to say the word flat, without any emphasis on either the "all" or "cock". You could write a Carry On about that alone.*

- *Larry Dann makes his first Carry On appearance as one of the student saboteurs. An accidental meeting with Gerald Thomas 15 years later led to his being invited to the team full-time from Carry On Behind.*

- *Morrissey's 1988 album "Viva Hate" features a song by the name "Late Night Maudlin Street", the title an amalgamation of the school from Carry On Teacher and Bill Naughton's book of short stories, "Late night on Watling Street".*

CARRY ON COCK-UPS:

Trivia	1m 40s	The clock on the front of the school building reads 4.30 - that's a late home time for the poor pupils at Maudlin - no wonder they're so militant.
Technical	7m 13s	Keep an eye on the chap sitting behind Kenneth Connor's left shoulder as he tries to keep a straight face.
Trivia	8m 05s	Needless to say the new school is as fictional as the town - there is no Offord New Town in Sussex.
Technical	41m 51s	Watch the door frame and wall as Leslie Phillips staggers back into the corridor. The whole wall moves as he tries to grab it for support.
Trivia	50m 10s	Those pupils can't be all bad - that's a gun on the mantel behind Kenneth Connor, thankfully untouched!
Technical	50m 33s	Look closely and you can see that the phone is attached to Kenneth Connor's hand by a hidden ring connecting it to his finger.
Technical	51m 11s	Charles Hawtrey was clearly under the impression that his screams would be dubbed in later. While he's mouthing dismay there's not a sound to be heard coming from his lips.
Continuity	1h 07m 04s	Who is the chap sitting between Leslie Phillips and Charles Hawtrey? Phillips specifically mentions there are five teachers in the room and the mysterious character isn't referred to in any way. Nevertheless, he is there throughout the entire scene, including the itchy conga.

LOCATIONS:

Time	Description	Address	Also seen in	Location Link
1m 40s	Maudlin Street School	South Lodge Pinewood Studios Iver Heath Bucks SL0 0NH	Drayton Green Primary School Drayton Grove Ealing London W13 0LA	

CARRY ON ABROAD:

Come On Professor – *Denmark*
Loud, Lovable Teacher – *Germany*
Go On, Sir – *Hungary*
Way to go, Teacher – *Portugal*

CARRY ON COLLECTING:

• As part of their "British Classics Series 1" collection. Postcard featuring UK One Sheet poster released in 1998 by The London Postcard Company.

• Die-cast 1:60 scale school bus featuring Carry On Teacher poster art by Lledo, 1998, as part of their "Days Gone" range.

SOUNDTRACK:

Main title theme available on "Carry On"
Various Artists, CD, Silva Screen 2005
Themes, cues and dialog taken from the original film soundtracks

"Carry On Suite" (incorporating music from Sergeant, Teacher and Nurse) available on "The Carry On Album, Music from the Films"
Gavin Sutherland & the Prague Philharmonic Orchestra, CD, ASV 1999
Newly performed renditions of classic Carry On themes

DVD:

Carry On Teacher
Warner Home Video, 2001
PAL, Region 2 (Europe, Middle East & Japan), Black & White

The Ultimate Carry On (Carry On Sergeant – Carry On Screaming!)
Warner Home Video, 2001
PAL, Region 2 (Europe, Middle East & Japan), Colour, Black & White
DeAgostini Carry On DVD partwork
DeAgostini/Carlton, 2003

PAL, Region 2 (Europe, Middle East & Japan), Colour, Black & White
Carry On – The Ultimate Collection
ITV Studios Home Entertainment, 2006
PAL, Region 2 (Europe, Middle East & Japan), Colour, Black & White
Special features as for individual ITV/Carlton/Optimum releases

Carry On Teacher
Optimum Home Releasing, 2007
PAL, Region 2 (Europe, Middle East & Japan), Black & White
Special Features: Commentary (Paul Cole, Larry Dann, Richard O'Sullivan), Stills, Trivia, Trailer

Carry On Collection Vol.1 (Sergeant / Teacher / Nurse / Constable)
Optimum Home Releasing, 2008
PAL, Region 2 (Europe, Middle East & Japan), Black & White
Special features as for individual ITV/Carlton/Optimum releases

Carry On – The Ultimate Collection
ITV Studios Home Entertainment, 2008
PAL, Region 2 (Europe, Middle East & Japan), Colour, Black & White
Special features as for individual ITV/Carlton/Optimum releases

VHS:

Carry On Teacher
Warner Home Video, 1988
PAL, Black & White

Carry On Screaming! / Carry On Teacher
Warner Home Video, 1993
PAL, Colour, Black & White

Carry On Teacher
Warner Home Video, 1997
PAL, Black & White

Carry On Screaming! / Carry On Teacher
Warner Home Video, 2001
PAL, Colour, Black & White

DeAgostini Carry On VHS partwork
DeAgostini/Carlton, 2003
PAL, Colour, Black & White

CARRY ON CONSTABLE

1960

Screenplay by Norman Hudis
Based on an idea by Brock Williams
Music Composed & Directed by Bruce Montgomery

CAST   CHARACTER

CAST	CHARACTER
Sidney James	Sergeant Frank Wilkins
Eric Barker	Inspector Mills
Kenneth Connor	Constable Charlie Constable
Charles Hawtrey	Special Constable Timothy Gorse
Kenneth Williams	Constable Stanley Benson
Leslie Phillips	Constable Tom Potter
Joan Sims	WPC Gloria Passworthy
Hattie Jacques	Sergeant Laura Moon
Shirley Eaton	Sally Barry
Cyril Chamberlain	Thurston
Joan Hickson	Mrs May
Irene Handl	Distraught Woman
Terence Longdon	Herbert Hall
Jill Adams	WPC Harrison
Freddie Mills	1st Crook
Brian Oulton	Store Manager
Victor Maddern	Criminal-looking Man
Joan Young	Suspect
Esma Cannon	Deaf Old Lady
Hilda Fenemore	Agitated Woman
Noel Dyson	Vague Woman
Tom Gill	1st Citizen
Anthony Sagar	2nd Citizen
Eric Corrie	3rd Citizen
Frank Forsyth	4th Citizen
John Antrobus	5th Citizen
Robin Ray	Assistant Manager
Michael Balfour	Matt
Diane Aubrey	Honoria
Ian Curry	Eric
Mary Law	1st Shop Assistant
Lucy Griffiths	Miss Horton
Peter Bennett	Passer-by
Jack Taylor	Cliff
Eric Boon	Shorty
Janetta Lake	Girl with Dog
Dorinda Stevens	Young Woman
Ken Kennedy	Wall-eyed Man

CREW

Production Manager .... Frank Bevis
Art Director .... Carmen Dillon
Director of Photography .... Ted Scaife
Editor.. John Shirley
Camera Operator... Alan Hume
Assistant Director .... Peter Manley
Sound Editor.. Leslie Wiggins
Sound Recordists .... Robert T MacPhee & Bill Daniels
Continuity.. Joan Davis
Make-up .... George Blackler
Hairdresser... Stella Rivers
Dress Designer .... Yvonne Caffin
Set Dresser .... Vernon Dixon
Casting Director... Betty White
Producer... Peter Rogers
Director.. Gerald Thomas

A Peter Rogers production.
Distributed by Anglo Amalgamated Film Distributors Ltd

PRODUCTION DETAILS:

Budget: £82,500
Filming: 9th November 1959 – 18th December 1959
Duration: 86m
Black & White
General Release: February 1960, Certificate A
TV Premiere: 24th June 1967, ITV (ABC Midland & North)
Home Video: 1988 (VHS), 2001 (DVD)

IN A NUTSHELL

"That hilarious Carry On shower in another riot of laughter"

The country is in the grip of a national flu epidemic. People everywhere are dropping like flies. Police Sergeant Wilkins is so short-staffed that he is forced to turn to raw recruits to police the area.

Help comes in the shape of three officers, fresh out of training school; Constable Charlie Constable (Kenneth Connor), Constable Stanley Benson (Kenneth Williams) and Constable Tom Potter (Leslie Phillips). Together with Special (very special) Constable Timothy Gorse (Charles Hawtrey), they patrol the streets bringing chaos where there was order, helping bank robbers and even indulging in a spot of accidental shoplifting. They may have the best of intentions, but the thin blue line looks decidedly shaky with these recruits on patrol.

REVIEW:

With Ted Ray now firmly back under contract to ABC, Rogers and Thomas had to find a new lead for their next Carry On and the craggy features of former Hancock botherer Sid James fitted the bill beautifully. But this is a very different Sid to the Carry On persona we've come to know and love. In Constable, and indeed in his next few Carry Ons, Sid is a fatherly, authoritarian figure. Left to handle the new recruits, he spends the film not leering and cackling but getting increasingly frustrated by the well-intentioned idiots under his command. As a foil for the rest of the team, Sid is perfectly cast.

Hawtrey, Williams, Connor and Phillips tread a beat that is all too familiar. There is little that is new in terms of the premise; bumbling fools thrust into a situation way above their capabilities – but the old Hudis magic is at work again. It's the banter, the set pieces and the hi-jinx that make Carry On Constable such a delight. We all know what we are going to get when we go to see a Carry On and audiences at the time did as well. But there's a definite evolution in the regular characters and their personas; Williams is more arch, louder and of course completely oblivious to his many faults, Hawtrey is a doe-eyed simpleton with not a bad word to say about anyone and Connor is a sexually frustrated bumbler.

Phillips takes the straight(er) role once again and plays the charmer we know and love. Everyone's growing into the personas with which they would later become so famous.

Constable also sees the Carry On team enjoy their first real taste of location filming and as they head into the streets of Ealing it's a genuine thrill to see them out and about in the "real" world. Treading the same streets as us doesn't make the Carry On team any more real. If anything it makes their antics seem even more surreal.

There is a lot going on in Carry On Constable. It is a film which covers an awful lot of ground, both in comedy and geographically. By now, there's a slightly more adult tone creeping into the films – the pursuit of sex is dealt with in not entirely innocent terms and it's dealt with quite a few times, albeit in a suggestive, cheeky way. Carry On Constable is a step onward from its predecessors. There's a great deal of confidence in the way the story is delivered in what is an accomplished, relaxed and tremendously fun – and funny - film.

VIEWING NOTES:

- *The title "Carry On Copper" was briefly considered as the title but it was pointed out to Peter Rogers that "Copper" could be considered a somewhat derisory name.*

- *The original outline submitted by Brock Williams for Constable became the basis for the Rogers/Thomas film, "The Big Job".*

- *For research purposes, Norman Hudis spent a week at a real police station, observing the real life antics of the Force for comic inspiration. Hudis found the process so depressing he reported back to Rogers that he'd rather forget the idea of a Police Carry On altogether.*

- *Once again, we hear the same theme music as was used in three previous three Carry On films. Bruce Montgomery was aiming for a more jazzy arrangement of the theme for this outing and struggling to get the right result, he turned to future Carry On composer Eric Rogers for help.*

- *Originally, the role of Sergeant Wilkins was intended for Ted Ray, who made such an impact in the previous film, Carry On Teacher. But with Ray under contract to ABC,*

Rogers was unable to use the actor in future projects and so a replacement was sought. Enter Sid James and the birth of a Carry On legend.

• *Carry On Constable was the first in the series to be given an A certificate, thanks in no small measure to the shower scene. The next time anyone tells you the Carry On films were sexist, remind them that the first nude scene in the series was a male one.*

CARRY ON COCK-UPS:

Continuity	2m 16s	Sid James is suddenly standing in a different position to the previous shot.
Continuity	15m 23s	Kenneth Williams is still walking the dog along South Ealing Road except he's further back down the same road than he was when he began. No wonder the dog bolts, it's probably fed up with going round the same block.
Continuity	15m 23s	There's a lone dog on the street behind Kenneth Williams which turns up again looking lost as he rounds the corner a few moments later.
Technical	18m 59s	The iron railings in a police station should be rather sturdier than the ones on display here. The banister wobbles alarmingly as Joan Sims turns to go back down.
Continuity	20m 17s	Take a look at the keys on the rack behind Leslie Phillips. When you see them a few moments later behind Kenneth Connor the large set is hanging on a different hook.
Technical	24m 30s	The chamber pot that Charles Hawtrey kicked getting out of bed won't stop rattling, so he ad-libs a "be quiet" at it.
Technical	25m 32s	You have to admire Charles Hawtrey's dedication to proper eyesight. Would you go into the shower wearing your glasses?
Continuity	38m 56s	The squad car, when driving is registered as 892 PPC. When parked, it's UUV 133.
Continuity	59m 27s	When Leslie Phillips runs up the drive he's holding the dog's lead in his left hand. When we see him enter the garden, it is in his right hand.
Continuity	1h 20m 26s	When Leslie Phillips falls from the landing down to the hall, you can see the mattress that has been put there to soften his fall.

LOCATIONS:

Time	Description	Address	Also seen in	Location Link
1m 31s	Police Station	Hanwell Library Cherington Road Ealing London W7 3HL		
4m 54s	Approaching the police station	Heading North at approx 3-27 South Ealing Road Ealing London W5 4QT		
5m 42s	Approaching police station	Then along the Avenue Ealing Approx 25 The Avenue Ealing London W13 8JR		
14m 00s	Walking the dog	North on the South Ealing Road Ealing London W5 4QT		
14m 08s	A distraught Irene Handl calls for help	10 Lothair Road Ealing London W5 4TA		
15m 48s	Kenneth chases the dog around the corner onto Lothair Road	Basement flat at 6A Lothair Road Ealing London W5 4TA		

22m 13s	Kenneth and Charles on patrol	Along Manor Road to the corner of Drayton Road Ealing London W13 0HY		
33m 27s	Police parade	West, along Pinewood Green and past 92 Pinewood Green Iver Heath Bucks SL0 0QH	Carry On Cabby Carry On Camping Carry On Behind	
34m 58s	Charles is stationed	Corner of Drayton Ave and Manor Road Ealing London W13 0JA		
35m 20s	Kenneth Connor's patrol begins	71-77 South Ealing Road Ealing London W5 4QB		
36m 11s	Kenneth is left outside the Drayton Road Post Office	He follows Victor Maddern East up Manor Road Ealing London W13 0HY		
38m 59s	Sid is picked by the squad car	Corner of Alacross Rd and Lothair Rd Ealing London W5 4HT		
39m 13s	Kenneth Connor hears a "murder"	39 The Avenue Ealing London W13 8JR		

41m 14s	Esma Cannon crosses the road	West Ealing Railway Station Drayton Green Rd London W13 0NQ		
48m 35s	Fluffy the cat goes missing	St. Mary's Church 135 Church Road Hanwell, London W7 3QP		
59m 17s	Leslie takes the dog for a walk to the boss' house	104 Pinewood Green Iver Heath Bucks SL0 0QH		
1h 02m 17s	Kenneth Connor and Joan Sims walk along Manor Road, Ealing - beside the railway tracks.	Manor Road, Ealing London W13 0HY The footbridge has disappeared behind the Access Self Storage depot on the Manor Road side but the bridge can be accessed via a replacement bridge to the rear of the building.		
1h 04m 37s	FH Rowse, where Kenneth and Charles drag up	96 Broadway, West Ealing London W13 0SY They exit via the side entrance on Green Man Lane and head back towards the Broadway.		
1h 09m 35s	Walking along the alleyway behind Church Gardens, an abandoned van is discovered	Entrance to Church Gardens, Ealing Approx 11 Church Place Ealing London W5 4HN		

1h 10m 04s		The wage snatch van is discovered outside the Rose & Crown pub Ealing London W5 4HN		
1h 16m 57s	The baddies' lair	Oakhurst House St Stephen's Road Ealing, London W13 8JB The old house was demolished in 1963 and on the location now stands the White Ledges Housing development.		

CARRY ON ABROAD:

Watch out for the Cops – *Denmark*
Watch out for the Police – *Finland*
These Sturdy Policemen – *Germany*
Go on, Policemen – *Hungary*
Four Agents of Disorder – *South America*

CARRY ON COLLECTING:

• Die-cast 1:60 scale Morris Police van featuring Carry On Constable poster art by Lledo, 1998, as part of their "Days Gone" range.

• Postcard featuring UK One Sheet poster released in 1998 by The London Postcard Company as part of their "British Classics Series 1" collection.

SOUNDTRACK:

Main title theme available on "Carry On"
Various Artists, CD, Silva Screen 2005
Themes, cues and dialog taken from the original film soundtracks

DVD:

Carry On Constable
Warner Home Entertainment, 2001
PAL, Region 2 (Europe, Middle East & Japan), Black & White

The Ultimate Carry On (Carry On Sergeant – Carry On Screaming!)
Warner Home Video, 2001
PAL, Region 2 (Europe, Middle East & Japan), Colour, Black & White

DeAgostini Carry On DVD partwork
DeAgostini/Carlton, 2003
PAL, Region 2 (Europe, Middle East & Japan), Colour, Black & White

Carry On – The Ultimate Collection
ITV Studios Home Entertainment, 2006
PAL, Region 2 (Europe, Middle East & Japan), Colour, Black & White
Special features as for individual ITV/Carlton/Optimum releases

Carry On Constable
Optimum Home Releasing, 2007
PAL, Region 2 (Europe, Middle East & Japan), Black & White
Special Features: Commentary (Leslie Phillips), Stills, Trivia, Trailer

Carry On Collection Vol.1 (Sergeant / Teacher / Nurse / Constable)
Optimum Home Releasing, 2008
PAL, Region 2 (Europe, Middle East & Japan), Black & White
Special features as for individual ITV/Carlton/Optimum releases

Carry On – The Ultimate Collection
ITV Studios Home Entertainment, 2008
PAL, Region 2 (Europe, Middle East & Japan), Colour, Black & White
Special features as for individual ITV/Carlton/Optimum releases

VHS:

Carry On Constable
Warner Home Video, 1988
PAL, Black & White

Carry On Constable / Carry On Jack
Warner Home Video, 1993
PAL, Black & White

Carry On Constable
Warner Home Video, 1997
PAL, Black & White

Carry On Constable / Carry On Jack
Warner Home Video, 2001
PAL, Black & White

DeAgostini Carry On VHS part work
DeAgostini/Carlton, 2003
PAL, Colour, Black & White

CARRY ON REGARDLESS

1961

Screenplay by Norman Hudis
Music Composed & Conducted by Bruce Montgomery

CAST	CHARACTER
Sidney James	Bert Handy
Kenneth Connor	Sam Twist
Charles Hawtrey	Gabriel Dimple
Joan Sims	Lily Duveen
Kenneth Williams	Francis Courtenay
Bill Owen	Mike Weston
Liz Fraser	Delia King
Terence Longdon	Montgomery Infield-Hopping
Hattie Jacques	Sister
Fenella Fielding	Penny Panting
Esma Cannon	Miss Cooling
Stanley Unwin	Landlord
Eleanor Summerfield	Mrs Riley
Ed Devereaux	Mr Panting
Ambrosine Phillpotts	Yoki's Owner
Cyril Chamberlain	Policeman
Joan Hickson	Matron
Terence Alexander	Trevor Trelawney
Norman Rossington	Referee
Sydney Tafler	Club Manager
Molly Weir	Bird Owner
June Jago	Sister
Eric Pohlmann	Sinister Man
Jerry Desmonde	Martin Paul
Jimmy Thompson	Mr Delling
Howard Marion-Crawford	Wine Organiser
Anthony Sagar	Bus Conductor
Fred Griffiths	Taxi Driver
Bernard Hunter	Wine Waiter
Nicholas Parsons	Wolf
Patrick Cargill	Raffish Customer
Michael Nightingale	Wine Bystander
Kynaston Reeves	Testy Old Man
Fraser Kerr	Houseman
Douglas Ives	Fanatic Patient
Maureen Moore	Pretty Probationer
Ian Whittaker	Shop Assistant
Betty Marsden	Mata Hari
Tom Clegg	Massive Mickey McGee

Freddie Mills ....Leftie
Julia Arnall ....Trudi Trelawney
Joe Robinson ....Dynamite Dan
Jack Taylor ....MC
Lucy Griffiths ....Auntie
Cyril Raymond ....Army Officer
George Street ....Club Reception Man
Ian Wilson ....Advertising Man
Michael Ward ....Photographer
Madame Yang ....Chinese Lady
Nancy Roberts ....Old Lady
Judith Furse ....Formidable Lady
Jack Taylor ....1st Railway Policeman
David Williams ....2nd Railway Policeman
David Stoll ....Distraught Manager
Victor Maddern ....1st Sinister Passenger
Denis Shaw ....2nd Sinister Passenger
Carl Conway ....Man in Health Club
Charles Julian ....Old Man in Ruby Room
Carol Shelley ....Helen Delling
Ian Curry ....Leonard Beamish
Eric Boon ....Second
David Lodge ....Connoisseur

CREW

Associate Producer ....Basil Keys
Art Director ....Lionel Couch
Director of Photography ....Alan Hume
Editor ....John Shirley
Camera Operator ....Dudley Lovell
Assistant Director ....Jack Causey
Unit Manager ....Claude Watson
Sound Editor ....Arthur Ridout
Sound Recordists ....Robert T MacPhee
                              & Gordon McCallum
Continuity ....Gladys Goldsmith
Make-up ....George Blackler
Hairdresser ....Biddy Chrystal
Costumer Designer ....Joan Ellacott
Casting Director ....Betty White
Producer ....Peter Rogers
Director ....Gerald Thomas

A Peter Rogers production
Distributed by Anglo Amalgamated Film Distribution Ltd

PRODUCTION DETAILS:

Budget: £100,000
Filming: 28th November 1960 – 17th January 1961
Duration: 90m
Black & White
General Release: March 1961, Certificate U
TV Premiere: 27th April 1968, ITV (Southern)
Home Video: 1988 (VHS), 2001 (DVD)

IN A NUTSHELL:

Jobs are scarce, but local entrepreneur Bert Handy (Sid James) has hit upon the perfect business idea - an agency where no job is too big or small. The Helping Hands Agency is born and as word spreads soon he is inundated with an influx of new recruits from the local labour exchange, including one of their clerks!

Sam Twist (Kenneth Connor), Gabriel Dimple (Charles Hawtrey), Francis Courtenay (Kenneth Williams), Lily Duveen (Joan Sims), Delia King (Liz Fraser), Mike Weston (Bill Owen) and Montgomery Infield-Hopping (Terence Longdon) find themselves taking on a bewildering series of increasingly odd jobs. A chimpanzee is taken for walkies; there's a disastrous visit to an Ideal Home Exhibition and a boxing match with an entirely unexpected result. Then there is the mysterious stranger (Stanley Unwin) who has an important message for Bert and the gang, if only they could understand a word he says.

REVIEW:

What do you do when you look down your list of standard professions and realise you have run out of ideas? In Carry On Regardless, the very premise of the film is its lack a story – it is a collection of disconnected sketches all loosely strung around the idea of an odd job agency where the employees will do anything, anytime. Proto-Goodies, if you will.

Within such a loose framework you can have Kenneths Connor and Williams playing at Richard Hannay or escorting chimpanzees. You can give Sid his first chance to properly leer at some scantily dressed ladies. There is even room to revive an old favourite with Hattie Jacques in a hospital scene. There's no on-going story as such, although Stanley Unwin does pop by every now and then to speak gobbledygook at the gang. But they cannot understand a word he says, so there's no reason why we should pay it any mind.

The disconnectedness of Carry On Regardless means there's not really much to care about in the film. We would like to think Kenneth Connor's character succeeds in kicking the fags but he probably won't and, if we are honest, we're not all that borthered. But that same disconnectedness means we do get to see Joan Sims getting drunk at a party and Charles Hawtrey in the boxing ring. There are some great routines, some lovely lines and a lot of laughs even if the film is really little more than a cabaret. The sketch format gives the Carry On team a chance to showcase what they can really do in terms of raising a laugh and they do it brilliantly.

The Ideal Home exhibition is a triumph of timing, delivery and sheer idiocy as the entire team manage to destroy every exhibit, all the while screaming with an infectious laughter that's impossible to resist. I honestly could quite happily listen to Joan Sims shrieking with laughter all day. So while *Regardless* is thin on story, it does give way to plenty of gags we wouldn't ordinarily get to see. The Helping Hands agency is an excuse to do any kind of Carry On Norman Hudis and the team could think up and not have to worry about little details like plot.

Carry On *Regardless* is a greatest hits of the Carry On series to date where everyone gets to show what they're best at and at their best the Carry Ons are untouchable.

VIEWING NOTES:

- *The success of the Carry On films worldwide had attracted a number of copycat projects by this time with rival studios, both at home and abroad talking up their own proposed "Carry On" films. "Carry On Doctor" was mooted by production companies in both the UK and US. In the event Peter Rogers issued a statement that the only films the public should consider as legitimate "Carry Ons" would be produced by him and distributed by Anglo Amalgamated.*

- *On a more cynical note, the 1960 film "Dentist in the Chair" was re-released in the US as "Carry On TV" in an attempt to cash in on the Carry Ons' success.*

- *Norman Hudis' original inspiration for the Helping Hands agency was the domestic assistance agency, Universal Aunts, first established in the 1920s and still going today. Find out more at http://www.universalaunts.co.uk.*

- *The shooting of Carry On Regardless was postponed because of the sudden illness of Hattie Jacques who was originally scripted to play a major role in the film. With Hattie out of action, substantial changes were made to the final script and Liz Fraser took on the female lead with Hattie appearing in little more than a cameo.*

- *Further delays to filming were caused by bad weather affecting location shoots. Original plans to film as far afield as West Drayton (oh, the glamour!) were eventually consolidated and instead all the main exteriors were shot in Windsor.*

- *The Role of Infield-Hopping was originally offered to Leslie Phillips, who turned the role down for fear of being typecast. Phillips wouldn't return to the Carry On fold until 1992's Carry On Columbus.*

- *Terence Longdon was offered a long-term contract to continue working on the Carry Ons, but with a US tour with the Old Vic looming and a growing number of offers from other studios, Regardless would become his final entry in the series.*

CARRY ON COCK-UPS:

Continuity	8m 55s	Liz Fraser has just undone her bra but it appears to be refastened when the client re-enters the room.
Continuity	16m 18s	Keep an eye on the cups on the table as Kenneth Williams shows us how attractive he is. Bill Owen's crockery seems to have a mind of its own as the camera switches between wide and close-up shots.

Technical	18m 03s	When Kenneth says "No offence" after the bus pulls away, in the next shot Yoki is seen to be molesting the woman standing behind. The woman, smiling, removes the chimp's offending arm.
Continuity	19m 06s	Look how frayed Yoki's collar is. In the next scene it's pristine.
Technical	22m 33s	Joan Sims crashes into the waiter carrying a tray full of glasses. The glasses are attached to the tray and don't fall off even when the waiter falls and throws it to the side.
Continuity	24m 06s	The flowers on Sid James' desk appear to have wilted somewhat since the previous shot.
Technical	27m 56s	A boom shadow creeps into shot and wiggles about on the top left of the screen as the nurse and doctor look out into the waiting room.
Continuity	37m 36s	The cigarettes and wrapping that Kenneth Connor discarded on the desk before he stood up are in a different position in this shot.
Continuity	46m 28s	As the fight announcer falls out of the ring he takes his microphone with him. In the next shot we see it on the floor of the ring.
Continuity	55m 12s	Kenneth Connor's jump from the train lands him in a puddle between the tracks. Before and after the jump the tracks appear to be laid on concrete but when we see him in the puddle, they're resting on ballast.
Technical	58m 50s	Kenneth Williams is already jumping up and screaming before Charles Hawtrey even appears in shot.
Continuity	58m 52s	Kenneth has also managed a quick costume change since leaving the see-saw and is no longer wearing baggy trousers.
Technical	59m 46s	The bed of the future doesn't look particularly safe or comfortable with wires running down both sides.
Continuity	1h 05m 28s	Take a good look at the fixings on the back of the card sorter that the cleaner has just knocked to the floor. When she puts it back on the shelf, the fixings are at the bottom of the box. In the next scene the box has been turned the other way and the fixings can be seen sticking out of the top.
Technical	1h 24m 48s	The door, entrance and floor have been substituted for a collapsible set. The floorboards can be seen to be falling away as soon as Charles Hawtrey approaches and have already disappeared when the door hits them. As the door falls, keep an eye on the gap to the right and you can see a stagehand pushing it over. When it finally crashes to the ground, the entire set is seen to wobble. Given the destruction surrounding him, Hawtrey does well to flinch as little as he does.

LOCATIONS:

Time	Description	Address	Also seen in	Location Link
2m 06s	Longdon's car pulls up on the corner, outside the labour exchange	1A Fairfield Road West Drayton UB7 8EY The original building is long since gone.		
4m 21s	The gang race towards the Helping Hands Agency	15 Park St Windsor Berks SL4 1LU	Carry On Cabby (opening credits) Carry On Again Doctor Carry On Loving	
16m 54s	Kenneth picks up Yoki the chimp	11 Clarence Crescent, Windsor Berks SL4 5DT	Carry On Up the Jungle	
17m 44s	Kenneth and Yoki are refused entry to the bus	Goswell Road Windsor Berks SL4 1RF Facing the railway bridge.		
18m 10s	Kenneth and Yoki hail a cab	Goswell Road Windsor Berks SL4 1RF On the opposite side of the road to the previous scene.		
18m 43s	The Zoological Gardens	Alexandra Gardens Goswell Road Windsor Berks SL4 1RF		

1h 07m 12s	Kenneth goes to pick up the schoolgirls	Windsor & Eton Central Railway Station, Thames Street Windsor, Berks SL4 1PJ Kenneth meets the girls on the concourse where Café Rouge now stands.	Carry On Loving	

CARRY ON CUTTING:

• *The most notable cut from the final print of Carry On Regardless was a lengthy scene where Charles Hawtrey's character, Gabriel Dimple, was hired to watch over a sleeping client to find out what she said in her sleep. Eleanor Summerfield played the part of Mrs Riley, who predictably fails to make Dimple understand quite why she wants him to spend the night with her.*

• *An additional scene inside the tobacconist's shop Kenneth Connor rushes to for smoky salvation was also cut from the final print.*

CARRY ON ABROAD:

We do Anything – *Denmark*
Carry On...Not Great, Sweetie – *Germany*
Carry On! – *Hungary*
Don't Worry, Go Ahead – *Romania*
Now We take Everything – *Sweden*

CARRY ON COLLECTING:

• Postcard featuring UK One Sheet poster released in 1998 by The London Postcard Company as part of their "British Classics Series 1" collection.

SOUNDTRACK:

Main title theme available on "Carry On"
Various Artists, CD, Silva Screen 2005
Themes, cues and dialog taken from the original film soundtracks

DVD:

Carry On Regardless
Warner Home Video, 2001
PAL, Region 2 (Europe, Middle East & Japan), Black & White

The Ultimate Carry On (Carry On Sergeant – Carry On Screaming!)
Warner Home Video, 2001
PAL, Region 2 (Europe, Middle East & Japan), Colour, Black & White

DeAgostini Carry On DVD partwork
DeAgostini/Carlton, 2003
PAL, Region 2 (Europe, Middle East & Japan), Colour, Black & White

Carry On – The Ultimate Collection
ITV Studios Home Entertainment, 2006
PAL, Region 2 (Europe, Middle East & Japan), Colour, Black & White
Special features as for individual ITV/Carlton/Optimum releases

Carry On Regardless
Optimum Home Releasing, 2007
PAL, Region 2 (Europe, Middle East & Japan), Black & White
Special Features: Commentary (Liz Fraser, Terence Longdon), Stills, Trivia, Trailer

Carry On Collection Vol.2 (Regardless / Cruising / Jack / Cabby)
Optimum Home Releasing, 2008
PAL, Region 2 (Europe, Middle East & Japan), Black & White
Special features as for individual ITV/Carlton/Optimum releases

Carry On – The Ultimate Collection
ITV Studios Home Entertainment, 2008
PAL, Region 2 (Europe, Middle East & Japan), Colour, Black & White
Special features as for individual ITV/Carlton/Optimum releases

VHS:

Carry On Regardless
Warner Home Video, 1988
PAL, Black & White

Carry On Regardless / Carry On Cowboy
Warner Home Video, 1993
PAL, Black & White

Carry On Regardless
Warner Home Video, 1997
PAL, Black & White

Carry On Regardless
Warner Home Video, 2001
PAL, Black & White

DeAgostini Carry On VHS partwork
DeAgostini/Carlton, 2003
PAL, Colour, Black & White

CARRY ON CRUISING

1962

Screenplay by Norman Hudis
from a story by Eric Barker
Music Composed & Directed by Bruce Montgomery & Douglas Gamley

CAST

CAST	CHARACTER
Sidney James	Captain Wellington Crowther
Kenneth Williams	First Officer Leonard Marjoribanks
Kenneth Connor	Doctor Arthur Binn
Liz Fraser	Glad Trimble
Dilys Laye	Flo Castle
Esma Cannon	Bridget Madderley
Lance Percival	Wilfred Haynes
Jimmy Thompson	Sam Turner
Ronnie Stevens	Drunk
Vincent Ball	Jenkins
Cyril Chamberlain	Tom Tree
Willoughby Goddard	Very Fat Man
Ed Devereaux	Young Officer
Brian Rawlinson	Steward
Anton Rodgers	Young Man
Anthony Sagar	Cook
Terence Holland	Handsome Passer-by
Mario Fabrizi	Cook
Marian Collins	Bride
Jill Mai Meredith	Shapely Miss
Alan Casley	Kindly Seaman
Evan David	Bridegroom

CREW

Production Manager	Bill Hill
Art Director	Carmen Dillon
Director of Photography	Alan Hume
Editor	John Shirley
Camera Operator	Dudley Lovell
Assistant Director	Jack Causey
Sound Editors	Arthur Ridout & Archie Ludski
Sound Recordists	Robert T MacPhee & Bill Daniels
Continuity	Penny Daniels
Make-up	George Blackler & Geoffrey Rodway
Hairdresser	Biddy Chrystal
Costume Designer	Joan Ellacott
Casting Director	Betty White
Beachwear for Miss Fraser & Miss Laye by "Silhouette"	

Producer ....Peter Rogers
Director ....Gerald Thomas

A Peter Rogers production. An Anglo Amalgamated film distributed through Warner-Pathe Distribution Ltd

PRODUCTION DETAILS:

Budget: £140,000
Filming: 8th January 1962 – 16th February 1962
Duration: 89m
Colour
General Release: April 1962, Certificate U
TV Premiere: 23rd December 1967; ITV (ABC Midland & North, Anglia)
Home Video: 1986 (VHS), 2001 (DVD)

IN A NUTSHELL:

"That Carry On crew in a luxury laughter-cruise!"

Captain Wellington Crowther (Sid James) runs a tight ship aboard the SS Happy Wanderer but when five crew members are replaced at short notice his latest voyage appears to be anything but smooth sailing.

The ship's new doctor, Arthur Binn (Kenneth Connor) has fallen for one of the female passengers. First Officer Leonard Marjoribanks (Kenneth Williams) causes chaos at every turn and the replacement chef, Wilfred Haynes (Lance Percival) is seasick. Worst of all, the new barman (Jimmy Thompson) doesn't know how to make captain Crowther's favourite tipple, an Aberdeen Angus.

Crowther promises his new crew positions aboard his next command if they manage to get through their inaugural voyage without incident, but with unrequited love on deck and a decidedly unappetising cake in the galley, it looks like his hopes for promotion are sunk.

REVIEW:

The Carry Ons explode into colour for the first time and we're given a tantalising glimpse of the kind of films they will ultimately become. Everything about Cruising is bigger and bolder. While the camaraderie, wide-eyed idiocy and sense of fun is certainly heightened by the fact that we're seeing the team's antics in colour, there's a magic to Carry On Cruising that's hard to define.

The plot, as with all the Hudis films (and this was to prove the last), centres once more around the tried-and-tested formula of an authority figure seeking his subordinates' help to go on to better things. But Sid's role in Cruising takes on a new dimension. He is not just the Captain or the father figure; he's also (gird yourselves) an object of sexual desire. Ironically, in Carry On Cruising, it is Sid who is chased while he tries to remain chaste.

As much as Carry On Nurse is responsible for the Carry On films becoming a series, Cruising is just as important for setting a new template which the films would build on in future instalments. The characters we know and love are fully formed in Cruising - Sid will become lewder, but he is as forthright, world-weary and explosive as ever. Kenneth Williams is arch and knowing - the snobbishness of earlier films is significantly toned down, even if he is rather more Snide than he will ultimately become. Connor is more self-contained and confident and of course he's "phwoar"ing all over the place.

Cruising is a stripped bare version of what the Carry Ons would later become under the authorship of Talbot Rothwell. The seeds of the bawdiness, the lewdness and the outrageousness are all here and Hudis's script is more cheeky, more knowing and far less sentimental than ever before.

Once again the team are thrown into a confined space to spark off each other but they do so in an entirely different style. The Carry Ons are coming of age.

Cruising is a remarkably accomplished film. It's polished, it's funny and it's written with a deftness of wit and charm that the series has only aspired to until now. Carry On Cruising takes the series to an entirely new level.

VIEWING NOTES:

- *Eric Barker's contribution to the film was an initial suggestion to Peter Rogers that a good subject for a Carry On would be a group of holidaymakers on a coach tour. Further refinement of Barker's original idea led to a proposal for "Carry On at Sea".*

- *Charles Hawtrey's absence from Carry On Cruising was exacerbated by a preview notice in the press which claimed that if a new Carry On was being filmed without Hawtrey then it wasn't worth seeing. The actor's agent used this argument as the basis for demands for him to be elevated to star status. Rogers wouldn't give in and, with Hawtrey unwilling to relent; he was omitted from the film. Lance Percival took over the role of chef, having previously been contracted to play the barman.*

- *Joan Sims was originally scheduled to play the role taken on by Dilys Laye but was taken ill just a few days before filming was due to commence.*

- *Vincent Ball, playing the role of Jenkins, became the face of a major advertising campaign for Silvikrin Hair Cream. The advertisements proclaimed that "The Carry On films have been a great success and Silvikrin Hair Cream has been a great success for Mr Ball".*

- *This is the last time we will hear Bruce Montgomery's distinctive Carry On theme. Montgomery was, by this point in his career, suffering with health problems and was unable to finish the score. Australian-born Douglas Gamley completed the music, assisted by Eric Rogers, who had already helped Montgomery with arrangements on previous films.*

- *Small screen stalwart Willoughby Goddard is on the receiving end of Kenneth Connor's George Formby gag. It is unusual to see an actor of Goddard's stature in such a minor role and his credit in the film's titles does lend credence to his having originally been cast in a more important scene. (See Carry On Cutting, below).*

- *The record that inspires Dr Binn's timeless classic "Bella Flo" is Roberto Cardinali's "Bella Marie" and was recorded especially for the production.*

- *P&O maintained a close relationship with the production team throughout the film. Gerald Thomas travelled down to Tilbury Docks to film some initial shots while P&O themselves supplied footage of their liners (watch and you can see the Happy Wanderer is played by more than just one liner).*

• *A premiere for cast and crew was held aboard a P&O liner moored at Southampton and the company even held a competition for when the film was launched to win a £500 luxury cruise to New York on the Canberra.*

CARRY ON COCK-UPS:

Technical	1m 40s	The footage at port in the opening scenes shows a different ship to the one used later in the film. The first liner appears to be the Orsova. Later at about the half-hour mark and throughout the remainder of the film we see the Oronsay, P&O's newest Orient Line ship, launched the same year.
Technical	4m 00s	As Lance Percival makes his first appearance, a boom shadow can be seen on his chef's hat.
Continuity	9m 20s	The piece of freshly carved ham that the chef picks up isn't the same piece he shows Lance Percival. That piece of "fresh" ham is as stiff as a board. No wonder Lance looks sick.
Continuity	29m 35s	When Ronnie Stevens is outside the bar, crowds are lined up along the railing outside, but when he goes through the door, there's nobody visible on deck through the window.
Continuity	32m 18s	Watch the vase on Sid James' desk - when the steward brings in the drinks, the flowers are in water. After Kenneth walks in, at 33m 02s the water is brown. The reason, and momentarily later the water will soon become clear.
Continuity	32m 24s	Keep an eye on the clock above Sid's desk during the alcohol scenes - the hands are fixed at 11.17.
Continuity	35m 05s	After filling the vase to the brim with discarded attempts at an Aberdeen Angus, when we next visit Sid the vase is now only three quarters full. When the vase explodes (and you can hardly blame it) a few seconds later, the liquid it contains is an entirely different colour.
Continuity	37m 38s	The barman has just poured a glass of vodka for Esma Cannon but when we next see her, the second glass is already on the bar, empty. Undaunted, Esma still picks it up as if to drink it.
Continuity	39m 47s	As Dilys Laye and Liz Fraser toast each other, two very full glasses have appeared in front of them (judging from the next shot they appear to be lager). After drinking both the whisky and the whiskey, both tall glasses are empty.
Continuity	1h 18m 15s	Kenneth Williams and Esma Cannon are conspiring about the Captain's party. Look in the background - among others you can see Kenneth Connor and Dilys Laye chatting. As the scene progresses, the extras remain in position, but Dilys' spot is suddenly taken by Sid James, who then walks over to Esma.

Continuity	1h 22m 25s	Keep an eye on the women behind Sid in the upcoming shots. They move around quite a bit from one shot to the next. The woman over his left shoulder (in the green dress) is particularly fidgety.

LOCATIONS:

Filmed entirely at Pinewood Studios with initial establishing shots at Tilbury Docks

CARRY ON CUTTING:

• *In a sequence cut from the final print, a beauty contest was held aboard the Happy Wanderer. Flo and Glad debate whether they should sign up.*

CARRY ON ABROAD:

Girls at Sea – *Denmark*
The Captain Makes Love – *Finland*
The Ship's Cook is Seasick – *Germany*
Mediterranean Cruise – *Greece*
Watch out for the Cabins – *South America*

CARRY ON COLLECTING:

• Postcard featuring UK Quad poster released in 1998 by The London Postcard Company as part of their "British Classics Series 5" collection.
• Promotional bookmark released in 1998 by The London Postcard Company featuring the Carry On Cruising and Carry On Don't Lose your Head Quad posters.

DVD:

Carry On Cruising
Warner Home Video, 2001
PAL, Region 2 (Europe, Middle East & Japan), Colour

The Ultimate Carry On (Carry On Sergeant – Carry On Screaming!)
Warner Home Video, 2001
PAL, Region 2 (Europe, Middle East & Japan), Colour, Black & White

DeAgostini Carry On DVD partwork
DeAgostini/Carlton, 2003
PAL, Region 2 (Europe, Middle East & Japan), Colour, Black & White

Carry On – The Ultimate Collection
ITV Studios Home Entertainment, 2006
PAL, Region 2 (Europe, Middle East & Japan), Colour, Black & White
Special features as for individual ITV/Carlton/Optimum releases

Carry On Cruising
Optimum Home Releasing, 2007
PAL, Region 2 (Europe, Middle East & Japan), Colour

Special Features: Commentary (Dilys Laye, Lance Percival), Stills, Trivia, Trailer

Carry On Collection Vol.2 (Regardless / Cruising / Jack / Cabby)
Optimum Home Releasing, 2008
PAL, Region 2 (Europe, Middle East & Japan), Black & White
Special features as for individual ITV/Carlton/Optimum releases

Carry On – The Ultimate Collection
ITV Studios Home Entertainment, 2008
PAL, Region 2 (Europe, Middle East & Japan), Colour, Black & White
Special features as for individual ITV/Carlton/Optimum releases

VHS:

Carry On Cruising
Warner Home Video, 1986
PAL, Colour

Carry On Spying / Carry On Cruising
Warner Home Video, 1993
PAL, Colour, Black & White

Carry On Cruising
Warner Home Video, 1997
PAL, Colour

Carry On Spying / Carry On Cruising
Warner Home Video, 2001
PAL, Colour, Black & White

DeAgostini Carry On VHS partwork
DeAgostini/Carlton, 2003
PAL, Colour, Black & White

CARRY ON CABBY

1963

Screenplay by Talbot Rothwell
Based on a story by Sid Green and Dick Hills
Music Composed & Directed by Eric Rogers

CAST   CHARACTER

Sidney James	Charlie Hawkins
Hattie Jacques	Peggy Hawkins
Kenneth Connor	Ted Watson
Charles Hawtrey	Terry "Pintpot" Tankard
Esma Cannon	Flo Sims
Liz Fraser	Sally
Bill Owen	Smiley Sims
Milo O'Shea	Len
Judith Furse	Battleaxe
Ambrosine Phillpotts	Aristocratic Lady
Renee Houston	Molly
Jim Dale	Expectant Father
Amanda Barrie	Anthea
Carole Shelley	Dumb Driver
Cyril Chamberlain	Sarge
Norman Chappell	Allbright
Peter Gilmore	Dancy
Michael Ward	Man in Tweeds
Noel Dyson	District Nurse
Michael Nightingale	Businessman
Ian Wilson	Clerk
Peter Byrne	Bridegroom
Darryl Kavann	Punchy
Peter Jesson	Car Salesman
Don McCorkindale	Tubby
Charles Stanley	Geoff
Marion Collins	Bride
Frank Forsyth	Chauffeur
Marian Horton	Glamcab Driver
Valerie van Ost	Glamcab Driver

CREW

Associate Producer	Frank Bevis
Art Director	Jack Stephens
Director of Photography	Alan Hume
Editor	Archie Ludski
Camera Operator	Godfrey Godar
Assistant Director	Peter Bolton

Unit Manager	Donald Toms
Sound Editor	Arthur Ridout
Sound Recordists	Bill Daniels & Gordon K McCallum
Continuity	Penny Daniels
Make-up	Geoffrey Rodway & Jim Hydes
Hairdresser	Biddy Chrystal
Costume Designer	Joan Ellacott
Producer	Peter Rogers
Director	Gerald Thomas

A Peter Rogers production
An Anglo Amalgamated film distributed by the Rank Organisation.

PRODUCTION DETAILS:

Budget: £150,000
Filming: 25th March 1963 – 7th May 1963
Duration: 91m
Black & White
General Release: June 1963, Certificate U
TV Premiere: 2nd November 1971, BBC1
Home Video: 1988 (VHS), 2001 (DVD)

IN A NUTSHELL:

"They're here again"

Speedee Taxis is the busiest taxi firm in town and owner Charlie Hawkins (Sid James) is the busiest cabby, much to the dismay of his wife, Peggy (Hattie Jacques). On the night of their wedding anniversary, Charlie is held up by an expectant father (Jim Dale) who demands that his wife be taken to hospital – twice! When she finally goes into labour, Charlie is kept out all night and misses his anniversary dinner. Vowing revenge, Peggy tells Charlie she's going to find a job.

Suddenly, a new cab firm arrives in town. Glamcabs offers a fleet of new, modern cars and sexy female drivers. Faced with that sort of competition, Charlie's battered old taxis and veteran drivers cannot hope to compete and before long he's facing bankruptcy. When he tries and spectacularly fails to sabotage the Glamcabs operation, Charlie is forced to visit their owner, the mysterious Mrs Glam, to propose a merger. But Charlie's troubles really begin when he discovers the identity of Mrs Glam.

REVIEW:

Carry On Cabby is a return to a more traditional style of comedy, with far less sauciness and pursuit of the opposite sex. Of course, the presence of Glamcabs means that sex is never far away, but it's the kind of innocent ogling and awkwardness with which Kenneth Connor's earlier characters indulged, rather than the leering and double-entendre that would become synonymous with Rothwell's scripts. This is a battle of- rather than for- the sexes.

Not conceived or initially filmed as a Carry On, Cabby can be forgiven for any dissimilarity with the overall tone of the series up to now. The decision to re-brand "Call me a Cab" as a Carry On is perfectly valid. There is a great deal more about Cabby that fits the Carry On house style than does not, but it feels more like an early Hudis film than any of its more recent predecessors.

Carry On Cabby is a gentle comedy of misunderstanding and rivalry and the heart of the film, the relationship between Charlie and Peggy is beautifully realised. They are the perfect couple and despite their increasingly bitter feud, all you want for them is to kiss and make up and move to Peggy's dream house to raise a family. Cabby is by far the most sentimental of the Carry On films, but it differs greatly from the earlier Hudis films in that the emotion never feels artificial or awkward.

There's plenty more to love, besides. Charles Hawtrey, by now firmly cast as the smiling simpleton is delightfully camp. In a break from his usual character (most likely due to the film's non-Carry On roots), Kenneth Connor is plays a more down-to-earth straight role (at least until he drags up as a Glamcabs girl, at which point all bets are well and truly off) and the supporting cast of other players are all perfectly cast, particularly Amanda Barrie, who simply sizzles as Anthea.

Carry On Cabby is a beautiful film - it's romantic and sentimental but it's also delightfully playful. While not typical of the direction the Carry On films have taken up to this point, it's a last reminder of the more innocent charms of the earlier films, written by a scriptwriter who, in Carry On terms at least, had yet to find his niche. Enjoy it while it lasts because when Rothwell finally cracked the formula the Carry Ons would never be the same again.

VIEWING NOTES:

- *Carry On Cabby didn't start life as a Carry On film. Peter Rogers and Gerald Thomas maintained a string of other successful comedies (see "Not a Carry On") which ran alongside the Carry Ons and newcomer Talbot Rothwell, having delighted Rogers with his script for "Poopdecker RN" (later to become Carry On Jack), was asked to re-write a script which Rogers had purchased from Sid Hills and Dick Green about feuding cabbies. The film went before the cameras as "Call me a Cab" and remained so throughout much of its production.*

- *The theme to Carry On Cabby is to the tune of the words "call me a cab"; the original title of the film and Sid's last line, following the successful rescue of Peggy. Before settling on the final title, "Carry On Taxi!" was also briefly considered and some publicity material went out under that name (see Carry On Collecting, below).*

- *Eric Rogers assumed full-time composing and conducting duties on the Carry On films for Cabby, having helped Bruce Montgomery with arrangements on the previous three films.*

- *Promotional consideration for Carry On Cabby came from the Ford Motor Company, who kindly lent the production their entire UK stock of the newly introduced Ford Cortina. Among the 25 cars loaned to the film, several can be seen as being two-door models which remain to this day illegal for use as taxis. Regal Petrol provided additional promotional support for the film.*

- *The role of Albright was originally offered to Kenneth Williams, but he turned down the role. Instead, Rothwell rewrote the part, giving many of Albright's original lines to Pintpot.*

- *Charles Hawtrey returned to the Carry On fold in Cabby after his dispute over billing in the previous film. Hawtrey agreed a deal with Peter Rogers that from Cabby onwards he would never be billed lower than third in the cast list. The policy didn't last long; while Hawtrey received third billing in many of the later films, by Carry On Jack, he was already in fourth place.*

- *Charles Hawtrey was unable to drive a car, or for that matter a motor scooter. He was given a crash course on the Pinewood lot in preparation for the film, where he succeeded in driving his scooter into Alan Hume's car.*

- *The chase sequence through the streets of Windsor was written by Sid Colin for another proposed film, "The Streets of Town". The final scene of the cabs coming over the crest of the hill at the end of the film was penned by Denis Norden.*

- *The 2011 BBC docu-drama "Hattie", which dramatised the life and loves of Hattie Jacques, featured recreations of a number of key scenes from Carry On Cabby.*

- *Carry On Cabby has, over the years, been the subject of discussion of a "lost" Carry On print. Several fans claim to have seen a colour print of the film but while colour photographs and lobby cards do exist for Carry On Cabby and although the previous film, Carry On Cruising, was filmed in colour, there is no colour print of Carry On Cabby.*

CARRY ON COCK-UPS:

Continuity	1m 59s	Watch as the two cars pull up at the lights. From Sid James' point of view there's a car parked on the other side of the road (which you can see through the window of the Rolls Royce) but the car isn't there in the long-shot.
Continuity	2m 32s	When Sid's taxi pulls up behind the driver who gives him the hand signal, you can see the lamppost through the car in front's window. In the next shot, there's a bike parked alongside it.
Continuity	23m 36s	Charles Hawtrey narrowly misses a car on a suburban street. In the shots before and after his near miss the backdrop outside the car shows open countryside through the driver's window.
Continuity	26m 38s	Look behind the newlywed as she hands Sid her suitcases. There's a lorry parked further down the road. In the next, close-up shot, the lorry has gone, only to return again in the next shot as Sid throws a suitcase to Charles.
Technical	27m 00s	Of course Hattie Jacques isn't really naked in the bath. Here you can see she is in fact wearing a bathing suit.
Continuity	27m 11s	The taxi pulls up outside London Airport departures in long-shot and has the departures lane to itself, bar a couple of other cars at the far end. Cut to a close-up of the cab and it's parked facing the opposite direction, in front of a van, with an entirely different building behind it.
Trivia	41m 55s	Peacock's of Balham was one of Ford's main London dealerships at the time. The firm was established in 1908 and finally closed in 2001. While it has some excellent product placement for the dealership, the interior was actually filmed at Maidenhead Autos in Taplow.

Continuity	44m 18s	Look at the pan on the cooker behind Sid James. When we see Sid in close-up, it has moved over to the right.
Continuity	44m 33s	The door behind Kenneth Connor is open wider than it was in the previous shot.
Technical	47m 12s	Take a look at the Glamcabs behind Hattie Jacques and Esma Cannon as they're talking - there are several 2-door models which were, and remain illegal for use as a taxi.
Technical	1h 17m 32s	Cyril Chamberlain's "****the union" in response to Albright is bleeped out but watch his lips – he only says "the union".
Continuity	1h 19m 35s	When Charles Hawtrey sits up after his cab is stolen his scarf is draped over his right arm. In the next shot it's behind his back.
Technical	1h 21m 45s	As the police car pulls away, you can see the reflections of the camera crew in the rear windows.
Continuity	1h 24m 14s	You can see a fence out of Peter Gilmore's car window. In the next shot they're shown to be driving on open land with nary a fence in sight.
Technical	1h 25m 00s	As the car nearest the camera drives past you can see the camera crew reflected in its bodywork.

LOCATIONS:

Time	Description	Address	Also seen in	Location Link
0m 27s	Gent hails Sid's cab	Corner of Trinity Place and St Leonard's Road Windsor Berks SL4 3AP		
1m 23s	Sid's cab rounds the corner of Sheet Street onto Thames St	Corner of Thames St & Sheet St, Windsor Berks SL4 1LU In the background you can see the same Victoria Wine shop that's next door to the Helping Hands Agency in Regardless.	Carry On Regardless Carry On Again Doctor Carry On Loving	
1m 54s	Sid's cab pulls up alongside a Rolls Royce	Corner of Bexley Street and Alma Road Windsor Berks SL4 5BP		

2m 32s	Sid almost rear-ends a car	Junction of Alma Road and Claremont Road Windsor Berks SL4 3HA		
8m 35s	Sid picks up the fearsome woman	The corner of Alma Road and Clarence Crescent Windsor, Berks SL4 3HP Directly opposite where Sid pulled up alongside the Rolls earlier.		
10m 50s	Sid's cab is almost hit by an oncoming car	East along St Mark's Road Windsor Berks SL4 3BD		
21m 45s	Kenneth's Cab pulls up alongside station	Windsor & Eton Riverside Station Datchet Road Windsor, Berks SL4 1DP You can see the Royal Oak pub in the background.		
23m 43s	Charles almost swerves off the road	St Mark's Road Windsor Berks SL4 3BD		
23m 51s	Charles' cab lesson takes him towards the roundabout, around a few times	Arthur Road roundabout Windsor Berks SL4 1RS		

26m 30s	The newlyweds depart	94 Pinewood Green Iver Heath Bucks SL0 0QP	Carry On Constable Carry On Camping Carry On Behind	
27m 06s	The newlyweds arrive at the airport	Heathrow Terminal 3 Departures Heathrow Airport Bath Road Hayes Middx UB3 5AP		
29m 27s	On the way to the hospital	Corner of Black Park Road and Rowley Lane Wexham Berks SL3 6DS		
30m 20s	Sid's taxi drives to the hospital	Bolton Avenue onto Nightingale Walk Windsor, Berks SL4 3HS The former hospital is now a private housing development.		
48m 18s	Charles' taxi rounds the corner of Datchet Road onto Farm Yard	Windsor & Eton Riverside Station Datchet Road Windsor Berks SL4 1DP The taxi rank was a prop built for the film. The entire block has since been redeveloped.		
54m 06s	Vying for the same customer	Corner of Queen's Road and Alma Road, outside the former Frogmore Hotel, 71 Alma Road Windsor SL4 3HD The Frogmore was demolished in early 2010.		

54m 25s	Two men compete for a Glamcab	Windsor & Eton Riverside Station Datchet Road Windsor Berks SL4 1DP		
58m 25s	Charles gets a call	The Royal Waiting Room Datchet Road Windsor Berks SL4 1QG		
1h 00m 25s	Sid sabotages a Glamcab	1 St Marks Road Windsor Berks SL4 3BD		
1h 00m 44s	Kenneth Connor comes to Amanda's aid	9 Dorset Rd Windsor Berks SL4 3BA		
1h 01m 44s	Sid comes to a Glamcab's aid - or so he thinks	Claremont Road into Alma Road. The cab stops outside 46 Alma Road Windsor Berks SL4 3HA		
1h 13m 54s	The robbers hijack Hattie's car	Down Duke St Windsor Berks SL4 1SH and around to the left where Duke St continues.		

1h 16m 12s	Speedee Cabs try to trap the stolen Glamcab on Rigby Road	Osborne Mews Windsor Berks SL4 3DE On the corner of St Leonard's Road. The cabs block the road further down where it becomes Queen's Road.		
1h 17m 11s	The hijacked Glamcab is blocked from going back up Wentworth Street	Pinewood Green, at the end of the road were the newlyweds were picked up earlier. Look in the background and you'll see the same parked truck from the earlier scene. The remainder of the chase takes place on the streets of the Pinewood Estate Iver Heath, Bucks SL0.		
1h 19m 05s	The thieves steal Charles' cab	Stovell Rd Windsor, Berks SL4 5JB Much of this area was demolished to make way for the A332 relief road.		
1h 22m 32s	The final chase	King Edward VII Avenue onto Romney Lock Road Windsor Berks SL4 6HX		

CARRY ON ABROAD:

Carry On Tired Taxi Driver – *Germany*
War of the Taxis – *South America*

CARRY ON COLLECTING:

- Die-cast 1:60 scale cab featuring the Speedee Taxis logo by Lledo, 1998, as part of their "Days Gone" range.
- Postcard featuring UK promotional Quad poster in association with Ford Motor Co released in 1998 by The London Postcard Company as part of their "British Classics Series 4" collection.
- Postcard featuring pre-release UK One Sheet poster for "Carry On Taxi" released in 1998 by The London Postcard Company as part of their "British Classics Series 5" collection.

SOUNDTRACK:

Main title theme available on "Carry On"
Various Artists, CD, Silva Screen 2005
Themes, cues and dialog taken from the original film soundtracks

Extended theme available on "The Carry On Album, Music from the Films"
Gavin Sutherland & the Prague Philharmonic Orchestra, CD, ASV 1999
Newly performed renditions of classic Carry On themes

"This is my Street" (cha-cha arrangement from Carry On Again Doctor) available on "What a Carry On"
Gavin Sutherland and the Royal Sinfonia, CD, Dutton Vocalion 2005
Newly performed renditions of classic Carry On themes

DVD:

Carry On Cabby
Warner Home Video, 2001
PAL, Region 2 (Europe, Middle East & Japan), Black & White

The Ultimate Carry On (Carry On Sergeant – Carry On Screaming!)
Warner Home Video, 2001
PAL, Region 2 (Europe, Middle East & Japan), Colour, Black & White

DeAgostini Carry On DVD partwork
DeAgostini/Carlton, 2003
PAL, Region 2 (Europe, Middle East & Japan), Colour, Black & White

Carry On – The Ultimate Collection
ITV Studios Home Entertainment, 2006
PAL, Region 2 (Europe, Middle East & Japan), Colour, Black & White
Special features as for individual ITV/Carlton/Optimum releases

Carry On Cabby / That's Carry On
Optimum Home Releasing, 2007
PAL, Region 2 (Europe, Middle East & Japan), Black & White, Colour

Carry On Collection Vol.2 (Regardless / Cruising / Jack / Cabby)
Optimum Home Releasing, 2008
PAL, Region 2 (Europe, Middle East & Japan), Black & White
Special features as for individual ITV/Carlton/Optimum releases

Carry On – The Ultimate Collection
ITV Studios Home Entertainment, 2008
PAL, Region 2 (Europe, Middle East & Japan), Colour, Black & White
Special features as for individual ITV/Carlton/Optimum releases

VHS:

Carry On Cabby
Warner Home Video, 1988
PAL, Black & White

Carry On Cabby / Carry On Nurse
Warner Home Video, 1993
PAL, Black & White

Carry On Cabby
Warner Home Video, 1997
PAL, Black & White

Carry On Cabby / Carry On Nurse
Warner Home Video, 2001
PAL, Black & White

DeAgostini Carry On VHS partwork
DeAgostini/Carlton, 2003
PAL, Colour, Black & White

CARRY ON JACK

1963

Screenplay by Talbot Rothwell
Music Composed & Conducted by Eric Rogers

CAST   CHARACTER

CAST	CHARACTER
Kenneth Williams	Captain Fearless
Bernard Cribbins	Midshipman Albert Poop-Decker
Juliet Mills	Sally
Charles Hawtrey	Walter Sweetley
Donald Houston	First Officer Jonathan Howett
Percy Herbert	Mr Angel
Carrier	Jim Dale
Patrick Cargill	Spanish Governor
Cecil Parker	1st Sea Lord
Ed Devereaux	Hook
Peter Gilmore	Patch
George Woodbridge	Ned
Ian Wilson	Ancient Carrier
Jimmy Thompson	Nelson
Anton Rodgers	Hardy
Michael Nightingale	Town Crier
Frank Forsyth	2nd Sea Lord
Barrie Gosney	Coach Driver
John Brooking	3rd Sea Lord
Jan Muzurus	Spanish Captain
Vivianne Ventura	Spanish Secretary
Marianne Stone	1st Woman at Dirty Dick's
Dorinda Stevens	2nd Woman at Dirty Dick's
Girls at Dirty Dicks:	Rosemary Manley, Sally Douglas, Jennifer Hill, Dominique Don,

Marian Collins, Jean Hamilton

CREW

Associate Producer	Frank Bevis
Art Director	Jack Shampan
Director of Photography	Alan Hume
Editor	Archie Ludski
Camera Operator	Godfrey Godar
Assistant Director	Anthony Waye
Unit Manager	Donald Toms
Sound Editor	Christopher Lancaster
Sound Recordist	Bill Daniels
Continuity	Penny Daniels
Make-up	Geoffrey Rodway & Jim Hydes

Hairdresser ....Olga Angelinetta
Costume Designer ....Joan Ellacott
Technical Advisor..Ian Cox
Producer ....Peter Rogers
Director ....Gerald Thomas

A Peter Rogers production.
An Anglo Amalgamated film distributed through Warner-Pathe Distribution Ltd

PRODUCTION DETAILS:

Budget: £152,000
Filming: 2nd September 1963 – 26th October 1963
Duration: 91m
Colour
General Release: November 1963, Certificate A
TV Premiere: 2nd October 1971, BBC1
Home Video: 1988 (VHS), 2001 (DVD)

IN A NUTSHELL:

Britain is locked in a bitter struggle with Spain. With the British fleet severely under-manned, the Admiralty takes the desperate step of sending recruits off to sea before they have completed training. Midshipman Albert Poop-Decker (Bernard Cribbins) is en route to join the crew of Captain Fearless (Kenneth Williams) when he is hoodwinked by Sally (Juliet Mills) a barmaid who is desperate to reach Spain to be reunited with her first love.

Poop-Decker is press-ganged into joining Fearless' crew where he finds himself below decks with the most un-seaman-like Walter Sweetley (Charles Hawtrey) and Sally, who has assumed not only his identity but also his position as a Midshipman.

Captain Fearless singularly fails to live up to his name and the crew grow increasingly mutinous. First Officer Howett (Donald Houston) and the Bosun, Mr Angel (Percy Herbert) stage a mutiny and cast Fearless, Sally, Albert and Walter adrift with only the ship's cow for company. But the Armada is coming so love and broken legs will have to wait.

REVIEW:

Carry On Jack is a tricky one. Taken at face value, you would be hard pressed to even identify it as a Carry On film. Kenneth Williams and Charles Hawtrey are the only cast members who by this stage could even be considered regular members of the Carry On team. Bernard Cribbins is flawlessly funny in every scene but this is his Carry On debut and he will only make one more in the next 28 years, so he is not what you might call a regular. Jim Dale gets a couple of very funny scenes early in the film but he is literally in it for a couple of minutes only. Donald Houston, Juliet Mills and particularly Peter Gilmore all put in sterling work. However, try as they might, they're not Carry On personalities and their antics do not a Carry On make.

Of course, Carry On Jack didn't start life as a Carry On film. "Poopdecker RN", as it was originally known, was the script Talbot Rothwell wrote to get Peter Rogers' attention. Viewed as intended, that is, as an historical comedy adventure, it is a perfectly good film. It's amusing, sumptuous and has a decent story which cracks along nicely. But the style of the comedy simply isn't Carry On. It is easy to see, from Carry On Jack, just why the Carry On team would go on to do so well at historical comedy, but here the balance all wrong. Carry On Jack focuses too much on plot and not enough on being funny and there is an awful lot of plot to get through. At the heart of any successful Carry On is a quick fire succession of one liners, physical comedy and double-entendres. There's not much of that in evidence in Carry On Jack. If anything, it's too well written.

Carry On Jack may not be a particularly great Carry On, but it is an excellent swashbuckling comedy adventure.

VIEWING NOTES:

• *Although it was filmed after Carry On Cabby, Carry On Jack was the first script that Talbot Rothwell delivered to Peter Rogers. It was sent unsolicited under its original title, "Poopdecker RN". Rogers was taken with the script and while further work was carried out, he commissioned Rothwell to complete work on the draft of "Call Me a Cab".*

• *Other names were considered for the film included "Carry On Sailor" and the team's favourite, "Up the Armada" but fears that the title wouldn't get past the censor led to its final title "Carry On Jack".*

• *Carry On Jack took longer than any other Carry On to complete. The film was made in just over 8 weeks, a positively lethargic pace by Rogers' usual standards.*

• *Liz Fraser was originally cast in the role of Sally, but decided against taking the part on the advice of her agent to avoid being typecast.*

• *The shipboard scenery was re-used from the 1962 film, HMS Defiant. The somewhat larger budget of the earlier film meant the set was able to move as if at sea, thanks to a system of hydraulic rollers. It's worth noting that Carry On Cruising had no such trickery to fall back on, nor did the much later Carry On Columbus.*

• *The use of stock footage of ships at sea is entirely understandable, but greater care could have been taken to match the footage with the studio sets. Among other things, the size of the ship's flag varies wildly between stock and studio shots.*

• *Filming at Frensham Ponds was delayed on numerous occasions while the production team waited for Army paratroopers to complete their manoeuvres. They were seen to be dropping in to shot on a number of occasions (none of which made the cut, so don't bother looking).*

CARRY ON COCK-UPS:

Trivia	1m 30s	The opening tableau is a faithful copy of Arthur William Devis' 1807 painting "The Death of Nelson, 21 October 1805.
Technical	5m 23s	The studio set for the George Inn coach station can't be very big. Once the coach departs and Bernard Cribbins climbs aboard the sedan chair, he, Jim Dale and the other bearer depart from a point several paces back into the set from where they met.

Trivia	9m 28s	Jim Dale's line "I'd get in if I were you - they'll be shut" was an ad-lib, something of a rarity in the Carry On films where Director Thomas was a stickler for the cast sticking rigidly to the script.
Continuity	25m 59s	When the ship's cat gets its close-up, it is being held in a different position to the long-shots when Kenneth Williams is at his desk.
Continuity	27m 33s	As Bernard Cribbins is tied and lashed, the dress he's wearing is ripped across his back but in the next shot he's wearing a different costume. The sleeves, the only part still attached to him, are significantly longer than before. Cribbins is also standing in an entirely different position (quite an achievement given that he's tied to the rack) with his arms fully outstretched.
Continuity	28m 15s	The vest worn by Bernard Cribbins was intact in the previous shot but now it's almost completely unravelled and entangled in the cat-o'nine tails. In the next shot, at 28m 22s, there's rather more of it than it was a few seconds before. The vest he wears in the next scene is different again.
Continuity	49m 47s	The cow in the boat isn't the same one used in filming for the scenes on land. This one is considerably less alive.
Technical	1h 10m 33s	The back projection when first Charles Hawtrey and then Bernard Cribbins are walking the plank is rather more active than could possibly ever be real.
Technical	1h 25m 47s	Keep an eye on the right of the screen and you'll see one of the extras waiting for her cue.

LOCATIONS:

Time	Description	Address	Also seen in	Location Link
53m 16s	Coming ashore	Frensham Great Pond Farnham Surrey GU10 2QD	Carry On Columbus	

CARRY ON ABROAD:

The Mutineers of the Venus – *Belgium*
Beware of the Pirates – *Denmark*
Pull Yourself Together Skipper! – *Finland*
The Unrigged Frigate / Carry On Venus – *Germany*
The Merry Mutineers of the Bounty – *Italy*
The Tremendous Mutineers of the Venus – *Spain*

CARRY ON COLLECTING:

- Postcard featuring UK Quad poster released in 1998 by The London Postcard Company as part of their "British Classics Series 1" collection.
- Swift Telecom, in 2001, issued a series of three Carry On-themed pre-paid phone cards, featuring the UK Quad artwork for Carry On Jack, Carry On Cleo and Carry On Screaming!

SOUNDTRACK:

Main title theme available on "Carry On"
Various Artists, CD, Silva Screen 2005
Themes, cues and dialog taken from the original film soundtracks

Extended theme available on "The Carry On Album, Music from the Films"
Gavin Sutherland & the Prague Philharmonic Orchestra, CD, ASV 1999
Newly performed renditions of classic Carry On themes

DVD:

Carry On Jack
Warner Home Video, 2001
PAL, Region 2 (Europe, Middle East & Japan), Colour

The Ultimate Carry On (Carry On Sergeant – Carry On Screaming!)
Warner Home Video
PAL, Region 2 (Europe, Middle East & Japan), Colour, Black & White

DeAgostini Carry On DVD partwork
DeAgostini/Carlton, 2003
PAL, Region 2 (Europe, Middle East & Japan), Colour, Black & White

Carry On – The Ultimate Collection
ITV Studios Home Entertainment, 2006
PAL, Region 2 (Europe, Middle East & Japan), Colour, Black & White
Special features as for individual ITV/Carlton/Optimum releases

Carry On Jack
Optimum Home Releasing, 2007
PAL, Region 2 (Europe, Middle East & Japan), Black & White, Colour
Special Features: Commentary (Bernard Cribbins), Stills, Trivia, Trailer, Textless titles

Carry On Collection Vol.2 (Regardless / Cruising / Jack / Cabby)
Optimum Home Releasing, 2008
PAL, Region 2 (Europe, Middle East & Japan), Black & White
Special features as for individual ITV/Carlton/Optimum releases

Carry On – The Ultimate Collection
ITV Studios Home Entertainment, 2008
PAL, Region 2 (Europe, Middle East & Japan), Colour, Black & White
Special features as for individual ITV/Carlton/Optimum releases

VHS:

Carry On Jack
Warner Home Video, 1988
PAL, Colour

Carry On Constable / Carry On Jack
Warner Home Video, 1993
PAL, Colour, Black & White

Carry On Jack
Warner Home Video, 1997
PAL, Colour

Carry On Constable / Carry On Jack
Warner Home Video, 2001
PAL, Black & White

DeAgostini Carry On VHS partwork
DeAgostini/Carlton, 2003
PAL, Colour, Black & White

CARRY ON SPYING

1964

Screenplay by Talbot Rothwell and Sid Colin
Music Composed & Conducted by Eric Rogers
Songs - "Too Late" by Alex Alstone & Geoffrey Parsons
"The Magic of Love" by Eric Rogers

CAST   CHARACTER

Kenneth Williams	Desmond Simpkins
Barbara Windsor	Daphne Honeybutt
Bernard Cribbins	Harold Crump
Charles Hawtrey	Charlie Bind
Eric Barker	The Chief
Dilys Laye	Lila
Jim Dale	Carstairs
Richard Wattis	Cobley
Eric Pohlmann	The Fat Man
Victor Maddern	Milchmann
Judith Furse	Dr Crow
John Bluthal	Head Waiter
Renee Houston	Madame
Tom Clegg	Doorman
Jack Taylor	1st Thug
Bill Cummings	2nd Thug
Gertan Klauber	Code Clerk
Norman Mitchell	Native Policeman
Frank Forsyth	Professor Stark
Derek Sydney	Algerian Gent
Anthony Baird	1st Guard
Patrick Durkin	2nd Guard
Jill Mai Meredith	Cigarette Girl
Angela Ellison	Cloakroom Attendant
Hugh Futcher	Scrawny Native
Norah Gordon	Elderly Woman
Funhouse Girls:	Virginia Tyler, Judi Johnson, Gloria Best
Amazon Guards:	Audrey Wilson, Vicki Smith, Jane Lumb, Marian Collins, Sally Douglas, Christine Rodgers, Maya Koumani

CREW

Associate Producer	Frank Bevis
Art Director	Alex Vetchinsky

Director of Photography ....Alan Hume
Editor...Archie Ludski
Camera Operator...Godfrey Godar
Assistant Director ....Peter Bolton
Unit Manager...Donald Toms
Sound Editor..Christopher Lancaster
Sound Recordists ....CC Stevens & Bill Daniels
Continuity...Penny Daniels
Make-up ....WT Partleton
Hairdresser...Biddy Chrystal
Costume Designer ....Yvonne Caffin
Producer...Peter Rogers
Director...Gerald Thomas

A Peter Rogers production.
An Anglo Amalgamated film distributed through Warner-Pathe Distribution Ltd.

PRODUCTION DETAILS:

Budget: £148,000
Filming: 8th February 1964 – 13th March 1964
Duration: 87m
Black & White
General Release: June 1964, Certificate A
TV Premiere: 3rd April 1972, BBC1
Home Video: 1988 (VHS), 2001 (DVD)

IN A NUTSHELL:

"They're at it again. O-O-Oh!"

A top-secret formula is stolen from a maximum security lab by the infamous spy Milchmann (Victor Maddern). Realising that he must be working for the evil Dr Crow's (Judith Furse) STENCH organisation, the British Operational Security Headquarters (BOSH) reluctantly send for the only agent available, the accident-prone Desmond Simpkins (Kenneth Williams).

Simpkins assembles his team - Charlie Bind (Charles Hawtrey), Harold Crump (Bernard Cribbins) and Daphne Honeybutt (Barbara Windsor), a group of fresh recruits with no field training. Simpkins leads his fellow spies in pursuit of Milchmann to recapture the secret formula and thwart Dr Crow's nefarious plot. The team liaise with top agent Carstairs (Jim Dale) in Vienna, who sends them to Algeria before locating Dr Crow's secret base which, after all that Carrying On, turns out to be underneath BOSH's own headquarters.

REVIEW

From the promotional artwork through to the characters and story, Carry On Spying is of course a spoof of the James Bond films which, at the time of release, were breaking new ground in popular cinema. With a direct target for Spying to ape, by necessity there is a strong focus on the plot and moving the story forward but like Carry On Jack before it, plot often comes at the expense of comedy. In many ways Carry On Spying is more Bond than Carry On. From its globe-trotting appearance (in reality it was anything but) to its super villain hideouts and criminal masterminds, it resembles more of a funny James Bond film than a Carry On in its own right.

Of course, at this point in the series' history, the Carry Ons didn't really adhere to any particular comedic style, so for audiences of the day this was exactly the right approach in terms of capitalising on the Bond films' success.

The most important criteria for any Carry On film is whether it is funny and Spying certainly raises plenty of laughs. There's not much in the way of a chuckle in terms of the story unless hermaphrodite evil genii tickle your fancy, but the main cast work brilliantly. Kenneth Williams falls back on his Snide character rather more than usual; a character of whom I am not particularly fond but it's easy to see from Babs' first Carry On appearance why the team were so keen to sign her up for more.

Throw in another top class performance from Bernard Cribbins and the ever-wonderful Charles Hawtrey and you have a team of idiots who blunder their way through the greatest criminal plot in history, defeating the bad guys through a combination of sheer luck and Kenneth's irresistible sex appeal. Sadly, the film runs out of steam when the gang reach the STENCH lair and from this point it becomes a simple knockabout farce, complete with speeded up visuals and comedy soundtrack.

The weak ending and the dense story leading up to it add up to a film which is underwritten in terms of character and humour but over-complicated in terms of set-up. The overall experience is certainly fun, but I always find my attention drifting by about the halfway mark. Carry On Spying is a great showcase for the Carry On team but the film as a whole is more than a little unsatisfactory. There is tremendous scope for comedy but it's not milked (or even milched) as much as it could be.

VIEWING NOTES

- *An early working title for Carry On Spying was "Come Spy with Me". However, Rogers had registered the title "Carry On Spying" as early as 1962, following the success of the first James Bond film, "Dr No".*

- *Norman Hudis was originally contracted to write the script for Carry On Spying but Peter Rogers was unhappy with the original treatment (which bears some resemblance to Harry Enfield's "Carry On Banging" sketch) and drafted Talbot Rothwell and Sid Colin to write the final script.*

- *Despite legal posturing from the James Bond team, Peter Rogers maintained that the decision to rename the lead character Charlie instead of the originally planned "James" Bind was purely for comedic reasons. But the film wears its heart on its sleeve - the UK poster is a direct homage to the poster art for "From Russia with Love".*

- *The Carry On films were famous for being delivered on time and under-budget, but a series of problems during production led to Carry On Spying coming in almost 10% over its initial budget. Peter Rogers attributed the over-spend to complications with the final sequences and injuries to the cast, most notably Charles Hawtrey and Kenneth Williams, which delayed production.*

- *Judith Furse's voice was re-dubbed by John Bluthal, whose manly tones gave the character of Doctor Crow a greater sense of being androgynous.*

CARRY ON COCK-UPS:

Technical	4m 16s	Someone or something knocks the lamp on Eric Barker's desk and it has a little wobble followed by a bigger one.
Technical	11m 07s	A stray body slips into shot beside Barbara Windsor as she stands to attention before The Chief.
Trivia	15m 14s	Eric Rogers pays homage to Anton Karas' distinctive theme from The Third Man in his accompanying music to the scenes on the streets (okay, street) of Vienna.
Continuity	29m 46s	Hitting that iron post hasn't just bent the barrel of the pistol Kenneth Williams is holding, it's made it quite a bit longer too.
Technical	30m 15s	Kenneth is clearly standing on a step or box below the window before climbing on to Charles Hawtrey's back. When he falls back a few seconds later, whatever it was has been removed.
Trivia	34m 18s	The musical theme Eric Rogers composed for the Algerian scenes can be heard again later in the series in Carry On Follow that Camel as the music accompanying Cork Tip's dance.
Technical	41m 24s	Bernard Cribbins drew the short straw when it came to gadgets - his aerial is clearly just a tape measure. The one he has in his bikini in Hakim's later is even more obvious.
Trivia	42m 00s	Looks like Barbara and Kenneth are doing a bit of shoplifting. Watch her pick up the slinky and him the cup and then a few moments later walk off without paying. They help themselves to a whole range of things in the next alleyway too!
Trivia	51m 33s	Yes, that is a Sega fruit machine in Hakim's Fun House - the same Sega who years later went on to produce the Megadrive and Sonic the Hedgehog.
Trivia	1h 08m 09s	The incidental music to the scene where Barbara is hypnotised also features in Carry On Screaming! as Valeria enters the lab.
Continuity	1h 09m 49s	That glass of water the henchman brings to Barbara is significantly more full when it arrives than it was when the henchman first picked it up.
Continuity	1h 14m 14s	Kenneth drops one of the tape spools on the floor, which of course is part of the plot. But keep watching…
Continuity	1h 14m 22s	When we next see our heroes, the spool that Kenneth dropped on the floor is back in his hand, together with a bundle of unwound tape. As he and the gang run away he drops the tape to the floor.
Technical	1h 14m 57s	Watch the set wobble as the henchman is pushed back into the wall.

Technical	1h 17m 09s	Look through the spinning blades and you'll see the conveyor is a relatively short moving platform with a painted backdrop on the other side. The next shot, coming out of the blades, is the same set reversed. Both Kenneth Williams and Charles Hawtrey were injured filming the scenes you're about to watch.

LOCATIONS:

Time	Description	Address	Also seen in	Location Link
10s	Entrance to the lab	Pinewood Road Iver Heath Bucks SL0 0NH		
38s	Research lab	North Gate and Hall of Fame Pinewood Studios Pinewood Road Iver Heath Bucks SL0 0NH		
2m 45s	BOSH HQ	HM Revenue & Customs Great George St London SW1	Carry On Emmannuelle	
1h 04m 54s	Entering STENCH	Pinewood Orchard Pinewood Studios Iver Heath Bucks SL0 0NH	Carry On Camping Carry On Behind Carry On England	

CARRY ON ABROAD:

Belgium – *Secret Agent O-O-Oh! Vs Dr Crow*
Carry On the Espionage – *Hungary*
Watch out for the Spies! – *South America*

CARRY ON COLLECTING:

- Postcard featuring UK One Sheet poster released in 1998 by The London Postcard Company as part of their "British Classics Series 1" collection.
- Postcard featuring UK Quad poster released in 1998 by The London Postcard Company as part of their "British Classics Series 3" collection.

SOUNDTRACK:

Main title theme available on "Carry On"
Various Artists, CD, Silva Screen 2005
Themes, cues and dialog taken from the original film soundtracks

Title theme and "The Magic of Love" available on "What a Carry On"
Gavin Sutherland and the Royal Sinfonia, CD, Dutton Vocalion 2005
Newly performed renditions of classic Carry On themes

DVD:

Carry On Spying
Warner Home Video, 2001
PAL, Region 2 (Europe, Middle East & Japan), Black & White

The Ultimate Carry On (Carry On Sergeant – Carry On Screaming!)
Warner Home Video, 2001
PAL, Region 2 (Europe, Middle East & Japan), Colour, Black & White

DeAgostini Carry On DVD partwork
DeAgostini/Carlton, 2003
PAL, Region 2 (Europe, Middle East & Japan), Colour, Black & White

Carry On – The Ultimate Collection
ITV Studios Home Entertainment, 2006
PAL, Region 2 (Europe, Middle East & Japan), Colour, Black & White
Special features as for individual ITV/Carlton/Optimum releases

Carry On Spying
Optimum Home Releasing, 2007
PAL, Region 2 (Europe, Middle East & Japan), Black & White, Colour
Special Features: Commentary (Bernard Cribbins, Dilys Laye), Stills, Trivia, Trailer, Textless titles

Carry On Collection Vol.3 (Spying / Cleo / Screaming! / Cowboy)
Optimum Home Releasing, 2008
PAL, Region 2 (Europe, Middle East & Japan), Black & White
Special features as for individual ITV/Carlton/Optimum releases

Carry On – The Ultimate Collection
ITV Studios Home Entertainment, 2008
PAL, Region 2 (Europe, Middle East & Japan), Colour, Black & White
Special features as for individual ITV/Carlton/Optimum releases

VHS:

Carry On Spying
Warner Home Video, 1988
PAL, Black & White

Carry On Spying / Carry On Cruising
Warner Home Video, 1993
PAL, Colour, Black & White

Carry On Spying
Warner Home Video, 1997
PAL, Black & White

Carry On Spying / Carry On Cruising
Warner Home Video, 2001
PAL, Colour, Black & White

DeAgostini Carry On VHS partwork
DeAgostini/Carlton, 2003
PAL, Colour, Black & White

CARRY ON CLEO

1964

Screenplay by Talbot Rothwell, from an original idea by William Shakespeare
Music Composed & Conducted by Eric Rogers

CAST

CHARACTER
Sidney James...Mark Antony
Kenneth Williams..Julius Caesar
Kenneth Connor ....Hengist Pod
Charles Hawtrey...Seneca
Joan Sims...Calpurnia
Jim Dale...Horsa
Amanda Barrie..Cleopatra
Victor Maddern...Sergeant Major
Julie Stevens ....Gloria
Sheila Hancock ....Senna Pod
Jon Pertwee..Soothsayer
Francis de Wolff..Agrippa
Michael Ward ....Archimedes
Brian Oulton ....Brutus
Tom Clegg ....Sosages
Tanya Binning..Virginia
David Davenport ....Bilius
Peter Gilmore..Galley Master
Ian Wilson ....Messenger
Brian Rawlinson ....Hessian Driver
Gertan Klauber ....Markus
Warren Mitchell..Spencius
Michael Nightingale..Caveman
Peter Jesson..Companion
Judi Johnson ....Gloria's Bridesmaid
Thelma Taylor ....Seneca's Servant
Norman Mitchell ....Heckler
Sally Douglas ....Dusky Maiden
Wanda Ventham ....Pretty Bidder
Peggy Ann Clifford ....Willa Claudia
Mark Hardy..Caesar's Guard
EVH Emmett ....Narrator
Cleo's Handmaidens: ....Christine Rodgers, Gloria Best, Virginia Tyler
Vestal Virgins: ....Gloria Johnson, Joanna Ford, Donna White, Jane Lumb, Vicki Smith

CREW

Associate Producer...Frank Bevis
Art Director ....Bert Davey
Director of Photography ....Alan Hume
Editor..Archie Ludski
Camera Operator...Godfrey Godar
Assistant Director ....Peter Bolton
Unit Manager..Donald Toms
Sound Editor...Christopher Lancaster
Sound Recordists ....Bill Daniels & Gordon K McCallum
Continuity...Olga Brook
Make-up ....Geoffrey Rodway
Hairdresser..Ann Fordyce
Costume Designer ....Julie Harris
Producer..Peter Rogers
Director..Gerald Thomas

A Peter Rogers production.
An Anglo Amalgamated film distributed through Warner-Pathe Distribution Ltd.

PRODUCTION DETAILS:

Budget: £194,500
Filming: 13th July 1964 – 28th August 1964
Duration: 92m
Colour
General Release: December 1964, Certificate A
TV Premiere: 26th December 1972, BBC1
Home Video: 1980 (VHS/Betamax), 2001 (DVD)

IN A NUTSHELL:

"The funniest film since 54BC"

Julius Caesar (Kenneth Williams) is having second thoughts about invading Britain. The constant rain is playing havoc with his health, but when his friend Mark Antony (Sid James) presents him with the captive Gloria (Julie Stevens) his laurels perk up.

Gloria's boyfriend Horsa (Jim Dale) and neighbour Hengist Pod (Kenneth Connor) mount a rescue attempt but they are soon captured by the Romans and shipped off to a slave market in Rome. Narrowly escaping an appointment with the lions in the coliseum, Hengist and Horsa make for Egypt, where Caesar and Mark Antony plan an alliance with the beautiful queen Cleopatra (Amanda Barrie). But unbeknown to Caesar, Mark Antony and Cleo are plotting his demise and an entirely different kind of alliance.

REVIEW:

Carry On Cleo is a tantalising glimpse of what the Carry On films could have looked like had they been filmed on the scale of the Hollywood blockbusters. By nibbling at the big-budget crumbs left over from the Richard Burton/Elizabeth Taylor epic, "Cleopatra", the team were able to inject some of the glamour of a $44m dollar film into their £200k romp.

The result is a visual and comedic feast which owes less to Hollywood glamour and more to the remarkable combination of one of Britain's finest comedy writers with a cast and crew at the very top of their game. Man meets woman, man falls in love with woman, woman persuades man to murder his best friend – it is an age-old tale. Everything else is just whimsy, but it's delivered with such flair and playfulness that Carry On Cleo is so much more than just another low budget British comedy. It is a genuinely epic tale of love and betrayal, taking in much of the civilised world (via the by-now traditional Pinewood lot).

Carry On Cleo shines with confidence and bravado. The solidly entertaining script from Talbot Rothwell doesn't dwell too heavily on the intricacies of plot but instead paints a broad story filled with Carry On set pieces which allow the cast to stretch their comedy muscles. The injection of big budget costumes and sets from its cinematic big brother is evident throughout so it's ironic, but hardly surprising given the end result, that the Carry On re-telling of Cleopatra is remembered with far greater affection than the original.

It's not quite the splendour that was Rome, but it's as decent a glimpse as you'll get for the price of a two bedroom semi.

VIEWING NOTES:

- *"Cleopatra" with Richard Burton and Elizabeth Taylor was shot at Pinewood Studios in 1963. The sets and costumes were still available at the time Carry On Cleo went into production so the Carry On team made good use of the more lavish trappings available to them. Sid James dons the costume worn by Richard Burton and Amanda Barrie wears Elizabeth Taylor's iconic head piece.*

- *Talbot Rothwell clearly knew his onions when it came to the ancient Britons. Hengist and Horsa are two characters from British mythology who led the Angles, Jutes and Saxons into battle and established the first British settlements in the 5th Century.*

- *Narrator EVH Emmett was a famous voice artist for the Gaumont British Newsreels. His distinguished tones lent gravity to a number of films of the period, including the Ealing classic, Passport to Pimlico.*

- *Sets and costumes were not the only things borrowed from the Burton/Taylor film. The original poster for Carry On Cleo aped the iconic image of Cleopatra reclining while Mark Anthony looked on - a painting commissioned by Fox from artist Howard Terpning.*

- *Twentieth Century Fox took Anglo Amalgamated to court over the image in a widely reported High Court case which serendipitously took place just days before the film's release and gave it a welcome boost in publicity. In the words of Sir Andrew Clark, on behalf of Fox: "They are entitled to make fun of our film, but for the purposes of advertising they have seen fit to make use of a poster which we say is quite clearly our poster but with different heads". The court ruled that the poster should be changed. The following day newspapers ran stories about emergency squads of bill posters replacing the offending posters, keeping the film firmly in the public eye.*

- *The "luxurious" bath in which Amanda Barrie spent so much of the film wallowing contained 1,000 gallons of skimmed milk and 2,000 gallons of water. The mixture was heated to 90 degrees Fahrenheit and rapidly took on a less than regal odour.*

- *Marks & Spencer also took issue with the film, not for its portrayal of slave traders by the name Marcus et Spencius, but for the Carry On's use of the M&S trademark's green and gold colours. Peter Rogers offered to make a public apology to the retailer in the Daily Express newspaper, but the matter was ultimately dropped after he apologised for the unintentional slight.*

- *Kenneth Williams' line, "Infamy! Infamy!" was, in 2007, voted the funniest line ever in a film by viewers of Sky Movies. But the line wasn't even written for Carry On Cleo – it was taken, by permission of the original writers, Frank Muir and Denis Norden, from the 1950s radio show "Take it From Here".*

CARRY ON COCK-UPS:

Continuity	1m 46s	The bar of soap left on the floor of Cleopatra's bathing room has moved by the time the Roman enters the room and slips on it a few seconds later.
Continuity	3m 17s	The position of the wheel that Kenneth Connor is working on differs between long-shot and close-up. When we switch to long-shot he's also holding a different tool to the one seen in the previous shot.
Technical	6m 01s	The Roman soldiers march to the then familiar cry "Sinister, Dexter" (trans. "Left, Right") but watch closely and you'll see that they're marching in opposite time.
Technical	24m 24s	Brian Oulton is visibly holding back laughter during Kenneth Williams' speech to the senate.
Technical	28m 58s	Close camera angles almost manage to disguise the fact that we're once again in Caesar's bathroom, this time complete with dining table. The budget couldn't stretch to more than a corridor and a room, so you'll be seeing a lot more of this set.
Technical	45m 11s	When Amanda Barrie first gets out of her bath, you can just see that she's wearing a below the waist garment to cover at least some of her modesty.
Technical	49m 58s	The pre-prepared breaks on the statue of Venus can be seen just before Kenneth Connor chops its arms off.
Technical	56m 18s	I can forgive the need to put Charles Hawtrey in underwear earlier in the film, but Jim Dale in striped pants is pushing credibility too far.
Technical	1h 25m 48s	Charles Hawtrey's dive off the balcony is disappointing. Watch the shadow of his vase on the "sky" behind the balcony, revealing it to be a much smaller set than it appears.

LOCATIONS:

Time	Description	Address	Also seen in	Location Link
05m 59s	English countryside	Chobham Common Woking Surrey GU24	Carry On Cowboy	

CARRY ON ABROAD:

OK, Cleo – *Belgium*
So, So, Cleopatra! – *Denmark*
Stop your Chariot, Cleo – *France*
Caesar Loves Cleopatra – *Germany*
Heroic Suckers in the Country of the Pharaoh – *Greece*
Cleopatra, the Works – *Poland*
Way to go, Cleopatra – *Portugal*

CARRY ON COLLECTING:

• Postcard featuring UK Quad poster released in 1998 by The London Postcard Company as part of their "British Classics Series 1" collection. An alternate Quad poster featured as part of their "British Classics Series 3" collection.
• Swift Telecom, in 2001, issued a series of three Carry On-themed pre-paid phone cards, featuring the UK Quad artwork for Carry On Jack, Carry On Cleo and Carry On Screaming!
• Carry On first class stamp and associated collectibles (presentation pack, postcard) featuring UK Quad poster for Carry On Cleo released in 2008 by Royal Mail.
• Product Enterprise, in 2005, released a 12" Kenneth Williams action figure, dressed in his character's costume from Carry On Cleo. The figure came with a Carry On branded base which would utter a selection of Kenneth's quotes from the film at the push of a button.

SOUNDTRACK:

Main title theme available on "Carry On"
Various Artists, CD, Silva Screen 2005
Themes, cues and dialog taken from the original film soundtracks

Extended theme available on "The Carry On Album, Music from the Films"
Gavin Sutherland & the Prague Philharmonic Orchestra, CD, ASV 1999
Newly performed renditions of classic Carry On themes

DVD:

Carry On Cleo
Warner Home Video, 2001
PAL, Region 2 (Europe, Middle East & Japan), Colour

The Ultimate Carry On (Carry On Sergeant – Carry On Screaming!)
Warner Home Video, 2001
PAL, Region 2 (Europe, Middle East & Japan), Colour, Black & White

DeAgostini Carry On DVD partwork
DeAgostini/Carlton, 2003
PAL, Region 2 (Europe, Middle East & Japan), Colour, Black & White

Carry On – The Ultimate Collection
ITV Studios Home Entertainment, 2006
PAL, Region 2 (Europe, Middle East & Japan), Colour, Black & White
Special features as for individual ITV/Carlton/Optimum releases

Carry On Cleo
Optimum Home Releasing, 2007
PAL, Region 2 (Europe, Middle East & Japan), Black & White, Colour
Special Features: Commentary (Amanda Barrie, Julie Stevens), Stills, Trivia, Trailer

Carry On Collection Vol.3 (Spying / Cleo / Screaming! / Cowboy)
Optimum Home Releasing, 2008
PAL, Region 2 (Europe, Middle East & Japan), Black & White
Special features as for individual ITV/Carlton/Optimum releases

Carry On – The Ultimate Collection
ITV Studios Home Entertainment, 2008
PAL, Region 2 (Europe, Middle East & Japan), Colour, Black & White
Special features as for individual ITV/Carlton/Optimum releases

VHS:

Carry On Cleo
Thorn EMI, 1980
PAL, Colour

Carry On Cleo
Warner Home Video, 1988
PAL, Colour

Carry On Cleo / Carry On Sergeant
Warner Home Video, 1993
PAL, Colour, Black & White

Carry On Cleo
Warner Home Video, 1997
PAL, Colour

Carry On Cleo / Carry On Sergeant
Warner Home Video, 2001
PAL, Colour, Black & White

DeAgostini Carry On VHS partwork
DeAgostini/Carlton, 2003
PAL, Colour, Black & White

BETAMAX:

Carry On Cleo
Thorn EMI, 1980
PAL, Colour

CARRY ON COWBOY

1965

Screenplay by Talbot Rothwell
Music Composed & Conducted by Eric Rogers
Carry On Cowboy, This is the Night for Love - Music Eric Rogers, Lyrics Alan Rogers

CAST	CHARACTER
Sidney James	Johnny Finger / The Rumpo Kid
Kenneth Williams	Judge Burke
Jim Dale	Marshall P Knutt
Charles Hawtrey	Big Heap
Joan Sims	Belle
Angela Douglas	Annie Oakley
Bernard Bresslaw	Little Heap
Peter Butterworth	Doc
Percy Herbert	Charlie
Jon Pertwee	Sheriff Albert Earp
Sydney Bromley	Sam Houston
Edina Ronay	Dolores
Lionel Murton	Clerk
Peter Gilmore	Curly
Davy Kaye	Josh the Undertaker
Alan Gifford	Commissioner
Brian Rawlinson	Stagecoach Guard
Michael Nightingale	Bank Manager
Simon Cain	Short
Sally Douglas	Kitikata
Cal McCord	Mex
Gary Colleano	Slim
Arthur Lovegrove	Old Cowhand
Margaret Nolan	Miss Jones
Tom Clegg	Blacksmith
Larry Cross	Perkins
Brian Coburn	Trapper
Hal Galili	Cowhand
Norman Stanley	Drunk
Carmen Dene	Mexican Girl
Andrea Allen	Minnie
Vicki Smith	Polly
Audrey Wilson	Jane
Donna White	Jenny
Lisa Thomas	Sally
Gloria Best	Bridget
George Mossman	Stagecoach Driver

Richard O'Brien .... Rider
Eric Rogers .... Pianist
The Ballet Montparnasse .... Dancing Girls

CREW

Production Manager .... Frank Bevis
Art Director .... Bert Davey
Director of Photography .... Alan Hume
Editor .... Rod Keys
Camera Operator .... Godfrey Godar
Assistant Director .... Peter Bolton
Unit Manager .... Ron Jackson
Continuity .... Gladys Goldsmith
Sound Editor .... Jim Groom
Sound Recordists .... Robert T MacPhee & Ken Barker
Make-up .... Geoffrey Rodway
Hairdresser .... Stella Rivers
Costumer Designer .... Cynthia Tingey
Assistant Editor .... Jack Gardner
Master of Horse .... Jeremy Taylor
Producer .... Peter Rogers
Director .... Gerald Thomas

A Peter Rogers production.
An Anglo Amalgamated film distributed through Warner-Pathe Distribution Ltd.

PRODUCTION DETAILS:

Budget: £195,000
Filming: 12th July 1965 – 3rd September 1965
Duration: 93m
Colour
General Release: November 1965, Certificate A
TV Premiere: 26th December 1971, BBC1
Home Video: 1981 (VHS), 2001 (DVD)

IN A NUTSHELL:

"How the West was lost!!"

Stodge City is being terrorised by the fiendish Johnny Finger, AKA the Rumpo Kid (Sid James) and his band of rustlers. When Rumpo takes up residence in the local saloon, owned by Belle (Joan Sims) and kills the sheriff (Jon Pertwee), Mayor Burke (Kenneth Williams) sends a desperate call for help.

A stagecoach speeds towards Stodge, carrying sanitation engineer (first class) Marshall P Knutt (Jim Dale) and the beautiful Annie Oakley (Angela Douglas). Knutt, mistakenly identified as a US marshal, has been sent to clean up Stodge but as he soon discovers, drain rods and a sink plunger aren't quite what the residents need.

Worried that a US Marshal will put an end to his crime spree, Rumpo forms an alliance with the local Indian tribe led by Chief Big Heap (Charles Hawtrey) but their attack on the stage is thwarted by Annie, a talented gunslinger who is in Stodge to avenge the death of her father, Sheriff Earp. When Annie discovers that Rumpo is her father's killer, she joins forces with Marshall.

REVIEW:

Wild West adventure is one of the more unusual and ambitious genres for the Carry On team to tackle. Unconvincing accents, stunts, action, gunplay, the wide open plains – there is a lot that could go wrong. But Carry On Cowboy is, on every level, cinematic and comedy perfection.

It is a triumph. Carry On Cowboy convinces as a Western thanks to some imaginative use of the British countryside and stunning set design on the Pinewood lot and its impeccable comedy credentials are thanks to Talbot Rothwell crafting a script which, again, relies on a simple premise that isn't too focused on the intricacies of plot.

The entire cast gives it everything they've got - the accents and action are brilliantly realised. The humour is loud, brash and confident, full of broad gags and Rothwell's increasingly delicate wordplay. Jim Dale gets his first proper starring role in Cowboy. He is a master of physical comedy, careering around the place and getting into deeper and deeper trouble with every step. Kenneth Williams adopts a voice and persona bigger than Texas in realising Judge Burke and hams his way through the film with such gusto that you hang off his every gnarled word. Then there is Sid James. His Rumpo Kid isn't the funniest character in the film but as a "Hollywood" bad guy he is perfection - he's gruff, menacing and when the occasion demands, charming and playful. The rest of the cast more than hold their own, from Joan Sims' vampish Belle to newcomer Angela Douglas' doe-eyed serial killer. Nobody puts a foot wrong. There's a confidence and gloss to Carry On Cowboy which elevates it above being just a great Carry On. Like Cleo before it and Screaming after, it's simply a great film.

VIEWING NOTES

- In 1965, the Carry On team briefly found themselves in competition for the biggest Western of the year when the Beatles announced that their next film project was to be an adaptation of Richard Condon's western "A Talent for Loving". Condon's novel is based on the true story of a race held in the Wild West of the 1870's where the first prize was a wealthy woman. Ultimately, the Fab Four passed on the film, but an adaptation did eventually hit cinemas in 1969.

- Carry On Cowboy was something of a rarity in terms of production in that it ran over-schedule by a day, when bad weather forced some early scenes to be re-staged.

- Compare the streets of Stodge City to any other Western and you'll notice that the Stodge City is built in a T-shape. This was to hide the fact that at the far end of the street, instead of the wide open spaces of the Midwest, there was a rather more modern-looking film studio.

- Bernard Bresslaw, Peter Butterworth and Angela Douglas all joined the regular Carry On team in Cowboy. Bresslaw, or at least part of him, had previously appeared in Carry On Nurse when his feet were used to double for Terence Longdon's.

- *Future Rocky Horror creator Richard O'Brien made his screen debut in Carry On Cowboy, playing one of the riders. O'Brien eventually returned to the world of the Carry Ons over 40 years later as presenter of the interactive DVD game, Carry On Quizzing.*

- *Kenneth Williams based the distinctive voice of his character, Judge Burke, on Hollywood pioneer Hal Roach.*

- *Angela Douglas' stunt double in Carry On Cowboy was Diana MacNamara. She later went on to play Princess Stephanie in Carry On Don't Lose your Head as well as the slightly more surprising role of Charles Hawtrey's stunt double.*

- *The stagecoach transporting Jim Dale and Angela Douglas in the film's early scenes was a replica which had already featured in a number of spaghetti westerns. It was driven in the film by George Mossman, owner of the Mossman Carriage Collection and can be seen, along with Mossman's entire collection (including a coach from Carry On Dick) at the Stockwood Discovery Centre in Luton (www.stockwooddiscoverycentre.com)*

- *During her scenes on horseback, Angela Douglas' guns had to be secured into their holsters with wire as they kept falling out.*

- *Angela was so terrified about her musical number that Joan Sims plied her with a couple of brandies beforehand and literally pushed her onto the set.*

- *The song, "This is the Night for Love" was written by Eric Rogers, with lyrics by his brother, Alan Rogers. Eric Rogers makes an appearance in the film as the piano player in the saloon.*

- *The Young Ones episode "Nasty" features a flash frame taken from Carry On Cowboy, inserted randomly into the episode.*

CARRY ON COCK-UPS:

Technical	2m 27s	The gun in Sid James' left hand goes off while it's still pointing at the ground.
Technical	2m 38s	Look over in the right hand window - you can see a man wearing a suit and tie.
Continuity	3m 14s	Take a look at the table in front of Kenneth Williams. When you see it in the next shot the glasses have moved.
Technical	10m 38s	Watch the saloon door as Jon Pertwee kicks it open - he smashes the glass on the "real" door behind.
Technical	13m 22s	Look closely at Jon Pertwee's glasses as they catch the light and you'll see the holes drilled in the centre of each lens so that the actor could see where he was going.
Technical	21m 24s	The Can-can is being played with great gusto - violins, horns, drums, the lot. Yet all you see on stage is a solitary pianist, played by Eric Rogers.
Technical	22m 56s	In a brilliant bit of continuity detail, the "Cashier Wanted" sign outside the bank has also been attached to the painted backdrop opposite the Saloon set.

Continuity	24m 47s	There are a few continuity gaffes in the scene at the bar, starting with Peter Gilmore's leaning on the bar with his right and left arms depending on the camera angle. Look also at the customers to the left of the bar. They move away as Sid tells Kenneth to go for his gun. When we cut, a couple of seconds later to the close-up of Kenneth, they can be seen to move away once again.
Technical	32m 23s	Angela Douglas declares "We've stopped" but look at the back projection through the coach window – it's still moving.
Technical	33m 31s	When the camera closes on Jim Dale, look closely at his hat - the wire for the arrow to travel along can be seen, along with a pre-marked hole for the eventual impact (and for the arrow to be pulled through). You may also want to ignore the fact that for the effect, Jim's standing in a different position to where we saw him a moment ago.
Technical	33m 38s	Just before the driver falls from the coach, his coat opens and you can see the arrow he's had tucked away in there before it springs up, appearing to shoot him in the chest.
Technical	54m 36s	As Jim Dale reacts to the banging on his door he knocks Kenneth Williams' hat with the tip of his gun.
Continuity	1h 02m 12s	Take a look at the seats and tables in the bar as the crowd rushes out. In the next shot, the close-up of Charles Hawtrey, they're arranged differently. The upturned stool behind him is upright in the previous long-shot and there's only a narrow gap for him to walk down. In subsequent shots, the gap widens and there's a growing number of upturned chairs.
Continuity	1h 02m 18s	Look too at exactly which accessories Charles Hawtrey has when he enters the saloon. A shovel and what looks like a dagger on his belt. When he's carried to the office Hawtrey's acquired a tomahawk.
Technical	1h 05m 34s	As he confronts Sid James downstairs in the bar, Jim Dale's holding up his gun belt - watch his hands.
Technical	1h 08m 59s	Look at the banister before Percy Herbert falls into it - you can see the breakaway section.
Trivia	1h 28m 28s	I know it's the entire premise for the film's finale but really - drains? In the Wild West? Continuity-wise, at least, the idea's sound. You can see a manhole cover right at the start of the film at 2m 23s

LOCATIONS:

Time	Description	Address	Also seen in	Location Link
0m 10s	The American plains	Chobham Common Surrey GU24	Carry On Cleo	

26m 43s		Black Park Black Park Rd Wexham Slough Berks SL3 6DR	Carry On Cabby Carry On Cleo Carry On Screaming! Carry On Don't Lose your Head Carry On Dick	

CARRY ON ABROAD:

Only Cowboys Next – *Croatia*
The Bold Cowboy – *Germany*
The Rumpo Kid wants a Duel – *Germany*
The Two Lightning Grand Canyon – *Greece*
From Joke to Revolver – *Norway*
The West is a Plague – *South America*

CARRY ON COLLECTING:

• Postcard featuring UK One Sheet poster released in 1998 by The London Postcard Company as part of their "British Classics Series 3" collection.

SOUNDTRACK:

"This is the Night for Love" (foxtrot arrangement from Again Doctor dance) available on "What a Carry On"
Gavin Sutherland and the Royal Sinfonia, CD, Dutton Vocalion 2005
Newly performed renditions of classic Carry On themes

DVD:

Carry On Cowboy
Warner Home Video, 2001
PAL, Region 2 (Europe, Middle East & Japan), Colour

The Ultimate Carry On (Carry On Sergeant – Carry On Screaming!)
Warner Home Video, 2001
PAL, Region 2 (Europe, Middle East & Japan), Colour, Black & White

DeAgostini Carry On DVD partwork
DeAgostini/Carlton, 2003
PAL, Region 2 (Europe, Middle East & Japan), Colour, Black & White

Carry On – The Ultimate Collection
ITV Studios Home Entertainment, 2006
PAL, Region 2 (Europe, Middle East & Japan), Colour, Black & White
Special features as for individual ITV/Carlton/Optimum releases

Carry On Cowboy
Optimum Home Releasing, 2007

PAL, Region 2 (Europe, Middle East & Japan), Black & White, Colour
Special Features: Commentary (Angela Douglas), Stills, Trivia, Trailer

Carry On Collection Vol.3 (Spying / Cleo / Screaming! / Cowboy)
Optimum Home Releasing, 2008
PAL, Region 2 (Europe, Middle East & Japan), Black & White
Special features as for individual ITV/Carlton/Optimum releases

Carry On – The Ultimate Collection
ITV Studios Home Entertainment, 2008
PAL, Region 2 (Europe, Middle East & Japan), Colour, Black & White
Special features as for individual ITV/Carlton/Optimum releases

VHS:

Carry On Cowboy
EMI, 1981
PAL, Colour

Carry On Cowboy
Thorn EMI, 1983

Carry On Cowboy
Warner Home Video, 1988
PAL, Colour

Carry On Regardless / Carry On Cowboy
Warner Home Video, 1993
PAL, Colour, Black & White

Carry On Cowboy
Warner Home Video, 1997
PAL, Colour

Carry On Regardless / Carry On Cowboy
Warner Home Video, 2001
PAL, Colour, Black & White

DeAgostini Carry On VHS partwork
DeAgostini/Carlton, 2003
PAL, Colour, Black & White

BETAMAX:

Carry On Cowboy
EMI, 1981
PAL, Colour

Carry On Cowboy
Thorn EMI, 1983
PAL, Colour

CARRY ON SCREAMING!

1966

Screenplay by Talbot Rothwell
Music Composed & Conducted by Eric Rogers
"Carry On Screaming!" by Myles Rudge & Ted Dick

CAST / CHARACTER

CAST	CHARACTER
Harry H Corbett	Detective Sergeant Sidney Bung
Kenneth Williams	Doctor Olando Watt
Jim Dale	Albert Potter
Fenella Fielding	Valeria Watt
Joan Sims	Emily Bung
Angela Douglas	Doris Mann
Bernard Bresslaw	Sockett
Peter Butterworth	Detective Constable Slobotham
Jon Pertwee	Dr Fettle
Charles Hawtrey	Dan Dann
Michael Ward	Vivian
Tom Clegg	Oddbodd
Billy Cornelius	Oddbodd Jr
Norman Mitchell	Cabby
Frank Thornton	Mr Jones
Frank Forsyth	Desk Sergeant
Anthony Sagar	Policeman
Sally Douglas	Girl
Marianne Stone	Mrs Parker
Denis Blake	Rubbatiti

CREW

Production Manager	Frank Bevis
Art Director	Bert Davey
Director of Photography	Alan Hume
Editor	Rod Keys
Camera Operator	Godfrey Godar
Assistant Director	Peter Bolton
Unit Manager	Ron Jackson
Sound Editor	Arthur Ridout
Sound Recordists	CC Stevens & Ken Barker
Continuity	Penny Daniels
Make-up	Geoffrey Rodway
Hairdresser	Stella Rivers
Costume Designer	Emma Selby-Walker
Producer	Peter Rogers
Director	Gerald Thomas

A Peter Rogers production.
An Anglo Amalgamated film distributed through Warner-Pathe Distribution Ltd.

PRODUCTION DETAILS:

Budget: £197,500
Filming: 10th January 1966 – 25th February 1966
Duration: 97m
Colour
General Release: August 1966, Certificate A
TV Premiere: 27th August 1973, BBC1
Home Video: 1988 (VHS), 2001 (DVD)

IN A NUTSHELL:

There's something nasty lurking in the woods. Young girls are being abducted by a mysterious creature. When Albert Potter's (Jim Dale) girlfriend Doris (Angela Douglas) goes missing, he turns to Detective Sergeant Sidney Bung (Harry H Corbett) and his trusty assistant Slobotham (Peter Butterworth) for help.

The trail of evidence leads the investigators to the mysterious Bide-a-Wee rest home where they meet the sinister Doctor Watt (Kenneth Williams) and his vamp-like sister Valeria (Fenella Fielding). Valeria convinces Bung of her innocence but as the evidence mounts up, it is clear that there's more to the Watts than meets the eye. Returning to interview Valeria, Bung is transformed into a hideous creature and sent to recover the mannequin into which young Doris has been transformed. But time is running out for the Watts and their dreams of shop window domination.

REVIEW:

Carry On Screaming! looks and feels every bit the Hammer pastiche it's meant to be. Director of photography Alan Hume, himself a Hammer veteran, creates an atmosphere perfectly in keeping with the Hammer style, adding a welcome authenticity. It's a magnificently creepy film, too. I can clearly remember being thrilled and terrified by Carry On Screaming! as a child and even today, the sight of Jon Pertwee's doctor, broken and discarded is a genuinely gruesome sight.

While there are genuine scares on offer, Carry On Screaming! strikes the perfect balance between comedy and horror. Talbot Rothwell's script takes in all the traditional Carry On tricks. Twelve films into the series and the Carry Ons have never been quite so accomplished, so daring and so out-and-out funny.

The sublime double act between leading man Harry H Corbett and the always-wonderful Peter Butterworth is the highlight of the film. Sid's absence from a role which was created for him is soon forgotten and, as much as it hurts me to say it, I don't think Sid could have done a better job. Throw in a literally smouldering performance from Fenella Fielding and the result is something very special indeed.

VIEWING NOTES:

- *Following the death of business partner Stuart Levy, Nat Cohen decided that the Carry On films were rather too low-brow for the direction he wanted to take Anglo Amalgamated. Thus, Carry On Screaming! was to be the final film in a long and record-breaking association.*

- *Sid James was unable to join the cast of Carry On Screaming! due to heavy work commitments. Tony Hancock was initially considered as a replacement for Sid but given their rather fractious professional relationship at the time it seems unlikely that Hancock would have seriously considered the idea.*

- *Harry H Corbett was reported to have been uncomfortable with some of the film's saucier lines and politely requested some of them be rewritten. By now, you can probably guess the reaction he received.*

- *In early drafts, Kenneth Williams' Doctor Watt was written as Valeria's father. When it was decided that Kenneth would play the role closer to his own age, the script was rewritten so that he appeared as her brother.*

- *In the original script, Jim Dale's character was named "Ken Connors". A clue, perhaps, as for whom the role was originally intended.*

- *To coincide with the launch of the film, ABC Cinemas struck a deal with novelty manufacturer, Plastech Ltd, to sell a range of Kreepy Kwiver plastic monster toys in the foyer of their cinemas.*

- *Carry On Screaming's title song is credited in the film to "Anon". For years, fans speculated whether Jim Dale was the mysterious singer, despite a single of the theme having been released by King Crimson/Bad Company's "Boz" Burrell. The theme was actually sung by Ray Pilgrim, a retired session singer who had left the notoriously fickle music business to pursue a career with the IBM Corporation.*

- *Bernard Bresslaw's character, Sockett, bears a striking resemblance to the Addams Family's faithful retainer, Lurch. Although the series was airing in the US, it had not been seen within the UK shores until Carry On Screaming! was some way into production, so the resemblance is purely coincidental.*

- *Originally, Charles Hawtrey was not cast in Carry On Screaming! In a rare instance of Peter Rogers' opinion being swayed by comments in the press, Charles was brought in to replace the originally cast Sydney Bromley (Sam Houston in Carry On Cowboy) after a critic suggested the film would be all the poorer without Hawtrey's presence.*

- *Talbot Rothwell began work on a novelisation of his script for Carry On Screaming! After a couple of chapters, he took the draft to Peter Rogers who, although delighted with the result, commented that based on the time Rothwell had spent on the novel, he would be lucky to make £500 should he ever complete it. Sadly the idea was dropped.*

- *Gerald Thomas makes his first Carry On vocal performance in this film, supplying the voice of Oddbod Jr.*

- *The car driven by Sergeant Bung is a 1904 Brushmobile, on loan to the studio, along with several other vehicles, from Lord Beaulieu's collection. Only six of these remarkable electric vehicles were ever made. Even more remarkably, the car survives to this day, although you'll have to travel to the National Motor Museum in Kuala Lumpur to see it. If you don't fancy making the trip, there's a photograph of the car on the Museum's website (http://www.jmm.gov.my/en/museum/national-automobile-museum).*

- *The budget for Carry On Screaming! wouldn't stretch to the rather striking ring that Fenella Fielding wears as part of her costume. Fenella bought the ring herself for £9.*

- *There are a couple of recognisable musical themes played throughout the film. When we see Bung behind the wheel, Eric Rogers included the strains of "Johnny Todd", the theme to popular TV detective show, Z Cars. Later, when Bung takes a ride on a horse and cart, the "Old Ned" theme from Steptoe & Son can be heard.*

- *The life-size waxwork dummies of Joan Sims and Angela Douglas are remarkably accurate creations. The two actresses had to endure hours of body casting in plaster to create the facsimiles. Look closely and you'll notice that the dummies' necks are rather fatter than their real-life counterparts; a consequence of the casts being taken when the actresses were lying down.*

- *In 2011, Time Out magazine published a list of the top 100 comedy films of all time, as chosen by a panel of comedians, writers, actors and other industry professionals. Carry On Screaming! was the only Carry On to make it into the list, at number 99.*

CARRY ON COCK-UPS:

Trivia	9m 55s	As the car pulls up in the woods, you can hear a few bars of "Johnny Todd", the theme to Z Cars, the most famous police TV show of the era.
Continuity	15m 10s	The note Harry H Corbett removed from the doorbell is in his left hand while he's in the hallway of Bide-a-Wee Rest Home. When we see him enter the drawing room his hand is empty.
Technical	17m 31s	The music played when Fenella Fielding enters the lab was first heard in Carry On Spying during the scene where Barbara Windsor is brainwashed.
Technical	27m 24s	Take a look at the houses on the road behind the police station and you'll see a collection of aerials eagerly awaiting the invention of the television.
Trivia	29m 27s	The Bless This House sign above Charles Hawtrey's bed also graced the Sheriff's bedroom in Carry On Cowboy.
Trivia	54m 58s	As the cart, driven by Harry H Corbett makes its way towards the shop to steal the dummy, we hear the familiar strains of "Old Ned", the theme to Steptoe & Son.
Technical	55m 13s	When Harry H Corbett dismounts from the cart, look closely at his "feet" during the close-up. As he starts to walk one of the rubber nails on his right foot gets crushed.
Technical	57m 29s	Yes, that's padding on the bottom of the water heater - just in case someone should bang their head.
Continuity	57m 37s	Harry H Corbett's costume is in a considerably better state than the night before. He's managed to find a pair of socks too.
Technical	58m 05s	As Harry H Corbett picks up the receiver on the phone he pulls open the front of the box.
Trivia	1h 02m 57s	Jim Dale leaves Bung's office without his shoes!

Technical	1h 17m 33s	The boom appears to be moving about quite a lot - the shadow falls across Harry H Corbett and Fenella Fielding several times during this series of two-shots.
Technical	1h 21m 44s	Sharing a bed with a real snake was one stunt Jim Dale wasn't prepared to do himself, as evinced by the rather unconvincing rubber one we see as he leaps out of bed.
Technical	1h 27m 23s	The boom shadow visible here is so obvious that a seasoned expert could probably name the precise model.
Technical	1h 31m 11s	You can clearly see a TV aerial on the roof behind where Jim Dale and Angela Douglas kiss.

LOCATIONS:

Time	Description	Address	Also seen in	Location Link
0m 00s	The spooky woods	Black Park Black Park Rd Wexham Slough Berks SL3 6DR	Carry On Cabby Carry On Cowboy Carry On Cleo Carry On Don't Lose your Head Carry On Dick	
13m 54s	Bide-a-Wee rest home	Fulmer Grange Framewood Road Wexham Slough Berks SL2 4QS		
27m 22s	Police Station	The Old Court Leonards Road Windsor Berks SL4 3BL		
27m 48s	Dan Dan's convenience	South Lodge Pinewood Studios Pinewood Road Iver Heath Bucks SL0 0NH	Carry On Nurse	

55m 58s	Bung's House	55 Queen's Road Windsor Berks SL4 3BH			

CARRY ON ABROAD:

Alarm in a Creepy Castle – *Germany*
Frankenstein Jr – *Greece*
With Pointed Teeth – *South America*
Between the Crazy Monsters – *Turkey*

CARRY ON COLLECTING

- Postcard featuring UK Quad poster released in 1998 by The London Postcard Company as part of their "British Classics Series 3" collection.
- Swift Telecom, in 2001, issued a series of three Carry On-themed pre-paid phone cards, featuring the UK Quad artwork for Carry On Jack, Carry On Cleo and Carry On Screaming!
- Carry On first class stamp and associated collectibles (presentation pack, postcard) featuring UK Quad poster for Carry On Screaming! released in 2008 by Royal Mail.

SOUNDTRACK:

7" single, "Carry On Screaming!" by Boz Burrell, Columbia DB 7972

Main title theme available on "Carry On"
Various Artists, CD, Silva Screen 2005
Themes, cues and dialog taken from the original film soundtracks

Title theme available on "What a Carry On"
Gavin Sutherland and the Royal Sinfonia, CD, Dutton Vocalion 2005
Newly performed renditions of classic Carry On themes

DVD:

Carry On Screaming!
Warner Home Video, 2001
PAL, Region 2 (Europe, Middle East & Japan), Colour

The Ultimate Carry On (Carry On Sergeant – Carry On Screaming!)
Warner Home Video, 2001
PAL, Region 2 (Europe, Middle East & Japan), Colour, Black & White

DeAgostini Carry On DVD partwork
DeAgostini/Carlton, 2003
PAL, Region 2 (Europe, Middle East & Japan), Colour, Black & White

Carry On – The Ultimate Collection
ITV Studios Home Entertainment, 2006

PAL, Region 2 (Europe, Middle East & Japan), Colour, Black & White
Special features as for individual ITV/Carlton/Optimum releases

Carry On Screaming!
Optimum Home Releasing, 2007
PAL, Region 2 (Europe, Middle East & Japan), Black & White, Colour
Special Features: Commentary (Angela Douglas, Fenella Fielding), Stills, Trivia, Trailer

Carry On Collection Vol.3 (Spying / Cleo / Screaming! / Cowboy)
Optimum Home Releasing, 2008
PAL, Region 2 (Europe, Middle East & Japan), Black & White
Special features as for individual ITV/Carlton/Optimum releases

Carry On – The Ultimate Collection
ITV Studios Home Entertainment, 2008
PAL, Region 2 (Europe, Middle East & Japan), Colour, Black & White
Special features as for individual ITV/Carlton/Optimum releases

VHS:

Carry On Screaming!
Warner Home Video, 1988
PAL, Colour

Carry On Screaming! / Carry On Teacher
Warner Home Video, 1993
PAL, Colour, Black & White

Carry On Screaming!
Warner Home Video, 1997
PAL, Colour

Carry On Screaming! / Carry On Teacher
Warner Home Video, 2001
PAL, Colour, Black & White

DeAgostini Carry On VHS partwork
DeAgostini/Carlton, 2003
PAL, Colour, Black & White

CARRY ON DON'T LOSE YOUR HEAD

1966

Screenplay by Talbot Rothwell
Music Composed & Conducted by Eric Rogers
"Don't Lose Your Head" by Bill Martin & Phil Coulter,
Executed by the Michael Sammes Singers

CAST

CAST	CHARACTER
Sidney James	Sir Rodney Ffing / The Black Fingernail
Kenneth Williams	Citizen Camembert
Jim Dale	Lord Darcy de Pue
Charles Hawtrey	Duc de Pommfrit
Peter Butterworth	Citizen Bidet
Joan Sims	Désirée Dubarry
Dany Robin	Jacqueline
Peter Gilmore	Robespierre
Marianne Stone	Landlady
Michael Ward	Henri
Leon Greene	Malabonce
David Davenport	Sergeant
Richard Shaw	Captain of Soldiers
Jennifer Clulow	1st Lady
Valerie van Ost	2nd Lady
Jacqueline Pearce	3rd Lady
Julian Orchard	Rake
Joan Ingram	Bald-headed Dowager
Elspeth March	Lady Binder
Billy Cornelius	Soldier
Nikki van der Zyl	Messenger
Ronnie Brody	Little Man
Diana MacNamara	Princess Stephanie
Hugh Futcher	Guard
Michael Nightingale	"What Locket?" Man
Patrick Allen	Narrator
Girls:	Monica Dietrich, Anna Willoughby, Penny Keen, Christine Pryor, June Cooper, Karen Young

CREW

Production Manager	Jack Swinburne
Art Director	Lionel Couch
Director of Photography	Alan Hume

Editor...Rod Keys
Camera Operator..Jimmy Devis
Assistant Director ....Jack Causey
Sound Editor..W Nelson
Sound Recordists ....Dudley Messenger & Ken Barker
Continuity...Rita Davidson
Make-up ....Geoffrey Rodway
Hairdresser..Stella Rivers
Costumer Designer..........................Emma Selby-Walker
Choreographer...Terry Gilbert
Master of Horse...Jeremy Taylor
Producer..Peter Rogers
Director..Gerald Thomas

A Peter Rogers production. Distributed through the Rank Organisation.

PRODUCTION DETAILS:

Budget: £200,000
Filming: 12th September 1966 – 28th October 1966
Duration: 90m
Colour
General Release: December 1966, Certificate A
TV Premiere: 19th September 1972, ITV (Westward)
Home Video: 1988 (VHS), 2001 (DVD)

IN A NUTSHELL:

"Carry On laughing until you have hysterics - but..."

France is in the grip of the Reign of Terror and the aristocracy are making the unwelcome acquaintance of Madame Guillotine. Sir Rodney Ffing (Sid James) and Lord Darcy de Pue (Jim Dale), alarmed at the plight of the French aristocrats vow to lift a finger or two to help bring justice back to French soil.

With Darcy on hand to distract onlookers, Sir Rodney, in the guise of the dashing Black Fingernail, rescues the Duc de Pommfrit (Charles Hawtrey) from the block moments before death. The trio flee to safety, with Citizens Camembert (Kenneth Williams) and Bidet (Peter Butterworth) in hot pursuit.

Once safely back in England, Sir Rodney holds one of his celebrated balls in aid of the beleaguered aristocrats but Camembert, with his sister Désirée (Joan Sims) and Bidet, trick their way in and reveal to Sir Rodney that they have captured the woman who helped him to flee their clutches, the beautiful Jacqueline. Sir Rodney, Darcy and the Duc head back over the channel to Camembert's chateau to mount a daring rescue.

REVIEW:

A new home for the Carry Ons. The Rank Organisation initially shied away from the Carry On moniker, but the sumptuous location filming, the familiar cast and, most importantly, a script that gleefully plays all sorts of games with established history all add up to a damn good laugh and a film which is every inch a Carry On.

Don't Lose your Head, in common with the later Anglo Amalgamated films displays a swaggering confidence. The Carry On team knows exactly how to raise a laugh out of a decidedly grim episode in history.

Sid James may be renowned as the most masculine bloke who ever walked the earth but his reputation has overshadowed the fact that he was also a fine actor when the role demanded it. Here, Sid plays the dual roles of The Black Fingernail and his foppish alter ego Sir Rodney with absolute conviction. He even makes for a surprisingly convincing woman. Sid, like the character (and characters) he plays, is a master of disguise and effortlessly slips in and out of each one.

Sadly, the film loses both momentum and conviction with its constant asides to camera, a device that appears rather novel at first but it is overly used, particularly in the sequence where Sir Rodney first bursts into Jacqueline's room. Both characters act out the scene, stopping every now and then to make sure that the audience is up to speed. It is over-long, awkward and takes the viewer out of the picture but if you can ignore these sequences (and there are more) then Don't Lose your Head is not only a joyful film but damned funny to boot.

There is a definite sense that the script runs out of steam towards the end. In particular, the sequence in the Chateau almost outstays its welcome. A touch of blood and thunder swashbuckling is all very well, but the fight does go on for quite some time. Then again, my own view of the film's ending is tainted somewhat by the awful version of "She Loves You". I'm sure to audiences of the time it was a hilarious piece of business, but it dates the film badly and like the earlier asides to camera, it takes the viewer out of the picture.

But of course, we don't love the Carry Ons for their realism and common sense and Don't Lose your Head is, for the most part, light, funny and anarchic. It's not one of the best Carry On films, but it is a long way from being one of the worst.

VIEWING NOTES:

• *Don't Lose your Head was the debut feature under Peter Rogers' new deal with The Rank Organisation. Despite assurances from Rogers, Rank was concerned that they may run into problems with the Monopolies & Mergers Commission by taking up the "Carry On" title, given the name's association with Anglo Amalgamated. Rogers explained that Nat Cohen and Anglo had assured him they no longer wanted to make any more Carry On films and that as far as he was concerned he was free to do with them as he pleased. Nevertheless, for this and the next film, Follow that Camel, the "Carry On" title was dropped.*

• *The tag line "'Carry On' Laughing until you have hysterics but...." was added to the poster to help audiences identify with the earlier films, but when box office receipts for both films were noticeably down on previous releases the title was eventually re-instated.*

• *Talbot Rothwell's original script contained a number of alternative titles, including "Short Back & Sides", "Heads You Lost", "Death of a Hat Salesman" and "Daddy Wouldn't buy me a Tourniquet". His playfulness with these titles would, in later films, become part of a running joke in the opening credits. A shame, then, that "A romance of the French Revolution" by Talbot Rothwell or "A script with cuts in it by Ivor Guillotine" didn't make the screen.*

• *Legal complications did arise when, in 1965, Sid James announced to the press that in the next Carry On he would be playing the Scarlet Pimpernel. Baroness Orczy, author of the original novel, was twenty years dead but her work was still very much within copyright. Peter Rogers drafted a hasty assurance to her estate that the film was in no way based on her earlier works. Let's face it, he was less than truthful. Overseas territories, including the USA, had no such qualms and re-titled the film "Carry On Pimpernel".*

- *French actress Dany Robin remained in the UK after completing Don't Lose your Head, eventually marrying Sid James' agent, Michael Sullivan.*

- *Charles Hawtrey's stunt double in Don't Lose your Head was Diana MacNamara, who also played Princess Stephanie, a French peasant and a solider on horseback. MacNamara had previously played Angela Douglas' stunt double in Carry On Cowboy.*

CARRY ON COCK-UPS:

Continuity	5m 50s	Jim Dale is holding his handkerchief differently between wide shots and close-ups.
Technical	11m 35s	When Peter Butterworth snatches the Marquis de Sade's book from Charles Hawtrey he accidentally tears the cover off.
Continuity	12m 29s	The girl drops the message in the basket for The Duc "to read later" (NB this gag is credited to Sid and Jim - another rare occasion where the films deviated from the original script). A couple of seconds later, we see into the basket and it's empty. When we next see inside at 14m 16s the letter has mysteriously appeared.
Continuity	12m 59s	Note where Sid James wedges the snuff box in the frame of the guillotine. When we see it again at 13m 24s it's considerably higher up.
Technical	13m 42s	Take a look at the dormer on the roof behind Kenneth Williams - you can see it's simply a prop added to the roofline. You can even see the original roof inside.
Continuity	14m 45s	Look at the position of the executioner's hands. Leon Greene's gripping the railings in close-up but in wide shots his arms are beside his sides.
Continuity	15m 34s	There's quite clearly no Black Fingernail attached to the guillotine but at 15m 46s it has appeared, despite Sid having long since departed the gallows.
Technical	21m 43s	After bumping hats a few times with Peter Butterworth as he leans out of the coach, Kenneth Williams takes stage directions into his own hands.
Trivia	22m 09s	In a nod to geographic accuracy the road signs in France denote kilometres. This cocks a snoop at historical accuracy as they weren't introduced until 1799, some six years after the Reign of Terror ended.
Continuity	22m 18s	The exterior of the Lit et Dejeuner do not match the interior. Most obviously, the window is in the wrong place in interior scenes.
Continuity	23m 37s	When Kenneth Williams helps Peter Butterworth off the floor, the chair he's just collapsed into has disappeared.

Continuity	23m 52s	Peter Butterworth's cummerbund is rather dishevelled when he leaves the inn, but he's immaculately turned out when he's seen walking through the door from the outside.
Continuity	33m 27s	Kenneth Williams moves the champagne glass to his left hand but when we see his hand behind Joan Sims in the next shot he's only holding the locket. The glass is on the table.
Continuity	35m 48s	Jim Dale talks to Sid James about the Duke and Duchess de la Plume de ma Tante but when they are finally introduced, Kenneth Williams introduces himself as The Count.
Technical	43m 02s	Jim Dale's sneeze is supplemented by an additional overdub which is slightly mistimed. The result is unfortunate for the poor dear if that's how he really sneezes.
Technical	43m 45s	As Charles Hawtrey turns away from the fountain, water can be seen to flow from the gargoyle's mouth. A few seconds later, when the he picks up the handkerchief, the water has been replaced by what looks like a glass rod.
Technical	44m 42s	The statue that Peter Butterworth hides behind wobbles as he touches it.
Trivia	45m 36s	Joan Sims' line "My brother....the count" was another of those lines which the censor allowed into the film only if there was a sufficient pause between the two words.
Continuity	59m 46s	Joan Sims can be seen, in long-shot, to walk after Sid and Jim but when we cut to the close shot she's still standing beside the cess pit.
Continuity	1h 00m 25s	Sid asks Charles Hawtrey where the Bastille is – but his character has already been there earlier in the film.
Technical	1h 00m 39s	You'll need a freeze frame for this one but as the carriage pulls up you can see the reflection of the film crew in its glass front. You get a better glimpse (in this case of a stage light) just before it pulls away again.
Technical	1h 06m 00s	Sid James does an uncanny impersonation of Robespierre, aided with nothing more than an overdub of Peter Gilmore's voice.
Trivia	1h 08m 52s	The song is, of course, based on The Beatles' "She Loves You". There has never been a worse cover version.
Continuity	1h 11m 04s	The barrel of gunpowder has been placed in the centre of the doorway, right where the two halves of the door meet. At 1h 12m 28s it's over to the left.
Continuity	1h 17m 58s	Sid's sword is pointing downwards when he jumps onto the banister. In the next shot he's holding it point-upwards and in the next it's back to its original position.
Technical	1h 19m 28s	The wire carrying Sid James' stunt double over to the chandelier is rather too obvious. You can also see the wire when Charles Hawtrey and Jim Dale do the same.

Technical	1h 19m 52s	Charles Hawtrey's lips don't match his dialogue (or his cackling).
Continuity	1h 21m 55s	Keep an eye on the soldier who just attacked Charles Hawtrey. In the next shot his hat is missing.
Continuity	1h 22m 42s	Peter Butterworth falls unconscious onto the floor. In a few moments, as Sid battles around the room, when we see the rug again, Butterworth has disappeared. Give it a couple of minutes, though, and he'll be back.
Technical	1h 22m 46s	The banister's taking quite a beating - it's wobbling under the strain.
Continuity	1h 23m 28s	The soldier slashes the tapestry with his sword. The next time we see it in 30 seconds time, the slashes will be in a different place, before we get to see the same soldier inflict the same damage all over again.
Continuity	1h 23m 38s	The harp has been well and truly unstrung. 20 seconds later it's intact as Kenneth Williams rushes over to save it
Technical	1h 25m 24s	Look at the pillar and you'll see the breakaway section, all ready for that axe.

LOCATIONS:

Time	Description	Address	Also seen in	Location Link
4m 23s	Sir Rodney's house	Cliveden House Taplow Maidenhead Bucks SL6 0JA		
34m 17s	Ballroom	Clandon Park West Clandon Guildford Surrey GU4 7RQ		
55m 51s	The duel	Pinewood Gardens Pinewood Studios Iver Heath Bucks SL0 0NH	Carry On Nurse Carry On Don't Lose your Head Carry On up the Khyber Carry On Camping Carry On Henry	

1h 07m 31s	Le Chateau Neuf	Waddesdon Manor Waddesdon Nr Aylesbury Bucks HP18 0JH		
1h 26m 35s	Church	St Mary's Church Village Road Denham Bucks UB9 5BH	Carry On Matron	

CARRY ON ABROAD:

The Black Fingernail – *Denmark*
Keep your Head – *Finland*
Just Don't Lose your Head – *Germany*
Carry On Revolutionary – *Hungary*
Carry On Pimpernel – *USA*

CARRY ON COLLECTING:

• Postcard featuring UK Quad poster released in 1998 by The London Postcard Company as part of their "Rank Classics Series 1" collection.
• Ethos, in 2007, released a series of mugs featuring the original UK Quad poster artwork for the Rank Carry Ons, including Carry On Don't Lose your Head.
• Promotional bookmark released in 1998 by The London Postcard Company featuring the Carry On Cruising and Carry On Don't Lose your Head Quad posters.

SOUNDTRACK:

Carry On Don't Lose your Head – complete audio soundtrack with additional linking narration by Patrick Allen

Original cast & crew, Audio Cassette, EMI 1996
Also released as a double-pack with Carry On Camping

DVD:

Carry On Don't Lose your Head
Cinema Club, 2001
PAL, Region 2 (Europe, Middle East & Japan), Colour

DeAgostini Carry On DVD partwork
DeAgostini/Carlton, 2003
PAL, Region 2 (Europe, Middle East & Japan), Colour, Black & White

Carry On Don't Lose your Head
ITV Studios Home Entertainment, 2003
PAL, Region 2 (Europe, Middle East & Japan), Colour
Special Features: Commentary (Jim Dale), Stills, Trivia, Trailer, Carry On Laughing – The Prisoner of Spenda
Carry On – The History Collection (Head, Dick, Jungle, Henry, England, Khyber)
ITV Studios Home Entertainment, 2005
PAL, Region 2 (Europe, Middle East & Japan), Colour
Special features as for individual ITV/Carlton/Optimum releases

Carry On – The Ultimate Collection
ITV Studios Home Entertainment, 2006
PAL, Region 2 (Europe, Middle East & Japan), Colour, Black & White
Special features as for individual ITV/Carlton/Optimum releases

Carry On Vol. 1 (Doctor, Follow that Camel, Don't Lose your Head, Up the Khyber)
Optimum Home Releasing, 2008
PAL, Region 2 (Europe, Middle East & Japan), Colour
Special features as for individual ITV/Carlton/Optimum releases

Carry On – The Ultimate Collection
ITV Studios Home Entertainment, 2008
PAL, Region 2 (Europe, Middle East & Japan), Colour, Black & White
Special features as for individual ITV/Carlton/Optimum releases

VHS:

Carry On Don't Lose your Head
Cinema Club, 1988
PAL, Colour

Carry On Don't Lose your Head
Cinema Club, 1992
PAL, Colour

Carry On Don't Lose your Head - Collector's Edition
Cinema Club, 1999
PAL, Colour

Carry On Follow that Camel / Carry On Don't Lose your Head
Cinema Club, 2000
PAL, Colour

The Carry On Collection (Don't Lose your Head – Carry On Emmannuelle)
Carlton Visual Entertainment, 2003
PAL, Colour

DeAgostini Carry On VHS partwork
DeAgostini/Carlton, 2003AL, Colour, Black & White

Carry On Don't Lose your Head
Carlton Visual Entertainment, 2003 PAL, Colour

CARRY ON FOLLOW THAT CAMEL

1967

Screenplay by Talbot Rothwell
Music Composed & Conducted by Eric Rogers

CAST / CHARACTER

CAST	CHARACTER
Phil Silvers	Sergeant Ernie Knocker
Kenneth Williams	Commandant Burger
Jim Dale	Bertram Oliphant "Bo" West
Charles Hawtrey	Captain Le Pice
Joan Sims	Zig-Zig
Angela Douglas	Lady Jane Ponsonby
Peter Butterworth	Simpson
Bernard Bresslaw	Sheikh Abdul Abulbul
Anita Harris	Corktip
John Bluthal	Corporal Clotski
William Mervyn	Sir Cyril Ponsonby
Peter Gilmore	Captain "Hump" Bagshaw
Julian Holloway	Ticket Collector
David Glover	Hotel Manager
Julian Orchard	Doctor
Vincent Ball	Ship's Officer
Peter Jesson	Lawrence
Gertan Klauber	Spiv
Michael Nightingale	Butler
Harold Kasket	Hotel Gentleman
Edmund Pegge	Bowler
Riffs at Abdul's Tent:	Richard Montez, Frank Singuineau, Larry Taylor, William Hurndell, Simon Cain
Harem Girls:	Carol Sloan, Gina Gianelli, Dominique Don, Anne Scott, Margot Maxine, Patsy Snell, Zorenah Osborne, Karen Young, Gina Warwick, Angela Grant, Sally Douglas, Helga Jones

CREW

Production Manager	Jack Swinburne
Art Director	Alex Vetchinsky
Director of Photography	Alan Hume
Editor	Alfred Roome
Camera Operator	Alan Hall

Assistant Director ....David Bracknell
Sound Recordists ....Dudley Messenger & Ken Barker
Dubbing Editor...Wally Nelson
Location Manager...Terry Clegg
Continuity..Joy Mercer
Assistant Editor..Jack Gardner
Make-up ....Geoffrey Rodway
Hairdresser ....Stella Rivers
Costume Designer...Emma Selby-Walker
Producer..Peter Rogers
Director...Gerald Thomas

A Peter Rogers production. Distributed through the Rank Organisation.

PRODUCTION DETAILS:

Budget: £288,500
Filming: 1st May 1967 – 23rd June 1967
Colour
General Release: September 1967, Certificate A
TV Premiere: 21st October 1972, ITV (ATV)
Home Video: 1984 (VHS/Betamax), 2001 (DVD)

IN A NUTSHELL:

"Bilko joins the Carry On legion!"

Accused of cheating at cricket, Bo West (Jim Dale) has just one option - to accept dishonour, turn his back on the life he knew and run away to join the Foreign Legion. With his faithful batman, Simpson (Peter Butterworth) in tow, Bo arrives to find the Legion locked in a bitter struggle with Sheikh Abdul Abulbul (Bernard Bresslaw).

Meanwhile, back in England, Bo's intended, Lady Jane Ponsonby (Angela Douglas) discovers that he was innocent all along and sets off to the desert to restore Bo's good name.

When Bo and Simpson reveal to the duplicitous Sergeant Nocker (Phil Silvers) that they had witnessed his heroic struggle, not with the local militia but with café owner, Zig-Zig (Joan Sims), life in the Legion becomes considerably more enjoyable. That is until Lady Jane is captured by the evil Sheikh.

When Bo and Nocker are themselves captured and taken to Abdul's camp, first Simpson and then Commandant Burger (Kenneth Williams) mount a daring rescue, only to discover that the Sheikh is preparing to attack the Legion's outpost at Fort Zuassantneuf.

REVIEW:

There is something not quite right about Carry On Follow that Camel. Of course, the absence of Sid and the flying in of Phil Silvers stands out but there is a bigger problem in that there are simply too many characters playing against type. With Kenneth Williams as the hard German commandant and Hawtrey as his uptight adjutant there is too much that is all at odds with what usually passes for a Carry On. Williams isn't arch enough, Hawtrey not silly enough and Silvers not Sid enough. But Bilko in a Carry On? Well, that at least does work. Silvers fits in perfectly with the rest of the team, sparking brilliantly off of the other cast members, especially Dale and Butterworth.

Jim Dale is the perfect romantic lead. He's a fine actor and manages an expressiveness of face and physique that enables him to deliver perfect slapstick as well as the film's more subtle line of comedy. There is one if you look for it. He plays beautifully opposite Peter Butterworth and alternates with ease between gormless idiot and man of action.

Meanwhile Peter Butterworth, the unsung hero of the Carry Ons, is never less than perfect. His presence can elevate a film from watchable to must-see and to see him with a meaty role is a quite a treat. Speaking of meaty roles, particular praise must also go to Bernard Bresslaw. The issue of him being blacked-up is a thorny one - such a thing would simply and quite rightly not be tolerated today. But Bresslaw throws everything he's got at the part and really does make a brilliant, scenery-chewing baddie. Such a shame, then, that in later films he would be too often reduced to playing a simple-minded giant.

So what's wrong with Follow that Camel? To my mind, it's an underlying but ever-present sense of desperation. Not so much in the script which crackles with Rothwell's customary wit, but in the very concept. Dishonour, lies, deceit, cuckolded lovers, even rape; these things are not the ingredients of a feel-good film. Add to that several of the core members playing characters they are not really suited for and the result is an entertaining and funny film which is undermined by too many factors which are anything but Carry On. While there are plenty of gags that work and some wonderful set pieces, Follow that Camel is ultimately rather a mean-spirited film.

VIEWING NOTES:

• *Talbot Rothwell's script was originally titled "Carry On Bo!" and once again included a number of alternative titles, most notably, "Across the Sahara with Spade & Bucket" and "You've Gotta be Tough when there's Nothing but Sand Paper".*

• *Like "Don't Lose your Head" before it, Follow that Camel was originally released without the "Carry On" prefix. The UK poster proclaimed via its tag line that "Bilko joins the 'Carry On' legion".*

• *The story of Phil Silvers' joining the Carry On team at the time at least, was one of happy coincidence. Sid James was committed to a TV sitcom, George & the Dragon and suffered a heart attack shortly after the film went into production. Thus, he was unable to join the cast despite the original starring role being ear-marked for him. As he wrote the script, Talbot Rothwell increasingly convinced that the Nocker role was essentially Bilko in the desert.*

• *The Rank Organisation, hoping to attract American audiences, suggested Phil Silvers would be an ideal addition to the cast although as producer Peter Rogers maintained, the films were already selling consistently well in America. The Carry Ons might never again achieve the record-breaking transatlantic success of Nurse, but they still enjoyed a modest, loyal audience across the Pond.*

• *Phil Silvers pocketed an enormous pay packet by Carry On standards – a whopping £30,000. By comparison, Kenneth Williams had only recently succeeded in increasing his pay to £6000.*

• *Charles Hawtrey was unhappy with the role of Le Pice, as originally offered and suggested to Peter Rogers that he would make a better Simpson. As the end result testifies, Rogers disagreed.*

- *Silvers' trademark glasses as worn in the film were fakes; the actor wore contact lenses to improve his poor eyesight. Silvers, whose health was failing during the production, had to resort to reading many of his lines from idiot boards.*

- *The camel ridden by Jim Dale in the film was hired from Chessington Zoo. Born in captivity, it had never walked on sand before, so filming was slightly delayed while it could be trained to walk on the unfamiliar surface.*

- *Anita Harris' character, Corktip, is named in homage to "Cigarette", as played by Claudette Colbert in the 1936 Foreign Legion adventure "Under Two Flags".*

- *In typical Carry On form, Camber Sands made for a convincing Sahara desert but the weather was particularly unseasonable that year. Instead of sweltering under a desert sky, the crew were snowed upon more often than not.*

- *To combat the appearance of cold, Peter Butterworth and Jim Dale, when buried in the sand, were fortified with brandy and wrapped in blankets. The sweat seen dripping down their faces as they bake under the desert "sun" was in fact glycerine.*

- *The feast at the Sheik's camp was filmed over a period of three days - with real food.*

- *As originally scripted, the baby at the end of the film was to have been played by Phil Silvers.*

CARRY ON COCK-UPS:

Continuity	2m 33s	When Jim Dale first approaches Peter Gilmore, the latter is holding his cricket pads with the knee end facing out. In the close-up shot that follows he's holding them the other way round.
Continuity	3m 53s	Angela Douglas picks up her napkin in her left hand when she holds the letter with her right. In the next close-up she has the napkin in her right and the letter in her left.
Technical	5m 15s	Take a look at the desert in the background as the camel comes through the archway. Painted backdrops are of course the norm in cinema but as the camel passes into the square you can see a seam running down the backdrop.
Continuity	9m 06s	Kenneth Williams has just turned the bloomers around in order to read the message written on them. In the long-shot from Abdul's tower, they are the other way around once more before reverting again just before Charles' hat is shot off.
Continuity	12m 26s	Kenneth Williams is talking to Jim Dale and Peter Butterworth from behind his desk. When Dale interrupts Butterworth's story about the gardener's daughter, there's a rather jarring cut. The conversation changes tone and Williams is suddenly standing beside Dale.
Continuity	16m 57s	Angela Douglas is sitting on the left hand side of the car when she talks to her father. In the next, wide shot, she's on the right and holding a parasol that wasn't there a moment ago.
Continuity	21m 47s	Peter Butterworth is seen to be fastening the buttons on Jim Dale's tunic. In the next shot, the tunic is still unfastened and Butterworth is standing to attention.

Technical	29m 08s	The music to which Anita Harris dances to is a re-arrangement of the Algerian theme Eric Rogers composed for Carry On Spying.
Continuity	29m 30s	Look at the table the gang are sitting around. There are two hats on it and one is upturned. In the close-up the second hat is the right way up and in a different position.
Continuity	36m 59s	When Anita Harris looks through the curtain at Phil Silvers and the boys, once again there are two hats on the table. Both are the right way up. When Joan gets to the table, one is upside down again.
Continuity	45m 30s	Phil Silvers is wearing his medals - remember that.
Continuity	48m 31s	Those medals are missing when we next see him at the Oasis El Nooki.
Continuity	50m 35s	Bernard Bresslaw is holding his whip at his side with his hand on his sword just after the first mention of Mustapha Leek but when we see him in close-up it is held to his chest with both hands.
Continuity	53m 16s	Jim Dale and Phil Silvers subdue the disguised Peter Butterworth. When we return there appears to have been a cut - there's no mention of the case of mistaken identity and the three carry on as if nothing has happened.
Continuity	54m 55s	Bernard Bresslaw's sword is now hung on his right side - it was on the left earlier.
Continuity	57m 41s	Now the sword is back on his left again.
Continuity	1h 00m 18s	Remember Phil Silvers lost his medals earlier? Well, they're back.
Technical	1h 09m 58s	Phil Silvers orders "Right turn" and the men turn to the left.
Continuity	1h 14m 58s	Small wonder the troops don't notice the bodies of their fallen comrades when they first enter the fort because they are not there when they first enter the fort. (at 1h 14m 41s).
Trivia	1h 25m 43s	The gramophone track played to fool Abdul and his men is the German military song "Durch die grüne Heide" ("By Heather Green").

LOCATIONS:

Time	Description	Address	Also seen in	Location Link
1m 32s	Cricket Match	Swakeleys House Milton Road Ickenham UB10 8NS		

3m 36s	Dinner in the house	Dining Room Osterley Park House Jersey Road Isleworth Middx TW7 4RB		
4m 38s	Hump hangs himself	Entrance hall Osterley Park House Jersey Road Isleworth Middx TW7 4RB		
47m 52s	Abdul's camp	Camber Sands Lydd Road Rye Sussex TN31 7RL		

CARRY ON ABROAD:

In the Desert, No Water Flows – *Germany*
Carry On with the Foreign Legion – *Hungary*
Carry On in the Legion – *USA*

CARRY ON CUTTING:

- *A scene was cut where Lawrence of Arabia, played by Peter Jesson, turns up in the desert asking Kenneth Williams for directions.*

- *Gertan Klauber filmed a brief scene in the film where he played a spiv, trying to sell naughty postcards to Bo and Simpson as they try to find the Legion HQ.*

- *Another brief gag cut from the final print features a level crossing for camels in the desert.*

- *A scene in which Jim Dale ran, bayonet at the ready at a strung-up dummy, reminiscent of Carry On Sergeant, was also cut from the final print.*

- *A scene was filmed following the arrival at Fort Zuassantneuf wherein Simpkins finds himself accidentally buried alongside the dead soldiers.*

CARRY ON COLLECTING:

- Postcard featuring UK Quad poster released in 1998 by The London Postcard Company as part of their "Rank Classics Series 1" collection.
- Promotional bookmark released in 1998 by The London Postcard Company featuring the Carry On Behind and Carry On Follow that Camel Quad posters.
- Ethos, in 2007, released a series of mugs featuring the original UK Quad poster artwork for the Rank Carry Ons, including Carry On Follow that Camel.

SOUNDTRACK:

Carry On Follow that Camel – complete audio soundtrack with additional linking narration by Patrick Allen
Original cast & crew, Audio Cassette, EMI 1996
Also released as a double-pack with Carry On Doctor

Main title theme available on "Carry On"
Various Artists, CD, Silva Screen 2005
Themes, cues and dialog taken from the original film soundtracks

Title theme available on "What a Carry On"
Gavin Sutherland and the Royal Sinfonia, CD, Dutton Vocalion 2005
Newly performed renditions of classic Carry On themes

DVD:

Carry On Follow that Camel
Cinema Club, 2001
PAL, Region 2 (Europe, Middle East & Japan), Colour

DeAgostini Carry On DVD partwork
DeAgostini/Carlton, 2003
PAL, Region 2 (Europe, Middle East & Japan), Colour, Black & White

Carry On Follow that Camel
ITV Studios Home Entertainment, 2003
PAL, Region 2 (Europe, Middle East & Japan), Colour
Special Features: Commentary (Jim Dale), Stills, Trivia, Trailer, Phil Silvers on-set interview

Carry On – The Holiday Collection (Camping, Abroad, Camel, Girls, Convenience, Behind)
ITV Studios Home Entertainment, 2005
PAL, Region 2 (Europe, Middle East & Japan), Colour
Special features as for individual ITV/Carlton/Optimum releases

Carry On – The Ultimate Collection
ITV Studios Home Entertainment, 2006
PAL, Region 2 (Europe, Middle East & Japan), Colour, Black & White
Special features as for individual ITV/Carlton/Optimum releases

Carry On Vol. 1 (Doctor, Follow that Camel, Don't Lose your Head, Up the Khyber)
Optimum Home Releasing, 2008
PAL, Region 2 (Europe, Middle East & Japan), Colour
Special features as for individual ITV/Carlton/Optimum releases

Carry On – The Ultimate Collection
ITV Studios Home Entertainment, 2008
PAL, Region 2 (Europe, Middle East & Japan), Colour, Black & White
Special features as for individual ITV/Carlton/Optimum releases

VHS:

Carry On Follow that Camel
Rank Video Library, 1984
PAL, Colour

Carry On Follow that Camel
Cinema Club, 1987
PAL, Colour

Carry On Follow that Camel
Cinema Club, 1992
PAL, Colour

Carry On Follow that Camel
Cinema Club, 1996
PAL, Colour

Carry On Follow that Camel - Collector's Edition
Cinema Club, 1999
PAL, Colour

Carry On Follow that Camel / Carry On Don't Lose your Head
Cinema Club, 2000
PAL, Colour

DeAgostini Carry On VHS partwork
DeAgostini/Carlton, 2003
PAL, Colour, Black & White

The Carry On Collection (Don't Lose your Head – Carry On Emmannuelle)
Carlton Visual Entertainment, 2003
PAL, Colour

Carry On Follow that Camel
Carlton Visual Entertainment, 2003
PAL, Colour

BETAMAX:

Carry On Follow that Camel
Rank Video Library, 1984
PAL, Colour

CARRY ON DOCTOR

Or...

NURSE CARRIES ON AGAIN

Or...

DEATH OF A DAFFODIL

Or...

LIFE IS A FOUR LETTER WORD
A BEDPANORAMA OF HOSPITAL LIFE

1967

Screenplay by Talbot Rothwell
Music Composed & Conducted by Eric Rogers

CAST

CAST	CHARACTER
Frankie Howerd	Francis Bigger
Sidney James	Charlie Roper
Charles Hawtrey	Mr Barron
Kenneth Williams	Doctor Kenneth Tinkle
Jim Dale	Doctor Jim Kilmore
Barbara Windsor	Nurse Sandra May
Joan Sims	Chloe Gibson
Bernard Bresslaw	Ken Biddle
Hattie Jacques	Matron
Anita Harris	Nurse Clarke
Peter Butterworth	Mr Smith
Dilys Laye	Mavis Winkle
June Jago	Sister Hoggett
Derek Francis	Sir Edmund Burke
Dandy Nichols	Mrs Roper
Peter Jones	Chaplain
Deryck Guyler	Surgeon Hardcastle
Gwendolyn Watts	Mrs Barron
Peter Gilmore	Henry
Harry Locke	Sam
Marianne Stone	Mother
Jean St.Clair	Mrs Smith
Valerie van Ost	Nurse Parkin
Julian Orchard	Fred
Brian Wilde	Man from Cox & Carter
Lucy Griffiths	Patient
Pat Coombs	Patient
Gertan Klauber	Wash Orderly
Julian Holloway	Simmons
Jenny White	Nurse in Bath

Helen Ford	Nurse
Gordon Rollings	Night Porter
Simon Cain	Tea Orderly
Penelope Keith	Plain Nurse
Cheryl Molineaux	Women's Ward Nurse
Alexandra Dane	Female Instructor
Bart Allison	Grandad
Jane Murdoch	Nurse
Stephen Garlick	Small Boy
Narrator	Patrick Allen

CREW

Production Manager	Jack Swinburne
Art Director	Cedric Dawe
Director of Photography	Alan Hume
Editor	Alfred Roome
Assistant Director	Terry Clegg
Camera Operator	Jim Bawden
Assistant Editor	Jack Gardner
Sound Recordists	Dudley Messenger & Ken Barker
Dubbing Editor	David Campling
Continuity	Joy Mercer
Make-up	Geoffrey Rodway
Hairdresser	Stella Rivers
Costume Designer	Yvonne Caffin
Titles by	"Larry"
Producer	Peter Rogers
Director	Gerald Thomas

A Peter Rogers production. Distributed through the Rank Organisation.

PRODUCTION DETAILS:

Budget: £214,000
Filming: 11th September 1967 – 20th October 1967
Duration: 94m
Colour
General Release: December 1967, Certificate A
TV Premiere: 11th September 1974, BBC1
Home Video: 1984 (VHS/Betamax), 2001 (DVD)

IN A NUTSHELL:

Faith healer Francis Bigger (Frankie Howerd) discovers that mind doesn't always conquer matter when he falls off stage during a lecture. Bigger is rushed into hospital where he finds himself at the mercy of the fearsome Matron (Hattie Jacques) and Dr Tinkle (Kenneth Williams), an eminent surgeon whose bedside manner leaves rather a lot to be desired.

Life on the wards becomes increasingly unpleasant for Bigger and his fellow patients, Charlie Roper (Sid James), Ken Biddle (Bernard Bresslaw) and Mr Barron (Charles Hawtrey) but things are far worse for the dashing young Doctor Kilmore (Jim Dale). When new nurse Sandra May (Barbara Windsor) arrives at the hospital, Kilmore uncovers her shady past with Dr Tinkle who, fearing his secret may come out, hatches a plot with Matron to disgrace the doctor and get him out of the way.

Bigger, believing that he is not much longer for this earth, agrees to marry his long-term assistant, the profoundly deaf Chloe Gibson (Joan Sims). The patients, meanwhile, come out in support of Dr Kilmore but when Matron and Dr Tinkle's tactics turn nasty, they are forced to take more drastic measures.

REVIEW:

Carry On Doctor is the finest of the medical Carry Ons. The gang really are all here and they are bolstered by the presence of Mr Francis Howerd, whose guest starring role would, in any other film, outshine every other character. But not when the Carry On gang is at its outrageous best. Carry On Doctor is a supremely confident film - it's not afraid to reference past glories and the Carry Ons have never been quite so saucy and suggestive.

Most of the cast are recumbent throughout, so there's not a great deal of action in Carry On Doctor but what action there is centres around the charismatic bungler played by Jim Dale. Sid, recovering from a heart attack, is allowed to take it easy and enjoys a somewhat smaller role than usual, but if we are honest, we are lucky to have him at all, given the severity of his illness at the time.

Doctor is the direct descendant of Carry On Nurse in tone as well as setting and it's the perfect way of heralding in a new era of Carry Ons under the Rank banner. It's easy to see why the team chose such a tried and tested formula and audiences for whom Carry On Nurse was such a fond memory, welcomed the re-invigorated and titularly re-instated Carry On team. The references to the past are brilliantly executed. Howerd in his private room is the Colonel, while the patients revolt in their beds under the reign of terror of the same Matron. The additional sub-plot of Kilmore is an added sophistication, but all the same basic ideas from Carry On Nurse are there.

After several years of visually more ambitious and grander productions, the Carry Ons come back down to earth in Doctor but the same beloved performers are all playing the roles we love best. It reassures the viewer that we are back on familiar ground but at the same time it ups the ante, making the sexual gags even nearer the knuckle and the performances more hilariously grotesque simply because they're rooted in our everyday reality. Quite simply, Carry On Doctor is a triumph.

VIEWING NOTES:

• *The Doctor films produced by Peter Rogers' wife Betty Box and directed by Gerald Thomas' brother, Ralph, were a well-established series, well on par with the Carry Ons. Rogers sought permission from his wife to use the "Doctor" title for this latest film and as a tribute to the series, a portrait of James Robertson Justice was placed between the lifts in the hospital foyer, bearing the words "Sir James R Justice, Founder". Permission was also sought, and granted, from Justice to use his likeness in the film.*

• *Rank's experience with their first two Carry Ons was a rather sobering affair. When Peter Rogers approached them, asking to call the next film "Carry On Doctor", Rank didn't hesi-*

tate in telling the producer that provided Betty Box saw no conflict with her long-running "Doctor" films, they agreed. The Rogers family coffers were swelled by a percentage of the takings of Carry On Doctor going to Betty Box by way of a royalty.

- Those additional joke titles that Rothwell habitually included on the cover of his scripts finally found their way on to the screen with Carry On Doctor. One that didn't make it to the final cut was "Hands off the Alimentary Canal". One of those additional titles was briefly considered as the name of the film. With Rank still uncertain about branding their film with a competitor's title, "Nurse Carries On Again" was an early potential title.

- In Peter Rogers' original notes, Joan Sims is pencilled in as a candidate for the role of Matron. This isn't as bizarre an idea as it sounds – Sims had played the Matron in the 1966 film, Doctor in Clover.

- The recumbent nature of Sid's role in Carry On Doctor was largely dictated by the fact that he was still recovering from a heart attack suffered earlier in the year.

- Much of the action in Carry On Doctor takes place on the Fosdick Ward, a name which Rothwell would resurrect in Carry On Again Doctor as the name of Patsy Rowlands' character.

- In 2006, the BBC Television programme Balderdash & Piffle launched a challenge to find the true origins of various words in the English language. "Phwoar" was championed by Carry On fans and selected for further investigation, with the ambulance driver's (Peter Gilmore) reaction to seeing Nurse May in Carry On Doctor suggested to be the earliest scripted example of the word's use. Sadly, like several other "phwoar"s over the years, Gilmore's comment wasn't scripted as such and the Carry Ons' place in literary history was lost to a schoolgirl in the 1970s writing in her diary about how attractive she found her teacher.

CARRY ON COCK-UPS:

Continuity	4m 39s	The ambulance parks diagonally across the parking bays when it arrives at the hospital. But when we see it reverse towards the doors it does so from an entirely different angle.
Continuity	4m 56s	The head of Sid's bed doesn't look particularly safe. It is not fixed properly and appears to be resting diagonally. It is inconsistently positioned throughout the film.
Continuity	6m 17s	We will put it down to hospital shenanigans when the porter pushes Frankie Howerd's bed from the top when they first enter the hospital but from the bottom when he enters the ward. But where is the blanket he had under his head?
Continuity	11m 39s	Frankie Howerd is fastening the collar of his gown when seen in close-ups over the next few minutes. When we cut to the wider shot of Hattie Jacques departing, he is lying in his earlier position with his hands inside the bedclothes, his collar undone.
Trivia	12m 19s	There is the portrait of James Robertson Justice.

Continuity	13m 56s	There's just a vase on Frankie Howerd's bedside table and, as we shall see in a moment, fruit on Charles Hawtrey's. At 14m 44s we see a bottle of yellow liquid (hopefully Lucozade) on Howerd's and a jar of water on Hawtrey's. The content of Hawtrey's fruit bowl has changed as well. Iin the first shot there is a black banana and what looks like a letter. By 14m 44s it is over flowing with ripe fruit and he's gained a bottle of cordial as well.
Trivia	14m 50s	Eric Rogers' music for when we first meet Charles Hawtrey borrows from Mussorgsky's "Ballet of the Chicks in their Shells".
Continuity	15m 48s	They're all at it – there's a bowl full of fruit on Sid's bedside table too, now.
Continuity	19m 14s	When Frankie Howerd turns over in bed, the bottle on the cabinet beside his bed is facing the camera. Moments later, when Jim Dale slips and plunges the syringe into his behind, the label is facing to the left.
Continuity	21m 18s	The porter approaches Sid James' bed with two cups but by the time he gets there, in the next shot, one has disappeared.
Continuity	29m 47s	Frankie Howerd's gown changes position in the upcoming sequence as we switch between shots.
Technical	30m 09s	There appear to be two charges for the X Ray explosion - look at the floor beneath the table and you'll see another one go off.
Continuity	30m 47s	A nurse can be seen holding open the door for Frankie Howerd's stretcher to go through. When we cut to the long shot there's no nurse in sight but one does then emerge behind the stretcher. When we next see Howerd on the floor she rushes to his help, but from the opposite direction.
Continuity	31m 12s	When Sid James is having his blood pressure taken the thermometer is to the right of the centre of the flowers. When it explodes it is dead centre.
Trivia	31m 33s	Frankie Howerd's reaction to the nurse with the daffodil is, of course, a reference to Wilfrid Hyde White's floral fate in Carry On Nurse.
Continuity	51m 26s	Keep an eye on the position of Kenneth Williams' stethoscope at the back of his neck through this scene - it changes from shot to shot.
Continuity	58m 21s	When Barbara Windsor climbs up to the roof, the window to the left of her is fully closed. In close-up shots the right pane of the window is open. When we see it again in long-shot the window is closed.
Technical	59m 45s	The whole roof wobbles when Jim Dale slams the skylight window open on to it.
Continuity	1h 00m 08s	Barbara Windsor undoes her bikini top to sunbathe. When she stands up in alarm it is fastened.
Continuity	1h 01m 55s	When Anita Harris runs up the stairs she has a seam up the back of her stockings. When we see her try to rescue Jim Dale on the roof they are seamless.

Continuity	1h 02m 46s	The curtains on the window that Jim Dale jumps through are open from the inside but drawn almost shut from the outside. When he first breaks the glass the window breaks cleanly leaving just one piece to the left but when he's in the bath you can see a few extra shards added to the broken frame.
Continuity	1h 04m 36s	In the wide shots of Charles Hawtrey at the pre-natal class, the floor in front of him is clean but there are scuff marks in the close-ups.
Trivia	1h 05m 49s	As Brian Wilde enters the room to measure up the bed, Eric Rogers borrows Gounod's "Funeral March of a Marionette".
Continuity	1h 10m 45s	Keep an eye on the wedding licence - it's in a different position between wide and close-up shots.
Technical	1h 21m 02s	There's a boom shadow moving about on the wall behind the girls.
Technical	1h 22m 15s	Kenneth Williams sits up on the bed after Hattie Jacques pushes him down and the pair accidentally hit faces. A hasty sound effect covers the gaffe although the pair, Hattie in particular, almost loses her composure.
Continuity	1h 22m 22s	When the door opens, Hattie Jacques and Kenneth Williams are sitting up on the bed where they were just seen mid-line to be lying down, with her on top.
Trivia	1h 27m 22s	Eric Rogers borrows a brief segment of Rossini's "The Barber of Seville" to accompany Bernard Bresslaw's comment about having been a barber.

LOCATIONS:

Time	Description	Address	Also seen in	Location Link
1m 37s	Church Hall	Old Masonic Temple New Windsor Street Uxbridge UB8 2TU		
4m 10s	Bigger's ambulance ride	High St Maidenhead Berks SL6	Carry On Camping	

4m 37s	Hospital exterior	Maidenhead Town Hall 11 St Ives Road, Maidenhead Berks SL6 1RF	Carry On Again Doctor Carry On Behind	
19m 32s	Nurses' quarters	Westbourne Street London W2 2TZ Opposite the Royal Lancaster Hotel, Hyde Park.		
58m 21s	Roof of nurses' quarters	Westbourne Street London W2 2TZ Opposite the Royal Lancaster Hotel, Hyde Park.		

CARRY ON CUTTING:

• A scene was filmed with Penelope Keith in the role of "Plain Nurse" who comes out to meet Henry the ambulance driver (Peter Gilmore) shortly after his encounter with Nurse May. Ms Keith is unflatteringly referred to as "plain" because in the script, Gilmore's character compared her attributes to those of Nurse May.

CARRY ON ABROAD:

Nurses in Heat – *Belgium*
The Sixth Section's Calling, Doctor! – *Denmark*
Go Ahead, Doctor! / A Mad Hospital – *Germany*
Physicians for All Jobs – *Greece*
Up with the Temperature! – *Norway*
Doc – get to work again! – *Poland*
Carry On in Hospital – *Spain*
Watch Out Doctor – *South America*
Take me on the Bed, Doctor – *Sweden*

CARRY ON COLLECTING:

• "Carry On Doctor – The wickedly funny story that starts where the film ends". A novel by Norman Giller
Andre Deutsch Ltd, 1996, ISBN 0233990275
• Postcard featuring UK Quad poster released in 1998 by The London Postcard Company as part of their "Rank Classics Series 1" collection.

- Promotional bookmark released in 1998 by The London Postcard Company featuring the Carry On Doctor and Carry On Matron Quad posters.
- Cartel International, in 1998, released a series of Carry On themed greetings cards bearing stills from the films together with suitably saucy texts. The series of 14 cards included stills from Carry On Doctor, Carry On Camping, Carry On Again Doctor, Carry On up the Jungle, Carry On Abroad and Carry On Girls.
- In 2001, Royal Doulton released a series of limited edition Carry On Toby jugs. The first pair, of which only 1000 were available, were of Hattie Jacques as Matron and Kenneth Williams as Dr Tinkle from Carry On Doctor.
- Cards Inc, in 2003, planned a series of Carry On trading cards. While the series was ultimately cancelled, a pack of eight preview cards were released featuring images from Carry On Doctor, Carry On up the Khyber, Carry On Camping, Carry On Again Doctor, Carry On up the Jungle, Carry On Abroad and Carry On Dick.
- Following the release of their Kenneth Williams Carry On Cleo action figure, Product Enterprise released details of a Barbara Windsor nurse figure, due for release in 2006. The product, which was incorrectly labelled as being from "Carry On Again Doctor" was dressed as Nurse May but was never released for sale.
- Ethos, in 2007, released a series of mugs featuring the original UK Quad poster artwork for the Rank Carry Ons, including Carry On Doctor.
- CollectablesMANIA, in 2007, released a series of Carry On-themed poker chips. Each set came in a presentation pack, complete with trivia notes and contained six individual plastic chips emblazoned with stills from the film. Five different sets were produced, representing Carry On Doctor, Carry On Up the Khyber, Carry On Camping, Carry On Henry and Carry On Matron.

SOUNDTRACK:

Carry On Doctor – complete audio soundtrack with additional linking narration by Peter Gilmore
Original cast & crew, Audio Cassette, EMI 1996
Also released as a double-pack with Carry On Follow that Camel

"Carry On Doctor / Doctor Again Suite" available on "The Carry On Album, Music from the Films"
Gavin Sutherland & the Prague Philharmonic Orchestra, CD, ASV 1999
Newly performed renditions of classic Carry On themes

Main title theme available on "Carry On"
Various Artists, CD, Silva Screen 2005
Themes, cues and dialog taken from the original film soundtracks

Title theme available on "What a Carry On"
Gavin Sutherland and the Royal Sinfonia, CD, Dutton Vocalion 2005
Newly performed renditions of classic Carry On themes

DVD:

Carry On Doctor
Cinema Club, 2001
PAL, Region 2 (Europe, Middle East & Japan), Colour

DeAgostini Carry On DVD partwork
DeAgostini/Carlton, 2003
PAL, Region 2 (Europe, Middle East & Japan), Colour, Black & White

Carry On Doctor
ITV Studios Home Entertainment, 2003
PAL, Region 2 (Europe, Middle East & Japan), Colour
Special Features: Commentary (Jim Dale), Stills, Trivia, Trailer, Carry On Laughing –
Baron Outlook

Carry On – The Doctors & Nurses Collection (Doctor, Matron, Again Doctor, That's
Carry On, Loving, Emmannuelle)
ITV Studios Home Entertainment, 2005
PAL, Region 2 (Europe, Middle East & Japan), Colour

Carry On – The Ultimate Collection
ITV Studios Home Entertainment, 2006
PAL, Region 2 (Europe, Middle East & Japan), Colour, Black & White
Special features as for individual ITV/Carlton/Optimum releases

Carry On Vol. 1 (Doctor, Follow that Camel, Don't Lose your Head, Up the Khyber)
Optimum Home Releasing, 2008
PAL, Region 2 (Europe, Middle East & Japan), Colour
Special features as for individual ITV/Carlton/Optimum releases

Carry On – The Ultimate Collection
ITV Studios Home Entertainment, 2008
PAL, Region 2 (Europe, Middle East & Japan), Colour, Black & White
Special features as for individual ITV/Carlton/Optimum releases

VHS:

Carry On Doctor
Rank Video Library, 1984
PAL, Colour

Carry On Doctor
Cinema Club, 1987
PAL, Colour

Carry On Doctor
Cinema Club, 1991
PAL, Colour

Carry On Doctor
Cinema Club, 1995
PAL, Colour

Carry On Doctor / Carry On Matron / Carry On Again Doctor
Cinema Club, 1997
PAL, Colour

Carry On Doctor - Collector's Edition

Cinema Club, 1999
PAL, Colour

Carry On Doctor / Carry On Again Doctor
Cinema Club, 2000
PAL, Colour

DeAgostini Carry On VHS partwork
DeAgostini/Carlton, 2003
PAL, Colour, Black & White

The Carry On Collection (Don't Lose your Head – Carry On Emmannuelle)
Carlton Visual Entertainment, 2003
PAL, Colour

Carry On Doctor
Carlton Visual Entertainment, 2003
PAL, Colour

BETAMAX

Carry On Doctor
Rank Video Library, 1984
PAL, Colour

CARRY ON UP THE KHYBER

Or

THE BRITISH POSITION IN INDIA

1968

Screenplay by Talbot Rothwell
Music Composed & Conducted by Eric Rogers

CAST   CHARACTER

Sidney James	Sir Sidney Ruff-Diamond
Kenneth Williams	The Khasi of Kalabar
Charles Hawtrey	Private James Widdle
Roy Castle	Captain Keene
Joan Sims	Lady Joan Ruff-Diamond
Bernard Bresslaw	Bunghit Din
Peter Butterworth	Brother Belcher
Terry Scott	Sergeant Major MacNutt
Angela Douglas	Princess Jelhi
Cardew Robinson	Fakir
Julian Holloway	Major Shorthouse
Peter Gilmore	Ginger
Leon Thau	Stinghi
Wanda Ventham	1st Wife
Alexandra Dane	Busti
Michael Mellinger	Chindi
Dominique Don	Belcher's Indian Girl
Derek Sydney	Major-Domo
Steven Scott	Burpa Guard
David Spenser	Servant
Liz Gold	2nd Wife
Vicki Woolf	3rd Wife
Anne Scott	4th Wife
Katherina Holden	5th Wife
Lisa Noble	8th Wife
Tamsin MacDonald	10th Wife
Eve Eden	11th Wife
Barbara Evans	13th Wife
Johnny Briggs	Sporran Soldier
Simon Cain	Bagpipe Soldier
Larry Taylor	Burpa at Door Grille
Patrick Westwood	Burpa in Crowd
John Hallam	Burpa on Rooftop
Patrick Allen	Narrator
Hospitality Girls:	Angela Grant, Josephine Blain,

Vicki Murden, Carmen Dene,
Valerie Leon, June Cooper,
Karen Young, Sue Vaughan

CREW

Production Manager .... Jack Swinburne
Art Director .... Alex Vetchinsky
Director of Photography .... Ernest Steward
Editor .... Alfred Roome
Camera Operator .... James Bawden
Camera Operator .... Neil Binney
Assistant Director .... Peter Weingreen
Assistant Editor .... Jack Gardner
Sound Recordists .... Robert T MacPhee & Ken Barker
Dubbing Editor .... Colin Miller
Continuity .... Yvonne Richards
Make-up .... Geoffrey Rodway
Hairdresser .... Stella Rivers
Costume Designer .... Emma Selby-Walker
Khyber location Director of Photography .... HAR Thomson
Titles by .... "Larry"
Producer .... Peter Rogers
Director .... Gerald Thomas

A Peter Rogers production Distributed through the Rank Organisation.

PRODUCTION DETAILS:

Budget: £260,000
Filming: 8th April 1968 – 31st May 1968
Duration: 88m
Colour
General Release: September 1968, Certificate A
TV Premiere: 23rd December 1975, BBC1
Home Video: 1981 (VHS/Betamax), 2001 (DVD)

IN A NUTSHELL:

"Enlist in the Carry On army and see the world of laughter!"

The British position in India has never been more uncomfortable. The Khasi of Kalabar's (Kenneth Williams) plan to overthrow the Colonialists is given an unexpected boost when local chief, Bunghit Din (Bernard Bresslaw) discovers that the British troops, the feared "Devils in Skirts" have taken to covering up their modesty and perhaps aren't quite so fearsome after all.

Fearing an uprising, Sir Sidney Ruff Diamond (Sid James) tries to quell the rumours, but when faced with Private Widdle's (Charles Hawtrey) offending underwear and the revelation that he is not the only one with something unexpected under his kilt, it looks like the British are under threat. Sir Sidney's problems worsen when his neglected wife, Lady Joan (Joan Sims), falls into the arms of the Khasi and gives him the proof he needs to spur the local chiefs into rising up against their Imperial overlords.

REVIEW:

The Carry Ons could never be described as epic productions: at their best they were intimate films, played out over a limited number of locations with beloved characters going through variations of the same beloved routines. Aside from the odd tweak here or adding a new character to work into the magic there, not much changed.

Then along came Carry On up the Khyber with its panoramic scenery, continent-spanning storyline, political and historical machinations and, well, I hate to say it but with white people blacked up to play baddies. But we'll come to that in a moment.

Carry On up the Khyber represents a new direction for the Carry Ons. A relatively sophisticated (and certainly adult in content) story with real historical significance is given a unique Carry On twist. The result is flawless. The story is beautifully constructed and the trappings so uniquely Carry On; the fate of an empire resting on a glimpse of a private's privates. Roy Castle's Captain Keene and Cardew Robinson's Fakir fit seamlessly into the team as if they have been there for years and it is a shame we never got to see more of them. There is not a single piece of Carry On up the Khyber that is less than comedy perfection.

The conflict that underlies the film is deftly managed and milked mercilessly for laughs but, unlike other films with a similar bitter conflict at their heart (particularly Camel, Henry and England); it does not sour the film in any way. Sir Sidney, the Khasi and Bunghit Din are all immensely likeable characters so our loyalties aren't important – it is easy to just sit back and enjoy the film.

When viewed today there is a definite discomfort in seeing Bernard Bresslaw blacked up to play Bunghit Din. But it is worth remembering that when the film was made, such things were far from unusual and of course the team have gone on record many times to say that they never set out to cause offence But putting aside the issue of colour, Bunghit Din is a staggering performance from Bernard Bresslaw and he imbues the character with the perfect mix of comedy and menace as he snarls his way through the film.

The story of the Carry Ons is often told as a slow decline into mediocrity but the truth is that over 31 films, there is a remarkable consistency in quality. With that said, few come close to the giddy heights of Carry On up the Khyber.

VIEWING NOTES:

• *Talbot Rothwell's initial script for Carry On up the Khyber was written before The Rank Organisation had re-instated the "Carry On" name for the films. It was simply called "Up the Khyber". Nevertheless, Rank were initially wary of the title for other reasons – in Cockney rhyming slang, "Khyber pass" is, of course, a substitute for the word "arse". Instead, they suggested "Carry On the Regiment" as a more suitable title.*

• *John Antrobus was once again contracted by Peter Rogers to contribute additional material to Rothwell's original script.*

- *The role of Captain Keene was written firmly with Jim Dale in mind but with Dale already committed elsewhere the role was offered to Roy Castle.*

- *Tommy Cooper was the team's first choice to play the role of the Fakir and he met with Rogers & Thomas to discuss what was originally going to be a much larger part. The eventual role was scaled back somewhat when Cooper was unable to join the cast.*

- *Stylistically, the opening credits to Carry On up the Khyber are unique in that they feature not just the names of the stars, but also the roles they play.*

- *Eric Rogers' theme to Up the Khyber is based on the traditional Scottish song "Cock O' the North", a theme which plays throughout the film.*

- *Location filming for Carry On up the Khyber took place in Snowdonia, the furthest the team travelled for a production. The Carry Ons never left British soil, although the abandoned 1980s film, Carry On Down Under was planned to have been filmed in Australia.*

- *Princess Margaret visited the set of Carry On up the Khyber during filming and was reported to have been less than amused by the "Dear Vicky" letter sent to Queen Victoria by Sir Sidney.*

- *Kenneth Williams declaration of "rank stupidity" when the gong is struck was a sly joke from Peter Rogers for The Rank Organisation. According to Rogers, the board of Rank loved it.*

- *The fakir became something of a delicate subject when it came to avoiding the censor – one line from Bernard Bresslaw about a "travelling fakir" was cut completely and the actor had to be sure to insert a suitable pause when, later in the film, he orders "Fakir...off".*

- *Joan Sims' declaration during the dinner scene at the end of the film that she had become "a little plastered" is another of those rare instances where an ad lib made it to the final print of a Carry On.*

- *The dinner scene itself was filmed over a period of three days - with real food.*

- *1969 was a record-breaking year for the Carry On films at the UK box office. Carry On up the Khyber was the UK's second highest grossing film that year. The first was Carry On Camping.*

- *During the 1990-1991 Gulf War, Carry On up the Khyber was deemed unsuitable for broadcasting on British television.*

CARRY ON COCK-UPS:

Continuity	2m 23s	The quantity of champagne in Sid James' glass varies between shots in the opening scenes of the film.
Technical	32m 27s	Look closely at the wall over Kenneth Williams' shoulder and you can see where some of the charges for bullet holes have been placed ready for the next round of gunshots.
Continuity	32m 51s	In close-up, there are a different number of bullet holes over Kenneth Williams left shoulder.
Trivia	37m 25s	The girl on the far right is future Carry On girl Valerie Leon.

Technical	42m 44s	The statue in the middle of the fountain doesn't look safe - it wobbles every time someone jumps into the water.
Trivia	43m 28s	Where did Charles Hawtrey get that rubber duck?
Continuity	43m 35s	Peter Butterworth ducks under the water when Bernard Bresslaw and the chiefs enter the harem but in the next shot he is standing up. In the shot after that he is seen emerging from the water.
Continuity	43m 58s	Keep your eye on Sid James' right arm as we switch between shots in this scene. From behind, his arm is outstretched but from the front his hands are crossed.
Technical	53m 46s	Look in the background to the right of centre and you can see Charles Hawtrey being helped back into his skirt. Nice of everyone to leave him alone while he sorts out his wardrobe.
Continuity	54m 39s	Cardew Robinson's basket is some way over to the left of where he does his levitation trick. After the offer of payment it has moved to just in front of where he was lying. His hoop magically appears behind his head before moving around the corner just as magically in the next shot.
Continuity	1h 02m 37s	Charles Hawtrey can be seen taking his fingers out of his ears in the wide shot, after the gun has fired. In the next close-up shot they're back in.
Technical	1h 03m 20s	There's a boom shadow on the wall behind Sid James. It's still there when he rounds the same spot a couple of seconds later.
Trivia	1h 04m 03s	Sid James adds a PS to his letter: "love to Albert". Prince Albert died in 1861, over 30 years before the film was set.
Continuity	1h 08m 28s	The circular window at the top of the residency is open. When we see the building next, the window is closed.
Technical	1h 14m 07s	When the Burpa cannonballs hit the wall it explodes outwards, rather than inwards.
Continuity	1h 15m 05s	The window behind the pianist is blown in by a shell. But it's back in the next interior shot ready for another go - and another, and another a few seconds after that. And yet another after that. At 1h 18m 47s the window is repaired and the blind has gone back up. A few seconds later and if you look over Sid James' shoulder the blind has gone but the window is still hanging on in there. Even after the whole orchestra's been blown up part of the window is still stubbornly in its frame.
Continuity	1h 15m 21s	Sid James is covered in dust but in the next shot his suit is clean. In the one after that it's dusty again. In fact, you could say the same for the entire cast - the dishevelment of cast and scenery varies from close-up to wide shot.
Technical	1h 19m 09s	When the window is blown out behind Joan Sims, the painted backdrop outside is seen to wobble.

Technical	1h 20m 29s	Of course it's not a real orchestra and they have just been blown up but the pianist could at least have tried to make his movements match the music.
Technical	1h 23m 28s	As the Burpa runs at Sid James, Sid is seen to mouth the words "do you wish to see me" but his voice is not heard. In the next shot he says the words again before shooting.
Continuity	1h 23m 53s	The pattern of blood on Roy Castle's face is different between the shots with Sid and the close-up that follows.

LOCATIONS:

Time	Description	Address	Also seen in	Location Link
2m 07s	Polo match	Pinewood Cricket Green Pinewood Studios Iver Heath Bucks SL0 0NH		
4m 31s	Khyber Pass	Watkin Path Cwm Llan Snowdonia Wales		The publishers have been advised not to include a direct link to this location as it is considered unsafe to visit unless suitably prepared and equipped. Readers are instead encouraged to visit http:// walkupsnowdon. co.uk
9m 17s	British Residency	Heatherden Hall Pinewood Studios Iver Heath Bucks SL0 0NH	Carry On Nurse Carry On Camping Carry On Again Doctor Carry On at your Convenience Carry On England	

CARRY ON CUTTING:

• *An additional scene outside the palace was filmed with Sir Sidney, Keene and MacNutt encountering the Fakir once again. They ask him to reveal their future which, of course he fails to do.*

CARRY ON ABROAD:

Carry On Gunga Din – *Denmark*
Everything's Under Control at the Khyber – *Germany*
Mad Conqueror Blundering in the Harem – *Greece*
Carry On the Khyber Strait – *Hungary*
Argument in the Khyber – *Poland*
Here Come the Men in Skirts! – *South America*

CARRY ON COLLECTING:

- "Carry On up the Khyber – The wickedly funny story that starts where the film ends".
  A novel by Norman Giller
  Andre Deutsch Ltd, 1996, ISBN 0233990305
- Postcard featuring UK Quad poster released in 1998 by The London Postcard Company as part of their "Rank Classics Series 1" collection.
- Promotional bookmark released in 1998 by The London Postcard Company featuring the Carry On up the Khyber and Carry On Girls Quad posters.
- In 2001, Royal Doulton released a series of Carry On Toby jugs. The second pair to be released, once more in a pair and once more in a limited edition of just 1000 were Sid James as Sir Sidney Ruff-Diamond and Charles Hawtrey as Private Widdle.
- Cards Inc, in 2003, planned a series of Carry On trading cards. Although the series was ultimately cancelled, eight preview cards were released featuring images from Carry On Doctor, Carry On up the Khyber, Carry On Camping, Carry On Again Doctor, Carry On up the Jungle, Carry On Abroad and Carry On Dick.
- In 2005, Cards Inc released a series of Carry On "Bobbin Head" dolls featuring characters from the films. Four were available from Carry On up the Khyber – Private Widdle, Bunghit Din, Sir Sidney Ruff-Diamond and the Khasi of Kalabar.
- Following the release of their Kenneth William's Carry On Cleo action figure, Product Enterprise released details of a Sir Sidney Ruff-Diamond figure due for release in 2006. Sadly, the product never made it to the shelves.
- Ethos, in 2007, released a series of mugs featuring the original UK Quad poster artwork for the Rank Carry On films including Carry On up the Khyber.
- CollectablesMANIA, in 2007, released a series of Carry On-themed poker chips. Each set came in a presentation pack, complete with trivia notes and contained six individual plastic chips emblazoned with stills from the film. Five different sets were produced, representing Carry On Doctor, Carry On Up the Khyber, Carry On Camping, Carry On Henry and Carry On Matron.

SOUNDTRACK:

Carry On up the Khyber – complete audio soundtrack with additional linking narration by Patrick Allen
Original cast & crew, Audio Cassette, EMI 1996
Also released as a double-pack with Carry On up the Jungle

Extended theme available on "The Carry On Album, Music from the Films"
Gavin Sutherland & the Prague Philharmonic Orchestra, CD, ASV 1999

Newly performed renditions of classic Carry On themes

Main title theme available on "Carry On"
Various Artists, CD, Silva Screen 2005
Themes, cues and dialog taken from the original film soundtracks

DVD:

Carry On up the Khyber
Cinema Club, 2001
PAL, Region 2 (Europe, Middle East & Japan), Colour

DeAgostini Carry On DVD partwork
DeAgostini/Carlton, 2003
PAL, Region 2 (Europe, Middle East & Japan), Colour, Black & White

Carry On up the Khyber
ITV Studios Home Entertainment, 2003
PAL, Region 2 (Europe, Middle East & Japan), Colour
Special Features: Commentary (Peter Rogers), Stills, Trivia, Trailer, Carry On Laughing –
The Sobbing Cavalier

Carry On – The History Collection (Head, Dick, Jungle, Henry, England, Khyber)
ITV Studios Home Entertainment, 2005
PAL, Region 2 (Europe, Middle East & Japan), Colour
Special features as for individual ITV/Carlton/Optimum releases

Carry On – The Ultimate Collection
ITV Studios Home Entertainment, 2006
PAL, Region 2 (Europe, Middle East & Japan), Colour, Black & White
Special features as for individual ITV/Carlton/Optimum releases

Carry On Vol. 1 (Doctor, Follow that Camel, Don't Lose your Head, Up the Khyber)
Optimum Home Releasing, 2008
PAL, Region 2 (Europe, Middle East & Japan), Colour
Special features as for individual ITV/Carlton/Optimum releases

Carry On – The Ultimate Collection
ITV Studios Home Entertainment, 2008
PAL, Region 2 (Europe, Middle East & Japan), Colour, Black & White
Special features as for individual ITV/Carlton/Optimum releases

VHS:

Carry On up the Khyber
Rank Video Library, 1981
PAL, Colour

Carry On up the Khyber
Cinema Club, 1987
PAL, Colour

Carry On up the Khyber
Cinema Club, 1991
PAL, Colour

Carry On up the Khyber
Cinema Club, 1995
PAL, Colour

Carry On up the Khyber - Collector's Edition
Cinema Club, 1999
PAL, Colour

Carry On up the Jungle / Carry On up the Khyber
Cinema Club, 2000
PAL, Colour

DeAgostini Carry On VHS partwork
DeAgostini/Carlton, 2003
PAL, Colour, Black & White

The Carry On Collection (Don't Lose your Head – Carry On Emmannuelle)
Carlton Visual Entertainment, 2003
PAL, Colour

Carry On up the Khyber
Carlton Visual Entertainment, 2003
PAL, Colour

BETAMAX

Carry On up the Khyber
Rank Video Library, 1981
PAL, Colour

CARRY ON CAMPING

Or...

LET SLEEPING BAGS LIE

1969

Screenplay by Talbot Rothwell
Music Composed & Conducted by Eric Rogers

CAST   CHARACTER

CAST	CHARACTER
Sidney James	Sid Boggle
Charles Hawtrey	Charlie Muggins
Joan Sims	Joan Fussey
Kenneth Williams	Doctor Kenneth Soaper
Terry Scott	Peter Potter
Barbara Windsor	Babs
Hattie Jacques	Miss Haggerd
Bernard Bresslaw	Bernie Lugg
Julian Holloway	Jim Tanner
Dilys Laye	Anthea Meeks
Peter Butterworth	Josh Fiddler
Betty Marsden	Harriet Potter
Trisha Noble	Sally
Amelia Bayntun	Mrs Fussey
Brian Oulton	Store Manager
Patricia Franklin	Farmer's Daughter
Derek Francis	Farmer
Michael Nightingale	Man in Cinema
Elizabeth Knight	Jane
George Moon	Scrawny Man
Sandra Caron	Fanny
Valerie Shute	Pat
Georgina Moon	Joy
Vivien Lloyd	Verna
Jennifer Pyle	Hilda
Lesley Duff	Norma
Jackie Poole	Betty
Anna Karen	Hefty Girl
Sally Kemp	Girl with Cow
Valerie Leon	Shop Assistant
Peter Cockburn	Commentator
Gilly Grant	Sally G-String
Lusty Youths:	Michael Low, Mike Lucas

CREW

Production Manager ....Jack Swinburne
Art Director ....Lionel Couch
Director of Photography ....Ernest Steward
Editor...Alfred Roome
Assistant Editor..Jack Gardner
Camera Operator...James Bawden
Assistant Director ....Jack Causey
Sound Recordists ....Bill Daniels & Ken Barker
Dubbing Editor ....Colin Miller
Continuity...Doreen Dernley
Make-up ....Geoffrey Rodway
Hairdresser..Stella Rivers
Costume Designer ....Yvonne Caffin
Titles by ...."Larry"
Producer..Peter Rogers
Director..Gerald Thomas

A Peter Rogers production. Distributed through the Rank Organisation.

PRODUCTION DETAILS:

Budget: £208,500
Filming: 7th October 1968 – 22nd November 1968
Duration: 88m
Colour
General Release: February 1969, Certificate A
TV Premiere: 15th February 1975, ITV
Home Video: 1981 (VHS/Betamax), 1999 (DVD)

IN A NUTSHELL:

"The Carry On team – refusing to let sleeping bags lie!"

Sid Boggle (Sid James) and his friend Bernie Lugg (Bernard Bresslaw) take their girlfriends Joan (Joan Sims) and Anthea (Dilys Laye) to the pictures for a night out. The girls are less than impressed with the nudist film that's playing, but it gives Sid an idea.

As the gang prepare for their upcoming camping trip, Sid spots a leaflet for what he believes to be the same nudist camp that featured in the film. Meanwhile Charlie Muggins (Charles Hawtrey) is preparing for a camping holiday of his own by testing out a cosy little two man tent with the shop assistant (Valerie Leon). Elsewhere, hen-pecked husband Peter Potter (Terry Scott) and his wife Harriet (Betty Marsden) are readying themselves for a camping trip despite Peter's ever increasing desire to abandon their tandem and tent for a luxury holiday in the sun. The girls of Chayste Place under the watchful tutelage of Doctor Soaper (Kenneth Williams) and Miss Haggerd (Hattie Jacques) are also off on a camping holiday.

Everyone is heading for Paradise, but one thing's for sure – not everyone is going to find it!

REVIEW:

Carry On Camping is, in many ways, the archetypal Carry On film. It's certainly the most identifiable of all the films, thanks to its bulging cast of Carry On regulars. From Harriet Potter's impossible braying laugh to Kenneth Williams' seeming ability to envelop vast swathes of the Buckinghamshire countryside with his flared nostrils, Carry On Camping is the world of Carry On in one gloriously neat 90 minute package. If somebody ever comes up to you and asks, "What are these Carry On films I've heard so much about?", this is the film you should sit them down to watch.

Camping is not the best of the Carry Ons; not by a long way, but it is the most typical. Sid is climbing over bodies to get at Babs. Meanwhile, Babs will take whatever she can get and if Sid is not quick enough, she will soon turn elsewhere. Bernie is the lovable idiot who wouldn't know what to do with it even if he had the chance. Joan is well on the way to becoming the Carry On battle-axe, Hattie is a sexually frustrated grotesque while Kenneth is a sexually repressed one and nobody quite knows what Charlie is. Everything the Carry On films represents is here in a muddy field at Pinewood. It's magnificent – there isn't a single joke that isn't milked (including the one about the bull) to within an inch of parody, not a stereotype is left un-poked.

It's far from flawless, but there really is not much to criticise in the film itself. Everyone's playing their most beloved Carry On stereotype and they all do it so well. The story is deliberately flimsy (although when it went before the cameras there was significantly more of a plot, but more on that later) but Talbot Rothwell's script is bursting with gags. While there's not as much subtlety or word-play as, for example, Carry On Henry or Doctor there is plenty of physical comedy and some classic set pieces. In Carry On terms, Camping is the perfect storm - a huge cast of regulars, a script that never lets up in its breathless pursuit of gags and a situation with which we can all identify. It is all here and it is exhaustingly funny.

VIEWING NOTES:

- While Carry On Camping is, of course, set during the summer, the fact that it was filmed in November of 1968 during a particularly cold spell meant that the cast and crew had a number of problems making the delights of Paradise look even remotely appealing. The leaves on the trees were sprayed green, as was the mud on the ground to try and give it the appearance of grass. You might be forgiven for thinking that some of the cast were having a crafty smoke between shots, but that is their breath condensing in the cold air.

- As scripted, Carry On Camping was to have gone in a rather different direction. A budding romance between Sally (Trisha Noble) and Jim Tanner (Julian Holloway) was intended to be a significant storyline, with the pair eventually running away together at the end of the film. However, Noble is said to have been repeatedly late for filming, angering Peter Rogers and Gerald Thomas, who ended up cutting most of her lines from the shooting script. Note Jim's absence in the final scenes of the film – the pair were due to have left together by that point. Incidentally, the role of Jim Tanner was originally offered to Jim Dale.

- Promotional consideration for Carry On Camping was supplied by Saxa Salt. The first prize in a competition which ran in conjunction with Saxa when the film was launched was £1000.

- The film that Sid and Bernie take the girls to at the start of the film is indeed called Nudist Paradise. This 1958 film was released in the USA as "Nature's Paradise" and when it *was released here in the UK it was billed as Britain's first nudist feature. There are a few changes made for the purposes of Carry On Camping, including a new voiceover and the character of Sally.*

- *Terry Scott later revealed that he had just undergone surgery on his rear end prior to filming Carry On Camping. Remember that when you see him riding that tandem, looking thoroughly miserable.*

- *The technical wizardry involved in making Barbara Windsor's bra fly off during the exercise scene came courtesy of an off-screen stagehand with a fishing line attached to the front of Babs' bra.*

- *Carry On Camping was Britain's biggest box office success in 1969.*

CARRY ON COCK-UPS:

Continuity	2m 08s	Keep an eye on Sid James' lolly. It appears in varying states of being eaten between wide and close-up shots. After devouring most of the lolly, at the end of the scene as Bernard Bresslaw leaves it's perfectly cut in half.
Continuity	5m 04s	Terry Scott is carrying his briefcase with the latch facing outwards as he approaches the door. When he gets inside it's the other way round.
Continuity	5m 10s	The front door of the Potter house is different outside to in. There's a row of windows on the outside which aren't there in the interior.
Continuity	7m 59s	Keep an eye on that blonde woman walking by as Sid James parks the van. Five seconds later she's walking by again.
Continuity	8m 02s	While we're here, look at where Sid James parks the van. In the next shot it's in a different spot.
Trivia	11m 24s	Eric Rogers borrows from Haydn's "String Quartet in F" for the music accompanying the first shot of Chayste Place.
Continuity	11m 35s	In the wide shot there three girls are stood close to the fireplace. In the close-up there are four. Back to the wide shot and the girls are standing apart again.
Trivia	12m 08s	Eric Rogers borrows from Saint-Saëns' "The Elephant" (from Carnival of the Animals) to accompany Hattie Jacques' appearance
Continuity	12m 18s	Hattie Jacques opens the door with her left hand. When we see her open it from the other side she's holding the doorknob with her right.
Continuity	16m 49s	The frying pan that Amelia Bayntun has just put on the front ring of the cooker can now be seen on the back ring, over Joan's shoulder. In the next shot it is back on the front ring. The loaf of bread on the table changes in size between shots as well. And it is a sliced loaf. Sliced – remember that, check for yourself at 17m 22s
Technical	17m 24s	Yes, Amelia Bayntun is slicing a sliced loaf.
Continuity	17m 49s	The pile of suitcases behind the front door has grown since we saw it through the kitchen doorway.

Continuity	19m 43s	Amelia Bayntun follows Sid James as he goes round the car to his door but as the car pulls off she has gone.
Continuity	23m 08s	Look at the white car on the side of the road that the Potters have just passed. When Charles Hawtrey asks "Why, what have you done, madam?" he is just about to walk past the very same car.
Continuity	24m 19s	The two girls sitting behind Barbara Windsor were standing up in the previous shot. Babs was wearing that coat that is now draped over the back of her chair.
Continuity	25m 15s	The girls are sitting in different positions aboard the coach to those they occupy in the interior shots. Then again, the coach driver is different as well. The chap driving looks nothing like Julian Holloway.
Continuity	28m 58s	That prop door on the farmhouse doesn't look quite right - the door on location (seen in the previous shot) had white beading around the window. When the farmer throws Charles Hawtrey out after confronting his daughter there's a wall visible outside the door which isn't on location.
Continuity	30m 24s	The farmer is leaning on the right door post facing Terry Scott when we see his face. From behind he's leaning on the other side of the door.
Continuity	39m 51s	Betty Marsden pulls Charles Hawtrey in through the right flap of the tent. The interior shot shows him coming in on the opposite site of the central pole.
Continuity	41m 54s	As Terry Scott runs out of the tent there's no sign of Charles Hawtrey on the camp bed he just sat down on in the previous shot.
Technical	42m 31s	Watch closely and you will see that Julian Holloway is falling before he even reaches Sandra Caron.
Continuity	42m 36s	Sandra Caron is lying on the floor after Julian Holloway fell over her and Holloway has a blue towel over his shoulder. In the next shot she is sitting up and smiling while Holloway's towel has disappeared.
Technical	45m 37s	As Betty Marsden and the others struggle to get undressed, watch her lips as she says "It'll be much better if I get my pants off" – the audio and video are un-synched.
Continuity	45m 55s	Terry Scott and Charles Hawtrey knock the central roof support out of the tent. In the next shot it's back in place.
Continuity	47m 29s	Charles Hawtrey climbs into Terry Scott's blue sleeping bag. When Scott and Betty Marsden leave him the next morning he's in a green and yellow patterned one. If you miss it you'll see it again being manhandled by the girls later. Hawtrey, by the time he's back in the Potters' tent later in the film, seems to have recovered the blue one.
Trivia	54m 10s	Charles Hawtrey brandishes a packet of Saxa Salt to keep the product guys happy.

Continuity	1h 00m 45s	This is the most famous blooper of all. We start with the revelation that Barbara Windsor isn't even in the line-up when we first see the girls exercising and neither is Hattie Jacques. At 1h 00m 58s we're ready to go. Windsor and Jacques are both there, and Hattie is without her headgear. 10 seconds later she has a towel wrapped around her head. In the next shot, the towel has gone. At 1h 01m 36s the bra doesn't fly off at all. It falls to the ground. A second later, defying gravity, the bra is in Kenneth Williams' face and Hattie's towel is back. As the girls all laugh at Barbara the one on the far left of the screen exclaims "Barbara" but her voice was lost in the dub. As Hattie Jacques takes them away you will notice that the tents and campers behind the girls have changed once again. Finally, keep an eye on the ground between the girls. It changes from luscious tufts of grass to grotty mud depending on the camera angle.
Continuity	1h 04m 46s	Bernard Bresslaw puts his wash bag down by the basin nearest the door. When Terry Scott comes into the washroom a few moments later it will have moved to the next sink along.
Technical	1h 05m 04s	Listen closely and you'll hear Barbara Windsor talking on the other side of the wall although what you're actually hearing is a replay of her apology to Kenneth Williams for walking in on him and Hattie the night before.
Technical	1h 05m 14s	The wall of the stall Sid James in has just disappeared. It pops back occasionally through the scene.
Technical	1h 06m 13s	The girl in the cubicle next to Barbara Windsor is clothed in a blue gown or towel.
Continuity	1h 15m 41s	Hattie Jacques' nightdress is done up to the top button. When we see her in the next shot the top button's undone.
Continuity	1h 15m 55s	Kenneth Williams was much further out of his tent a moment ago.
Trivia	1h 17m 46s	Hattie Jacques is referring to Carry On Doctor's Dr Tinkle when describing her former love.
Technical	1h 20m 11s	In case you haven't noticed the band aren't playing in time with the music.

LOCATIONS:

Time	Description	Address	Also seen in	Location Link
1m 41s	Cinema	Odeon Cinema Ethorpe Crescent Gerrards Cross Bucks SL9 8PN		
4m 53s	Approaching Peter Potter's house	8 Pinewood Close Pinewood Estate Iver Heath Bucks SL0 0QS	Carry On Behind Carry On Emmannuelle	
7m 54s	Driving up to Courts	13-17 High Street Maidenhead Berks SL1 5QA	Carry On Doctor	
11m 24s	Chayste Place	Heatherden Hall Pinewood Studios Iver Heath Bucks SL0 0NH	Carry On Nurse Carry On up the Khyber Carry On Again Doctor Carry On at your Convenience Carry On England	
14m 26s	Snogging under a tree	Clubhouse entrance (back of Heatherden Hall) Pinewood Studios Iver Heath Bucks SL0 0NH	Carry On Nurse Carry On up the Khyber Carry On Henry	
15m 57s	Approaching Mrs Fussey's House	Pinewood Green Pinewood Estate Iver Heath Bucks SL0 0QP	Carry On Cabby	

18m 04s	Mrs Fussey's house	94 Pinewood Green Pinewood Estate Iver Heath Bucks SL0 0QP	Carry On Cabby (the house next door) Carry On Behind	
21m 58s	Sid's car pulls up in the lane to turn corner	Black Park Road Wexham Berks SL3	Carry On Cabby	
28m 46s	Farmhouse	Sauls Farm Sevenhills Road Iver Heath Bucks SL0 0NY		
32m 22s	Paradise park gate exterior version	Dromenagh Farm Sevenhills Road Bucks SL0 0PA		
32m 45s	Interior of gate to Paradise Park	Peace Road Pinewood Studios Iver Heath Bucks SL0 0NB		
37m 23s	Balsworth Youth Hostel	TV Complex Pinewood Studios Iver Heath Bucks SL0 0NH		

CARRY ON CUTTING:

- One notable scene that was filmed as part of the abandoned Sally/Jim romance took place in the ladies' ablutions where Sally was scared by the same ram that appears later in the film. Jim Tanner, of course, came to the rescue.

CARRY ON ABROAD:

A Completely Mad Camping Paradise – *Germany*
Girls Camping – *Netherlands*
Leave the Sleeping Bag at Home! – *Norway*
Holidays! Let's go! – *Poland*
The Trouble with Camping – *Portugal*
Control Yourself, Hiker – *Spain*
I Want a Nudist Girlfriend – *South America*

CARRY ON COLLECTING:

- Die-cast 1:60 scale VW camper van featuring Carry On Camping logo by Lledo, 1998, as part of their "Days Gone" range.
- Postcard featuring UK Quad poster released in 1998 by The London Postcard Company as part of their "Rank Classics Series 1" collection.
- In 1998, Cartel International released a series of Carry On-themed greeting cards bearing stills from the films together with suitably saucy text. The series of 14 cards included stills from Carry On Doctor, Carry On Camping, Carry On Again Doctor, Carry On up the Jungle, Carry On Abroad and Carry On Girls.
- Cards Inc, in 2003, planned a series of Carry On trading cards. While the series was ultimately cancelled, a set of eight preview cards were released, featuring images from Carry On Doctor, Carry On up the Khyber, Carry On Camping, Carry On Again Doctor, Carry On up the Jungle, Carry On Abroad and Carry On Dick.
- In 2005, Cards Inc released a series of Carry On "Bobbin Head" dolls featuring characters from the films. Three were available from Carry On Camping – Sid Boggle, Dr Soaper and Barbara.
- Following the release of their Kenneth Williams' Carry On Cleo action figure, Product Enterprise released details of a Charlie Muggins' figure due for release in 2006. The product never was released for sale.
- Ethos, in 2007, released a series of mugs featuring the original UK Quad poster artwork for the Rank Carry On films, including Carry On Camping.
- In 2008, Ethos released a 16 piece Carry On Camping picnic set, comprising of bowls, saucers, plates and beakers all emblazoned with Carry On Camping stills. The items are all available separately, together with a Carry On Camping tray.
- CollectablesMANIA, in 2007, released a series of Carry On-themed poker chips. Each set came in a presentation pack, complete with trivia notes and contained six individual plastic chips emblazoned with stills from the film. Five different sets were produced, representing Carry On Doctor, Carry On Up the Khyber, Carry On Camping, Carry On Henry and Carry On Matron.

SOUNDTRACK:

Carry On Camping – complete audio soundtrack with additional linking narration by Joan Sims

Original cast & crew, Audio Cassette, EMI 1996
Also released as a double-pack with Carry On Don't Lose your Head

"Carry On Camping Suite" available on "The Carry On Album, Music from the Films"
Gavin Sutherland & the Prague Philharmonic Orchestra, CD, ASV 1999
Newly performed renditions of classic Carry On themes

Title theme available on "What a Carry On"
Gavin Sutherland and the Royal Sinfonia, CD, Dutton Vocalion 2005
Newly performed renditions of classic Carry On themes

DVD:

Carry On Camping
Carlton Visual Entertainment, 1999
PAL, Region 2 (Europe, Middle East & Japan), Colour

DeAgostini Carry On DVD partwork
DeAgostini/Carlton, 2003
PAL, Region 2 (Europe, Middle East & Japan), Colour, Black & White

Carry On Camping
ITV Studios Home Entertainment, 2003
PAL, Region 2 (Europe, Middle East & Japan), Colour
Special Features: Commentary (Dilys Laye, Sandra Caron), Stills, Trivia, Trailer, Carry On Laughing – Orgy & Bess

Carry On – The Holiday Collection (Camping, Abroad, Camel, Girls, Convenience, Behind)
ITV Studios Home Entertainment, 2005
PAL, Region 2 (Europe, Middle East & Japan), Colour
Special features as for individual ITV/Carlton/Optimum releases

Carry On – The Ultimate Collection
ITV Studios Home Entertainment, 2006
PAL, Region 2 (Europe, Middle East & Japan), Colour, Black & White
Special features as for individual ITV/Carlton/Optimum releases

Carry On Camping (UMD Mini for PSP)
ITV Studios Home Entertainment, 2006
Colour

Carry On Vol. 2 (Henry, Up the Jungle, Again Doctor, Camping)
Optimum Home Releasing, 2008
PAL, Region 2 (Europe, Middle East & Japan), Colour
Special features as for individual ITV/Carlton/Optimum releases

Carry On – The Ultimate Collection
ITV Studios Home Entertainment, 2008
PAL, Region 2 (Europe, Middle East & Japan), Colour, Black & White
Special features as for individual ITV/Carlton/Optimum releases

VHS:

Carry On Camping
Rank Video Library, 1981
PAL, Colour

Carry On Camping
Rank Video Library, 1986
PAL, Colour

Carry On Camping
Pickwick Video Ltd, 1990
PAL, Colour

Carry On Camping
Rank Classics, 1992
PAL, Colour

Carry On Camping
Carlton Visual Entertainment, 1997
PAL, Colour

DeAgostini Carry On VHS partwork
DeAgostini/Carlton, 2003
PAL, Colour, Black & White

The Carry On Collection (Don't Lose your Head – Carry On Emmannuelle)
Carlton Visual Entertainment, 2003
PAL, Colour

Carry On Camping
Carlton Visual Entertainment, 2003
PAL, Colour

BETAMAX:

Carry On Camping
Rank Video Library, 1981
PAL, Colour

CARRY ON AGAIN DOCTOR

Or...

WHERE THERE'S A PILL THERE'S A WAY

Or...

THE BOWELS ARE RINGING

Or...

IF YOU SAY IT'S YOUR THERMOMETER I'LL HAVE TO BELIEVE YOU, BUT IT'S A FUNNY PLACE TO PUT IT

1969

Screenplay by Talbot Rothwell
Music Composed & Conducted by Eric Rogers

CAST   CHARACTER

CAST	CHARACTER
Sidney James	Gladstone Screwer
Kenneth Williams	Doctor Frederick Carver
Charles Hawtrey	Doctor Ernest Stoppidge
Jim Dale	Doctor James Nookey
Joan Sims	Ellen Moore
Barbara Windsor	Goldie Locks
Hattie Jacques	Matron
Patsy Rowlands	Miss Fosdick
Peter Butterworth	Shuffling Patient
Wilfrid Brambell	Mr Pullen
Elizabeth Knight	Nurse Willing
Alexandra Dane	Stout Woman
Peter Gilmore	Henry
Pat Coombs	New Matron
Patricia Hayes	Mrs Beasley
William Mervyn	Lord Paragon
Lucy Griffiths	Old Lady in Headphones
Harry Locke	Porter
Gwendolyn Watts	Night Sister
Valerie Leon	Deirdre
Frank Singuineau	Porter
Valerie van Ost	Out-Patients Sister
Billy Cornelius	Patient in Plaster
Simon Cain	X-Ray Man
Elspeth March	Hospital Board Member
Valerie Shute	Nurse
Ann Lancaster	Patient
Shakira Baksh	Scrubba
Georgina Simpson	Men's Ward Nurse

Faith Kent .... Berkeley Matron
Frank Forsyth .... Mr Bean
Donald Bisset .... Patient
Bob Todd .... Pump Patient
Heather Emmanuel .... Plump Native Girl
Yutte Stensgaard .... Trolley Nurse
George Roderick .... Waiter
Jenny Counsell .... Night Nurse
Hugh Futcher .... Cab Driver
Rupert Evans .... Stunt Orderly

CREW

Production Manager .... Jack Swinburne
Art Director .... John Blezard
Director of Photography .... Ernest Steward
Editor... Alfred Roome
Camera Operator .... James Bawden
Assistant Director .... Ivor Powell
Assistant Editor... Jack Gardner
Sound Recordists .... Bill Daniels & Ken Barker
Dubbing Editor .... Colin Miller
Continuity.. Susanna Merry
Make-up .... Geoffrey Rodway
Hairdresser.. Stella Rivers
Costume Designer .... Anna Duse
Producer.. Peter Rogers
Director.. Gerald Thomas

A Peter Rogers production. Distributed through the Rank Organisation.

PRODUCTION DETAILS:

Budget: £219,000
Filming: 17th March 1969 – 2nd May 1969
Duration: 86m
Colour
General Release: August 1969, Certificate A
TV Premiere: 1st January 1976, ITV
Home Video: 1984 (VHS/Betamax), 2001 (DVD)

IN A NUTSHELL:

"Poking their diagnoses into other people's business!"

Dr Frederick Carver (Kenneth Williams) dreams of turning his back on the National Health and setting up a private clinic of his own to cater for his own particular brand of medicine – the kind that pays.

Together with his old college roommate, Dr Stoppidge (Charles Hawtrey), Carver rules Long Hampton hospital, swanning about the place as if he owns it. When an opportunity to establish his own clinic arises, courtesy of private patient Ellen Moore (Joan Sims), Carver sees in young Dr Nookey (Jim Dale) the perfect candidate to take over her late husband's practice in the Beatific Islands. This would earn him favour with the rich widow and perhaps the money he needs to set up a foundation of his own. But Nookey's not interested. He's fallen in love with Goldie Locks (Barbara Windsor), a model who has fallen on hard times, or more specifically a hard surface.

But the path of true love never runs smooth, particularly when your boss wants you out of the way and his best friend spikes your drink at a posh soirée. The disgraced Nookey is banished to the Beatific Islands where the natives all have one thing in common - the shapeliest of figures. Nookey makes a deal with the local medic, Gladstone Screwer (Sid James), inventor of a miracle slimming potion, which Nookey takes with him back to England to make his fortune. Everything would be perfect if Carver didn't keep trying to steal the potion.

REVIEW:

The medical meme has become particularly treasured in Carry On terms but Again Doctor is really quite a poor relation to the other hospital-based films. Nurse was the film that established the Carry On series as a going concern. Doctor heralded a return to traditional Carry On values and the later Matron signalled the new direction, with a cast of younger stars mingling with their Carry On elders.

Carry On Again Doctor has little to distinguish it from those other films. It is something of a mishmash of ideas with little in the way of a cohesive on-going narrative. In fact, the film stops halfway through and takes an entirely unexpected, though not unwelcome, change of direction. You would be forgiven for confusing the first half of the film with the earlier Carry On Doctor as once again Jim Dale's young dashing doctor is victimised by the hospital elders, in the shape of Kenneth Williams and Hattie Jacques in precisely the same way as in the earlier film.

But let's not completely devalue the film's opening. That the earlier segments in the hospital are similar to Carry On Doctor is high praise. They're funny...very funny indeed. The ongoing plot of Dr Carver's seduction of Ellen Moore is brilliantly handled by Williams and Sims, Patsy Rowlands is delightful as the squirming Miss Fosdick and Charles Hawtrey gives, as Dr Stoppidge, one of his finest performances. It's in their hate campaign against Dr Nookey where the first half of the film fails to deliver. When victimisation and double dealing creep in to the Carry Ons, the films lose some of their shine. These are characters and actors we all love and seeing them be less than lovable quickly becomes uncomfortable.

Turning to the second half of the film, while the scenes aboard Dr Nookey's island retreat are grim by their very nature, the fact that Sid's character is having such a wonderful time lifts the whole piece. But the film really takes off when Nookey returns to Blighty. The Moore-Nookey cure is a marvel and as punters flock to their door, the increasingly desperate antics of Carver and Stoppidge to get to the bottom of the mysterious potion are hilariously misguided. Hawtrey, it has to be said, makes for a gruesomely convincing grand dame.

Sadly, the film ends on something of a duff note, with an unimaginative runaround which only compounds the overall feeling that there's something not quite finished, not properly thought-out about the whole affair. That's not to say Carry On Again Doctor is a bad film, rather that it's a jumble of ideas all vying for their own place in the limelight.

VIEWING NOTES:

• *Talbot Rothwell's original script for Carry On Again Doctor made the Rank lawyer, Hugh J Parton, nervous. Rothwell had previously written a script for Betty Box's "Doctor" series and Parton was concerned that the dialogue for Dr Carver was rather too reminiscent of that which, he thought, may have been previously written for James Robertson Justice. Adding further concern was the fact that in the original Doctor books, by Richard Gordon, there was also a story where a doctor was sent to a remote tropical island. In the event, the legal issues were overcome and the script went ahead with just one slight modification - Sir Frederick lost his originally planned knighthood.*

• *Patsy Rowlands makes her first Carry On appearance in Carry On Again Doctor as the put-upon (and drawn-upon) Miss Fosdick. Her character is named after the ward featured in Carry On Doctor.*

• *Pat Coombs was originally cast in the role of Mrs Armitage, but the sudden unavailability of Ambrosine Phillphotts meant that she was instead offered the role of the new Matron.*

• *Jim Dale famously insisted on doing all of his stunts personally. After several takes rattling down those stairs attached to a metal trolley, Jim severely hurt his arm and was rushed to hospital. The actor sustained further injuries during the scene where he first arrives on the Beatific Islands.*

• *Jim's wasn't the only newsworthy mishap on the production. Alexandra Dane, seen in the film as the victim of a slimming machine gone haywire, made the headlines when the belt on the machine broke loose and flung her through the air.*

CARRY ON COCK-UPS:

Continuity	2m 45s	Jim Dale lets go of his towel and we see it drop to the floor. In the very next shot it's still suspended around his waist and we see it fall once more. Answers on a postcard as to what was holding it up.
Continuity	3m 22s	Billy Cornelius, the man in the leopardskin pyjamas (yes, that's right, leopardskin pyjamas) pulls himself into a seated position, in preparation for Kenneth Williams' rounds. When Williams and Charles Hawtrey enter the ward a few moments later (3m 32s) he can be seen not just laying down but fast asleep in his bed.
Continuity	6m 54s	The contents of Patricia Hayes' shopping bag have rearranged themselves in the time it takes her to to walk into Dr Nookey's office.
Continuity	7m 11s	Take a look at the lamp on Jim Dale desk – the lid is closed. In the upcoming close-up shots of Patricia Hayes it's open.
Trivia	9m 08s	Listen closely as the camera first alights on Wilfrid Brambell and you can hear the familiar strains of "Old Ned", the theme to Steptoe & Son.
Technical	17m 57s	The first explosion in the X-ray room goes off before Jim Dale has pressed the button.
Technical	18m 19s	Look closely at the floor polisher as the porter is pulled along under the beds and you can see the wire pulling him, and it, across the floor.

Technical	20m 41s	The files in the cabinet Patsy Rowlands is examining outside the office are all empty.
Trivia	21m 55s	The clarinet player at the dinner/dance is none other than Carry On composer Eric Rogers.
Trivia	24m 02s	The tune of the general excuse may be familiar - it's the theme from Carry On Cabby, Jim Dale's first Carry On.
Trivia	25m 39s	A brief scene appears to have been cut here - we go from Kenneth Williams and Joan Sims sitting at a table in one shot and seconds later they're standing next to Charles Hawtrey (see Carry On Cutting).
Trivia	28m 35s	Listen to the music playing as Jim makes his way back from the buffet. It's "The Magic of Love" from Carry On Spying.
Technical	33m 43s	Jim Dale escapes from Kenneth Williams and co by running through one of the wards. Despite appearances, he emerges from the same doorway he entered and into the exact same corridor he was in a moment ago. The signage, fuse box and discarded trolley are all exactly where they were in the "other" corridor moments ago.
Continuity	34m 00s	As Jim Dale plummets down the stairs on the hospital trolley, Charles Hawtrey declares "Oh no!" and he and the others turn back to try and get out of the way. We then cut back to Dale on the trolley whereupon he descends the flight of stairs (until he's parallel with the sign advertising the dance). But in the next shot, Hawtrey and crowd are once more seen to be running down the same flight of stairs and we cut back **again** to Dale on the trolley.
Trivia	37m 27s	The theme from Carry On Cabby gets another reworking as the tropical music playing when Jim Dale first arrives on the Beatific Islands.
Technical	38m 42s	The trick panel which Jim Dale falls through as he enters the mission (and the ones his hammock falls through in a few moments) are very obvious. If it is caused by woodworm, as Sid James claims, they're experts at woodwork.
Technical	44m 28s	The hurricane blowing outside Jim Dale's bedroom seems rather tame - the flag is barely fluttering and what are those clumps of vegetation being thrown up in the air. Looks like the Pinewood wind machine was otherwise engaged that day.
Trivia	46m 28s	Scrubba is played by the future Mrs Michael Caine, Shakira Baksh.
Continuity	47m 33s	Keep your eye on the limp flag outside Jim Dale's window. In the time it takes him to cross into the next room, the wind's back up and blowing in the opposite direction.
Trivia	55m 49s	Matron's name in Carry On Again Doctor is "Soaper" - the same as Kenneth Williams' character in the previous film, Carry On Camping. Put any thoughts of an ongoing romance among their characters out of your head, though – she states quite clearly that she's a "Miss".

| Continuity | 1h 07m 05s | Sid James sits down and removes a bottle of scotch. Without pausing to fill it, the glass is instantly full. |
| Technical | 1h 15m 46s | Despite undressing, Joan Sims can be seen to be wearing flesh-coloured underwear beneath her nightie. |

LOCATIONS:

Time	Description	Address	Also seen in	Location Link
1m 41s	Long Hampton hospital	Maidenhead Town Hall St Ives Road Maidenhead, Berks SL6 1RF	Carry On Again Doctor Carry On	
9m 38s	Berkley Nursing Home - Mrs Moore's nursing home	Iver Grove Langley Park Road Iver Bucks SL0 0LB		
9m 51s	Interior of Mrs Moore's nursing home	Heatherden Hall Pinewood Studios Iver Heath Bucks SL0 0NH	Carry On Emmannuelle	
43m 45s	Clinic for sale (later to become the Moore-Nookey clinic)	Heatherden Hall Pinewood Studios Iver Heath Bucks SL0 0NH	Carry On Nurse Carry On up the Khyber Carry On Camping Carry On Again Doctor Carry On at your Convenience Carry On England	
52m 27s	Dr Nookey's consulting rooms	12 Park Street, Windsor Berks SL4 1LU	The Helping Hands agency (Regardless) and Wedded Bliss (Loving) are on the same street	

CARRY ON CUTTING:

• *The scene where Dr Carver visits Ellen in bed after her operation was originally quite a protracted sequence with her reminding him that he'd agreed to save her removed appendix. In a panic he speaks to Miss Fosdick about where he put it and ends up grabbing a piece of chicken, putting it in a jar and giving her that, instead.*

• *The scene where Ellen Moore tells Dr Carver to stop reading his notes was cut. It originally went on to see him accidentally set light to the notes on the candle and then the entire table.*

• *Another cut was from when Dr Nookey and Goldie are dancing. In the longer edit, Nookey accidentally tears off the skirt from a fellow dancer, with predictable ire from those watching.*

CARRY ON ABROAD:

A Complete Madhouse – *Germany*
A Crazy Gynaecologist – *Greece*
Doctor...Now's the Rub – *Portugal*
Watch Out Doctor – *South America*

CARRY ON COLLECTING:

• Postcard featuring UK Quad poster released in 1998 by The London Postcard Company as part of their "Rank Classics Series 1" collection.
• Cartel International, in 1998, released a series of Carry On themed greetings cards bearing stills from the films together with suitably saucy text. The series of 14 cards included stills from Carry On Doctor, Carry On Camping, Carry On Again Doctor, Carry On up the Jungle, Carry On Abroad and Carry On Girls.
• Cards Inc, in 2003, planned a series of Carry On trading cards. While the series was ultimately cancelled, eight preview cards was released, featuring images from Carry On Doctor, Carry On up the Khyber, Carry On Camping, Carry On Again Doctor, Carry On up the Jungle, Carry On Abroad and Carry On Dick.
• Ethos, in 2007, released a series of mugs featuring the original UK Quad poster artwork for the Rank Carry Ons, including Carry On Again Doctor.
• The same year, Ethos also released a series of colour changing mugs. Two of the set featured images from Carry On Again Doctor; one of Dr Stoppidge helping Ellen with her corsets and another of Dr Nookey examining Goldie Locks.

SOUNDTRACK:

"Carry On Doctor / Doctor Again Suite" available on "The Carry On Album, Music from the Films"
Gavin Sutherland & the Prague Philharmonic Orchestra, CD, ASV 1999
Newly performed renditions of classic Carry On themes

Main title theme available on "Carry On"
Various Artists, CD, Silva Screen 2005
Themes, cues and dialog taken from the original film soundtracks

Selection of arrangements from the dinner dance scenes available on "What a Carry On"
Gavin Sutherland and the Royal Sinfonia, CD, Dutton Vocalion 2005
Newly performed renditions of classic Carry On themes

DVD:

Carry On Again Doctor
Cinema Club, 2001
PAL, Region 2 (Europe, Middle East & Japan), Colour

DeAgostini Carry On DVD partwork
DeAgostini/Carlton, 2003
PAL, Region 2 (Europe, Middle East & Japan), Colour, Black & White

Carry On Again Doctor
ITV Studios Home Entertainment, 2003
PAL, Region 2 (Europe, Middle East & Japan), Colour
Special Features: Commentary (Jim Dale), Stills, Trivia, Trailer, Carry On Laughing – One
in the Eye for Harold

Carry On – The Doctors & Nurses Collection (Doctor, Matron, Again Doctor, That's
Carry On, Loving, Emmannuelle)
ITV Studios Home Entertainment, 2005
PAL, Region 2 (Europe, Middle East & Japan), Colour

Carry On – The Ultimate Collection
ITV Studios Home Entertainment, 2006
PAL, Region 2 (Europe, Middle East & Japan), Colour, Black & White
Special features as for individual ITV/Carlton/Optimum releases

Carry On Vol. 2 (Henry, Up the Jungle, Again Doctor, Camping)
Optimum Home Releasing, 2008
PAL, Region 2 (Europe, Middle East & Japan), Colour
Special features as for individual ITV/Carlton/Optimum releases

Carry On – The Ultimate Collection
ITV Studios Home Entertainment, 2008
PAL, Region 2 (Europe, Middle East & Japan), Colour, Black & White
Special features as for individual ITV/Carlton/Optimum releases

VHS:

Carry On Again Doctor
Rank Video Library, 1984
PAL, Colour

Carry On Again Doctor
Cinema Club, 1987
PAL, Colour

Carry On Again Doctor
Cinema Club, 1992
PAL, Colour

Carry On Again Doctor
Cinema Club, 1996
PAL, Colour

Carry On Doctor / Carry On Matron / Carry On Again Doctor
Cinema Club, 1997
PAL, Colour

Carry On Again Doctor – Collector's Edition
Cinema Club, 1999
PAL, Colour

Carry On Doctor / Carry On Again Doctor
Cinema Club, 2000
PAL, Colour

DeAgostini Carry On VHS partwork
DeAgostini/Carlton, 2003
PAL, Colour, Black & White

The Carry On Collection (Don't Lose your Head – Carry On Emmannuelle)
Carlton Visual Entertainment, 2003
PAL, Colour

Carry On Again Doctor
Carlton Visual Entertainment, 2003
PAL, Colour

BETAMAX:

Carry On Again Doctor
Rank Video Library, 1984
PAL, Colour

CARRY ON UP THE JUNGLE

Or

THE AFRICAN QUEENS

Or

STOP BEATING ABOUT THE BUSH

Or

SHOW ME YOUR WATERHOLE AND I'LL SHOW YOU MINE

1970

Screenplay by Talbot Rothwell
Music Composed & Conducted by Eric Rogers

CAST   CHARACTER

Frankie Howerd	Professor Inigo Tinkle
Sidney James	Bill Boosey
Charles Hawtrey	Walter Bagley / King Tonka
Joan Sims	Lady Evelyn Bagley
Terry Scott	Jungle Boy / Cecil Bagley
Kenneth Connor	Claude Chumley
Bernard Bresslaw	Upsidaisi
Jacki Piper	June
Valerie Leon	Leda
Reuben Martin	Gorilla
Edwina Carroll	Nerda
Valerie Moore	Lubi Lieutenant
Cathi March	Lubi Lieutenant
Danny Daniels	Nosha Chief
Yemi Ajibadi	Witch Doctor
Verna Lucille MacKenzie	Gong Lubi
Heather Emmanuel	Pregnant Lubi
Lincoln Webb	Nosha with Girl
Noshas:	Roy Stewart, Jean Hamilton, Chris Konyils, Willie Jonah, Nina Baden-Semper

CREW

Production Manager	Jack Swinburne
Art Director	Alex Vetchinsky
Director of Photography	Ernest Steward
Editor	Alfred Roome
Camera Operator	James Bawden
Assistant Director	Jack Causey
Assistant Editor	Jack Gardner

Sound Recordists ....RT MacPhee & Ken Barker
Dubbing Editor ....Colin Miller
Continuity..Josephine Knowles
Make-up ....Geoffrey Rodway
Hairdresser..Stella Rivers
Costume Designer ....Courtenay Elliott
Titles...GSE Ltd
Producer...Peter Rogers
Director...Gerald Thomas

A Peter Rogers production. Distributed through the Rank Organisation.

PRODUCTION DETAILS:

Budget: £210,000
Filming: 13th October 1969 – 21st November 1969
Duration: 89m
Colour
General Release: March 1970, Certificate A
TV Premiere: 3rd April 1976, ITV (Thames & Southern)
Home Video: 1981 (VHS/Betamax), 2001 (DVD)

IN A NUTSHELL:

"The Carry On team in starkest Africa"

Professor Inigo Tinkle (Frankie Howerd) leads an expedition into darkest Africa in search of the rare Oozlum Bird (rare because it keeps disappearing up its own ****). He is joined in his search by fellow twitcher Claude Chumley (Kenneth Connor) and the Great White Tin Opener, Bill Boosey (Sid James). Also joining the expedition are Lady Evelyn Bagley (Joan Sims), searching for her son who went missing in the jungle as a baby, and her maid June (Jacki Piper).

Tinkle's expedition is hindered by a troublesome gorilla and the incompetent Jungle Boy (Terry Scott), who has taken a shine to June. Fleeing the cannibalistic Nosha tribe, the intrepid explorers are ensnared by the glamorous Lubidubis. Lady Evelyn is stunned to discover that their leader, Tonka (Charles Hawtrey), is none other than her estranged husband. However, there is an even bigger surprise for the men as they are forced to become sex slaves for the Lubidubis. Things are looking up for Boosey and his fellow explorers, but a diet of non-stop lovemaking can be too much for even the most hardened of men.

REVIEW:

With Sid James as the great white hunter, Frankie Howerd as the mad professor and Joan Sims as the English upper class dame there's so much to love about Carry On up the Jungle. The plot is nonsense, of course, but it hardly matters.

Frankie Howerd's Carry On appearances are all too infrequent but, as always, he lifts the entire team. Sid is on rare form too; his gnarled and world-weary Boozey is a joy. Joan Sims plays a desperate fading beauty and I suggest you treasure her appearance, because in the films to come she rarely gets to play such a sparkling, well rounded character. Jungle also sees the welcome return of Kenneth Connor although, because the Carry On team dynamic changed during his six year absence, he no longer appears to own a distinctive persona. Too old for the romantic lead and not quite ready for the frustrated old man that he later played so well, Connor is something of a spare part although he remains as much fun to watch as ever. Bernard Bresslaw is blacked-up once again for his role and as in Follow that Camel and Up the Khyber that may make for a little discomfort. But let's leave the logic of that decision firmly in the past where it belongs.

But Terry Scott - oh what a joy. He doesn't get many lines but those he does have are delivered so simply, so bluntly that you can't help but stifle a giggle every time he opens his mouth. And, let's face it, with a physique like that, who else would you get to play Jungle Boy?

Once again, the film runs out of steam towards the end as the explorers meet up with the Lubidubis. By this point, the script is running on empty and one can't help but think that the film would have done just as well without such a protracted sequence. But it does give us a chance to see Hawtrey as a Love-God, so it's not all bad. Somewhat more alarmingly especially for those of us of a more delicate sensibility, Carry On up the Jungle is the first film to really enter the realms of proper adult humour. The very idea of our heroes being held as sex slaves sets a precedent on which the films to come would build throughout the 1970s.

Nevertheless, despite the shortcomings of the later scenes, Up the Jungle remains a true classic among the Carry Ons.

VIEWING NOTES:

- *Early titles for Carry On up the Jungle included "Carry On Tarzan" (but the Tarzan character remained under copyright to the estate of Edgar Rice Burroughs) and "Carry On Jungle Boy".*
- *Talbot Rothwell went overboard on the additional titles for Carry On up the Jungle. His original script is littered with more, including "Don't Shoot 'til you see the Whites of their Thighs", "The Game's the Thing" and "The Lust Continent".*
- *Kenneth Williams was originally offered the role of Inigo Tinkle, but his work commitments meant that he would have only been able to take on a minor role in the film. Angered at being subsequently offered a role which he thought (rightly) had been written for Charles Hawtrey, he declined altogether.*
- *The role of Jungle Boy was originally offered to Jim Dale, but the actor thought the role was a step backwards in terms of what would be demanded of him.*
- *Bernard Bresslaw went to the trouble of learning all his lines in the South African Ndebele language, only to later discover that the actors playing the natives were all from the West Indies.*
- *On completing Carry On up the Jungle, Jacki Piper made the headlines with the signing of a two year contract to stay with the series. She would go on to star in Carry On Loving, Carry On at your Convenience and Carry On Matron.*
- *Joan Sims, playing the role of Terry Scott's mother in Up the Jungle, was actually three years younger than him.*
- *The Carry On team's personal gorilla was Reuben Martin who would go on to play similar roles in both Carry On Emmanuelle and the Carry On Laughing television episode "Lamp Posts of the Empire".*
- *The BBC's long-running Film Night series visited the set of Carry On up the Jungle, to film a special 30 minute documentary entitled "Carry On Forever". The programme aired on 12 April 1970 on BBC2 (See "Carry On Television" for more details).*

CARRY ON COCK-UPS:

Technical	1m 30s	Take a close look at the windows on the right of the library as the punters go in and you will spot some then-futuristic strip lights inside.
Technical	4m 39s	Joan Sims calls Sid James "Mr Woosey".
Technical	5m 22s	Amazingly, this is not a real gorilla so let's just get that out of the way early, because you'll be seeing a lot of him, and not just in this film.
Technical	9m 22s	Needless to say, that is a body double in the shower and not Joan Sims. Joan was reported to have watched the scene being filmed, commenting on how good she was looking.
Continuity	10m 54s	The person in the shower pretending to be Joan Sims, when viewed from above, appears to have mislaid her towel.
Technical	11m 05s	Watch Bernard Bresslaw as he "says" the line "Big White Hunter… big white tin opener" - his lips don't move. The line was clearly dubbed later.
Technical	12m 47s	Frankie Howerd calls Joan Sims "Lady Badly".
Technical	15m 59s	Sid James' cry to Jungle Boy is a dub of Terry Scott's original. You can see Sid's mouth isn't even moving in time with the sound.
Technical	20m 40s	Look closely at the bottom of the vine Terry Scott's swinging on. The film is being played in reverse.
Technical	20m 52s	All the shots of Terry Scott swinging from a rope (those that aren't of a stuntman) are less than convincing, but this is about the worst of the lot. He steps onto a platform at the bottom of the rope and is lifted, rather than swung out of shot.
Continuity	26m 53s	Savour the last moments of Jacki Piper wearing specs. From this point, true love cures her short-sightedness and you don't see them again.
Technical	27m 00s	The addition of foam to the waterfall suddenly makes that pool far less enticing as a place to swim.
Continuity	28m 04s	Jacki Piper's singlet and hair are dirty and wet from her rescuing Jungle Boy. A quick trip behind the bushes and she's nice and clean again ready for another swim.
Technical	32m 30s	The underwear Jacki Piper wears to cover her modesty as she leaves the pool definitely isn't in keeping with the period.
Continuity	33m 54s	As Jacki says goodbye to Terry Scott, she's covered in sand but as she turns to find her clothes the magic jungle dry cleaners have already been hard at work and her singlet is almost spotless once more.
Continuity	41m 42s	Joan Sims' gown is pulled tight in close-up shots but thrown open to the jungle in wider ones.

Technical	50m 05s	The lamp knocked over by the gorilla is, of course, electric. That's why it extinguishes immediately instead of engulfing the tent in fire.
Continuity	52m 21s	Frankie Howerd lights a match to get a better look at his bed mate. Watch how he holds it - from one shot to the next the match changes orientation from down to up.
Technical	52m 23s	In case there was any doubt left by this time, you get a good look at the eyes behind the gorilla mask.
Technical	59m 16s	The brief snippet of explosion is lifted from the longer shot a few moments later.
Technical	1h 06m 08s	Nice to see you can still get a decent pair of mules for your delicate Amazonian feet even in the remotest jungles. Many of the Lubidubis are wearing stylish footwear in the upcoming scenes.
Continuity	1h 22m 21s	Valerie Leon unveils the symbol of perpetuity but in the very next shot the cage is covered up. It is unveiled once more in the next one.

LOCATIONS:

Time	Description	Address	Also seen in	Location Link
1m 30s	Tinkle's lecture	Former site of Maidenhead Library St Ives Road Maidenhead Berks SL6 1RF	Carry On Doctor The site is directly opposite Maidenhead Town Hall, although the original building was demolished in 1974.	
1h 26m 12s	Jungle boy's home	11 Clarence Crescent Windsor Berks SL4 5DT	Carry On Regardless	

CARRY ON CUTTING:

• *A scene was cut where Joan Sims goes into Frankie's tent looking for comfort and a little bit of passion. Frankie completely misreads the situation, thinks that she is ill and offers her some pills.*

• *In another brief gag removed from the final cut, Sid James is stopped in the jungle by a man who mistakes him for Dr Livingstone.*

CARRY ON ABROAD:

Carry On Tarzan – *Denmark*
Queen of the Amazons – *Germany*
Carry On through the Jungle – *Hungary*

Full speed ahead...Safari – *Poland*
Watch out for the Jungle – *South America*
Adventures in Africa – *Sweden*

CARRY ON COLLECTING:

- Postcard featuring UK Quad poster released in 1998 by The London Postcard Company as part of their "Rank Classics Series 1" collection.
- In 1998, Cartel International released a series of Carry On-themed greetings cards bearing stills from the films together with a suitably saucy text. The series of 14 cards included stills from Carry On Doctor, Carry On Camping, Carry On Again Doctor, Carry On up the Jungle, Carry On Abroad and Carry On Girls.
- In 2003, Cards Inc planned a series of Carry On trading cards. While the series was ultimately cancelled, eight preview cards were released featuring images from Carry On Doctor, Carry On up the Khyber, Carry On Camping, Carry On Again Doctor, Carry On up the Jungle, Carry On Abroad and Carry On Dick.

SOUNDTRACK:

Carry On up the Jungle – complete audio soundtrack with additional linking narration by Patrick Allen
Original cast & crew, Audio Cassette, EMI 1996
Also released as a double-pack with Carry On up the Khyber

Title theme available on "What a Carry On"
Gavin Sutherland and the Royal Sinfonia, CD, Dutton Vocalion 2005
Newly performed renditions of classic Carry On themes

DVD:

Carry On Up the Jungle
Cinema Club, 2001
PAL, Region 2 (Europe, Middle East & Japan), Colour

DeAgostini Carry On DVD part-work
DeAgostini/Carlton, 2003
PAL, Region 2 (Europe, Middle East & Japan), Colour, Black & White

Carry On up the Jungle
ITV Studios Home Entertainment, 2003
PAL, Region 2 (Europe, Middle East & Japan), Colour
Special Features: Commentary (Jacki Piper, Valerie Leon), Stills, Trivia, Trailer, Carry On Laughing – The Nine Old Cobblers

Carry On – The History Collection (Head, Dick, Jungle, Henry, England, Khyber)
ITV Studios Home Entertainment, 2005
PAL, Region 2 (Europe, Middle East & Japan), Colour

Carry On – The Ultimate Collection
ITV Studios Home Entertainment, 2006
PAL, Region 2 (Europe, Middle East & Japan), Colour, Black & White
Special features as for individual ITV/Carlton/Optimum releases

Carry On Vol. 2 (Henry, Up the Jungle, Again Doctor, Camping)
Optimum Home Releasing, 2008
PAL, Region 2 (Europe, Middle East & Japan), Colour
Special features as for individual ITV/Carlton/Optimum releases

Carry On – The Ultimate Collection
ITV Studios Home Entertainment, 2008
PAL, Region 2 (Europe, Middle East & Japan), Colour, Black & White
Special features as for individual ITV/Carlton/Optimum releases

VHS:

Carry On up the Jungle
Rank Video Library, 1981
PAL, Colour

Carry On up the Jungle
Cinema Club, 1986
PAL, Colour

Carry On up the Jungle
Cinema Club, 1991
PAL, Colour

Carry On up the Jungle
Cinema Club, 1995
PAL, Colour

Carry On up the Jungle – Collector's Edition
Cinema Club, 1999
PAL, Colour

Carry On up the Jungle / Carry On up the Khyber
Cinema Club, 2000
PAL, Colour

DeAgostini Carry On VHS partwork
DeAgostini/Carlton, 2003
PAL, Colour, Black & White

The Carry On Collection (Don't Lose your Head – Carry On Emmannuelle)
Carlton Visual Entertainment, 2003
PAL, Colour

Carry On up the Jungle
Carlton Visual Entertainment, 2003
PAL, Colour

BETAMAX:

Carry On up the Jungle
Rank Video Library, 1981
PAL, Colour

CARRY ON LOVING

Or

IT'S NOT WHAT YOU FEEL – IT'S THE WAY THAT YOU FEEL IT

Or

TWO'S COMPANY BUT THREE'S QUITE GOOD FUN TOO

Or

LOVE IS A FOUR LETTER WORD

Or

IT'S JUST ONE THING ON TOP OF ANOTHER

1970

Screenplay by Talbot Rothwell
Music Composed & Conducted by Eric Rogers

CAST   CHARACTER

Sidney James	Sidney Bliss
Kenneth Williams	Percival Snooper
Charles Hawtrey	James Bedsop
Hattie Jacques	Sophie Bliss / Plummett
Joan Sims	Esme Crowfoot
Terry Scott	Terry Philpott
Richard O'Callaghan	Bertram Muffett
Bernard Bresslaw	Gripper Burke
Jacki Piper	Sally Martin
Imogen Hassall	Jenny Grubb
Patsy Rowlands	Miss Dempsey
Peter Butterworth	Client
Julian Holloway	Adrian
Joan Hickson	Mrs Grubb
Janet Mahoney	Gay
Ann Way	Aunt Victoria Grubb
Bill Maynard	Mr Dreery
Gordon Richardson	Uncle Ernest Grubb
Amelia Bayntun	Corset Lady
Valerie Shute	Girl Lover
Michael Grady	Boy Lover
Tom Clegg	Trainer
Lucy Griffiths	Woman
Harry Shacklock	Lavatory Attendant
Anthony Sagar	Man in Hospital
Derek Francis	Bishop
Alexandra Dane	Emily
Philip Stone	Robinson

Sonny Farrar .... Violinist
Patricia Franklin .... Mrs Dreery
Hilda Barry .... Grandma Grubb
Josie Bradley .... Pianist
Bart Allison .... Grandpa Grubb
Anna Karen .... Wife
Dorothea Phillips .... Aunt Beatrice Grubb
Lauri Lupino Lane .... Husband
Bill Pertwee .... Barman
Colin Vancao .... Cousin Wilberforce Grubb
Gavin Reed .... Window Dresser
Ken Lowe.. Maître d'Hotel
Joe Cornelius .... 2nd Maître d'Hotel
Fred Griffiths .... Taxi Driver
Ronnie Brody.. Henry
Kenny Lynch .... Bus Conductor
Norman Chappell .... Mr Thrush
James Beck .... Mr Roxby
Yutte Stensgaard .... Mrs Roxby
Robert Russell.. Policeman

CREW

Production Manager .... Jack Swinburne
Art Director .... Lionel Couch
Director of Photography .... Ernest Steward
Editor... Alfred Roome
Camera Operator.. James Bawden
Assistant Director .... David Bracknell
Assistant Editor.. Jack Gardner
Sound Recordists .... JWN Daniel & Ken Barker
Dubbing Editor .... Marcel Durham
Assistant Art Director .... William Alexander
Continuity.. Josephine Knowles
Make-up .... Geoffrey Rodway
Hairdresser... Stella Rivers
Costume Designer .... Courtenay Elliott
Set Dresser .... Peter Howitt
Titles .... GSE Ltd
Producer... Peter Rogers
Director.. Gerald Thomas

A Peter Rogers production. Distributed through the Rank Organisation.

PRODUCTION DETAILS:

Budget: £215,000
Filming: 6th April 1970 – 15th May 1970

Duration: 88 minutes
Colour
General Release: September 1970, Certificate A
TV Premiere: 15th December 1976, BBC1
Home Video: 1984 (VHS/Betamax), 2001 (DVD)

IN A NUTSHELL:

"Doing their bit for laughter!"

Sidney (Sid James) and Sophie Bliss (Hattie Jacques) run the Wedded Bliss Agency, a lonely hearts' bureau which uses the latest cutting edge computer technology to match clients with the ideal partner – or so it seems. In truth, Sid and Sophie aren't even married and their computer is as real as their relationship. Clients are matched completely at random, assuming of course that Sid doesn't get to them first.

Bertram Muffett (Richard O'Callaghan) pays Wedded Bliss a visit, hoping to find his ideal woman. Sophie pairs him up with Sid's "special" client, Esme Crowfoot (Joan Sims), but a mix up over milk bottle tops and glamour photography finds Muffett going home with model Sally Martin (Jacki Piper).

Terry Philpott (Terry Scott) is sent on a date with Jenny Grubb (Imogen Hassall) but is less than pleased to discover that within the space of one disastrous date he's already betrothed to both Jenny and her family of hangers-on. Philpott later demands his money back but is reunited with a newly liberated Jenny who, tired of her oppressive family, has decided to strike out on her own.

Meanwhile, confirmed bachelor and marriage guidance counsellor Percival Snooper (Kenneth Williams), faces unemployment if he doesn't find a wife so he turns to Wedded Bliss for help. Sophie, outraged at Sid's infidelities turns her attention to Snooper the moment she claps eyes on him and before the long the pair are engaged.

When Esme's ex-boyfriend, wrestler Gripper Burke (Bernard Bresslaw) returns to claim his love, Sid finds himself alone. Vowing to win Sophie back, he enlists Esme and an unwitting Gripper to further his plan and the pair finally tie the knot, surrounded by their happy (and not so happy) clients.

REVIEW:

In Carry On Loving, the team take a definitive step towards sex comedy. Innuendo is jettisoned in favour of sexual freedom, loose morals and a general feeling that this is an entirely more grown-up and rather less family friendly Carry On film than we have ever seen before. Sex, or rather a tongue in cheek, boggle-eyed appreciation of it, had been one of the mainstays of the Carry On films since the early 1960s. During the more liberated late 60s and early 70s, it became inevitable that to move with the times the Carry Ons would have to become more overtly sexual.

With all that in mind, it's a relief to see the result be every bit as charming, entertaining and genuinely hilarious as the best of the Carry Ons up to this point. Unlike later dalliances with more direct adult content, Carry On Loving never feels uncomfortably sexual. While the on-going gag of the young couple canoodling in all sorts of public places feels rather more like a Confessions film than a Carry On, it is at least done relatively tastefully. In fact, Carry On

Loving is one of the few 70s Carry Ons with absolutely no nudity. There's sex all over the place - they're all at it, but we don't get to see any of it. It's as surprising as it is ingenious that a film that deals as much with attitudes to sex as the act itself is so clean.

Sid and Hattie are the lynchpins around whom the film revolves as, invoking the spirit of the earlier Carry On that was set in the very same building, a series of set pieces are constructed around the loose scenario of the Wedded Bliss agency. It is Carry On Regardless for the free-love generation.

Richard O'Callaghan takes on the awkward romantic role and does so beautifully - his innocent gormlessness is delightful. Meanwhile, Kenneth Williams, Sid, Hattie and Charles are our links to the world of the Carry Ons we know so well. In a film where so much is new and out of the ordinary in terms of cast and tone, they anchor us to the fact that we are still basically on familiar territory.

But it's the remarkably bold, skilful and funny treatment of the very idea of free love that sets Carry On Loving among the greatest of the series. The film doesn't shy away from the subject of sex, nor does it stray too far into adult territory. Loving is a Carry On masterpiece.

VIEWING NOTES:

- *The film was originally commissioned under the title "Carry On Courting".*
- *The new young male lead, Richard O'Callaghan is the son of Carry On Again Doctor actress (and Tony Hancock's very own Mrs Cravatte), Patricia Hayes.*
- *Charles Hawtrey originally turned down the role of Bedsop because of a dispute over billing - an issue which plagued Hawtrey throughout his Carry On career and which saw him ultimately leave the series after Abroad. Eventually, Rogers relented in this case and Hawtrey received third billing, above Joan Sims and Hattie Jacques.*
- *Peter Butterworth agreed to appear in a cameo as the mysterious, murderous character Sid jokingly calls "Crippen". Butterworth's name is absent from the film's credits as per agreement with Rogers.*
- *Charles Hawtrey's character in the film invariably appears to the accompaniment of Eric Rogers' adaptation of Gounod's "Funeral March of a Marionette", a tune better known (particularly at the time) as the theme to "Alfred Hitchcock Presents". The same theme was used in Carry On Doctor to accentuate the strangeness of Brian Wilde's character.*
- *The computers which make up the Wedded Bliss dating system were previously used for an altogether more serious purpose in the Gerry Anderson series, "UFO". Among other places they can be seen in the series' opening title sequence.*
- *The spectacular food fight that takes place at the end of Carry On Loving was filmed over a period of three days. The cream used on the cakes was real and after three days under studio lights the cast and crew were in something of a rush to get out of there.*
- *The famous food fight scene at the end of the film was lifted for a 2007 advertising campaign for Bounty kitchen towels. In it, the long-running Bounty "women" (actually two burly men in drag) were edited in to the fight. The tag line - Carry On Cleaning, of course!*

CARRY ON COCK-UPS:

Continuity	1m 54s	Terry Scott's train has just left the station but in the next shot, as he is talking to the vicar, the scenery outside depicts open countryside. If only trains could run that quickly these days.

Technical	12m 38s	There's a minor typo on the sign outside the Citizens' Advice Bureau. The apostrophe should be after the "S". On the door to Snooper's office, the apostrophe is in the correct place.
Continuity	13m 08s	The clock on Kenneth Williams' mantel appears to have stopped – it reads 6.55 throughout the scene. According to the sign outside, the office should be closed at that time of day.
Technical	18m 03s	As Terry Scott walks away from the mini parked outside the Grubbs' house you can see the shadow of a microphone boom disappear up and out of shot.
Trivia	18m 45s	Eric Rogers uses an arrangement of Chopin's "Funeral March" as Terry Scott enters the house. He uses the same arrangement later in Carry On Abroad.
Continuity	19m 35s	The man sitting at the back of the room, over Jenny's shoulder, by the window is holding his cup differently in the next shot.
Continuity	20m 37s	Keep an eye on that tea trolley. When Imogen Hassall goes to prepare the tea it's in front of the organ. By the time Terry Scott goes to leave, it has wandered in front of the door.
Technical	23m 29s	By the time Sid James goes to talk to Sophie about cancelling Muffett's date, he has reverted to calling him "Muffin".
Continuity	27m 27s	The newspaper Charles Hawtrey is hiding behind has two eye-holes cut out when Sid James enters the bar. In every shot before and after the holes are not present. In fact the very next time you see him he appears to be holding up a different paper altogether.
Trivia	29m 35s	As Charles Hawtrey follows Sid, Eric Rogers borrows Gounod's "Funeral March of a Marionette" as last heard in Carry On Doctor.
Trivia	29m 46s	As Sid James walks down towards the station, watch the lady in the blue coat at the top of the road. Having spotted there's some filming going on she is determined to have a good look.
Continuity	29m 54s	Watch the bus outside the station entrance. When Sid James enters it completely covers the doorway but when Charles Hawtrey follows him it is set back allowing you to see the Parkway Hotel, this time minus the fake sign put up for filming.
Continuity	30m 05s	A young boy walks out in front of the bus that's parked behind Charles. In the next shot, that boy, in the twinkling of an eye has grown into a balding middle aged man.
Continuity	30m 19s	As Charles checks his reflection in the mirror of the photo booth we can see the policeman reflected behind him. However, the reflected policeman isn't standing in the same place as the one we are shown in close-up a moment later.
Continuity	30m 46s	As we cut to the close-up of Sid looking over the top of the cubicle, you can see him holding the top of the frame with his hands. Cut to the wide shot and his hands are elsewhere.

Technical	35m 45s	Sid James presses the button for the sixth floor when he goes into the lift at Rogerham Mansions. From the outside you can see quite clearly that it's only a four storey building.
Continuity	36m 13s	Sid James gives himself a thorough soaking - yet his suit is dry when we switch to the interior of Joan's flat.
Trivia	51m 21s	Eric Rogers reprises his hospital theme from Carry On Doctor for the scene with Richard O'Callaghan and Jacki Piper in the hospital.
Continuity	1h 17m 18s	Sid James moves outside the window to watch the seduction inside. Through the entire scene he's not visible in the shots from the inside looking out despite the curtains being drawn and it being daylight outside.
Continuity	1h 23m 18s	There are a number of continuity slips during the food fight. Watch closely and you can see cakes changing between shots, violinists covered in food one minute and spotlessly clean the next. Shooting such a complex scene over a number of days proved problematical in many ways.

LOCATIONS:

Time	Description	Address	Also seen in	Location Link
1m 37s	Much Snogging on the Green	Windsor & Eton Central Railway Station Thames Street Windsor Berks SL4 1PJ The station has changed radically over the years. Much of the station concourse is now a variety of cafes and market stalls.	Carry On Regardless	
2m 24s	The bus goes round the roundabout	Former site of Slough Greyhound stadium Wellington Street Slough Berks SL1 1RP		
3m 40s	Bertram looks in the shop window	38 Thames Street Windsor Berks SL4 1PR		

Time	Scene	Address	Films	QR
4m 00s	The Wedded Bliss Agency	15 Park St Windsor Berks SL4 1LU	Carry On Regardless Carry On Cabby Carry On Again Doctor	
12m 38s	The Citizen's (ad)Vice Bureau	75 Frances Road Windsor Berks SL4 3AJ		
17m 31s	Philpott's car pulls up outside Jenny Grubb's house	26 Queen's Road Windsor Berks SL4 3BH		
25m 18s	Bertram enters the Parkway Hotel Cocktail Bar	31 High Street Windsor Berks SL4 1PH The entrance can be found on Thames Street		
29m 35s	Philpott follows Sid up Thames St, towards the station entrance	Windsor & Eton Central Railway Station Thames Street, Windsor Berks SL4 1PJ		
29m 54s	Sid enters Windsor Central railway station. Bedsop can be seen hanging around the entrance.	Windsor & Eton Central Railway Station Thames Street Windsor Berks SL4 1PJ Behind him you can see the Parkway Hotel entrance, which has since had its set dressing removed and is revealed to be a coffee shop.	Carry On Regardless	

31m 32s	Sid exits Windsor & Eton Central Station via the main entrance and hails a cab	Windsor & Eton Central Railway Station Thames Street Windsor Berks SL4 1PJ		
35m 06s	Sid's taxi pulls up outside Rogerham Mansions	Atherton Court Meadow Lane Windsor & Eton Berks SL4 6BN		
1h 10m 02s	Percy Snooper's house	32 Adelaide Square Windsor Berks SL4 2AQ		
1h 22m 00s	The wedding reception	Ballroom Pinewood Studios Iver Heath Bucks SL0 0NH		

CARRY ON CUTTING:

- James Beck and Yutte Stensgaard filmed a scene in Kenneth Williams' marriage guidance office playing the Roxbys. Mr Roxby had caught his wife in bed with another man and, thanks to some typically confused logic from Snooper, is made to realise that it was his fault for not letting her know he was on his way.

- The scene where Hattie rings Charlie was originally longer. In the original, Charlie was seen to be having a debriefing session with client Mr Thrush (played by Norman Chappell).

CARRY ON ABROAD:

Love, Love, etc – *Germany*
The Brides Cry Out – *Greece*

CARRY ON COLLECTING:

- "Carry On Loving – The wickedly funny story that starts where the film ends". A novel by Norman Giller
  Andre Deutsch Ltd, 1996, ISBN 0233990291
- Postcard featuring UK Quad poster released in 1998 by The London Postcard Company as part of their "Rank Classics Series 1" collection.

- In 2007, Ethos released a series of mugs featuring the original UK Quad poster artwork for the Rank Carry Ons, including Carry On Loving.
- The same year, Ethos also released a series of colour changing mugs. One of the set features a still of Sid James taken from Carry On Loving.

SOUNDTRACK:

Title theme available on "What a Carry On"
Gavin Sutherland and the Royal Sinfonia, CD, Dutton Vocalion 2005
Newly performed renditions of classic Carry On themes

DVD:

Carry On Loving
Cinema Club, 2001
PAL, Region 2 (Europe, Middle East & Japan), Colour

DeAgostini Carry On DVD partwork
DeAgostini/Carlton, 2003
PAL, Region 2 (Europe, Middle East & Japan), Colour, Black & White

Carry On Loving
ITV Studios Home Entertainment, 2003
PAL, Region 2 (Europe, Middle East & Japan), Colour
Special Features: Commentary (Jacki Piper, Richard O'Callaghan), Stills, Trivia, Trailer, Carry On Laughing – Under the Round Table

Carry On – The Doctors & Nurses Collection (Doctor, Matron, Again Doctor, That's Loving, Emmanuelle)
ITV Studios Home Entertainment, 2005
PAL, Region 2 (Europe, Middle East & Japan), Colour

Carry On – The Ultimate Collection
ITV Studios Home Entertainment, 2006
PAL, Region 2 (Europe, Middle East & Japan), Colour, Black & White
Special features as for individual ITV/Carlton/Optimum releases

Carry On Vol. 3 (Abroad, At your Convenience, Loving, Matron)
Optimum Home Releasing, 2008
PAL, Region 2 (Europe, Middle East & Japan), Colour
Special features as for individual ITV/Carlton/Optimum releases

Carry On – The Ultimate Collection
ITV Studios Home Entertainment, 2008
PAL, Region 2 (Europe, Middle East & Japan), Colour, Black & White
Special features as for individual ITV/Carlton/Optimum releases

VHS:

Carry On Loving
Rank Video Library, 1984
PAL, Colour

Carry On Loving
Cinema Club, 1987
PAL, Colour

Carry On Loving
Cinema Club, 1991

Carry On Loving
Cinema Club, 1996
PAL, Colour

Carry On Loving – Collector's Edition
Cinema Club, 1999
PAL, Colour

Carry On Loving / Carry On Behind
Cinema Club, 2000
PAL, Colour

DeAgostini Carry On VHS partwork
DeAgostini/Carlton, 2003
PAL, Colour, Black & White

The Carry On Collection (Don't Lose your Head – Carry On Emmannuelle)
Carlton Visual Entertainment, 2003
PAL, Colour

Carry On Loving
Carlton Visual Entertainment, 2003
PAL, Colour

Carry On Loving
Rank Video Library, 1984
PAL, Colour

CARRY ON HENRY

Or

MIND MY CHOPPER!

1971

Screenplay by Talbot Rothwell
Music Composed & Conducted by Eric Rogers

CAST	CHARACTER
Sidney James	King Henry VIII
Kenneth Williams	Thomas Cromwell
Charles Hawtrey	Sir Roger de Lodgerley
Joan Sims	Queen Marie of Normandy
Terry Scott	Cardinal Wolsey
Barbara Windsor	Bettina
Kenneth Connor	Lord Hampton of Wick
Peter Butterworth	Earl of Bristol
Julian Holloway	Sir Thomas
Peter Gilmore	Francis, King of France
Julian Orchard	Duc de Poncenay
Gertan Klauber	Bidet
David Davenport	Major Domo
Margaret Nolan	Buxom Lass
William Mervyn	Physician
Norman Chappell	1st Plotter
Derek Francis	Farmer
Bill Maynard	Guy Fawkes
Douglas Ridley	2nd Plotter
Dave Prowse	Torturer
Monica Dietrich	Katherine Howard
Marjie Lawrence	Serving Maid
Patsy Rowlands	Queen
Billy Cornelius	Guard
Alan Curtis	Conte di Pisa
Leon Greene	1st Warder
John Bluthal	Royal Tailor
William McGuirk	Flunky
Anthony Sagar	Heckler
David Essex	Page Boy
Jane Cardew	Henry's 2nd Wife
John Clive	Dandy
Brian Wilde	2nd Warder
Valerie Shute	Maid
Henrys' Courtiers:	Peter Rigby, Trevor Roberts, Peter Munt

CREW

Production Manager ....Jack Swinburne
Art Director ....Lionel Couch
Director of Photography ....Alan Hume
Editor...Alfred Roome
Camera Operator...Derek Browne
Assistant Director ....David Bracknell
Assistant Editor...Jack Gardner
Sound Recordists ....Danny Daniel & Ken Barker
Dubbing Editor...Brian Holland
Continuity..Rita Davidson
Make-up ....Geoffrey Rodway
Hairdresser..Stella Rivers
Set Dresser ....Peter Howitt
Costume Designer ....Courtenay Elliott
Costumes ....L&H Nathan Ltd
Assistant Art Director ....William Alexander
Titles..GSE Ltd
Producer..Peter Rogers
Director...Gerald Thomas

A Peter Rogers production. Distributed through the Rank Organisation.

PRODUCTION DETAILS:

Budget: £223,000
Filming: 12th October 1970 – 27th November 1970
Duration: 89m
Colour
General Release: February 1971, Certificate A
TV Premiere: 9th October 1976, ITV (Southern)
Home Video: 1981 (VHS/Betamax), 2001 (DVD)

IN A NUTSHELL:

"A great guy with his chopper"

Despite the best efforts of a string of wives, King Henry (Sid James) still hasn't managed to sire an heir to his throne. His new wife, Queen Marie of Normandy (Joan Sims) is keen to get started in the bedchamber, but her insistence on consuming vast quantities of garlic means Henry just can't get near her. In despair, he orders two of his courtiers, Thomas Cromwell (Kenneth Williams) and Cardinal Wolsey (Terry Scott), to arrange another divorce but while they are happy enough to follow the King's every whim (particularly if they can make a profit out of it) they are wary of offending Rome. Meanwhile, Sir Roger de Lodgerley (Charles Hawtrey), the King's taster, has a taste of Marie and she falls pregnant.

King Henry meets Bettina (Barbara Windsor), daughter of Charles, Earl of Bristol (Peter Butterworth) and falls hopelessly in love. Despatching Queen Marie to the tower, Henry sets his sights on young Bettina. But things get complicated when Francis, King of France (Peter Gilmore) unexpectedly arrives and threatens war against England if the King's relationship with his sister, Marie, turns sour. With a wife up the tower and a mistress in his bed, Henry has got some fast talking to do.

REVIEW:

An historical Carry On always offers something different. There's a great deal of mileage in taking famous historical events or characters and putting a saucy twist on tales we all know. It adds an immediacy and familiarity to the proceedings as well as giving the team some obvious hooks on which to hang the trademark Carry On humour. So, why does Carry On Henry fall flat? We have Sid James (who else?) as the bawdy King Henry and the sublime double act of Kenneth Williams and Terry Scott. Joan Sims and Babs add some welcome glamour and do all they can to make the men appear fools. But somehow, despite all these delicious ingredients, Carry On Henry leaves a sour taste.

Talbot Rothwell's script is just as clever, knowing and multi-dimensional as always. There are times where his playfulness with the English language makes me want to clap with glee, such as the introduction of Butterworth's Charles, Earl of Bristol and his well-endowed daughters. That's your triple-entendre right there - Charlies or Bristols (Tolly goes for the former). The dialogue in Carry On Henry is among the finest the series has to offer, but there's an underlying sense of maliciousness in this film which is at odds with the comedy.

Consider a story where the lead character spends most of his time trying to dispose of the female lead; where she gets pregnant by another man and then blackmails her cuckolded husband; where another character spends the bulk of the proceedings in a torture chamber undergoing untold ignominy. All these things work against the gloriously scripted lines and the wonderful performances to produce a film which feels more than a little heartless and cynical.

Nevertheless, there are many elements of Carry On Henry that do stand out. Eric Rogers' score, based on the music of the time, is a delightfully sophisticated backdrop to a sumptuous visual feast. The costumes and sets all look beautiful and as a period piece it's hard to find fault. There are wonderful performances from the lead actors and the trusty Carry On rep - most notably Peter Gilmore, whose King of France is a joyously camp and menacing character. All these things deserve praise. But Carry On Henry is a film at odds with itself. The lasting impression is one of cynicism and deceit and these do not a cosy comedy make.

VIEWING NOTES:

- *Early drafts of the script played with King Henry's love of music and included a number of saucy madrigals. While they were ultimately dropped from the film, these ideas did resurface in the 1972 Carry On Christmas television special and the Carry On London stage play. That same year, Kenneth Connor and Glennis Beresford released an album of highly suggestive madrigals, so if that's the kind of thing that floats your Mary Rose, you can track down the album, "Much Ado About Love" (Avenue Recordings, AVE 085).*
- *One of Talbot Rothwell's additional titles for the film was to have been "Anne of a Thousand Lays" - playing typically suggestive homage to the 1969 Richard Burton film, "Anne of The Thousand Days".*
- *There was concern prior to shooting that Sid James would be unavailable due to work commitments. Harry Secombe was considered a likely replacement if Sid should be unable to join the production.*

- *The Crown Estates Office granted permission for the Carry On team to film at Windsor on the strict proviso that there would be "no publicity or mention of Windsor Great Park or the Long Walk". I don't suppose they'll mind now though.*
- *Talbot Rothwell received a surprise on the set of Carry On Henry when, on 28th October, Eamonn Andrews confronted him with the infamous red book and informed him that "This is Your Life".*
- *Sid James once again gets to don Richard Burton's cast offs. The cloak that he wears in the film is the same that Richard Burton wore in the 1969 film "Anne of the Thousand Days".*
- *Southern Television visited the set of Carry On Henry on 5th November 1970. An extensive set report was produced featuring interviews with Sid James, Kenneth Williams and Terry Scott. The full report can be found on the Carry On Henry DVD.*

CARRY ON COCK-UPS:

Carry On Henry, like all the historical Carry Ons, is awash with historical inaccuracies (Guy Fawkes was not born until after Henry's death, for example), anachronisms (features of Windsor castle not built until much later) and so on but we'll ignore all of those. Here, I focus purely on the logic (or lack of it) within the film itself.

Trivia	0m00s	The theme of Carry On Henry is, of course, an arrangement by Eric Rogers of "Greensleeves", the tune (allegedly) composed by Henry VIII.
Trivia	3m 15s	Listen out for Eric Rogers' familiar wedding theme (as heard in Carry On Loving) when Henry prepares to tie the knot again.
Technical	6m 02s	That's a very un-Tudor pair of underpants beneath Sid James' nightgown. They get another airing at 16m 46s.
Continuity	11m 52s	The window panes are clear the King leaves to go hunting yet when, in the next shot, we see Charles Hawtrey turn away from them the panes are opaque.
Technical	17m 04s	As Sid James escapes the farmer, running from the barn, he shouts "Give me my money back!" but his lips aren't moving. The reason, of course, is clear…
Continuity	17m 04s	Sid James' stunt double is wearing different coloured leggings to those that Sid wore in the barn sequence.
Technical	29m 26s	The cameraman appears to have a spot of trouble negotiating the trunk at the bottom of the bed. Watch the shot as we pull back to witness Kenneth Connor and his cronies enter the room and you'll spot the camera shake as it moves backwards.
Technical	29m 52s	Sid James and the conspirators are all standing still, Joan Sims is in bed. So whose shadow is that moving along the back wall of the bedchamber?
Technical	55m 03s	As Barbara Windsor bows, there's an obvious boom shadow
Technical	1h 14m 57s	The trail of gunpowder stops a couple of inches short of the barrel so it's hardly surprising that it fails to ignite.

| Technical | 1h 15m 27s | Bill Maynard doesn't have a chance to even drop the lighted match before the barrel explodes. In fact, in a physics-defying explosion, the flash of light comes first, then the smoke, then the explosion. All the while, Maynard is still holding that match. |

LOCATIONS:

Time	Description	Address	Also seen in	Location Link
13m 20s	Henry goes hunting	The Long Walk Windsor Castle Windsor Berks SL4 2HH		
13m 33s	Henry chases a wench	Windsor Great Park Windsor Berks SL4 2HT		
13m 55s	Henry corners the wench in a barn	Southlea Farm Southlea Rd Datchet Slough Berks SL3 9BZ		
1h 02m 05s	In the garden with Bettina	Pinewood Gardens Pinewood Studios Iver Heath Bucks SL0 0NH	Carry On Nurse Carry On Don't Lose your Head Carry On up the Khyber Carry On Camping	

CARRY ON CUTTING:

- *David Essex filmed a scene as a pageboy in a scene set at Speaker's Corner where Kenneth Connor's Lord Hampton of Wick spoke out against the King's Sex Enjoyment Tax.*

- *The scene in the throne room where Henry refers to the family motto originally included a gag where he spots a busty maiden at the far end of the room and suggests to Wolsey and Cromwell that she has the perfect figure and might be a candidate for his next wife. Henry is reminded by Cromwell that the woman (played by Jane Cardew) was, in fact, Henry's second wife and that her voluptuous curves weren't entirely natural.*

- *The sequence in the gardens was originally embellished with an additional scene on the croquet lawn with Sid inevitably suggesting (and losing at) strip croquet.*

- *A scene was cut where Wolsey takes Henry through a series of portraits of Europe's most eligible queens-in-waiting while Henry himself turns each down with increasing bluntness.*

CARRY ON ABROAD:

Henry's Bedtime Stories, or How the garlic came to England – *Germany*
Carry On Henry VIII – *USA*

CARRY ON COLLECTING:

- "Carry On Henry – The wickedly funny story that starts where the film ends". A novel by Norman Giller
  Andre Deutsch Ltd, 1996, ISBN 0233990321
- Postcard featuring UK Quad poster released in 1998 by The London Postcard Company as part of their "Rank Classics Series 2" collection.
- In 2007, Ethos released a series of mugs featuring the original UK Quad poster artwork for the Rank Carry Ons, including Carry On Henry.
- CollectablesMANIA, in 2007, released a series of Carry On-themed poker chips. Each set came in a presentation pack, complete with trivia notes and contained six individual plastic chips emblazoned with stills from the film. Five different sets were produced, representing Carry On Doctor, Carry On Up the Khyber, Carry On Camping, Carry On Henry and Carry On Matron.

SOUNDTRACK:

Title theme available on "What a Carry On"
Gavin Sutherland and the Royal Sinfonia, CD, Dutton Vocalion 2005
Newly performed renditions of classic Carry On themes

DVD:

Carry On Henry
Cinema Club, 2001
PAL, Region 2 (Europe, Middle East & Japan), Colour

DeAgostini Carry On DVD partwork
DeAgostini/Carlton, 2003
PAL, Region 2 (Europe, Middle East & Japan), Colour, Black & White

Carry On Henry
ITV Studios Home Entertainment, 2003
PAL, Region 2 (Europe, Middle East & Japan), Colour
Special Features: Commentary (Alan Hume), Stills, Trivia, Trailer, Location report

Carry On – The History Collection (Head, Dick, Jungle, Henry, England, Khyber)
ITV Studios Home Entertainment, 2005
PAL, Region 2 (Europe, Middle East & Japan), Colour

Carry On – The Ultimate Collection
ITV Studios Home Entertainment, 2006
PAL, Region 2 (Europe, Middle East & Japan), Colour, Black & White
Special features as for individual ITV/Carlton/Optimum releases

Carry On Vol. 2 (Henry, Up the Jungle, Again Doctor, Camping)
Optimum Home Releasing, 2008
PAL, Region 2 (Europe, Middle East & Japan), Colour
Special features as for individual ITV/Carlton/Optimum releases

Carry On – The Ultimate Collection
ITV Studios Home Entertainment, 2008
PAL, Region 2 (Europe, Middle East & Japan), Colour, Black & White
Special features as for individual ITV/Carlton/Optimum releases

VHS:

Carry On Henry
Rank Video Library, 1981
PAL, Colour

Carry On Henry
Cinema Club, 1987
PAL, Colour

Carry On Henry
Cinema Club, 1991
PAL, Colour

Carry On Henry – Collector's Edition
Cinema Club, 1999
PAL, Colour

Carry On Dick / Carry On Henry
Cinema Club, 2000
PAL, Colour

DeAgostini Carry On VHS partwork
DeAgostini/Carlton, 2003
PAL, Colour, Black & White

The Carry On Collection (Don't Lose your Head – Carry On Emmannuelle)
Carlton Visual Entertainment, 2003
PAL, Colour

Carry On Henry
Carlton Visual Entertainment, 2003
PAL, Colour

BETAMAX:

Carry On Henry
Rank Video Library, 1981
PAL, colour

CARRY ON AT YOUR CONVENIENCE

Or

DOWN THE SPOUT

Or

LADIES PLEASE BE SEATED

Or

UP THE WORKERS

Or

LABOUR RELATIONS ARE THE PEOPLE WHO COME TO SEE YOU WHEN YOU'RE HAVING A BABY

1971

Screenplay by Talbot Rothwell
Music Composed & Conducted by Eric Rogers

CAST   CHARACTER

CAST	CHARACTER
Sidney James	Sid Plummer
Kenneth Williams	WC Boggs
Charles Hawtrey	Charles Coote
Joan Sims	Chloe Moore
Hattie Jacques	Beattie Plummer
Bernard Bresslaw	Bernie Hulke
Kenneth Cope	Vic Spanner
Patsy Rowlands	Hortence Withering
Jacki Piper	Myrtle Plummer
Richard O'Callaghan	Lewis Boggs
Bill Maynard	Fred Moore
Davy Kaye	Benny
Renee Houston	Agatha Spanner
Marianne Stone	Maud
Margaret Nolan	Popsy
Geoffrey Hughes	Willie
Hugh Futcher	Ernie
Simon Cain	Barman
Leon Greene	Chef
Harry Towb	Doctor in Film
Peter Burton	Hotel Manager
Larry Martyn	Rifle Range Owner
Shirley Stelfox	Bunny Waitress
Bill Pertwee	Manager
Philip Stone	Mr Bulstrode
Jan Rossini	Hoopla Girl
Amelia Bayntun	Mrs Spragg

Alec Bregonzi .... Photographer
Anouska Hempel .... New Canteen Girl

CREW

Production Manager .... Jack Swinburne
Art Director .... Lionel Couch
Director of Photography .... Ernest Steward
Editor .... Alfred Roome
Camera Operator .... James Bawden
Assistant Director .... David Bracknell
Assistant Editor .... Jack Gardner
Sound Recordists .... Danny Daniel & Ken Barker
Dubbing Editor .... Brian Holland
Continuity .... Rita Davidson
Make-up .... Geoffrey Rodway
Hairdresser .... Stella Rivers
Costume Designer .... Courtenay Elliott
Set Dresser .... Peter Howitt
Assistant Art Director .... William Alexander
Titles .... GSE Ltd
Producer .... Peter Rogers
Director .... Gerald Thomas

A Peter Rogers production. Distributed through the Rank Organisation.

PRODUCTION DETAILS:

Budget: £220,000
Filming: 22nd March 1971 – 7th May 1971
Duration: 90m
Colour
General Release: December 1971, Certificate A
TV Premiere: 26th December 1976, BBC1
Home Video: 1981 (VHS/Betamax), 2001 (DVD)

IN A NUTSHELL:

"Flushed with success – the Carry On team carries on round the bend!"

WC Boggs (Kenneth Williams) is the troubled owner of a company which manufactures traditional lavatories. Threatened by modern manufacturing techniques and changing markets, Boggs is under pressure from the industry and his own workers. Militant unionists, led by Vic Spanner (Kenneth Cope), threaten production and walk out on strike at the slightest provocation - usually when there's a match on.

When Boggs' son, Lewis (Richard O'Callaghan) secures a large overseas order, Boggs is forced to swallow his pride and accept, but the bank won't lend him the capital to start production. Luckily works foreman Sid Plummer (Sid James) has had an amazing run of luck on the horses and comes to Boggs' aid. But just as production's about to begin, the union protests at unfair working conditions and walks out once more.

When the annual works' outing to Brighton comes around, the workers flood back to the factory and a thoroughly good time is had by all. But does this newfound goodwill mean the factory can stay open? It does if the workers' wives have anything to say about it.

REVIEW:

Carry On at your Convenience was derided and shunned by the public on release for its supposedly negative portrayal of trade unions but in recent years it has quite deservedly gained a reputation for epitomising all that is best about the Carry Ons. And who am I to argue? I might as well get this out of the way early – Carry On at your Convenience is my favourite Carry On film.

The gang's all here and Talbot Rothwell's script positively crackles with one liners. There is a decent story to keep things moving along and some of the most rounded, sympathetic characters the Carry Ons have ever seen. Come on, who didn't shed a little tear at the goodnight scene between Sid and Joan? But best of all there's a right good booze up to really get us into the spirit of things.

Poking fun at the unions in the 1970s was never going to be a particularly popular idea, so minus points to the team for thinking that they could get away with it. While the intent of the film is every bit "up the workers" as management fight the stupid bureaucracy that would all too often bring the country to a standstill, the press and public saw the film as an "up yours" to the workers.

But Convenience doesn't poke fun at unions; it pokes fun at the same targets as always - petty officialdom in all its many forms. It just happens that in this particular case the officialdom comes in the shape of Kenneth Cope and his self-serving NUCIE rules.

Every single member of the team is at the top of their game in Carry On at your Convenience. Supporting characters like Renee Houston light up the screen while established regulars push their comedy characters further than ever before. The scene in the works' canteen is breathlessly and relentlessly hilarious and it's just one among so many classic moments.

The day trip to Brighton epitomises the Carry On films - cheeky, anarchic, the very definition of saucy and just plain damned funny.

VIEWING NOTES:

- Carry On at your Convenience was originally announced to the press in 1971 as the 21st Carry On film. But with media interest growing around the films' anniversary, Peter Rogers decided to bestow the honour on a more prestigious production, bringing Carry On Henry forward in the production schedule.
- The original title for Carry On at your Convenience was "Carry on Comrade" but the somewhat militant title was soon changed to "Carry On Working".
- Renee Houston's role in At your Convenience was almost recast as the actress was suffering ill health at the time.
- The hotel visited by the WC Boggs workers is Clarges Hotel in Brighton, then owned by former Carry On star, Dora Bryan. The same location would be revisited in the later Carry On Girls.
- Gerald Thomas would later maintain that the first Carry On to lose money would be the last Carry On the team would make. Carry On at your Convenience came close to being

just that. The film alienated the working class audience by poking fun at the trade union movement and box office takings for the film were down significantly on previous Carry Ons. The film finally broke even in 1976.

CARRY ON COCK-UPS:

Continuity	2m 24s	Charles Hawtrey's neckerchief is fastened tightly around his throat when we first see him, but it's loose in the next shot. By the time we see him again, it has been refastened.
Technical	3m 23s	Watch Charles Hawtrey as we cut from close-up to wide shot. He can be seen to mouth the word "room" again.
Continuity	9m 01s	Several supporting actors sit in different positions throughout this scene, depending on the camera angle.
Trivia	13m 51s	Richard O'Callaghan's maths aren't clear - 16x4.5 = 72 minutes. That's 6 hours per worker per 5 day week, not the 15 that he claims.
Continuity	17m 37s	Look at the sofa. There's a large newspaper on the left, leaning against the back of the seat. When Sid sits down in a moment it's nowhere to be seen.
Continuity	17m 47s	Take a look at the inside of Joey's cage. When you see it in close-up Joey's no longer a stuffed bird and the toys and ladder are in different positions. In the next shot with Sid and Hattie, when the cage is between them, they've moved again.
Continuity	18m 17s	Sid James has just put his jacket down and covered the knitting needles on the sofa. Notice that the newspaper that was leaning on the seat to the left of him a moment ago is no longer there. In the close-up shot that you're about to see you'll spot both needles sticking up on either side of Sid's jacket. You'll see them appear and disappear as we switch shots through the rest of the scene.
Continuity	19m 30s	When Sid James stands up to speak to Joey there's only one feeder on the cage. There were two just moments ago.
Continuity	22m 40s	Look at the chap in the suit and tie just walking past the Mini. In the next shot, after Kenneth Cope gets off the bike you can see him again walking past the lorry at the far end of the street – the lorry which itself wasn't there a moment ago. The green car that was parked on the left of the street has also disappeared, along with the man on the left who's crossing by the pub.
Continuity	23m 03s	Oh look, the green car is still there - it's just parked further down the street that it was a moment ago. And watch, at 23m 14s – there's our old friend "man in suit" again.
Continuity	23m 21s	He REALLY gets about – here he is again walking past Kenneth Cope.
Continuity	28m 17s	Did you see the woman in the green dress who just walked past on the opposite side of the road? When Kenneth Cope and Bernard Bresslaw depart at 28m 25s she's moved further back down the road.

Technical	28m 29s	Watch the neighbour after Mrs Spanner tells her to mind her own bloody business. She says something, but there's an abrupt cut so we see her about to speak and then jump to her shutting her window.
Continuity	29m 28s	Bernard Bresslaw stops the bike in the middle of the road. When he pulls away in a few moments he's closer to the kerb.
Continuity	47m 03s	Watch Davy Kaye's cigar in this scene – when we see him from behind the cigar is considerably shorter than in the shots where he's facing the camera.
Continuity	49m 04s	When the workers down tools in the yard they leave a few pieces of toilet-ware on the ground. When Sid James looks out the window they've gone.
Continuity	50m 22s	Geoffrey Hughes is leaning on the bidet differently between close-up and wide shots.
Continuity	52m 08s	Patsy Rowlands is standing alongside Kenneth Williams as she pleads. Then, when she asks what is to become of her she's directly in front of him. After she says he's never pinched her bottom we cut to another shot and she's back alongside.
Trivia	54m 33s	In Carry On world, coaches only go one way. This is the exact same stretch of road the Chayste Place girls travelled along on their coach trip to Paradise Campsite.
Continuity	54m 54s	Look at the back of the coach and you'll see Margaret Nolan sitting in the centre seat. In the next shot she's moved along to sit beside Bernard Bresslaw.
Continuity	57m 14s	The coach and car are on a dual carriageway. By the time Richard O'Callaghan's car has pulled in behind the coach to wave they're on a motorway. In the very next shot it's a dual carriageway again.
Technical	1h 08m 38s	The sound effect of Kenneth Cope's moans as he is being beaten up can be heard again later when he's having his bottom smacked at 1h 20m 54s.
Technical	1h 10m 00s	The same footage of the team getting off and back onto the coach is re-used for every pub. Note the reflection of the other coach.
Technical	1h 10m 40s	That's a very un-coach-like sound effect as the coach pulls away from the bus stop. It's the same sound effect used for Lewis' car at 29m 40s. You can hear the coach's MG impersonation again in a few moments.
Continuity	1h 15m 02	Kenneth Williams has the covers drawn up to his neck. In the next shot he's pointing at Patsy Rowlands and in the one after that the covers are back up to his neck again and his arm is under the cover.
Continuity	1h 19m 00s	As we look at out of the office window at the picket, you can see Renee Houston smacking Kenneth Cope's bottom over a tea crate - at this point in the film that hasn't happened yet. In fact when we cut to the next shot at the picket line Cope's speaking to the troops and there's not a woman in sight.

Continuity	1h 19m 00s	Now - look at the parked cars. You can see the white van and green car that were parked on Kenneth Connor's street earlier in the film. The red car is parked facing toward the factory gate. At 1h 19m 53s when the women appear there's a Morris Minor parked behind the red car which itself has now turned 180 degrees.
Technical	1h 21m 38s	Look at the back window of Sid's car and you'll see the reflection of a microphone boom.
Continuity	1h 22m 04s	The Morris Minor has gone and the van is back, along with the green car. The red car is facing in the other direction once more.

LOCATIONS:

Time	Description	Address	Also seen in	Location Link
1m 32s	WC Boggs	Timber Store Pinewood Studios Iver Heath Bucks SL0 0NH		
15m 47s	Sid's & Joan's houses	82 & 84 Pinewood Green Iver Heath Bucks SL0 0QP		
22m 40s	Vic Spanner's house	Don't bother looking - it was a set made for Billy Wilder's 1970 film The Private Life of Sherlock Holmes.		
29m 15s	Odeon cinema Uxbridge	Fitness First High Street Uxbridge UB8 1GD		
	Vic's trouser incident	Same location, facing the other way.		

39m 26s	The Whippit Inn	Heatherden Hall Pinewood Studios Iver Heath Bucks SL0 0NH	Carry On Nurse Carry On up the Khyber Carry On Camping Carry On Again Doctor Carry On at your Convenience Carry On England	
57m 36s	Brighton. Marine Parade and Clarges	Clarges Hotel 115-119 Marine Drive Brighton East Sussex BN2 1DD	Carry On Girls	
1h 01m 14s	Palace Pier	Brighton Pier Madeira Drive Brighton East Sussex BN2 1TW		
1h 09m 33s	Horse Drawn carriage	Madeira Drive Brighton East Sussex BN2 1PS		

CARRY ON CUTTING:

- *A lengthy boardroom scene was shot where the NUCIE General Manager, Terry Scott met with WC and Lewis Boggs, Sid Plummer and Vic Spanner to discuss the on-going union troubles.*

- *WC Boggs' dismay at the bank refusing to give the firm a bridging loan was originally expanded upon with a scene where Boggs visits his bank manager, Mr Bulstrode (played by Philip Stone).*

- *Bill Pertwee filmed a scene as the manager of The Whippit Inn which was also cut from the final print. A still from this scene was distributed in the Carry On at your Convenience press pack.*

- *A gag with a photographer on the pier (played by Alec Bregonzi) was cut, although a truncated version appears in the final print. In the original version, two characters were to have emerged from behind the novelty screen wearing the exact same clothes as their cartoon counterparts.*

- *Further pier shenanigans cut from the film also included a hoopla stall where Charles Coote manages to throw a hoop onto the stallholder's (Jan Rossini) breasts. A still from this missing scene can be found in the 2012 Carry On Calendar.*

CARRY ON ABROAD:

Carry On Round the Bend – *Australia (& USA)*
A Dangerous Strike – *Germany*
Carry On Your Way – *Hungary*
How do you Make your Bed? – *Poland*

CARRY ON COLLECTING:

- Postcard featuring UK Quad poster released in 1998 by The London Postcard Company as part of their "Rank Classics Series 2" collection.
- In 2007, Ethos released a series of mugs featuring the original UK Quad poster artwork for the Rank Carry Ons, including Carry On at your Convenience.

SOUNDTRACK:

Extended theme available on "The Carry On Album, Music from the Films".
Gavin Sutherland & the Prague Philharmonic Orchestra, CD, ASV 1999
Newly performed renditions of classic Carry On themes

DVD:

Carry On at your Convenience
Cinema Club, 2001
PAL, Region 2 (Europe, Middle East & Japan), Colour

DeAgostini Carry On DVD partwork
DeAgostini/Carlton, 2003
PAL, Region 2 (Europe, Middle East & Japan), Colour, Black & White

Carry On at your Convenience
ITV Studios Home Entertainment, 2003
PAL, Region 2 (Europe, Middle East & Japan), Colour
Special Features: Commentary (Jacki Piper, Richard O'Callaghan), Stills, Trivia, Trailer,
Carry On Laughing – The Case of the Screaming Winkles

Carry On – The Holiday Collection (Camping, Abroad, Camel, Girls, Convenience, Behind)
ITV Studios Home Entertainment, 2005
PAL, Region 2 (Europe, Middle East & Japan), Colour

Carry On – The Ultimate Collection
ITV Studios Home Entertainment, 2006
PAL, Region 2 (Europe, Middle East & Japan), Colour, Black & White
Special features as for individual ITV/Carlton/Optimum releases

Carry On Vol. 3 (Abroad, At your Convenience, Loving, Matron)
Optimum Home Releasing, 2008
PAL, Region 2 (Europe, Middle East & Japan), Colour
Special features as for individual ITV/Carlton/Optimum releases

Carry On – The Ultimate Collection
ITV Studios Home Entertainment, 2008
PAL, Region 2 (Europe, Middle East & Japan), Colour, Black & White
Special features as for individual ITV/Carlton/Optimum releases

VHS:

Carry On at your Convenience
Rank Video Library, 1981
PAL, Colour

Carry On at your Convenience
Cinema Club, 1987
PAL, Colour

Carry On at your Convenience
Cinema Club, 1991
PAL, Colour

Carry On at your Convenience
Cinema Club, 1996
PAL, Colour

Carry On at your Convenience – Collector's Edition
Cinema Club, 1999
PAL, Colour

Carry On Matron / Carry On at your Convenience
Cinema Club, 2000
PAL, Colour

DeAgostini Carry On VHS partwork
DeAgostini/Carlton, 2003
PAL, Colour, Black & White

The Carry On Collection (Don't Lose your Head – Carry On Emmannuelle)
Carlton Visual Entertainment, 2003
PAL, Colour

Carry On at your Convenience
Carlton Visual Entertainment, 2003
PAL, Colour

BETAMAX:

Carry On at your Convenience
Rank Video Library, 1981
PAL, Colour

CARRY ON MATRON

Or

FROM HERE TO MATERNITY

Or

FAMILIARITY BREEDS

Or

WOMB AT THE TOP

Or

THE PREGGERS OPERA

1972
Screenplay by Talbot Rothwell
Music Composed & Conducted by Eric Rogers

CAST	CHARACTER
Sidney James	Sid Carter
Kenneth Williams	Sir Bernard Cutting
Charles Hawtrey	Doctor Francis A Goode
Joan Sims	Mrs Tidey
Hattie Jacques	Matron
Bernard Bresslaw	Ernie Bragg
Kenneth Cope	Cyril Carter
Terry Scott	Doctor Prodd
Barbara Windsor	Nurse Susan Ball
Kenneth Connor	Mr Tidey
Jacki Piper	Sister
Bill Maynard	Freddy
Patsy Rowlands	Evelyn Banks
Derek Francis	Arthur
Amelia Bayntun	Mrs Jenkins
Valerie Leon	Jane Darling
Brian Osborne	Ambulance Driver
Gwendolyn Watts	Frances Kemp
Valerie Shute	Miss Smethurst
Margaret Nolan	Mrs Tucker
Michael Nightingale	Pearson
Wendy Richard	Miss Willing
Zena Clifton	Au Pair Girl
Bill Kenwright	Reporter
Robin Hunter	Mr Darling
Jack Douglas	Expectant Father
Madeline Smith	Mrs Pullitt
Marianne Stone	Mrs Putzova
Juliet Harmer	Mrs Bentley

Gilly Grant	Nurse in Bath
Lindsay March	Shapely Nurse
Laura Collins	Nurse

CREW

Production Manager	Jack Swinburne
Art Director	Lionel Couch
Director of Photography	Ernest Steward
Editor	Alfred Roome
Camera Operator	James Bawden
Assistant Editor	Jack Gardner
Continuity	Joy Mercer
Sound Recordists	Danny Daniel & Ken Barker
Dubbing Editor	Peter Best
Make-up	Geoffrey Rodway
Hairdresser	Stella Rivers
Costume Designer	Courtenay Elliott
Assistant Art Director	William Alexander
Set Dresser	Peter Lamont
Wardrobe	Vi Murray & Maggie Lewin
Titles	GSE Ltd
Producer	Peter Rogers
Director	Gerald Thomas

A Peter Rogers production Distributed through the Rank Organisation.

PRODUCTION DETAILS:

Budget: £225,000
Filming: 11th October 1971 – 26th November 1971
Duration: 87m
Colour
General Release: May 1972, Certificate A
TV Premiere: 4th June 1977, ITV (Channel, Southern, Westward)
Home Video: 1980 (VHS), 2001 (DVD)

IN A NUTSHELL:

Sid Carter (Sid James) and his gang of small time crooks plan to steal Finisham Maternity Hospital's entire stock of contraceptive pills for sale overseas. The key to Carter's plan is his son, Cyril (Kenneth Cope) disguising himself as a nurse and infiltrating the hospital. Finisham is governed by the neurotic Sir Bernard Cutting (Kenneth Williams), who becomes increasingly convinced that he's turning into a woman; a conviction which is compounded by psychiatrist Dr F A Goode (Charles Hawtrey). Meanwhile, Matron (Hattie Jacques) has more than enough to contend with on the wards. Mrs Tidey (Joan Sims) is long overdue but appears to be quite content to lie in bed and dine on hospital food while her husband (Kenneth Connor) waits patiently in the waiting room.

Cyril's attempt to secure a plan of the hospital goes awry when he is forced to attend local film star, Jane Darling (Valerie Leon), who's about to give birth. In fact, the longer Cyril spends on the wards, the more he realises that Sid's nefarious plan simply isn't right. Before he can call the whole thing off, Nurse Ball (Barbara Windsor) outs him as a man, and the pair begin an illicit affair. Deciding that he is unable to wait any longer, Sid and the rest of the gang visit the hospital with a heavily "pregnant" Ernie Bragg (Bernard Bresslaw) in tow and a plan to smuggle out the pills.

REVIEW:

Carry On Matron is an early attempt at portraying a more mature Carry On team. Slap and tickle is most definitely not the order of the day and instead, we're presented with what is essentially a comedy heist. That it is dressed in the trappings of the earlier, cosier medical Carry Ons means some of the impact of this new direction is lost when Kenneth, Charles and Hattie get up to their usual tricks.

But at the heart of Carry On Matron is a new dynamic. Sid's criminal mastermind is a much darker character than he's played in the past. He's not in it for a bit of fun and a flash of skin. In fact, the closest Sid and his goons get to the opposite sex is a bit of light cross-dressing but even that is driven by criminal intent. Sex, or rather having it, is the furthest thing from Sid's mind.

The team at Finisham, on the other hand, are carrying on like they always have. Dr Prodd terrorises the young nurses, Cyril's busy trying to keep his stockings up, Matron and Dr Goode share an altogether stranger passion and Sir Bernard's convinced he's turning into a woman. That's all traditional, farcical, wonderful Carry On fare but thrown into that familiar world is a much darker plot. It's a brilliant way of mixing things up. The hospital scenario is both the film's foundation and its undoing.

Another odd note is Barbara Windsor's Nurse May. There's simply no reason for her to even be in the film. The character's sole purpose is to out the cross-dressing Cyril, but by the time that happens, Cyril has taken steps to bring the whole charade to an end anyway. What's worse is that the time spent looking at Babs takes attention from other, far worthier candidates like Terry Scott's brilliant Doctor Prodd or Sir Bernard and his mounting insanity.

Despite these shortcomings, Carry On Matron is a lovely, funny film. Part-heist, part-hospital comedy and all Carry On, it manages to take an old idea and inject new humour, tension and lovability into a series which, so far, shows no evidence of running out of steam.

VIEWING NOTES:

- *Additional titles from Talbot Rothwell, under the Carry On Matron banner, also included "If in Doubt – Have it Out" and "If No Doubt – Up the Spout".*
- *Peter Butterworth was originally cast in the role of Freddy but was unable to join the production because of work commitments.*
- *Future Carry On regular, Jack Douglas, makes his first appearance in the Carry Ons as the twitching father in the waiting room. Douglas later claimed that his appearance was unpaid, but he was in fact granted a one-off fee of £25 for a single day's work.*
- *The name of Bernard Bresslaw's character, Ernie Bragg, would be revived for Jack Douglas in Carry On Behind.*
- *If the "story so far" from the medical drama Matron and Dr Goode are so entranced by*

sounds familiar, that's because it's taken directly from the 1946 Alastair Sim film "Green for Danger", a film which gave Hattie one of her first major screen credits.

CARRY ON COCK-UPS:

Continuity	2m 03s	The windscreen wipers on the front of Sid James' car have vanished. They'll be back again later at 19m 26s.
Continuity	3m 31s	Kenneth Williams enters the hospital via the door to the left. When we cut to the interior, the door on the left is closed and he enters via the right.
Continuity	3m 32s	Kenneth's car has disappeared from the front of the hospital.
Continuity	6m 32s	Note the position of the phone on the table to the left. Next time you see it, when Jack Douglas picks it up, it has moved to the other side of the table.
Continuity	8m 16s	The blanket covering Madeline Smith's baby's head differs in position between shots.
Continuity	9m 45s	Sid James' hand moves up the door frame between shots.
Continuity	18m 24s	The container of urine is still on Terry Scott's desk. When Hattie Jacques comes in it has vanished.
Technical	20m 31s	As the student nurses enter the hospital, Derek Francis can be heard to say "Over to the desk, girls" but his lips don't move.
Continuity	24m 15s	Keep an eye on the woman behind Hattie Jacques and remember the name of the ward they're in. If you can't remember from earlier, you can see through the window when Terry Scott's in shot – the Bunn Ward.
Trivia	38m 25s	The announcer on television is of course none other than Kenneth Williams.
Continuity	40m 38s	Pay attention to the trophy photographs on the wall. In the close-up Barts and Charing Cross have changed places.
Trivia	50m 56s	The journalist at the desk is played by none other than theatrical impresario and Everton FC Chairman, Bill Kenwright.
Continuity	51m 42s	Watch the mugs in front of Bernard Bresslaw and Bill Maynard. In this scene Bresslaw's hands are alternately holding or nowhere near his mug. The mug in front of Maynard moves of its own accord several times.
Continuity	53m 31s	Bill Maynard is reading out the story of the miracle birth from the front page of the newspaper. When we next see him, he's reading the same story from the back page.
Continuity	55m 35s	The two women in the corridor are the same two we saw in the scene with Kenneth Connor at the start of the film. They're standing in the exact same spot.
Continuity	56m 46s	Remember that glass of urine on Terry Scott's desk earlier? It's back.

Continuity	58m 13s	The woman we saw behind Hattie Jacques earlier is now in the Oven Ward – you can see her through the glass behind Hattie.
Continuity	1h 03m 03s	Sid James walks in on Barbara Windsor and Kenneth Cope on the bed. The wig Cope discarded moments ago has gone. At 1h 03m 28s it is back on the bed once more.
Continuity	1h 05m 51s	The cars in the hospital car park as seen from Kenneth Williams' window differ from those seen at ground level as Hattie Jacques chases Sid James to his car.
Trivia	1h 05m 58s	That brown Maxi is very badly parked.
Trivia	1h 06m 02s	The Psychology of Jealousy is written by Ernest Steward - the very same Ernest Steward who is Director of Photography on this, and other Carry On films. A nice little in-joke from the production team.
Technical	1h 07m 36s	You can see the Velcro seams on Patsy Rowlands' stunt dress.
Continuity	1h 13m 13s	Bernard Bresslaw seems to have grown a few inches just for this close-up.
Technical	1h 19m 12s	The dynamite blows up before Sid James turns the detonator handle.
Continuity	1h 19m 34s	There are significantly more packets of pills left on the shelf in the close-up of Bernard Bresslaw than there are in the wide shot.
Continuity	1h 22m 26s	It has already been established that the hospital doors are locked. When Terry Scott wakes up and looks out of the ambulance's windscreen they're open. As indeed they are in the very next interior shot.
Technical	1h 23m 40s	Hattie Jacques is heard to say "give it to me", referring to the suitcase, but her lips do not move.

LOCATIONS:

Time	Description	Address	Also seen in	Location Link
1m 52s	Finisham Maternity Hospital	Heatherwood Hospital London Road Ascot Berks SL5 8AA		
48m 05s	Jane Darling's house	The White House Village Road Denham Bucks UB9 5BE		

1h 24m 20s	The church	St Mary's Church, Village Road Denham Bucks UB9 5BH	Carry On Don't Lose your Head	

CARRY ON CUTTING:

- Cyril's conversation with the hospital receptionist was originally part of a longer scene featuring another new nurse, played by Laura Collins.

- A brief scene with Juliet Harmer as Mrs Bentley was cut from the film. In it, Mrs Bentley politely refused to have her baby's father present during the birth because her husband wouldn't like it!

- As originally filmed, the wedding scene at the end of Carry On Matron was longer. An extended piece was cut from the ending where Sir Bernard has another attack of hypochondria.

CARRY ON ABROAD:

A Crazy Nurse – *Germany*
Mom, the Works – *Poland*
Be Careful with the Pill – *South America*

CARRY ON COLLECTING:

- Die-cast 1:60 scale ambulance featuring Carry On Matron poster art by Lledo, 1998, as part of their "Days Gone" range.
- Postcard featuring UK Quad poster released in 1998 by The London Postcard Company as part of their "Rank Classics Series 2" collection.
- Promotional bookmark released in 1998 by The London Postcard Company featuring the Carry On Matron and Carry On Doctor Quad posters.
- In 2007, Ethos released a series of mugs featuring the original UK Quad poster artwork for the Rank Carry Ons, including Carry On Matron.
- CollectablesMANIA, in 2007, released a series of Carry On-themed poker chips. Each set came in a presentation pack, complete with trivia notes and contained six individual plastic chips emblazoned with stills from the film. Five different sets were produced, representing Carry On Doctor, Carry On Up the Khyber, Carry On Camping, Carry On Henry and Carry On Matron.

SOUNDTRACK:

Main title theme available on "Carry On"
Various Artists, CD, Silva Screen 2005
Themes, cues and dialog taken from the original film soundtracks

Title theme available on "What a Carry On"
Gavin Sutherland and the Royal Sinfonia, CD, Dutton Vocalion 2005
Newly performed renditions of classic Carry On themes

DVD:

Carry On Matron
Cinema Club, 2001
PAL, Region 2 (Europe, Middle East & Japan), Colour

DeAgostini Carry On DVD partwork
DeAgostini/Carlton, 2003
PAL, Region 2 (Europe, Middle East & Japan), Colour, Black & White

Carry On Matron
ITV Studios Home Entertainment, 2003
PAL, Region 2 (Europe, Middle East & Japan), Colour
Special Features: Commentary (Jacki Piper, Valerie Leon, Patsy Rowlands), Stills, Trivia, Trailer, Carry On Laughing – And in my Lady's Chamber

Carry On – The Doctors and Nurses Collection (Doctor, Matron, Again Doctor, That's Loving, Emmannuelle.
ITV Studios Home Entertainment, 2005
PAL, Region 2 (Europe, Middle East & Japan), Colour

Carry On – The Ultimate Collection
ITV Studios Home Entertainment, 2006
PAL, Region 2 (Europe, Middle East & Japan), Colour, Black & White
Special features as for individual ITV/Carlton/Optimum releases

Carry On Vol. 3 (Abroad, At your Convenience, Loving, Matron)
Optimum Home Releasing, 2008
PAL, Region 2 (Europe, Middle East & Japan), Colour
Special features as for individual ITV/Carlton/Optimum releases

Carry On – The Ultimate Collection
ITV Studios Home Entertainment, 2008
PAL, Region 2 (Europe, Middle East & Japan), Colour, Black & White
Special features as for individual ITV/Carlton/Optimum releases

VHS:

Carry On Matron
Rank Video Library, 1980
PAL, Colour

Carry On Matron
Cinema Club, 1987
PAL, Colour

Carry On Matron
Cinema Club, 1991
PAL, Colour

Carry On Matron
Cinema Club, 1995
PAL, Colour

Carry On Doctor / Carry On Matron / Carry On Again Doctor
Cinema Club, 1998
PAL, Colour

Carry On Matron – Collector's Edition
Cinema Club, 1999
PAL, Colour

Carry On Matron / Carry On at your Convenience
Cinema Club, 2000
PAL, Colour

DeAgostini Carry On VHS partwork
DeAgostini/Carlton, 2003
PAL, Colour, Black & White

The Carry On Collection (Don't Lose your Head – Carry On Emmannuelle)
Carlton Visual Entertainment, 2003
PAL, Colour

Carry On Matron
Carlton Visual Entertainment, 2003
PAL, Colour

CARRY ON ABROAD

Or

WHAT A PACKAGE

Or

IT'S ALL IN

Or

SWISS HOLS IN THE SNOW

1972

Screenplay by Talbot Rothwell
Music Composed & Conducted by Eric Rogers

CAST

CHARACTER

Sidney James	Vic Flange
Kenneth Williams	Stuart Farquhar
Charles Hawtrey	Eustace Tuttle
Joan Sims	Cora Flange
Bernard Bresslaw	Brother Bernard
Barbara Windsor	Sadie Tomkins
Kenneth Connor	Stanley Blunt
Peter Butterworth	Pepe
Jimmy Logan	Bert Conway
June Whitfield	Evelyn Blunt
Hattie Jacques	Floella
Derek Francis	Brother Martin
Sally Geeson	Lily
Ray Brooks	Georgio
Carol Hawkins	Marge
John Clive	Robin
Jack Douglas	Harry
Patsy Rowlands	Miss Dobbs
Gail Grainger	Moira
David Kernan	Nicholas
Amelia Bayntun	Mrs Tuttle
Alan Curtis	Police Chief
Gertan Klauber	Postcard Seller
Brian Osborne	Stallholder
Hugh Futcher	2nd Policeman
Olga Lowe	Madame Fifi

CREW

Production Manager	Jack Swinburne
Art Director	Lionel Couch

Director of Photography	Alan Hume
Editor	Alfred Roome
Camera Operator	Jimmy Devis
Continuity	Joy Mercer
Assistant Director	David Bracknell
Assistant Editor	Jack Gardner
Sound Recordists	Taffy Haines & Ken Barker
Dubbing Editor	Peter Best
Make-up	Geoffrey Rodway
Hairdresser	Stella Rivers
Costume Designer	Courtenay Elliott
Assistant Art Director	Bill Bennison
Set Dresser	Don Picton
Titles	GSE Ltd
Producer	Peter Rogers
Director	Gerald Thomas

A Peter Rogers production. Distributed through the Rank Organisation.

PRODUCTION DETAILS:

Budget: £225,000
Filming: 17th April 1972 – 26th May 1972
Duration: 88m
Colour
General Release: December 1972, Certificate A
TV Premiere: 8th January 1978, ITV
Home Video: 1980 (VHS/Betamax), 2001 (DVD)

IN A NUTSHELL:

"The holiday of a laugh-time!"

Vic Flange (Sid James) is planning another of his regular package holidays, leaving his wife Cora (Joan Sims), who doesn't like flying, at home. But when she discovers that saucy Sadie Tompkins (Barbara Windsor) happens to be going on the same holiday, Cora reconsiders and the next day the pair set off for the Spanish resort of Els Bels. Also heading off for a few days in the sun are holiday rep Stuart Farquhar (Kenneth Williams) and his assistant Moira (Gail Grainger), hen-pecked Stanley Blunt (Kenneth Connor) and his uptight wife Evelyn (June Whitfield), mummy's boy Eustace Tuttle (Charles Hawtrey) and a group of monks who plan to visit a shrine near the resort.

On arriving at the hotel, the holidaymakers are dismayed to discover the place is only partially built. Hotel manager Pepe (Peter Butterworth), and his wife Floella (Hattie Jacques), do their best to cater for the tourists' every need but when the weather takes a turn for the worse it looks like the holiday, and the hotel, is at an end.

REVIEW:

Abroad is the last film in the series to feature the cosy family unit that the Carry Ons had become. Charles Hawtrey had periodic fallings-out with the Rogers and Thomas but the actor finally burned his bridges by walking out on that year's Carry On Christmas special just days before filming. The definitive end to such a key Carry On regular's career with the series is a rather sad milestone. Things would never be quite the same again.

As a last hurrah, Carry On Abroad is a sparkling 90 minutes of proper Carry On fun. The cast deliver Talbot Rothwell's marvellous dialogue with mounting and infectious comic hysteria. Everything about Abroad works, from the lengthy but brilliant set up at the Wundatours office, to the slow realisation that the Palace Hotel is about to fail spectacularly to live up to its name. Above it all, and this is an important distinction in terms of the later films, Abroad manages to retain an air of good clean fun even when all the participants are leaping into bed left right and centre. In fact, it is the last of truly family-oriented Carry Ons. Carry On Girls is rather too suggestive, Dick's obsessed with its eponymous member and the last few entries are far more obviously adult in tone.

Carry On Abroad successfully recaptures at least some of the magic of Convenience - the whole gang are off on a coach trip to who knows where with fun and disaster waiting at the other end. There is also a noticeable lack of the new generation of Carry On stars. Kenneth Cope, Richard O'Callaghan, Jacki Piper, Angela Douglas - all the wonderful actors who flitted in and out for a few films during the late 60s and 70s have moved on to pastures new and we find ourselves back with the old guard. The Carry On greats are together again one last time and they're on rare form.

VIEWING NOTES:

- *Madeline Smith had so impressed Peter Rogers in her role as Mrs Pullitt in Carry On Matron that she was invited to join Carry On Abroad in the role of Lily. Work commitments forced her to decline and the role was subsequently offered to Sally Geeson.*
- *Hattie Jacques was originally planned to have a significant role in Carry On Abroad, but continuing health problems meant the production insurers would not agree to cover her more active participation in the film.*
- *In Rothwell's original outline several character names were different to their eventual screen counterparts – Cora Flange was originally "Clara", Stuart Farquhar was "Kenneth Stuart-Farquhar" and Eustace Tuttle was "Charles Makepeace". Els Bels also underwent a change of name. As originally outlined, it would have been Costa Bomm.*
- *The opening titles of Carry On Abroad credit the technical advisor – the dubiously named Sun Tan Lo Tion.*
- *Eustace Tuttle's continual drinking in the film was consciously included by Rothwell as a humorous slight against the actor's own dependency on the bottle.*
- *The somewhat uncoordinated dancing of the holidaymakers in the final scenes of the film can be forgiven. There was no music played into the set while the scene was filmed.*
- *The Daily Express newspaper ran a competition to celebrate the launch of Carry On Abroad, offering one lucky winner a trip on the P&O cruise ship, Canberra, with £1000 of spending money.*

CARRY ON COCK-UPS:

Continuity	4m 21s	Joan Sims is standing in a different position behind the bar to the last shot.
Continuity	7m 54s	Take a look through the coach window at the badly parked van further down the road. By 9m 05s, when we see it behind Charles Hawtrey, it's slightly less badly parked.
Continuity	9m 03s	Now, ignore the badly parked van and look at the alleyway beside Wundatours. There's a big lorry parked there. There's also a bright red coach or lorry parked behind the badly parked van. At 9m 28s both have disappeared.
Continuity	10m 07s	The badly parked van has now disappeared and the red lorry is in its place. Sanity is restored by 10m 35s and the street immediately in front of the coach is now empty.
Continuity	11m 44s	Look behind Barbara Windsor as she boards the coach. Through the window you can see a white van parked before the coach. Seconds later, there's another lorry there.
Technical	13m 08s	With all the continuity confusion boarding the coach at Wundatours, you have to take your hat off to the team for being continuity-savvy enough to secure a left-hand drive coach for the scenes in Spain.
Technical	14m 43s	As the scene cuts to Hattie Jacques in the kitchen, look to the far left of your screen. Very briefly there's a shadow of someone moving past the cupboard - more on that in a moment.
Technical	15m 39s	At the end of Peter Butterworth and Hattie Jacques' conversation, just as he nears the cupboard on the left of the screen, hit pause and take a deep breath. The shadow you saw running out of shot at 14m 43s, above, was Butterworth leaving this very shot.
Trivia	16m 03s	A zealous edit means that a lovely gag is lost. Pepe is wearing shoes while out on the building site but when we see him next inside the hotel, he's barefoot (and has his right trouser rolled up - but we'll ignore that continuity slip). Now, when the coach party enters the hotel a few moments later, he makes a comment about wet cement and there, on the step we see his shoes from the earlier scene stuck in the cement on the steps. There they remain for much of the film.
Continuity	16m 04s	There was stepladder beside the table & chairs outside the hotel's main door. When Butterworth emerges to greet the holidaymakers it has gone.
Continuity	21m 34s	June Whitfield goes into the bathroom carrying an item of blue clothing - when we see her enter the bathroom it has disappeared.
Technical	26m 13s	Stupid What indeed! Farquhar calls Peter Butterworth's character "Monsieur Pepe" despite the fact that he's Spanish but then again and so does everyone else throughout the film. Señor Pepe would have made for a much dirtier gag.

Technical	26m 45s	Look at the second stair up behind the switchboard and you can see the flash-pot that will create the explosive effect of the switchboard blowing up. A second explosion goes off under the staircase but the switchboard itself remains intact.
Technical	30m 55s	Listen to Sid James' line - what the heck is "biahhrea"?
Technical	33m 34s	As Barbara Windsor finds her table and sits down to dinner, listen to the background noise – you'll hear Joan Sims' dialogue from a few moments earlier looped in as part of the background chatter.
Technical	38m 55s	No wonder the place is falling apart if they're using porridge instead of cement.
Technical	40m 15s	That's a boom shadow on the wall next to Peter Butterworth.
Technical	47m 48s	Whose giggle is that when Sid James goes after Joan Sims? He's got nothing to laugh at and Jimmy Logan's looking anything but amused.
Continuity	48m 05s	When Kenneth Connor sits on the sun lounger there's a plank of wood behind him to the right.
Continuity	48m 34s	Kenneth Connor's sitting in a rather macho position. In the next shot, we see him sitting quite differently before switching back to his previous position in the next. The plank of wood has also disappeared in the confusion.
Continuity	49m 32s	Kenneth Williams is seen to be holding the umbrella but in the next shot he has moved to the left of the table.
Technical	58m 05s	Look behind the market stall and you can see a concealed crash mat for Kenneth Connor to fall on.
Technical	58m 53s	If you fancy a look at Kenneth Williams' legs you'll also spot the stunt trousers with the Velcro seam. Kenneth's screams are not in synch with his lip movements.
Trivia	1h 02m 20s	Eric Rogers uses the same arrangement of Chopin's "Funeral March" from Carry On Loving.
Continuity	1h 09m 25s	There's not much champagne punchings in that bowl. Thankfully it magically tops itself up by the time Gail Grainger arrives. One of the glasses on the table next to the bowl moves between shots.
Continuity	1h 12m 49s	It looks like June Whitfield's had a wardrobe malfunction. That's one of her shoes on the dance floor.
Technical	1h 15m 54s	You can see the cutaway section of floor that's ready to collapse when Peter Butterworth steps onto it.
Technical	1h 19m 56s	Look at the hole in the dining room floor and you can see black drapes beneath to create the illusion of darkness. They move when Peter Butterworth falls in.
Technical	1h 22m 26s	You can see another boom shadow as Jimmy Logan heads towards the window.
Technical	1h 22m 44s	The collapsing pillar is helped on its way by an explosive charge.

LOCATIONS:

Time	Description	Address	Also seen in	Location Link
5m 00s	Wundatours	52-54 High Street Slough Berks SL1 1EY		
13m 08s	Els Bels airport	Security block Pinewood Studios Iver Heath Bucks SL0 0NH	Carry On Spying	
13m 35s	Approaching the hotel	Back lot Pinewood Studios Iver Heath Bucks SL0 0NH		

CARRY ON CUTTING:

- *Bill Maynard was cast as the manager of Wundatours, Mr Fiddler, for a brief scene at the start of the film. There, he was in conference with Stuart Farquhar and Moira, discussing Farquhar's disastrous exploits on other holidays.*

- *A couple of lines were excised at the BBFC's request. Early TV screenings had these lines re-instated but when the cinema print was used for subsequent DVD and video releases they were lost to the public.*

CARRY ON ABROAD:

Looking for the Sun Abroad – *Belgium*
What a Holiday! – *Denmark*
A Completely Mad Holiday – *Germany*
Girls' Room – *Italy*
The Shopping Spree! – *Portugal*

CARRY ON COLLECTING:

- "Carry On Abroad – The wickedly funny story that starts where the film ends". A novel by Norman Giller
Andre Deutsch Ltd, 1996, ISBN 0233990313
- Postcard featuring UK Quad poster released in 1998 by The London Postcard Company as part of their "Rank Classics Series 2" collection.

- In 1998, Cartel International released a series of Carry On themed greetings cards bearing stills from the films together with suitably saucy text. The series of 14 cards included stills from Carry On Doctor, Carry On Camping, Carry On Again Doctor, Carry On up the Jungle, Carry On Abroad and Carry On Girls.
- In 2007, Ethos, released a series of mugs featuring the original UK Quad poster artwork for the Rank Carry Ons, including Carry On Abroad.
- The same year, Ethos also released a series of colour changing mugs. One of the set featured an image of Kenneth Williams as Stuart Farquhar with his trousers down.

SOUNDTRACK:

Title theme available on "What a Carry On"
Gavin Sutherland and the Royal Sinfonia, CD, Dutton Vocalion 2005
Newly performed renditions of classic Carry On themes

DVD:

Carry On Abroad
Cinema Club, 2001
PAL, Region 2 (Europe, Middle East & Japan), Colour

DeAgostini Carry On DVD partwork
DeAgostini/Carlton, 2003
PAL, Region 2 (Europe, Middle East & Japan), Colour, Black & White

Carry On Abroad
ITV Studios Home Entertainment, 2003
PAL, Region 2 (Europe, Middle East & Japan), Colour
Special Features: Commentary (John Clive, Sally Geeson, Carol Hawkins, David Kernan), Stills, Trivia, Trailer, Carry On Laughing – Short Knight, Long Daze

Carry On – The Holiday Collection (Camping, Abroad, Camel, Girls, Convenience, Behind)
ITV Studios Home Entertainment, 2005
PAL, Region 2 (Europe, Middle East & Japan), Colour

Carry On – The Ultimate Collection
ITV Studios Home Entertainment, 2006
PAL, Region 2 (Europe, Middle East & Japan), Colour, Black & White
Special features as for individual ITV/Carlton/Optimum releases

Carry On Vol. 3 (Abroad, At your Convenience, Loving, Matron)
Optimum Home Releasing, 2008
PAL, Region 2 (Europe, Middle East & Japan), Colour
Special features as for individual ITV/Carlton/Optimum releases

Carry On – The Ultimate Collection
ITV Studios Home Entertainment, 2008
PAL, Region 2 (Europe, Middle East & Japan), Colour, Black & White
Special features as for individual ITV/Carlton/Optimum releases

VHS:

Carry On Abroad
Rank Video Library, 1980
PAL, Colour

Carry On Abroad
Cinema Club, 1987
PAL, Colour

Carry On Abroad
Cinema Club, 1991
PAL, Colour

Carry On Abroad
Cinema Club, 1995
PAL, Colour

Carry On Abroad – Collector's Edition
Cinema Club, 1999
PAL, Colour

Carry On Abroad / Carry On England
Cinema Club, 2000
PAL, Colour

DeAgostini Carry On VHS partwork
DeAgostini/Carlton, 2003
PAL, Colour, Black & White

The Carry On Collection (Don't Lose your Head – Carry On Emmannuelle)
Carlton Visual Entertainment, 2003
PAL, Colour

Carry On Abroad
Carlton Visual Entertainment, 2003
PAL, Colour

BETAMAX:

Carry On Abroad
Rank Video Library, 1980
PAL, Colour

CARRY ON GIRLS

1973

Screenplay by Talbot Rothwell
Music Composed & Conducted by Eric Rogers

CAST	CHARACTER
Sidney James	Sidney Fiddler
Barbara Windsor	Hope Springs
Joan Sims	Connie Philpotts
Kenneth Connor	Mayor Frederick Bumble
Bernard Bresslaw	Peter Potter
June Whitfield	Augusta Prodworthy
Peter Butterworth	Admiral
Jack Douglas	William
Patsy Rowlands	Mildred Bumble
Joan Hickson	Mrs Dukes
David Lodge	Police Inspector
Valerie Leon	Paula Perkins
Margaret Nolan	Dawn Brakes
Sally Geeson	Debra
Jimmy Logan	Cecil Gaybody
Angela Grant	Miss Bangor
Wendy Richard	Ida Downs
Arnold Ridley	Alderman Pratt
Robin Askwith	Larry
Patricia Franklin	Rosemary
Brian Osborne	1st Citizen
Bill Pertwee	Fire Chief
Marianne Stone	Miss Drew
Brenda Cowling	Matron
Zena Clifton	Susan Brooks
Mavis Fyson	Francis Cake
Laraine Humphrys	Eileen Denby
Pauline Peart	Gloria Winch
Caroline Whitaker	Mary Parker
Barbara Wise	Julia Oates
Carol Wyler	Maureen Darcy
Billy Cornelius	Constable
Edward Palmer	Elderly Resident
Michael Nightingale	City Type
Hugh Futcher	2nd Citizen
Elsie Winsor	Cloakroom Attendant
Ron Tarr	Bearded Man in Audience
Nick Hobbs	Stunt Double

CREW

Production Manager ....Roy Goddard
Art Director ....Robert Jones
Director of Photography ....Alan Hume
Editor..Alfred Roome
Camera Operator...Jimmy Devis
Assistant Director ....Jack Causey
Assistant Editor...Jack Gardner
Sound Recordists ....Paul Lemare & Ken Barker
Dubbing Editor...Patrick Foster
Continuity...Marjorie Lavelly
Make-up ....Geoffrey Rodway
Hairdresser..Stella Rivers
Costume Designer...Courtenay Elliott
Set Dresser ....Kenneth McCallum Tait
Titles by ...."Larry"
Titles...GSE Ltd
Producer..Peter Rogers
Director...Gerald Thomas

A Peter Rogers production. Distributed through Fox / Rank Distribution Ltd

PRODUCTION DETAILS:

Budget: £206,000
Filming: 16th April 1973 – 25th May 1973
Duration: 88m
Colour
General Release: November 1973, Certificate A
TV Premiere: 27th December 1978, BBC1
Home Video: 1981 (VHS/Betamax), 2001 (DVD)

IN A NUTSHELL:

"When it comes to beauty queens it's Carry On and bust!"

The seaside resort of Fircombe is on its uppers. Another miserable summer means the tourists are staying away in droves. Local counsellor, Sidney Fiddler (Sid James) comes up with the perfect way to generate interest in the town - a Miss Fircombe beauty pageant.

Sid volunteers the services of his girlfriend Connie Philpotts' (Joan Sims) hotel as the perfect place for the bathing beauties to stay in preparation for the big day. Much to Connie's dismay, none of them will be paying. Meanwhile, local counsellor Augusta Prodworthy (June Whitfield) is outraged to hear of the contest, which was agreed upon in her absence. Rousing her fellow feminists, Augusta protests to the Mayor, Frederick Bumble (Kenneth Connor) but he refuses to cancel the pageant.

Unable to halt the contest via official channels, Prodworthy and the local feminists stage a dirty campaign. When an insider informs them that one of the contestants is, in reality, a man (Bernard Bresslaw), it looks like she has all the ammunition she needs. Or she would, if it wasn't a carefully staged publicity campaign by Fiddler and his co-conspirators.

REVIEW:

While lewdness, nudity and sexual shenanigans are all on the up in Carry On Girls, at its heart, it's a traditional tale of power and betrayal. While scheming Sid aims to get his hands on the money and the girls, all at the expense of long-suffering girlfriend Connie, the right-thinking feminists of the town are burning their bras. Any serious political message the film might have had is dealt with swiftly by portraying the feminists under Augusta's command as a bunch of dowdy lesbians and cross dressers. They're not there to be taken seriously, but when their chief opponent is the most repressed and ineffectual little man ever to hold the post of Mayor you realise they're probably their own worst enemies anyway.

If one word sums up Carry On Girls, it's desperation. Sid's desperate to get his end away and Connie is desperate for him to start taking their relationship more seriously. Meanwhile, the Bumbles live in quiet desperation, with an unbearable tension simmering just below the surface of their drab lives. Prodworthy and her cronies are just desperate for a good seeing to, or so we're led to believe. In short, everyone's living a miserable life until Sid tries to inject a bit of fun, a bit of a spark back into the town. It is one-dimensional sexist stuff but it's done with such style, such a sense of "we're only in it to make you laugh" that the end result is two parts melodrama, three parts Benny Hill.

There's plenty of fun to be had, albeit with a more adult tone than in the earlier films. The Carry Ons aren't bordering on sex comedy territory yet, but they're definitely giving it the glad eye. But Carry On Girls is an inconsistent film and Talbot Rothwell's script contains a few clunkers. The Cecil Gaybody character is horribly written and there are too many instances of double-entendre being reduced to the level of a one-track-mind.

The star performance is Kenneth Connor as Mayor Bumble. While I personally never found Connor particularly entertaining as the romantic lead in earlier films, I adore his later portrayals of endlessly frustrated, world-weary characters. He battles the forces of feminism with a barely concealed yet entirely impotent rage, every facet of his life a crushing disappointment.

Augusta Prodworthy and her harpies are less convincing, but given the nature of the Carry Ons and attitudes towards sexual equality in popular culture at the time the feminists were never going to be anything more than lesbians in men's clothing. Despite the best efforts of June Whitfield and co, they're contemptible upstarts and it's hard to sympathise with their cause.

However, in a Carry On whose very premise is out and out sexism there is a delicate balance to tread and, by today's standards, the team do a pretty decent job. Of course, the sheer insanity of anyone finding Bernard Bresslaw remotely attractive as a woman (down boy!) helps enormously. The Grand Guignol that underlines Carry On humour is rarely more obvious.

Carry On Girls is a good film, but it is far from a great one. It's particularly lovely to see the team out on location again and any film made in Brighton, the ultimate dirty post-card resort, will always have something to recommend it. The Carry On team look at home amidst the saucy postcards which inspired them. While some of the gags are forced and while some of the actors are looking past their prime, Girls at least feels like a proper Carry On.

VIEWING NOTES:

• *An early title proposed for Carry On Girls was "Carry On Beauty Queen".*

- *Renee Houston was originally contracted to play the role of Mrs Dukes but was forced to pull out of the production because of ill health.*
- *Bill Maynard was originally cast in the role of the police inspector, but filming clashed with a recently signed TV commitment.*
- *While the character of Cecil Gaybody appears to have been written with Charles Hawtrey in mind, the actor was never approached for the role.*
- *Rothwell re-uses another classic Carry On character name – Bernard Bresslaw's character Peter Potter shares a moniker with Terry Scott's distressed husband in Carry On Camping.*
- *The Carry On team once again made use of former Carry On star Dora Bryan's Clarges Hotel for location shooting. The dog that urinates on the pillar early in the film was Dora's own dog, Dougal.*
- *Although much of the film takes place on Brighton's now derelict West Pier, the pier itself was closed at the seaward end following the 1970 summer season. While the theatre on the pier remained open, it was not used for the final beauty contest scenes.*
- *A motorbike was donated by Honda for use in the film in return for promotional consideration, but Barbara Windsor was unable to ride with any confidence. Stuntman Nick Hobbs makes for a less than convincing stand-in.*

CARRY ON COCK-UPS:

Continuity	2m 32s	The position of the paperwork in front of Sid and the level of water in his glass differ between shots.
Trivia	7m 31s	There is our old friend the trusty switchboard from Carry On Abroad.
Technical	8m 22s	There's a boom shadow on the wall behind Jack Douglas throughout this scene.
Continuity	9m 01s	Take a look at the brochures on the stand in reception by the phones. They're different in the close-up of Sid James as he makes his phone call.
Technical	9m 16s	You're looking at Valerie Leon. However, you're not listening to her. Valerie 's entire performance was re-dubbed by June Whitfield.
Continuity	13m 24s	Keep your eye on the cigarette that Patsy Rowlands has just put in her mouth throughout the next scene. When she opens the door it's in her hand. When she closes it again, she puts it back in her mouth but when we cut to the next shot it is back in her hand. While there are quite a few cigarette-related gaffes in the film, Patsy herself was a non-smoker so she may be entirely forgiven.
Continuity	13m 27s	Keep an eye on the interior of the hallway. There's a door to the right of Patsy Rowlands and a short length of wall before it. On the shot from the outside into the hall the wall is much longer, with white trim and not an interior door in sight. The piece of wall by the door as seen from the outside can be seen to move as Patsy leans against it.
Continuity	14m 02s	If you can tear your eyes from the sight of Kenneth Connor in his bath, keep an eye on that soap in the dish on the wall. In the next shot (the close-up of Connor) it has moved. Both it and the sponge (when he puts it on the dish) move between close and wide shots.

Continuity	15m 05s	Clearly this scene was filmed in multiple takes. Keep an eye on the doors behind Bernard Bresslaw throughout the scene.
Continuity	21m 57s	Robin Askwith's arms were crossed just a moment ago. His hand movements from behind do not match them from the front through this sequence as Sid James talks to Wendy Richard.
Continuity	22m 11s	Wendy Richard goes upstairs to change into her costume. It takes her 18 seconds. If there is ever a Miss Quick Change she should get the prize.
Continuity	23m 32s	Margaret Nolan's top is different to the one she wore on the train earlier. There, the left shoulder was torn off and the right intact. Here, the right is almost torn through while the left is still hanging on. The front is also torn differently.
Technical	24m 38s	That motorcyclist looks nothing like Barbara Windsor. Or indeed, a woman.
Continuity	24m 39s	"Miss Easy Rider" rides past the hotel, almost running Jack Douglas and Joan Hickson over. In the next shot she pulls up outside the hotel she has just ridden straight past.
Trivia	25m 05s	Here's a lovely gag. As Sid James comes down the stairs past Peter Butterworth he pretends that his bottom has been pinched.
Continuity	31m 21s	Barbara Windsor pushes Sid James towards the hotel door and away from the donkey, but when we switch shots he's falling back towards the animal.
Technical	31m 41s	The combined momentum of Barbara Windsor and Margaret Nolan isn't enough to push the sofa over, so the old lady sitting on it gives them a helping hand, or foot, and shoves the thing backward.
Continuity	33m 22s	Margaret Nolan pulls the mayor's trousers down and puts her left hand to her mouth in surprise. In the next shot her left hand is still holding the trousers and she has her right hand to her mouth.
Continuity	33m 53s	Patsy Rowlands' cigarette grows in length as she passes from the hall to the kitchen.
Continuity	35m 05s	As Patsy Rowlands sits down there's a cigarette in her mouth. By the time she's sat down on the chair it's nowhere to be seen.
Continuity	51m 23s	When Jack Douglas calls June Whitfield he asks if she has ever seen a young woman using a gents' toilet. Whitfield says she hasn't. Earlier in the film, she and a bunch of her friends were "squatting" in one.
Continuity	1h 04m 07s	Patsy Rowlands is sitting reading the paper (with the inevitable cigarette in her hand). When we cut back to her after Kenneth Connor enters, the paper is open at a different page (and of course her fag is in a different hand). In the closing shot of the scene the paper's on a different page again and we can see another visible boom shadow.

Trivia	1h 05m 29s	That is indeed a plan of Brighton's West Pier.
Technical	1h 10m 19s	There's a very Gerald Thomas-like reflection in the window behind Robin Askwith.
Technical	1h 20m 29s	Zena Clifton doesn't even bother stepping on the washing up liquid on the ramp, she just steps right out and falls flat on her back.
Continuity	1h 22m 41s	Sid James' suit is inevitably dry when he leaves the theatre.
Technical	1h 24m 02s	Once again, that motorcyclist looks nothing like Barbara Windsor.
Continuity	1h 24m 06s	The person sitting in the promenade pagoda on the left wasn't there in the previous shot. You probably didn't notice that before as you were too busy marvelling at how they could ever think that motorcyclist could be mistaken for Barbara Windsor.

LOCATIONS:

Time	Description	Address	Also seen in	Location Link
1m 38s	Rainy Fircombe	Opposite Clarges Hotel 115-119 Marine Drive Brighton East Sussex BN2 1DD		
1m 53s	Fircombe Town Hall	Slough Town Hall Bath Road Slough Berks SL1 3UQ		
5m 41s	Palace Hotel	Clarges Hotel 115-118 Marine Parade Brighton East Sussex BN2 1DD		
12m 40s	Mayor Bumble's house	38 Lansdowne Avenue Slough Berks SL1 3SJ		

Time	Scene	Location		QR
15m 05s	Train station	Marylebone Station Melcombe Place London NW1 6JJ		
18m 24s	Flagpole on the seafront	Marine Parade Brighton East Sussex BN2 1DD		
42m 04s	Nude photo-shoot on the beach	Beach opposite Brunswick Lawns Kingsway Hove East Sussex BN3		
1h 09m 36s	Fire station	Slough Fire Station Tuns Lane Slough Berks SL1 2XA		
1h 10m 48s	Beauty Pageant	West Pier King's Road Brighton East Sussex BN3		
1h 24m 01s	Escape from the pier	King's Road Brighton East Sussex BN3		
1h 24m 10s	Escaping along main road	Datchet Road just outside Slough (B376)		

CARRY ON CUTTING:

- *The girl fight in the hotel lobby was trimmed judiciously to avoid the film being tagged with an AA rating.*

CARRY ON ABROAD:

Let's Go Girls – *Finland*
Carry On English – *Germany*
Go Girls! – *Hungary*
Come on, Girls – *Sweden*

CARRY ON COLLECTING:

- Postcard featuring UK Quad poster released in 1998 by The London Postcard Company as part of their "Rank Classics Series 2" collection.
- Promotional bookmark released in 1998 by The London Postcard Company featuring the Carry On up the Khyber and Carry On Girls Quad posters.
- In 1998, Cartel International released a series of Carry On-themed greetings cards bearing stills from the films together with suitably saucy text. The series of 14 cards included stills from Carry On Doctor, Carry On Camping, Carry On Again Doctor, Carry On up the Jungle, Carry On Abroad and Carry On Girls.
- In 2007, Ethos, released a series of mugs featuring the original UK Quad poster artwork for the Rank Carry Ons, including Carry On Girls.

SOUNDTRACK:

Title theme available on "What a Carry On"
Gavin Sutherland and the Royal Sinfonia, CD, Dutton Vocalion 2005
Newly performed renditions of classic Carry On themes

DVD:

Carry On Girls
Cinema Club, 2001
PAL, Region 2 (Europe, Middle East & Japan), Colour

DeAgostini Carry On DVD partwork
DeAgostini/Carlton, 2003
PAL, Region 2 (Europe, Middle East & Japan), Colour, Black & White

Carry On Girls
ITV Studios Home Entertainment, 2003
PAL, Region 2 (Europe, Middle East & Japan), Colour
Special Features: Commentary (Jack Douglas, Patsy Rowlands, June Whitfield), Stills, Trivia, Trailer, On Location – the Carry Ons

Carry On – The Holiday Collection (Camping, Abroad, Camel, Girls, Convenience, Behind)
ITV Studios Home Entertainment, 2005
PAL, Region 2 (Europe, Middle East & Japan), Colour

Carry On – The Ultimate Collection
ITV Studios Home Entertainment, 2006

PAL, Region 2 (Europe, Middle East & Japan), Colour, Black & White
Special features as for individual ITV/Carlton/Optimum releases

Carry On Vol. 4 (Girls, England, Dick, Behind)
Optimum Home Releasing, 2008
PAL, Region 2 (Europe, Middle East & Japan), Colour
Special features as for individual ITV/Carlton/Optimum releases

Carry On – The Ultimate Collection
ITV Studios Home Entertainment, 2008
PAL, Region 2 (Europe, Middle East & Japan), Colour, Black & White
Special features as for individual ITV/Carlton/Optimum releases

VHS:

Carry On Girls
Rank Video Library, 1981
PAL, Colour

Carry On Girls
Cinema Club, 1987
PAL, Colour

Carry On Girls
Cinema Club, 1991
PAL, Colour

Carry On Girls
Cinema Club, 1996
PAL, Colour

Carry On Girls – Collector's Edition
Cinema Club, 1999
PAL, Colour

Carry On Emmannuelle / Carry On Girls
Cinema Club, 2000
PAL, Colour

DeAgostini Carry On VHS partwork
DeAgostini/Carlton, 2003
PAL, Colour, Black & White

The Carry On Collection (Don't Lose your Head – Carry On Emmannuelle)
Carlton Visual Entertainment, 2003
PAL, Colour

Carry On Girls
Carlton Visual Entertainment, 2003
PAL, Colour

BETAMAX:

Carry On Girls
Rank Video Library, 1981
PAL, Colour

CARRY ON DICK

1974

Screenplay by Talbot Rothwell
Based on a treatment by Lawrie Wyman and George Evans
Music Composed & Conducted by Eric Rogers

CAST   CHARACTER

Sidney James	The Reverend Flasher / Big Dick Turpin
Barbara Windsor	Harriet
Kenneth Williams	Captain Desmond Fancey
Hattie Jacques	Martha Hoggett
Bernard Bresslaw	Sir Roger Daley
Joan Sims	Madame Desiree
Kenneth Connor	Constable
Peter Butterworth	Tom
Jack Douglas	Sergeant Jock Strapp
Patsy Rowlands	Mrs Giles
Bill Maynard	Bodkin
Margaret Nolan	Lady Daley
John Clive	Isaak
David Lodge	Bullock
Marianne Stone	Maggie
Larry Taylor	Tough Man
Billy Cornelius	Tough Man
Patrick Durkin	William
Sam Kelly	Sir Roger's Coachman
George Moon	Mr Giles
Michael Nightingale	Squire Trelawney
Brian Osborne	Browning
Anthony Bailey	Rider
Brian Coburn	Highwayman
Jeremy Connor	Footpad
Max Faulkner	Highwayman
Nosher Powell	Footpad
Joy Harrington	Lady
Oiseaux de Paradis:	Laraine Humphrys, Linda Hooks, Penny Irving, Eva Reuber-Staier

CREW

Production Manager	Roy Goddard
Art Director	Lionel Couch
Director of Photography	Ernest Steward
Editor	Alfred Roome
Camera Operator	Jimmy Devis

Assistant Director	David Bracknell
Sound Recordists	Danny Daniel & Ken Barker
Dubbing Editor	Peter Best
Continuity	Jane Buck
Make-up	Geoffrey Rodway
Hairdresser	Stella Rivers
Costume Design	Courtenay Elliott
Set Dresser	Charles Bishop
Master of Horse	Gerry Wain
Assistant Editor	Jack Gardner
Casting Director	John Owen
Stills Cameraman	Tom Cadman
Wardrobe	Vi Murray & Maggie Lewin
Coach & Horses	Supplied by George Mossman
Titles	GSE Ltd
Producer	Peter Rogers
Director	Gerald Thomas

A Peter Rogers production. Distributed through Fox / Rank Distribution Ltd.

PRODUCTION DETAILS:

Budget: £245,000
Filming: 4th March 1974 – 11th April 1974
Duration: 91m
Colour
General Release: July 1974, Certificate A
TV Premiere: 31st December 1979, ITV
Home Video: 1984 (VHS/Betamax), 2001 (DVD)

IN A NUTSHELL:

"Dick carries on with his flintlock cocked!"

The mysterious highwayman, Big Dick Turpin (Sid James), and his band of cut-throats are at large. With his enormous weapon and his cry of "Stand and Deliver" nobody is safe on the highways of England.

Sir Roger Daley (Bernard Bresslaw), humiliated after being robbed of everything apart from his shoes, vows vengeance against Turpin and puts his top man on the case. However, with an opponent like Captain Desmond Fancey (Kenneth Williams), Turpin doesn't appear to have too much to worry about.

Captain Fancey and his sidekick, Jock Strapp (Jack Douglas), set out to trap the highwayman by any means necessary. Whether it means hiding in the bushes or spying in men's conveniences, they leave no stone unturned but it's a safe bet that nobody will be getting their hands on Dick anytime soon.

REVIEW:

On the surface, Carry On Dick has all the ingredients that have made so many other Carry Ons so memorable and yet the end result is something of a disappointment.

There's a lot to love about Carry On Dick. Sid James plays the dual roles of the growling Dick Turpin and the "butter-wouldn't-melt" Reverend Flasher brilliantly and there are similarly great performances from Kenneth Williams, Bernard Bresslaw, Jack Douglas and the rest of the Carry On regulars. The script has plenty of good honest laughs and visually it depicts the period well (concrete bollards and road-markings notwithstanding). But there's something not quite right about the way it all hangs together.

For a start, the sexual gags are rather too direct, with none of Rothwell's trademark subtlety. There's little in the way of spark to the dialogue or in the way it's delivered and the whole film exudes an air of what I can only describe as exhaustion. To some extent, this is understandable, given the context of Carry On Dick. Many of the cast were exhausted – after each day's filming they would rush back to town for the Carry On London stage show.

Personally, my biggest problem with Carry On Dick is that so many great actors are relegated to relatively minor roles. Kenneth Connor doesn't get much to do and Hattie Jacques' character is, frankly, pointless. Miss Haggerd is an irrelevant inclusion but the fact that she is in the script means Hattie should have had some decent material to work with. The sad truth is that she does not. Her role appears to be little more than walking bromide to the Reverend's ardour.

Of course, by this point, it is also obvious that several of the team are too old for the roles they have been given. The idea of Sid, by then well into his 60s, chasing young fillies just isn't as fun as it once was. His scenes with Harriet are almost on the wrong side of seediness and occasionally make for uncomfortable viewing, even if what we see on screen is pretty much what we're told the pair of them were getting up to behind the scenes.

The whole gang is giving it everything they've got and it's easy to get swept along by the fun of it all, particularly when Kenneth Williams is in full flow but I cannot shake the feeling that their hearts are not really in this one. Carry On Dick has all the ingredients of a classic Carry On but they're delivered in such a way as to make the whole significantly less than the sum of the by now rather sagging parts.

VIEWING NOTES:

• *With Talbot Rothwell's contract coming to an end, Peter Rogers originally turned to "The Navy Lark" writers Lawrie Wyman and George Evans for the next Carry On script. Their initial proposal, Carry On Sailor, was deemed unsuitable but the pair's next idea, Carry On Dick (with Sid as the "hero" Dick Twirpin) was picked up by Rogers for further development.*
• *In the event, Rothwell's contract was renewed for a further three pictures but the writer suffered a breakdown during the writing process and the final script had to be dictated to his daughter. Sadly, Carry On Dick was Rothwell's last contribution to the Carry On films.*
• *The casting of the Birds of Paradise made the news headlines in 1974. Eva Reuber-Staier won the Miss World contest in 1969 and her fellow Oiseau, Linda Hooks, was a former Miss International.*
• *The coaches seen in the film are part of the Mossman Collection. Many of Mossman's coaches, including those from Carry On Cowboy and Carry On Dick, can be seen at the Stockwood Discovery Centre in Luton (http://www.stockwooddiscoverycentre.com).*
• *There isn't really any timing for this as it is a slow realisation, but look at the exterior of the church and compare it to the interior. The belfry is in the wrong place. Where the door is there should be a bell tower on the left but instead there is a wall. The interior of the church doesn't match the exterior at all.*

• *The bawdier nature of the script called for some judicious cuts to the dialogue in the final print in order to secure an A certificate.*
• *Carry On Dick was banned in South Africa for several years because of the religious offence potentially caused by having a bandit who was really a vicar.*

CARRY ON COCK-UPS:

Technical	3m 21s	The road surface and concrete bollards running by the roadside take away from the authenticity of the piece when we see the initial hold up.
Technical	3m 29s	The barbed wire on the wall behind Sid James doesn't help matters either.
Continuity	3m 50s	Take a close look at the driver of Bernard Bresslaw's coach. Depending on whether they're actually driving or not, throughout the film you'll see either the actor Sam Kelly or the coach's owner, George Mossman.
Trivia	3m 56s	Bernard Bresslaw insisted on a closed set for his nude scene following Dick's hold-up. The fact that there are several highly publicised shots taken of the scene will tell you what the crew thought about that.
Continuity	8m 27s	When we last saw the coach driver, he was wearing a hessian mat hung from his neck. This blue cloth is much more fetching. While their driver is permitted to hide his modesty, you will note in a moment that Bresslaw and Nolan are still both naked.
Continuity	8m 31s	It looks like Dick's stolen the lamps that were on the original carriage as well.
Technical	12m 26s	Where to begin? Look at the road - it's a modern tarmac surface with white lines down the middle - you can also see the lines on the entrance to the churchyard. There are concrete bollards lining the approach to the church and a massive one by the entrance. There is also a war memorial just behind the "St Michael's" sign.
Continuity	12m 55s	The windows inside the church do not match those on the outside.
Continuity	19m 46s	Keep an eye on the candle on Kenneth Williams' table - it changes size a few times between shots during the Old Cock Inn scenes.
Continuity	25m 22s	Take a look at the wide shot and you'll see Peter Butterworth, Barbara Windsor, Sid James and Bill Maynard with Marianne Stone sitting in front. In the close-up, we see a man sitting on either side of Marianne. Not only that, her pipe has been replaced by a tankard. But there's more. Look behind Barbara Windsor and you'll notice the barmaid has disappeared too.
Continuity	28m 44s	Where has Jack Douglas gone? He was there literally a second ago.
Technical	33m 55s	Much of the underwear you're about to see wasn't even invented in the 16th century. Brassieres are a 19th century invention and yet les Oiseaux all seem to be wearing them.

Continuity	52m 07s	Keep an eye on Sid James' clothes as we alternate between shots in this scene. Shot from the front he's wearing his coat but in the shots over his shoulder he's wearing only a waistcoat.
Continuity	56m 51s	It looks like Bernard Bresslaw and the coachman both got to keep their underpants this time.
Continuity	58m 30s	That's a lovely modern frosted door and guttering at the Old Cock Inn. Compare the window Peter Butterworth and Barbara Windsor peer through for their view from the inside. The panes, particularly the middle right one, are different.
Continuity	58m 44s	Bernard Bresslaw is pouring himself a glass of wine as he talks. In the very next shot he can be seen to pour himself another. It's thirsty work.
Continuity	1h 01m 42s	Keep an eye on the red garment on the bed behind Barbara Windsor. When she starts to undress it's crumpled on the bed behind her. In the next shot it has moved.
Continuity	1h 24m 16s	Jack Douglas catches his right leg in the bell rope as he climbs the ladder but when we see him swinging from the rope a few moments later it's his left leg that has been caught on the rope.

LOCATIONS:

Time	Description	Address	Also seen in	Location Link
0m 00s	Opening titles - Dick on horseback	Black Park Black Park Rd Wexham Slough Berks SL3 6DR	Carry On Cabby Carry On Cowboy Carry On Cleo Carry On Screaming Carry On Don't Lose your Head	
1m 59s	Bow St	Pinewood Studios Iver Heath Bucks SL0 0NH		
12m 26s	Rev Flasher's Church	St Mary's Church Hitcham Lane Burnham Slough Bucks SL1 7DP		

16m 52s	Old Cock Inn	The Jolly Woodman Littleworth Road Littleworth Common Bucks SL1 8PF		
40m 51s	Police Station	Servants' quarters Stoke Poges Manor house Park Road Stoke Poges Slough Berks SL2 4PG		
42m 41s	Fancey and Strapp at the blasted oak	Langley Park Country Park Billet Lane Iver Heath Bucks SL0 0LS		
44m 36s	Rev Flasher's home	Stoke Poges Manor House Park Road Stoke Poges Slough Berks SL2 4PG All interiors filmed on location.		
51m 33s	Outside Rev Flasher's home	Stoke Poges Manor House Park Road Stoke Poges Slough Berks SL2 4PG		

CARRY ON ABROAD:

Carry On Mugger – *Germany*

CARRY ON COLLECTING:

- Postcard featuring UK Quad poster released in 1998 by The London Postcard Company as part of their "Rank Classics Series 2" collection.
- In 2003, Cards Inc planned a series of Carry On trading cards. While the series was ultimately cancelled, a set of six preview cards was released, featuring images from Carry On Doctor, Carry On up the Khyber, Carry On Camping, Carry On Again Doctor, Carry On up the Jungle and Carry On Dick.

• In 2007, Ethos, released a series of mugs featuring the original UK Quad poster artwork for the Rank Carry Ons, including Carry On Dick.

SOUNDTRACK:

Title theme available on "What a Carry On"
Gavin Sutherland and the Royal Sinfonia, CD, Dutton Vocalion 2005
Newly performed renditions of classic Carry On themes

DVD:

Carry On Dick
Cinema Club, 2001
PAL, Region 2 (Europe, Middle East & Japan), Colour

DeAgostini Carry On DVD partwork
DeAgostini/Carlton, 2003
PAL, Region 2 (Europe, Middle East & Japan), Colour, Black & White

Carry On Dick
ITV Studios Home Entertainment, 2003
PAL, Region 2 (Europe, Middle East & Japan), Colour
Special Features: Commentary (Jack Douglas), Stills, Trivia, Trailer, Carry On Laughing – The Case of the Coughing Parrot

Carry On – The History Collection (Head, Dick, Jungle, Henry, England, Khyber)
ITV Studios Home Entertainment, 2005
PAL, Region 2 (Europe, Middle East & Japan), Colour

Carry On – The Ultimate Collection
ITV Studios Home Entertainment, 2006
PAL, Region 2 (Europe, Middle East & Japan), Colour, Black & White
Special features as for individual ITV/Carlton/Optimum releases

Carry On Vol. 4 (Girls, England, Dick, Behind)
Optimum Home Releasing, 2008
PAL, Region 2 (Europe, Middle East & Japan), Colour
Special features as for individual ITV/Carlton/Optimum releases

Carry On – The Ultimate Collection
ITV Studios Home Entertainment, 2008
PAL, Region 2 (Europe, Middle East & Japan), Colour, Black & White
Special features as for individual ITV/Carlton/Optimum releases

VHS:

Carry On Dick
Rank Video Library, 1984
PAL, Colour

Carry On Dick
Cinema Club, 1987
PAL, Colour

Carry On Dick
Cinema Club, 1991
PAL, Colour

Carry On Dick
Cinema Club, 1996
PAL, Colour

Carry On Dick – Collector's Edition
Cinema Club, 1999
PAL, Colour

Carry On Dick / Carry On Henry
Cinema Club, 2000
PAL, Colour

DeAgostini Carry On VHS partwork
DeAgostini/Carlton, 2003
PAL, Colour, Black & White

The Carry On Collection (Don't Lose your Head – Carry On Emmannuelle)
Carlton Visual Entertainment, 2003
PAL, Colour

Carry On Dick
Carlton Visual Entertainment, 2003
PAL, Colour

BETAMAX

Carry On Dick
Rank Video Library, 1984
PAL, Colour

CARRY ON BEHIND

1975

Screenplay by Dave Freeman
Music Composed & Conducted by Eric Rogers

CAST	CHARACTER
Elke Sommer	Professor Anna Vooshka
Kenneth Williams	Professor Roland Crump
Bernard Bresslaw	Arthur Upmore
Kenneth Connor	Major Leep
Jack Douglas	Ernie Bragg
Joan Sims	Daphne Barnes
Windsor Davies	Fred Ramsden
Peter Butterworth	Henry Barnes
Liz Fraser	Sylvia Ramsden
Patsy Rowlands	Linda Upmore
Ian Lavender	Joe Baxter
Adrienne Posta	Norma Baxter
Patricia Franklin	Vera Bragg
Donald Hewlett	Dean
Carol Hawkins	Sandra
Sherrie Hewson	Carol
David Lodge	Landlord
Marianne Stone	Mrs Rowan
George Layton	Doctor
Brian Osborne	Bob
Larry Dann	Clive
Georgina Moon	Sally
Diana Darvey	Maureen
Jenny Cox	Veronica
Larry Martyn	Electrician
Linda Hooks	Nurse
Kenneth Waller	Barman
Billy Cornelius	Man with Salad
Melita Manger	Woman with Salad
Hugh Futcher	Painter
Helli Louise Jacobson	Nudist
Jeremy Connor	Student with Ice Cream
Alexandra Dane	Lady in Low-cut Dress
Sam Kelly	Projectionist
Johnny Briggs	Plasterer
Lucy Griffiths	Woman with Hat
Stanley McGeach	Short-Sighted man
Brenda Cowling	Wife

Sidney Johnson .... Man in Glasses
Drina Pavlovic .... Courting Girl
Caroline Whitaker .... Student
Ray Edwards .... Man with Soapy Water

CREW

Production Manager .... Roy Goddard
Art Director .... Lionel Couch
Director of Photography .... Ernest Steward
Editor .... Alfred Roome
Camera Operator .... Neil Binney
Assistant Director .... David Bracknell
Sound Recordists .... Danny Daniel & Ken Barker
Dubbing Editor .... Pat Foster
Assistant Editor .... Jack Gardner
Continuity .... Marjorie Lavelly
Make-up .... Geoffrey Rodway
Hairdresser .... Stella Rivers
Costume Designer .... Courtenay Elliott
Set Dresser .... Charles Bishop
Titles .... GSE Ltd
Producer .... Peter Rogers
Director .... Gerald Thomas

A Peter Rogers production. Distributed through Fox / Rank Distribution Ltd.

PRODUCTION DETAILS:

Budget: £217,000
Filming: 10th March 1975 – 18th April 1975
Duration: 90m
Colour
General Release: December 1975, Certificate A
TV Premiere: 20th December 1980, ITV
Home Video: 1981 (VHS/Betamax), 2001 (DVD)

IN A NUTSHELL:

"The Carry On team looking for a site for sore thighs!"

Fred (Windsor Davies), and Ernie (Jack Douglas), are off on a weekend fishing trip to the country but when two busty young cyclists (Sherrie Hewson and Carol Hawkins) pitch their tent in the shadow of Fred's caravan, he decides to go after an altogether different catch.

Meanwhile, Professor Crump (Kenneth Williams) and his glamorous colleague Dr Vooshka (Elke Sommer) are examining the remains of a mysterious Roman encampment, recently discovered beneath the site.

As the excavations continue, the weather gets progressively worse and the campsite grows increasingly treacherous – if the rain doesn't get the campers, the mysterious holes appearing in the ground surely will.

For Daphne Barnes (Joan Sims), there is an even bigger discovery. After years of being estranged from her husband (Peter Butterworth), he is revealed to be none other than the down-at-heel camp handyman.

REVIEW:

The Carry Ons were never afraid to re-invent themselves. Carry On Behind finally acknowledges that people grow old and responds with rather bittersweet portrayals of many classic Carry On characters. The gang are no longer running around like randy teenagers. Physically, if not mentally, they have grown up.

There is a more mature, somewhat less family friendly edge to Carry On Behind, compared to many of the earlier films, but the end result is absolutely hilarious. Centre stage goes to Carry On newcomer Windsor Davies, who is paired up with Jack Douglas in his biggest Carry On role to date. Essentially, they are playing Sid and Bernie from Carry On Camping in what is little more than a re-tread of that same film. What distinguishes Carry On Behind from Camping and so many of the films that have gone before is its maturity, not just in terms of increased nudity but also in more direct sexual humour.

Kenneth Williams is decidedly greyer around the temples. Bernie's a married man with a mother-in-law in tow. Kenneth Connor has retired to a life of obscurity, grabbing the occasional bit of fun when he can but basically living the quiet life. Joan has ended up as the harridan you always knew her Carry On persona would become and good old Josh Fiddler's still living at the back of the campsite in a bashed up caravan, scheming his get-rich schemes.

Even Sid and Bernie, sorry, Fred and Ernie, have become respectable. Suddenly released from their domestic chains for a couple of days, they are off on a boys' weekend to recapture some lost youth. They're not the young tearaways they once were and, truth be told, they're too old to get up to the sort of stuff they used to, even if they could remember how. There lies much of the comedy in Carry On Behind because no matter how hard they try, like so many of the other characters, they are past it.

There's also a rather touching continuity to Carry On Behind. Dr Crump, the eternal frump, is Dr Soaper thrown forward 10 years. He is just as repressed, histrionic and neurotic as he ever was but by the end of the film he's finally abandoned his old hang-ups and allowed himself to have a bit of fun. Joan's battle-axe character re-discovers her love of yester-year in a beautifully moving scene and even old Fiddler finally re-joins the real world.

Dave Freeman's script is tonally quite different from the sort of romps Talbot Rothwell used to write. The characters live slightly more in the real world, the humour is less nuanced, there's less archness and the story is more straightforward.

Seeing the characters we have come to love finally acting their age adds a sentimentality to Carry On Behind that overshadows its other, more adult trappings. If Carry On Dick was a last hurrah for the old ways, Behind can be seen as a fresh start. There are enough of the old gang present to remind you that you're still watching a Carry On, but there is a fresh wave of newcomers and with them a feeling that this is quite a different way of carrying on. Carry On Behind is the "Star Trek Generations" of the Carry On films. We have the old guard looking as if they're getting ready to bow out and a new wave of performers stepping into their mud-soaked loafers. The end result is a feeling that if this is the direction the Carry Ons are going to move into then it will do very nicely indeed.

Carry On Behind is a vastly underrated Carry On. The widely held notion that as the 70s moved on the Carry Ons lost their appeal and became one-note "smut-a-thons" simply isn't true. Carry On Behind shows that "adult" entertainment isn't all just naked flesh and romps under the covers.

VIEWING NOTES:

- *Bless This House screenwriter Dave Freeman's script was originally intended as a non-Carry On under the title "Love on Wheels". It bore several suggested Carry On titles, including "Carry On Carrying On", "Carry On in a Caravan" and "Carry On Caravanning".*
- *Eric Rogers' score for Carry On Behind exhibits his typical playfulness. The main score throughout the film is based on the keys B, E and B, in honour of Peter Rogers' wife Betty Evelyn Box.*
- *Elke Sommer's top billing in the film came with a sizeable pay-packet. She pocketed £30,000 for her performance as Dr Vooshka.*
- *Larry Dann's return to the Carry Ons came about purely by chance. Dann went for an audition for the filming of an advert, which was being directed by Gerald Thomas. Gerald took Dann aside and told him that while he wasn't right for the advert, he was working on a new Carry On film and invited the actor to join the cast.*
- *The camp's barman was originally to have been played by Chris Gannon (recognisable to Doctor Who fans as Casey in The Talons of Weng Chiang). Gannon was forced to pull out of the film due to a clash with other work commitments.*
- *It is worth keeping an eye on the ground as you watch the film – every now and then you'll notice an actor with green feet. History repeats itself - in Camping they were spraying trees green to make winter look like summer. In this one they were spraying the snow green.*
- *The film bears many similarities to Carry On Camping, starting with the location. The very same orchard at Pinewood was used for the campsite sequences.*
- *Promotional consideration for Carry On Behind was provided by caravan manufacturer, CI. You'll see their logo quite a bit throughout the film, in addition to the opening credits.*
- *Director Gerald Thomas' dulcet tones can be heard as the voice of the mynah bird.*

CARRY ON COCK-UPS:

Technical	3m 05s	The man with the pipe burns his finger as he tries to light it but the flame goes nowhere near his fingers.
Continuity	6m 57s	There's a woman with a headscarf at the counter when we first see into the shop. In the next shot, inside the shop as Windsor Davies talks to Marianne Stone, the woman has vanished.
Technical	8m 22s	Jack Douglas has got holes drilled in the centre of his spectacles so he can see.
Trivia	10m 42s	As the car pulls away, we're treated to another of Eric Rogers' musical jokes. The theme here, and throughout the film to accompany the antics of Carry On newcomer Windsor Davies, borrows from the overture of Carl Otto Nicolai's "The Merry Wives of Windsor".
Technical	10m 45s	Windsor Davies is heard to say goodbye to his wife and laugh at her joke about his rods as they drive off. But if you look through the window of the car you'll see that his lips aren't moving.

Continuity	18m 29s	Keep an eye on Kenneth Connor's grip on his stick - it changes between shots, as does the mud on the steps behind him.
Continuity	22m 24s	It looks like someone has stolen the girls' bikes while they were in Windsor Davies' caravan. They were there a moment ago.
Continuity	23m 04s	Look at the awning on Bernard Bresslaw's caravan as Joan and Patsy walk towards it. It's closed when filmed from the outside but for interior shots like the one you'll see in a moment, it is open.
Technical	25m 20s	Look in the window of the door of the caravan as Elke Sommer first talks to Bernard Bresslaw and you'll see the reflection of a couple of members of the film crew.
Continuity	28m 41s	Notice how Peter Butterworth writes the word "Men" on the shower wall. That'll change a few times throughout the film.
Continuity	29m 37s	Ian Lavender's plain orange towel is on his right shoulder as he stands outside the shower block. He also appears to be holding a wash bag in his right hand. By the time he gets inside, the towel is has moved to his right shoulder and is now red with a distinct pattern. The wash bag is now in his left hand.
Continuity	36m 28s	Kenneth Williams' right top pocket is open. In the upcoming wide shot of him with Elke Sommer it is closed. After he gets up off the floor in a few moments the pocket is open once again.
Continuity	53m 05s	Peter Butterworth picks up just one egg and puts it in the helmet. So what's that in his hand that explodes?
Continuity	54m 11s	The awning has disappeared from Bernard Bresslaw's caravan. It'll be back in a couple of minutes.
Trivia	1h 01m 37s	The music playing in the background of the bar is a gentle arrangement of the film's theme.
Continuity	1h 03m 03s	There are four empty glasses on the boys' table. Look again after Kenneth Connor and Joan Sims have their chat.
Trivia	1h 08m 59s	As the titles explain, the caravans for the film were supplied by CI. In the clubhouse behind Kenneth Connor you'll spot a bit of subtle product placement.
Continuity	1h 10m 42s	Earlier in the film when Kenneth Connor uses the tannoy he pressed the button to speak. He doesn't bother this time.
Technical	1h 17m 29s	The stripper's music is great but it is not coming from the tape recorder - the spools are not moving.
Trivia	1h 17m 29s	This, by the way, is the same stripper we saw at the start of the film in Kenneth Williams' presentation.
Trivia	1h 26m 15s	The missing piece of the mosaic really is quite rude! However, if you look closely at the design, you can see that it's not a mosaic at all, simply a painting made to look like one.

LOCATIONS:

Time	Description	Address	Also seen in	Location Link
4m 47s	University of Kidburn	Maidenhead Town Hall St Ives Road Maidenhead Berks SL6 1RF	Carry On Doctor Carry On Again Doctor	
6m 48s	Fred Ramsden's shop	2/3 Robin Parade, Rosewood Way Farnham Royal Bucks SL2 3QL		
8m 43s	Bernie's house	8 Pinewood Close Pinewood Estate Iver Heath Bucks SL0 0QS	Carry On Camping Carry On Emmannuelle	
9m 37s	Joe & Norma Baxter's House	94 Pinewood Green Pinewood Estate Iver Heath Bucks SL0 0QP	Carry On Camping Carry On Cabby	
11m 36s	Campsite	Pinewood Orchard Pinewood Studios Iver Heath Bucks SL0 0NH	Carry On Camping Carry On England	

CARRY ON CUTTING:

- To secure an A certificate, a number of minor cuts were made to the film, including some trimming of the stripper sequence at the beginning and a number of the film's more suggestive lines.

- A scene where Kenneth Connor's Major criticises the decorating of the camp clubhouse was also trimmed. In this scene, Johnny Briggs plays the plasterer defending his work. In the final print, you can see Briggs in the background struggling with a wall fixing.

CARRY ON ABROAD:

The Wacky Campers – *Denmark*
Everything Backfires   – *Germany*
Carry On Digging! – *Hungary*
Camping Cheerleader – *Italy*
The Roman Camp – *Poland*
Watch out for the Women – *South America*
Now we take the Romans – *Sweden*
A Taste of Honey – *Turkey*

CARRY ON COLLECTING:

- Postcard featuring UK Quad poster released in 1998 by The London Postcard Company as part of their "Rank Classics Series 2" collection.
- Promotional bookmark released in 1998 by The London Postcard Company featuring the Carry On Behind and Carry On Follow that Camel Quad posters.
- In 2007, Ethos released a series of mugs featuring the original UK Quad poster artwork for the Rank Carry Ons, including Carry On Behind.

SOUNDTRACK:

Title theme available on "The Carry On Album, Music from the Films"
Gavin Sutherland & the Prague Philharmonic Orchestra, CD, ASV 1999
Newly performed renditions of classic Carry On themes

DVD:

Carry On Behind
Cinema Club, 2001
PAL, Region 2 (Europe, Middle East & Japan), Colour

DeAgostini Carry On DVD partwork
DeAgostini/Carlton, 2003
PAL, Region 2 (Europe, Middle East & Japan), Colour, Black & White

Carry On Behind
ITV Studios Home Entertainment, 2003
PAL, Region 2 (Europe, Middle East & Japan), Colour
Special Features: Commentary (Larry Dann, Jack Douglas, Dave Freeman, Patsy Rowlands), Stills, Trivia, Trailer, Carry On Laughing – Who Needs Kitchener?

Carry On – The Holiday Collection (Camping, Abroad, Camel, Girls, Convenience, Behind)
ITV Studios Home Entertainment, 2005
PAL, Region 2 (Europe, Middle East & Japan), Colour

Carry On – The Ultimate Collection
ITV Studios Home Entertainment, 2006
PAL, Region 2 (Europe, Middle East & Japan), Colour, Black & White
Special features as for individual ITV/Carlton/Optimum releases

Carry On Vol. 4 (Girls, England, Dick, Behind)
Optimum Home Releasing, 2008

PAL, Region 2 (Europe, Middle East & Japan), Colour
Special features as for individual ITV/Carlton/Optimum releases

Carry On – The Ultimate Collection
ITV Studios Home Entertainment, 2008
PAL, Region 2 (Europe, Middle East & Japan), Colour, Black & White
Special features as for individual ITV/Carlton/Optimum releases

VHS:

Carry On Behind
Rank Video Library, 1981
PAL, Colour

Carry On Behind
Cinema Club, 1987
PAL, Colour

Carry On Behind
Cinema Club, 1991
PAL, Colour

Carry On Behind
Cinema Club, 1996
PAL, Colour

Carry On Behind – Collector's Edition
Cinema Club, 1999
PAL, Colour

Carry On Loving / Carry On Behind
Cinema Club, 2000
PAL, Colour

DeAgostini Carry On VHS partwork
DeAgostini/Carlton, 2003
PAL, Colour, Black & White

The Carry On Collection (Don't Lose your Head – Carry On Emmannuelle)
Carlton Visual Entertainment, 2003
PAL, Colour

Carry On Behind
Carlton Visual Entertainment, 2003
PAL, Colour

BETAMAX:

Carry On Behind
Rank Video Library, 1981
PAL, Colour

CARRY ON ENGLAND

1976

Screenplay by David Pursall & Jack Seddon
Music Composed & Conducted by Max Harris

CAST   CHARACTER

Kenneth Connor	Captain S Melly
Windsor Davies	Sergeant Major "Tiger" Bloomer
Judy Geeson	Sergeant Tilly Willing
Patrick Mower	Sergeant Len Able
Jack Douglas	Bombardier Ready
Joan Sims	Private Jennifer Ffoukes-Sharp
Melvyn Hayes	Gunner Shorthouse
Peter Butterworth	Major Carstairs
Peter Jones	Brigadier
Diane Langton	Private Alice Easy
Julian Holloway	Major Butcher
David Lodge	Captain Bull
Larry Dann	Gunner Shaw
Brian Osborne	Gunner Owen
Johnny Briggs	Melly's Driver
Patricia Franklin	Corporal Cook
John Carlin	Officer
Linda Hooks	Army Nurse
Michael Nightingale	Officer
Vivienne Johnson	Freda
Peter Banks	Gunner Thomas
Richard Bartlett	Gunner Drury
Jeremy Connor	Gunner Hiscocks
Richard Olley	Gunner Parker
Billy J Mitchell	Gunner Childs
Peter Quince	Gunner Sharpe
Paul Toothill	Gunner Gale
Louise Burton	Private Evans
Jeannie Collings	Private Edwards
Barbara Hampshire	Private Carter
Linda Regan	Private Taylor
Tricia Newby	Private Murray
Barbara Rosenblat	ATS Girl

CREW

Production Manager	Roy Goddard
Art Director	Lionel Couch
Director of Photography	Ernest Steward

Editor	Richard Marden
Camera Operator	Godfrey Godar
Assistant Director	Jack Causey
Sound Recordists	Danny Daniel & Gordon McCallum
Dubbing Editor	Pat Foster
Assistant Editor	Jack Gardner
Continuity	Marjorie Lavelly
Make-up	Geoffrey Rodway
Hairdresser	Stella Rivers
Wardrobe	Vi Murray & Don Mothersill
Casting Director	John Owen
Stills Cameraman	Ken Bray
Costume Designer	Courtenay Elliott
Set Dresser	Don Picton
Titles	GSE Ltd
Producer	Peter Rogers
Director	Gerald Thomas

A Peter Rogers Production. Distributed by Fox / Rank Distributors Ltd.

PRODUCTION DETAILS:

Budget: £250,000
Filming: 3rd May 1976 – 4th June 1976
Duration: 89m
Colour
General Release: October 1976, Certificate A (originally AA)
TV Premiere: 25th May 1983, BBC1
Home Video: 1981 (VHS/Betamax), 2001 (DVD)

IN A NUTSHELL:

"It's the biggest bang of the War!"

It is World War II and England expects every man and woman to do their bit. The latest initiative from the War Office is a new combined anti-aircraft battery, bringing male and female recruits together in one unit.

Captain S Melly (Kenneth Connor) is given command of the experimental unit in the hope that his leadership skills will knock them into shape. But Melly's ideas about what makes an efficient battery differ from those under his command, who would rather make love than war.

REVIEW:

If Carry On Behind offered a glimpse of a bright new future for the Carry Ons, England shows us another, less attractive alternative. It's not that it's a badly made film. There are certainly plenty of decent performances from the team and while it may not boast a full complement of Carry On regulars, there are a few familiar faces and they are all great in the roles they play. But, at its core, Carry On England is a mean-spirited and cynical film which is flawed from the outset.

It is hard to sympathise with any of the characters in Carry On England. The troops are single-minded sex maniacs with no respect for anything other than their own genitals or the next person to get their hands on them. Captain Melly is equally one-dimensional in his desire to knock the troops into shape. Clearly the two will never agree and what follows is basically a hate campaign. The recruits really are only interested in one thing and when Melly tries to take it away they turn on him like cheeky-grinned Rottweilers. Melly, in return, escalates his campaign and the whole film becomes a bitter war of attrition. While there has always been conflict in the Carry On films, it has mostly been accompanied by a general sense of fun, of silliness and abandonment. There is very little of this spirit evident in Carry On England.

Of course, the role fulfilled by Melly isn't uncommon in the Carry On world. Connor's own Mayor Bumble in Carry On Girls is ineffectual, arrogant, self-aggrandising and thoroughly unlikeable. But in Girls, Bumble is just one character amongst many, all of whom are to some extent incorrigible idiots and deceitful rogues. They are also characters for whom you can at last feel a little sympathy. In England, with the sole exception of the sublime Sergeant Major Bloomer, every character is unlikeable. Worse still, further ignominy is heaped on long-term Carry On favourites like Joan Sims and Jack Douglas, who are shoe-horned into roles they are clearly too old and too dignified for.

Carry On England is an unpleasant experience which glories in ignominy being relentlessly heaped upon just one, admittedly unlikeable, character. It rarely shows any of the charm and warmth of the earlier films and it's sad to see this once great series being reduced to a film where the only comedy is in victimisation.

VIEWING NOTES:

- Carry On England began life as a script for the Carry Laughing television series. Pursall and Seddon had submitted a script under the name "The Busting of Balsy" which ATV had decided would be too expensive to produce. Rather than abandon the idea altogether, Rogers suggested that the pair adapt the script for use as a film.
- Financing issues beset Carry On England from the start. With The Rank Organisation only putting up half the required budget and a proposed deal with Pink Floyd for the remainder having fallen through, Rogers and Thomas took the decision to fund the rest of the money themselves.
- Budgets, then, were unusually tight on Carry On England, even by the team's usual standards. Composer, Eric Rogers, declined to take part in the project when he was informed he would be only be able to use half his usual orchestra of 40 musicians.
- Carry On England was the shortest Carry On to complete. Filming wrapped in less than five weeks.
- Kenneth Williams was approached to play the role of the Brigadier but was unable to join the production due to theatre commitments.
- Other actors shortlisted for roles in the film included Penelope Keith (presumably as Ffoukes-Sharpe) and Richard O'Sullivan as Len Able.
- Carry On England was originally released in cinemas with an AA certificate, firmly placing the film outside of the traditional family audience with nobody under the age of 14 being allowed to see it. Takings were so poor that Gerald Thomas re-edited the print and it was subsequently re-released as an A. The material cut from the "mature" print centred primarily on the topless parade and a joke about "Fokkers". The Special Edition DVD

of Carry On England contains both prints but for the purposes of this book, all timings are based on the uncut version of the film. If I had to sit all the way through it there's no reason why you shouldn't.

- *The prop gun featured (eventually) in the film was on loan to the production from the Imperial War Museum.*

CARRY ON COCK-UPS:

Continuity	3m 40s	The shot of the underwear hanging on the line is the same one we saw moments earlier at 3m 24s.
Continuity	3m 46s	Take a look at the bag on the table behind David Lodge. On it you'll see an upturned cap and a helmet. By the time Kenneth Connor crosses the room the helmet has found its way under the cap which is now the right way up.
Continuity	4m 06s	David Lodge leaves his bottle of Haig on the desk in his hurry to escape. When we next see the desk at 5m 04s it's gone. (Spirited away?).
Continuity	5m 04s	The lanyard was over Windsor Davies' right shoulder when he was outside a moment ago. Here, it appears on his left. Throughout the film, whenever Davies appears inside the hut the lanyard will be on his left. In every other shot it will be on his right.
Trivia	11m 47s	Kenneth Connor's line "I've been regular for 18 years" is a lovely in-joke referring to his tenure on the Carry Ons.
Continuity	15m 11s	Kenneth Connor transfers his stick to his left hand to lift his ear defenders. In the next shot, the close-up, it's in his right hand. When we switch back to the two-shot it is back in his left.
Continuity	30m 15s	Patrick Mower's shirt is open to his navel when Kenneth Connor approaches but keep an eye on it throughout the scene and you will see it open and close depending on the shot.
Continuity	33m 27s	Kenneth Connor and Patrick Mower are holding Judy Geeson's bra, reading the label. After the camera cuts briefly to Geeson and back, the bra is gone and never referred to again.
Continuity	35m 37s	The door at the far end of the hut is closed but Kenneth Connor, sliding across the floor, goes through an open door.
Continuity	45m 31s	Connor is standing in a different position to a moment ago. When he was pinned to the wall, the clipboard that he was leaning on with his elbow was behind his head.
Trivia	55m 19s	There are a couple of notable omissions from the line-up of topless troops. Neither Judy Geeson nor Diane Langton would consent to baring their breasts for the film so they were excused this particular parade.
Continuity	57m 25s	The end of Kenneth Connor's rant to the troops is accompanied by a few bars of the Deutschlandlied, the German national anthem.

Continuity	1h 20m 16s	There is nobody at the air raid siren when we see Kenneth Connor walking towards the hut. After a quick cut to the Brigadier and back and there's someone there winding the siren.
Continuity	1h 22m 15s	Melvyn Hayes loads the gun, but doesn't close the breach. Nevertheless, the gun still fires.
Continuity	1h 23m 01s	Kenneth Connor's hand is nowhere near the trigger or breach when he is injured - you can see the trigger miss his hand by several inches.

LOCATIONS:

Time	Description	Address	Also seen in	Location Link
2m 03s	Captain Melly arrives.	Heatherden Hall Pinewood Studios Iver Heath Bucks SL0 0NH	Carry On Nurse Carry On up the Khyber Carry On Camping Carry On Again Doctor Carry On at your Convenience	
2m 53s	Entrance to the camp	Peace Road Iver Heath Iver Bucks SL0 0NB To this day there remains a building where the gatehouse stands.	Carry On Camping Carry On Behind	
3m 29s	The camp	Pinewood Orchard Pinewood Studios Iver Heath Bucks SL0 0NH	Carry On Spying Carry On Camping Carry On Behind	

CARRY ON CUTTING:

- *For the A certificate version of the film, the topless parade scene was cut to reveal less flesh. An additional gag was changed to reference "Bristols" instead of "Fokkers".*

- *The mess scene was slightly trimmed for the final cut. In the longer version, Able engages in some characteristically insulting banter with the cook.*

CARRY ON ABROAD:

Let's Go, England – *Finland*
Saviour of the Nation – *Germany*
Mixed Barracks – *Italy*

CARRY ON COLLECTING:

- "Carry On England – The wickedly funny story that starts where the film ends", a novel by Norman Giller.
Andre Deutsch Ltd, 1996, ISBN 0233990283
- Postcard featuring UK Quad poster released in 1998 by The London Postcard Company as part of their "Rank Classics Series 2" collection.
- In 2007, Ethos, released a series of mugs featuring the original UK Quad poster artwork for the Rank Carry Ons, including Carry On England.

SOUNDTRACK:

Main title theme available on "Carry On"
Various Artists, CD, Silva Screen 2005
Themes, cues and dialog taken from the original film soundtracks

DVD:

Carry On England
Cinema Club, 2001
PAL, Region 2 (Europe, Middle East & Japan), Colour

DeAgostini Carry On DVD partwork
DeAgostini/Carlton, 2003
PAL, Region 2 (Europe, Middle East & Japan), Colour, Black & White

Carry On England
ITV Studios Home Entertainment, 2003
PAL, Region 2 (Europe, Middle East & Japan), Colour
Special Features: Commentary (Patrick Mower), Stills, Trivia, Trailer, Carry On England – The Censored Edition

Carry On – The History Collection (Head, Dick, Jungle, Henry, England, Khyber)
ITV Studios Home Entertainment, 2005
PAL, Region 2 (Europe, Middle East & Japan), Colour

Carry On – The Ultimate Collection
ITV Studios Home Entertainment, 2006
PAL, Region 2 (Europe, Middle East & Japan), Colour, Black & White
Special features as for individual ITV/Carlton/Optimum releases

Carry On Vol. 4 (Girls, England, Dick, Behind)
Optimum Home Releasing, 2008
PAL, Region 2 (Europe, Middle East & Japan), Colour
Special features as for individual ITV/Carlton/Optimum releases

Carry On – The Ultimate Collection
ITV Studios Home Entertainment, 2008
PAL, Region 2 (Europe, Middle East & Japan), Colour, Black & White
Special features as for individual ITV/Carlton/Optimum releases

VHS:

Carry On England
Rank Video Library, 1981
PAL, Colour

Carry On England
Cinema Club, 1987
PAL, Colour

Carry On England
Cinema Club, 1991
PAL, Colour

Carry On England
Cinema Club, 1996
PAL, Colour

Carry On England – Collector's Edition
Cinema Club, 1999
PAL, Colour

Carry On Abroad / Carry On England
Cinema Club, 2000
PAL, Colour

DeAgostini Carry On VHS partwork
DeAgostini/Carlton, 2003
PAL, Colour, Black & White

The Carry On Collection (Don't Lose your Head – Carry On Emmannuelle)
Carlton Visual Entertainment, 2003
PAL, Colour

Carry On England
Carlton Visual Entertainment, 2003
PAL, Colour

BETAMAX:

Carry On England
Rank Video Library, 1981
PAL, Colour

THAT'S CARRY ON

1978

Script by Tony Church
Music Arranged by Eric Rogers

CAST   CHARACTER

CAST	CHARACTER
Kenneth Williams	Himself
Barbara Windsor	Herself

CREW

Production Manager	Roy Goddard
Director of Photography	Tony Imi
Editor	Jack Gardner
Dubbing Editor	Christopher Lancaster
Sound Recordists	Danny Daniel & Ken Barker
Titles	GSE Ltd
Compiled by	Gerald Thomas
Producer	Peter Rogers
Director	Gerald Thomas

A Rank / EMI Production distributed by the Rank Organisation.

PRODUCTION DETAILS:

Budget: £30,000
Filming: April 1977
Duration: 95m
Colour
General Release: February 1978, Certificate A
TV Premiere: 25th May 1981, ITV
Home Video: 1980 (VHS/Betamax), 2003 (DVD)

IN A NUTSHELL:

"Everyone who's anyone is in it...right in it!"

Kenneth Williams and Barbara Windsor play themselves, a couple of old friends enjoying a gossip and sharing fond memories about the Carry On films, as well as introducing some highlights from the series' 19 year history.

REVIEW:

When a film encompasses all that is great about the Carry On films, how can it fail to be anything other than spectacular? That's Carry On is a fitting tribute to a series which has delighted viewers around the world for decades and the selection of clips chosen includes just about every classic Carry On moment you could ever hope to see.

However, there is a definite air of finality to the production and that alone makes That's Carry On something of a disappointment. Kenneth and Barbara are the perfect hosts. They tease each other affectionately and in doing so welcome the viewer into their cosy little world to share a few laughs and happy memories. But the continual references to the Carry Ons in the past tense add a somewhat gloomy air to an otherwise glorious celebration of our most beloved comedy institution.

VIEWING NOTES:

- *The disastrous box office performance of Carry On England left the Carry Ons with an uncertain future. A conversation with former Anglo Amalgamated studio boss Nat Cohen (now part of EMI) inspired Rogers & Thomas to relive some of the Carry Ons' past glories and remind the film-going public that at their best the Carry On films were still the nation's favourite comedies. Taking the template of the phenomenally successful 1974 compilation "That's Entertainment" Thomas began compiling a "greatest hits" of the Carry Ons to date.*
- *The original title for the film was to have been "The Best of Carry On".*
- *The only film missing from the roll call of Carry On classics is the most recent, and financially least successful entry, Carry On England. The film's sole mention is in the credits.*
- *Distributor confidence in That's Carry On wasn't strong enough to warrant a major release and so it was paired with the Richard Harris thriller "Golden Rendezvous".*

LOCATIONS:

The Kenneth Williams / Barbara Windsor linking sequences were filmed at Pinewood's projection room 7.

CARRY ON COLLECTING:

- Postcard featuring UK One Sheet poster released in 1998 by The London Postcard Company as part of their "British Classics Series 3" collection.

DVD:

DeAgostini Carry On DVD partwork
DeAgostini/Carlton, 2003
PAL, Region 2 (Europe, Middle East & Japan), Colour, Black & White

That's Carry On
ITV Studios Home Entertainment, 2003
PAL, Region 2 (Europe, Middle East & Japan), Colour
Special Features: Commentary (Peter Rogers), Stills, Trivia, Trailer, Carry On Laughing – Lamp Posts of the Empire

Carry On – The Doctors and Nurses Collection (Doctor, Matron, Again Doctor, That's Loving, Emmannuelle)
ITV Studios Home Entertainment, 2005
PAL, Region 2 (Europe, Middle East & Japan), Colour

Carry On – The Ultimate Collection
ITV Studios Home Entertainment, 2006

PAL, Region 2 (Europe, Middle East & Japan), Colour, Black & White
Special features as for individual ITV/Carlton/Optimum releases

Carry On Cabby / That's Carry On
Optimum Home Releasing, 2007
PAL, Region 2 (Europe, Middle East & Japan), Black & White, Colour

Carry On – The Ultimate Collection
ITV Studios Home Entertainment, 2008
PAL, Region 2 (Europe, Middle East & Japan), Colour, Black & White
Special features as for individual ITV/Carlton/Optimum releases

VHS:

That's Carry On
Rank Video Library, 1980
PAL, Colour

That's Carry On
Rank Video Library, 1986
PAL, Colour, Black & White

That's Carry On
Weintraub, 1991
PAL, Colour

DeAgostini Carry On VHS partwork
DeAgostini/Carlton, 2003
PAL, Colour, Black & White

The Carry On Collection (Don't Lose your Head – Carry On Emmannuelle)
Carlton Visual Entertainment, 2003
PAL, Colour

That's Carry On
Carlton Visual Entertainment, 2003
PAL, Colour

BETAMAX:

That's Carry On
Rank Video Library, 1980
PAL, Colour

CARRY ON EMMANNUELLE

1978

Screenplay by Lance Peters
Music Composed & Conducted by Eric Rogers
"Love Crazy" by Kenny Lynch, sung by Masterplan

CAST	CHARACTER
Kenneth Williams	Emile Prevert
Kenneth Connor	Leyland
Joan Sims	Mrs Dangle
Jack Douglas	Lyons
Peter Butterworth	Richmond
Larry Dann	Theodore Valentine
Suzanne Danielle	Emmannuelle Prevert
Beryl Reid	Mrs Valentine
Tricia Newby	Nurse in Surgery
Albert Moses	Doctor
Henry McGee	Harold Hump
Howard Nelson	Harry Hernia
Claire Davenport	Blonde in Pub
Tim Brinton	BBC Newscaster
Corbet Woodall	ITN Newscaster
Robert Dorning	Prime Minister
Bruce Boa	US Ambassador
Eric Barker	Ancient General
Victor Maddern	Man in Launderette
Norman Mitchell	Drunken Husband
Jack Lynn	Admiral of the Fleet
Michael Nightingale	Police Commissioner
Llewellyn Rees	Lord Chief Justice
Steve Plytas	Arabian Official
Joan Benham	Cynical Lady
Marianne Maskell	Nurse in Hospital
Louise Burton	Girl at Zoo
Dino Shafeek	Immigration Officer
David Hart	Customs Officer
Gertan Klauber	German Soldier
Malcolm Johns	Sentry
John Carlin	French Parson
Guy Ward	Dandy
James Fagan	Concorde Steward
John Hallett	Substitute Footballer
Deborah Brayshaw	French Buxom Blonde

Suzanna East ....Colette
Bruce Wyllie..Football Referee
Philip Clifton ....Injured Footballer
Stanley McGeagh ....Journalist
Bill Hutchinson ....1st Reporter
Neville Ware ....2nd Reporter
Jane Norman ....3rd Reporter
Nick White ....Sent-off Footballer

CREW

Production Manager ....Roy Goddard
Art Director ....Jack Shampan
Director of Photography ....Alan Hume
Editor..Peter Boita
Camera Operator ....Godfrey Godar
Assistant Director ....Gregory Dark
Assistant Editor..Jack Gardner
Sound Recordists ....Danny Daniel & Otto Snel
Dubbing Editor ....Peter Best
Continuity..Marjorie Lavelly
Make-up ....Robin Grantham
Hairdresser..Betty Sherriff
Costume Designer ....Courtenay Elliott
Wardrobe..Margaret Lewin
Set Dresser ....John Hoesli
Stills Cameraman ....Ken Bray
Titles ....GSE Ltd
Production Executive for Cleeves Investments ....Donald Langdon
Producer..Peter Rogers
Director..Gerald Thomas

Cleeves Investments Ltd presents a Pete Rogers Production.
A Gerald Thomas film distributed by Hemdale International Films

PRODUCTION DETAILS:

Budget: £320,000
Filming: 10th April 1978 – 15th May 1978
Duration: 88m
Colour
General Release: November 1978, Certificate AA
TV Premiere: 5th December 1992, Sky Movies +
Home Video: 1981 (VHS/Betamax), 2001 (DVD)

IN A NUTSHELL:

"When it comes to foreign 'affairs' it's..."

Following a particularly nasty naked skydiving incident, Emile Prevert (Kenneth Williams) is unable to satisfy his wife, Emmannuelle (Suzanne Danielle). This presents something of a problem because Emmannuelle was already insatiable to begin with. The couple reach an understanding, whereby Emmannuelle can indulge her sexual urges however she chooses, provided she leaves Emile to his own amusements.

Emmannuelle seduces Theodore Valentine (Larry Dann), in the lavatory aboard Concorde when she flies to England to join her beloved husband. It may be a casual fling for her, but Valentine falls instantly in love with the temptress and sets out on a campaign to convince her that he, not Emile, is her one true love.

Arriving in London, Emmannuelle embarks on a diplomatic mission to smooth foreign relations in an entirely novel and thoroughly pleasurable way – by sleeping with every man who comes near her. The British press gets wind of Emmannuelle's antics and declares her a national scandal.

Emile, distraught at not being able to satisfy his wife's increasingly public sexual desires, decides to take action and give her what she really wants.

REVIEW:

I must be honest – I hadn't even bothered to watch Carry On Emmannuelle until I started work on this book. The received wisdom (if you listen to your mates or believe what you read on Web forums) is that Emmannuelle is so bad, so denigrating to the memory of our beloved Carry Ons that it is best ignored.

That's all nonsense. Carry On Emmannuelle is a wonderful film and, if anything it's the perfect end to the series. Maybe people are put off by the concept of a Carry On that is all about a slut who can't keep her knickers on. But, to some degree, is that not what all the Carry Ons are about when you boil them down to basics?

Carry On Cleo is about a randy queen who uses sex to get her own way. In Carry On Camping Babs is gagging for it and they're all at it in Abroad. Even Dora Bryan in Sergeant would have put out for Kenneth Connor if he had only had the courage to ask. The Carry Ons have always been about sex, but each era has dealt with the subject in the language of its time. By the late 1970s, people were practically doing it in the streets if you believe popular British cinema of the time. Carry On Emmannuelle simply told the same old story in a way with which contemporary audiences were responding.

Admittedly, the Carry Ons had stopped being good old fashioned family entertainment by this point, but sex comedies were big business during the period and Emmannuelle simply went after the most lucrative market. As it turned this was wrong but you can't keep making references to sex if you're not actually going to show it sooner or later.

At its heart, Carry On Emmannuelle is a deeply sentimental and thoroughly charming film as the Preverts and their retainers take a misty-eyed look at their lives and loves and try to rekindle some of their old passions. It is a love letter to past glories and a fitting end to the series. It is also extremely funny. Once you get past the embarrassing Concorde gag in the opening credits, there is plenty of good old-fashioned Carry On fun: Victor Maddern flaunting his Y-fronts in a West London launderette; Kenneth Connor and Clare Davenport getting frisky in a grotty bedsit; a naked skydiving Kenneth Williams. There are some brilliant gags in Carry On Emmannuelle and most of them, usually the ones not directly involving sexual contact, are very funny indeed.

There's a lot to love about Carry On Emmannuelle, if you'll only give it a chance. I'm not ashamed to say it has become one of my favourite Carry Ons.

VIEWING NOTES:

- *Lance Peters' original script for Carry On Emmannuelle was considerably more lewd than the film that eventually bore its name. Vince Powell and Willie Rushton were brought in to tone down some of the naughtier bits and supply additional material, but both writers' contributions remained un-credited. Lance Peters' novel of the same name gives a flavour of what the film could have been. Thank goodness for Messrs Powell & Rushton.*
- *Peters' original script was entitled "Carry On Emmanuelle" (with one "n"). The additional consonant was added later to fend off any potential legal trouble.*
- *Elements of Lance Peters' original script found their way into press reports prior to the launch of Carry On Emmannuelle. In August 1978, the Daily Express billed Joan Sims' character Mrs Dangle as being the owner of a brothel in the up-coming film.*
- *Contrary to reports that Rank weren't interested in a Carry On with such an adult theme, Rogers didn't even approach his former studio bosses and instead struck a deal with Hemdale for a £400,000 investment in the project.*
- *Incredibly, Peter Rogers and Gerald Thomas originally went to the British Board of Film Censors seeking a U certificate for the film. Even more incredibly, the BBFC was prepared to grant one, provided certain cuts be made. Ultimately, though, the film was granted an AA certificate, meaning nobody under the age of 14 could see it.*
- *A serious early contender for the role of Emmannuelle was a 16-year old Kelly Le Brock.*
- *To this day rumours persist that Barbara Windsor had been cast in Carry On Emmannuelle but that she had walked off the set in disgust. The truth is that while Barbara Windsor had been approached (more on that in a moment) she was unable to commit to the film due to scheduling conflicts and in reality had never set foot in the studio.*
- *Had she joined the cast, Barbara Windsor would have played a single object of desire in all the male sexual fantasy scenes as well as the nurse holding Emmannuelle's babies at the end of the film.*
- *Rogers and Thomas were unhappy with Howard Nelson's performance as body-builder Harry Hernia. The actor's lines were re-dubbed by Kenneth Connor to give the performance a more manly tone.*
- *Kenneth Williams requested a car to take him to the studios when filming Emmannuelle. Uncharacteristically, Peter Rogers agreed to Kenneth's request, but as the star later discovered, the £250 booking fee was subtracted from Kenneth's £6000 fee for making the film.*
- *Arrow Books released a tie-in novel based on Lance Peters' original script, infuriating Peter Rogers who feared that the public would buy what he thought to be an X-rated novel and be misled about the content of his AA-rated film. Consequently, he decreed that no Carry On imagery or logo be allowed to appear on the novel itself.*

CARRY ON COCK-UPS:

Continuity	7m 11s	We have just seen Jack Douglas pull the door behind him. It remains so throughout his conversation with Suzanne Danielle - at least in his close-ups. In the over-shoulder shots of Danielle the door is wide open.
Continuity	14m 04s	The glasses Peter Butterworth is holding aren't the same broken ones he wore when he was looking through the peephole. This pair are not cracked.

Continuity	17m 23s	Look out of the car window behind Suzanne Danielle and you'll see a blue Ford Transit van and in front of that, two yellow cars and a blue one, all parked in the central reservation. There they are again at 17m 41s. At 17m 53s, Danielle's car pulls up alongside the Transit.
Technical	17m 33s	Watch the right hand side of the screen and you can see there's someone sitting in the seat beside Danielle. At 17m 40s their hand will come into shot.
Continuity	19m 07s	The limousine drives along the south side of Trafalgar Square, past Nelson's Column 4 times in the space of just a few lines of dialogue.
Trivia	21m 26s	In some of the worst green screen in cinema history we can surmise that Suzanne Danielle is not really showing her bottom to a guard outside St James' Palace – it is actually the car park at Pinewood. .
Technical	22m 38s	Listen to Suzanne Danielle's dialogue here. Being French, she would never mispronounce "Chanel" as "Sharnel" and no self-respecting French woman would ever pronounce the "s" on the end of "Paris".
Technical	25m 12s	Kenneth Williams' mouth is moving but the over-dubbed dialogue doesn't match his lips.
Technical	28m 54s	Suzanne Danielle didn't have to go far to get to know the Arabian ambassador better - the house they used for the exterior location is directly opposite Emmannuelle's own. You can see it behind her when she first arrives home and again when Larry Dann follows her on her tour of London.
Technical	32m 48s	A boom shadow runs over the wall behind Joan Sims.
Trivia	42m 43s	The music accompanying the scene with Joan and Victor Maddern is the same striptease music from Carry On Behind. You'll hear another arrangement of the same music later.
Continuity	46m 30s	The two parachutists jump out of the plane in blue overalls. In the next shot, one of them is wearing a red jumpsuit and the other yellow.
Technical	49m 29s	Whose shadow is that in the mirror? It doesn't match Kenneth Williams' movements and Suzanne Danielle is lying down.
Continuity	52m 58s	Watch how Suzanne Danielle is holding her towel. Now look again at the reflection of her holding the towel a couple of seconds later – it doesn't match.
Horror	54m 12s	If you really, really have to - take a close look at the right leg of Kenneth Williams' shorts. There's something poking out and I don't want to think about what it might be.
Technical	1h 4m 40s	I think Suzanne Danielle and the footballer are supposed to be making love in the team's medical room. How many medical rooms do you know with showers and soap trays running all across the walls?
Trivia	1h 20m 17s	The music accompanying the nurse's brief striptease is the same used for the stripper in Carry On Behind.

LOCATIONS:

Time	Description	Address	Also seen in	Location Link
6m 50s	Pulling up outside Emile's house	78 Addison Road Kensington London W14 8EB		
14m 56s	Valentine comes home	8 Pinewood Close Pinewood Estate Iver Heath Bucks SL0 0QS		
18m 04s	Tour of London	Emmannuelle's car travels down Regent Street, crossing Oxford Circus London W1		
18m 43s		Parliament Square London SW1 That's the headquarters of BOSH from Spying over on the left.	Carry On Spying	
19m 07s		Trafalgar Square London W1		
19m 51s		The Mall London W1		

Time	Scene	Location		QR
21m 04s		St James' Palace London W1		
28m 54s	Arabian Embassy	This is the house directly opposite 78 Addison Road Kensington London W14 8EB		
39m 05s	Richmond's encounter in the church.	St Mary's Church Church Hill Harefield Middx UB9 6DU		
40m 15s	Lyons' fantasy	Regent's Park Zoo Regent's Park London NW1 4RY		
42m 43s	Mrs Dangle's fantasy	21 The Parade Bourne End Bucks SL8 5SB		
47m 21s	Emile's encounter with a church spire	St Peter's Church Church Lane Cassington Oxon OX29 4BN		

CARRY ON CUTTING:

• A brief scene where Emmannuelle was intimately questioned by a customs officer (David Hart) was cut from the final film. In it, Emmannuelle consents to a strip search, provided the customs officer strips off as well.

CARRY ON ABROAD:

Emmannuelle at Play – *Spain*
Hot Emmannuelle – *South America*

CARRY ON COLLECTING:

* Masterplan – Love Crazy / Since I've Been Away from my Love, 7" single, Satril SAT 136, 1978
* Carry On Emmannuelle by Lance Peters
  Arrow Books, 1978, ISBN: 0099182203

DVD:

Carry On Emmannuelle
Cinema Club, 2001
PAL, Region 2 (Europe, Middle East & Japan), Colour

DeAgostini Carry On DVD partwork
DeAgostini/Carlton, 2003
PAL, Region 2 (Europe, Middle East & Japan), Colour, Black & White

Carry On Emmannuelle
ITV Studios Home Entertainment, 2003
PAL, Region 2 (Europe, Middle East & Japan), Colour
Special Features: Commentary (Larry Dann, Jack Douglas), Stills, Trivia, Trailer, What's a Carry On?

Carry On – The Doctors and Nurses Collection (Doctor, Matron, Again Doctor, That's Loving, Emmannuelle)
ITV Studios Home Entertainment, 2005
PAL, Region 2 (Europe, Middle East & Japan), Colour

Carry On – The Ultimate Collection
ITV Studios Home Entertainment, 2006
PAL, Region 2 (Europe, Middle East & Japan), Colour, Black & White
Special features as for individual ITV/Carlton/Optimum releases

Carry On – The Ultimate Collection
ITV Studios Home Entertainment, 2008
PAL, Region 2 (Europe, Middle East & Japan), Colour, Black & White
Special features as for individual ITV/Carlton/Optimum releases

VHS:

Carry On Emmannuelle
CBS/Fox, 1981
PAL, Colour

Carry On Emmannuelle
Cinema Club, 1991
PAL, Colour

Carry On Emmannuelle

Cinema Club, 1995
PAL, Colour

Carry On Emmannuelle – Collector's Edition
Cinema Club, 1999
PAL, Colour

Carry On Emmannuelle / Carry On Girls
Cinema Club, 2000
PAL, Colour

DeAgostini Carry On VHS partwork
DeAgostini/Carlton, 2003
PAL, Colour, Black & White

The Carry On Collection (Don't Lose your Head – Carry On Emmannuelle)
Carlton Visual Entertainment, 2003
PAL, Colour

Carry On Emmannuelle
Carlton Visual Entertainment, 2003
PAL, Colour

BETAMAX:

Carry On Emmannuelle
CBS/Fox, 1981
PAL, Colour

CARRY ON COLUMBUS

1992

Screenplay by Dave Freeman
Additional material by John Antrobus
Music by John Du Prez

CAST	CHARACTER
Jim Dale	Christopher Columbus
Bernard Cribbins	Mordecai Mendoza
Maureen Lipman	Countess Esmeralda
Peter Richardson	Bart Columbus
Alexei Sayle	Achmed
Rik Mayall	The Sultan
Charles Fleischer	Pontiac
Nigel Planer	The Wazir
Leslie Phillips	King Ferdinand
June Whitfield	Queen Isabella
Julian Clary	Don Juan Diego
Sara Crowe	Fatima
Keith Allen	Pepi the Poisoner
Richard Wilson	Don Juan Felipe
Rebecca Lacey	Chiquita
Jon Pertwee	The Duke of Costa Brava
Larry Miller	Big Chief
Jack Douglas	Marco the Cereal Killer
Andrew Bailey	Genghis
Burt Kwouk	Wang
Philip Herbert	Ginger
Tony Slattery	Baba the Messenger
Martin Clunes	Martin
David Boyce	Customer with Ear
Sara Stockbridge	Nina the Model
Holly Aird	Maria
James Faulkner	Torquemada
Don MacLean	Inquisitor with Ham Sandwiches
Peter Grant	Cardinal
Su Douglas	Countess Joanna
John Antrobus	Manservant
Lynda Baron	Meg
Allan Corduner	Sam
Nejdet Saleh	Fayid
Mark Arden	Mark
Silvestre Tobias	Abdullah
Danny Peacock	Tonto the Torch

Don Henderson...Bosun
Harold Berens..Cecil the Torturer
Peter Gilmore...Governor of the Canaries
Marc Sinden...Captain Perez
Charles Fleischer..Pontiac
Chris Langham...Hubba
Reed Martin...Poco Hontas
Prudence Solomon..Ha Ha
Peter Gordeno..Shaman
Stunt Double...Paul Jennings
Inquisitors: ....Dave Freeman, Duncan Duff,
Jonathan Taffler, James Pertwee,
Toby Dale, Michael Hobbs

CREW

Production Supervisor..Joyce Herlihy
Costume Designer...Phoebe De Gaye
Editor...Chris Blunden
Production Designer...Harry Pottle
Director of Photography...Alan Hume
Casting...Jane Arnell
Choreographer...Peter Gordeno
Production Cooordinator...Lorraine Fennell
Art Director...Peter Childs
Script Supervisor..Maggie Unsworth
Assistant Director...Gareth Tandy
Assistant Director...Terry Bamber
Assistant Director...Becky Harris
Camera Operator..Martin Hume
Clapper Loader...Sean Connor
Camera Grip..Colin Manning
Sound Recordist...Chris Munro
Sound Maintenance...Graham Nieder
Chief Dubbing Editor...Otto Snel
Dubbing Mixers..Kevin Taylor, Michael Carter
Assistant Editor..Steve Maguire
2nd Assistant Editor..Natalie Baker
Dialogue Editor..Alan Paley
Assistant Dialogue Editor..Andrew Melhuish
Dubbing Editor...Peter Horrocks
Assistant Dubbing Editor..Christine Newell
Footsteps Editor...Richard Hiscott
Wardrobe..Ken Crouch, Sue Honeyborne,
Jane Lewis, Jo Korer
Make-up...Sarah Monzani, Amanda Knight
Hairdresser..Sue Love, Sarah Love

Set Decorator	Denise Exshaw
Assistant Art Director	Edward Ambrose
Scenic Artist	Ted Mitchell
Production Buyer	Brian Winterborn
Art Department Assistant	Peter Francis
Gaffer	Denis Brock
Best Boy	Billy Poccetty
Assistant to John Goldstone	Lisa Bonnichon
Assistant to Peter Rogers & Gerald Thomas	Audrey Skinner
Production Accountants	Bob Blues, Gordon Davis, Jacky Holding
Stunt Arranger	Jason White
Unit Nurse	Nicky Gregory
Production Runner	Stuart Gladstone
Floor Runner	Natasha Gladstone
Unit Publicist	Ann Tasker
Casting Assistant	Gina Jay
Boat Consultant	David Raine
Construction Manager	Ken Pattenden
Chargehand Carpenter	Bill Hearn
Chargehand Rigger	Les Beaver
Chargehand Painter	Michael Gunner
Chargehand Plasterer	Ken Barley
Stand-by Props	Philip McDonald
Stand-by Carpenter	David Williams
Stand-by Painter	Peter Mounsey
Stand-by Rigger	Gordon Humphrey
Stand-by Stagehand	Leonard Serpant
Special Effects	Effects Associates
Title Design	Gillie Potter
Stills	Keith Hamshere
Property Master	Charles Torbett
Costumes Supplied by	Angels and Bermans
Unit Driver	Keith Horsley, Brian Baverstock
Lighting Services	Michael Samuelson Lighting
Titles	General Screen Enterprises
Stills Processing	Pinewood Studios
Cameras	Camera Associates
Title Backgrounds	C&P Graphics Enterprises
Insurance Arranged by	Rollins Burdick Hunter Ltd
Production Legal Services	Marriott Harrison
Completion Guarantee	The Completion Bond Company
Prosthetics (Ear)	Aaron Sherman
Computer Services	Sargent-Disc Ltd
Glasses	Onspec
Hair Products supplied by	Paul Mitchell Systems

Executive Producer ....Peter Rogers
Producer..John Goldstone
Director...Gerald Thomas

A Comedy House Production in association with Peter Rogers Productions.
A Gerald Thomas Film

PRODUCTION DETAILS:

Budget: £2,500,000
Filming: 21st April 1992 – 27th May 1992
Duration: 91m
Colour
General Release: October 1992, Certificate PG
TV Premiere: 20th August 1994 (The Movie Channel)
Home Video: 1993 (VHS)

IN A NUTSHELL:

"Up your anchor for a well crewed voyage!"

Map maker Christopher Columbus (Jim Dale) is visited by Mordechai Mendoza (Bernard Cribbins), a scholar who claims to have a map showing a route to the Far East which circumvents the lands owned by the Sultan of Turkey (Rik Mayall). Bypassing Turkey means travellers can avoid the Sultan's exorbitant taxes. The King and Queen of Spain (Leslie Phillips and June Whitfield) commission Columbus to lead an expedition to the Indies via this new route. Prison Governor Don Juan Diego (Julian Clary) agrees to join Columbus and brings with him a motley crew of criminals and cut-throats. But the Sultan's spies present an even greater danger. Achmed (Alexei Sayle) smuggles himself aboard together with the beautiful Fatima (Sara Crowe), disguised as a cabin boy.

When Columbus finally sights land the natives aren't quite what he expected. Conned out of his provisions and even his clothes by the devious Big Chief (Larry Miller) and his men, Columbus returns to Spain with a consignment of fool's gold. But there's a different kind treasure on offer when Columbus unfrocks the cabin boy.

REVIEW:

It is difficult to know quite where to begin describing how wrong Carry On Columbus is. I have never been opposed to the idea of a Carry On revival – the recent success of the St Trinian's films shows that much-loved comedy franchises can come back from the dead and still retain the same old magic, but Columbus is executed so dispassionately, so awkwardly that it fails on almost every level.

Let us start with the cast. Given the age of the many of our beloved Carry On regulars it is understandable to want to inject the film with some fresh new blood. We have seen before in films like Behind or Matron that such a policy can produce magnificent results. But in Carry On Columbus, rather than look to comedy performers, the team hired the cream of that generation's new "alternative" comedians, the majority of whom simply were not competent as actors. To make matters worse, there's absolutely no chemistry between the cast – it's not just a case of the old guard not mixing with the new – nobody seems to mix with anyone.

With just a few rare exceptions, every performance is leaden and, quite frankly, dull. Julian Clary saves the day with every line he utters but he, Jim Dale and Bernard Cribbins simply could not carry the film between them.

Carry On Columbus is joyless. The story, and there really isn't much of one, plods around confusingly before the team finally reach America at which point the remainder of the film is basically an over long sketch about how the gang are conned by the natives. But we knew that would happen the moment we first clapped eyes on Big Chief and his admittedly rather brilliantly conceived natives. The big payoff takes so long to happen that by the time it does, the only emotion left is relief. Any comedy potential disappeared long ago.

Atmospherically, there is a vacuum at the heart of Carry On Columbus left by an almost total absence of incidental music. There's an occasional musical sting every now and then, but it's invariably at odds with the action on screen. With a decent musical accompaniment, the film could have salvaged at least some goodwill. As it is, the jokes fall flat as silence greets almost every attempt at a punch line.

Carry On Columbus is a charmless attempt to breathe life into an old favourite. I tried to like it when it came out and I've tried again a number of times since but, no matter how hard I try to find some redeeming feature to make the effort worthwhile, I cannot.

VIEWING NOTES:

- *John Goldstone established the Comedy House production company with a view to promoting British comedy films in America. Gerald Thomas met with Goldstone in 1991 to discuss potential projects and an initial concept was agreed of a revival of the "Road..." films. Writers Andrew Marshall and David Renwick originally signed up to pen the script but following a number of abortive attempts to get the project off the ground, the writers departed.*

- *Thomas' next proposal was a revival of the Carry On franchise. With the anniversary of Columbus' discovery of America on the horizon, the explorer's historic journey seemed an ideal target for the Carry On treatment.*

- *Scriptwriter Dave Freeman was given just three weeks to deliver his initial script for Carry On Columbus.*

- *While Carry On Columbus is generally considered to have been an artistic and comedic flop, at the box office the film was relatively successful and, with UK box office takings of £1.6m it out-performed the two other Columbus-related films released in 1992, John Glenn's "Christopher Columbus – The Discovery" and Ridley Scott's "1492: Conquest of Paradise".*

- *The role of the Duke of Costa Brava was originally offered to Kenneth Connor. Other Carry On regulars considered for the film included Frankie Howerd as the King of Spain and Joan Sims as Queen Isabella. Howerd is reported to have agreed up to appear in the film, but the star died shortly before filming was due to start. Producers also approached Bernard Bresslaw and Barbara Windsor for the roles.*

- *Jonathan Ross was originally cast as the customer whose ear is cut off by Alexei Sayle but work commitments meant he was unable to appear.*

- *The Cardinal is played by legendary former Led Zeppelin manager, Peter Grant.*

- *Dave Freeman and Jim Dale's son, Toby played inquisitors in Columbus. Following a whirlwind on-set romance, Toby Dale married actress Sara Crowe shortly after filming. Remember that the next time you watch the scene where she seduces Toby's dad.*

CARRY ON COCK UPS:

Continuity	5m 29s	The messenger asks permission to take his boot off and then doesn't - he pulls the message out instead.
Continuity	8m 49s	Sara Crowe's cloak goes through various levels of being fully wrapped from one shot to the next during the scene in Achmed's shop.
Continuity	9m 09s	The model is wearing a mermaid's bottom and sitting down. So in the next scene who is Alexei Sayle looking at through that peep-hole?
Continuity	10m 48s	Bernard Cribbins places the velvet sleeve on the counter facing one way. When he picks it up its facing a different way.
Continuity	21m 17s	In wide shot there's no lantern swinging behind Jim Dale and he is further away from the gangplank than in the close-up.
Technical	36m 07s	Look at the sea over the side of the boat. Those waves are part of the painted backdrop. Similarly unconvincing is that although the boat is "moving" with the ocean, the horizon and the hand rail does not move in relation to each other.
Technical	45m 26s	Tonto The Andalusian Arsonist would be delighted to discover that he's about to accidentally set that rope on fire – it just starts to catch as he's calling "pirates".
Technical	57m 47s	Jim Dale remains suspended in the air for a second before falling when Sara Crowe cuts the rope around his neck.
Continuity	59m 39s	The oars in the boat are stowed in a different angle across the next few shots.
Technical	1h 00m 52s	When Richard Wilson & Maureen Lipman look out at the coast, the crew are nowhere to be seen. It's the same shot as was seen at 58m 44s.
Continuity	same time	The lantern behind Richard Wilson and Maureen Lipman has gained glass panels that weren't there earlier.

LOCATIONS:

Time	Description	Address	Also seen in	Location Link
58m 44s	Landing in the New World	Frensham Great Pond Farnham Surrey GU10 2QD	Carry On Jack	

CARRY ON CUTTING:

- *A scene featuring TP McKenna as the Archbishop of Canterbury, marrying Jon Pertwee's Duke of Costa Brava and Holly Aird's Maria was cut from the final film.*

CARRY ON ABROAD:

Chris Columbus' Crazy Gang – *Spain*

CARRY ON COLLECTING:

Soundtrack:
* Carry On Columbus by Fantastic Planet (Malcolm McLaren) CD Single, A&M Records, 1992, AMCD 065
* Carry On Columbus by Fantastic Planet (Malcolm McLaren) 2x12" Promo Single, A&M Records, 1992, AMY0065DJ
* Carry On Columbus by Fantastic Planet (Malcolm McLaren) 12" Single, A&M Records, 1992, AMY0065

VHS:

Carry On Columbus
Warner Home Video, 1993
PAL, Colour

Carry On Columbus
Warner Home Video, 1999
PAL, Colour

CARRY ON TELEVISION & RADIO

From the giddy heights of the Carry On Christmas specials to the subterranean lows of the mid-1970s Carry On Laughing series some of the Carry Ons' best moments – and most of their worst – took place on the small screen.

The Carry On team's television legacy is over 40 years old. In 1969, with the production on Carry On up the Jungle recently wrapped, the team moved to an altogether more intimate studio to create a TV tradition that would delight audiences for the next five years. Carry On Christmas spearheaded the early stages of ITV's ratings war against the BBC for Christmas audiences.

In 1975, the team returned to television screens in a series of 13 half-hour mini Carry Ons. It's fair to say that not every episode lived up to the standard of their big screen counterparts but the series contained plenty of surprising comedy gems and, more importantly, it provided an opportunity for the gang to take on new and more interesting roles. Overall, Carry On Laughing scored more misses than hits but stories like the sublime Orgy & Bess almost, but not quite, makes up for dross like Lamp Posts of the Empire.

In the 1980s, Carry On clip shows were a quick and cheap way for broadcasters to fill half an hour in their schedule and it seemed at the time that they were never off the air. What a Carry On! and Carry On Laughing regularly attracted audiences of over 10 million viewers every week and the addition of the 1993 series, Laugh with the Carry Ons, ensured that the Carry On team were never too far from our screens more than a decade after the last film was made.

When asked about the possibility of new Carry On films in the mid-1980s, Gerald Thomas joked that there was no need for he and Peter to make more because it was far easier to carry on making audiences laugh with the TV compilations. By the mid-1990s, Peter Rogers had begun talking about bringing the Carry Ons back to the small screen in a new series of comedy adventures but while plans took on various shapes and formats over the next few years, none ultimately came to fruition.

Today, with the Carry On team firmly established as British cultural icons you are never too far away from a fresh insight into the films and the people who made them.

The Carry Ons grew up on British television screens and today those same screens are playing back their own interpretation of the Carry On legend.

THE CARRY ON TELEVISION PRODUCTIONS:

Starting with one which, strictly speaking, isn't....

OUR HOUSE

11/09/1960 – 21/04/1962
An ABC Weekend Television Production for ITV
26 x 45 minutes, 13 x 55 minutes

Hattie Jacques	Georgina Ruddy
Charles Hawtrey	Simon Willow
Joan Sims	Daisy Burke
Bernard Bresslaw	William Singer
Norman Rossington	Gordon Brent
Ina de la Haye	Louise Illiffe
Frank Pettingell	John Illiffe
Trader Faulkner	Stephen Hatton
Leigh Madison	Marcia Hatton
Frederick Peisley	Herbert Keane

CREW:

Created by	Norman Hudis
Writers	Norman Hudis, Brad Ashton, Bob Block
Music	Norman Percival
Designer	Tom Spaulding, Paul Bernard
Producer	Ernest Maxin

Nearly a decade before the first of the team's official television outings, Carry On scriptwriter Norman Hudis created what is, to all intents and purposes, a Carry On television series. With more regulars than some of the films, Our House delivered domestic Carry On fun every week on the small screen.

Our House features a group of misfits thrown together in unusual circumstances. The set up makes as much - or as little - sense as it did in Hudis' Carry On film scripts. A group of strangers meet at an estate agent's and decide that if they cannot afford to buy their own houses individually, they should club together and buy one together. Hattie Jacques led the cast as librarian Georgina Ruddy; Charles Hawtrey played town clerk Simon Willow and Joan Sims the serially unemployable Daisy Burke. They were joined by an eclectic group of other eccentrics, including a newlywed couple, an artist, a retired sea captain and a singer. For the next two years, the Carry On team would enjoy a new adventure every week in our very own homes.

Following a successful first year, Our House returned late in 1961. Bernard Bresslaw, Hylda Baker and Johnny Vyvyan took up residence when a number of cast members, including Joan Sims and Norman Rossington, packed their bags and moved on. Our House performed significantly less well with audiences during the early weeks of its second series and a number of ITV franchises took the decision to drop the programme. A popular show in its first year, Our House was forced into obscurity while it was still in production and was cancelled after just two series.

AVAILABILITY

DVD:

Our House: The Three Surviving Episodes
Network, 2012
PAL, Region 2 (Europe, Middle East & Japan), Black & White

CARRY ON CHRISTMAS

24/12/1969, 9.10pm
A Thames Television Production for ITV
50 minutes

Sid James	Ebenezer Scrooge
Terry Scott	Dr Frank N Stein, Convent Girl, Mr Barrett, Baggie
Charles Hawtrey	Spirit of Christmas Past, Angel, Convent Girl, Buttons
Hattie Jacques	Elizabeth Barrett, Nun, Passer-by
Barbara Windsor	Cinderella, Fanny, Spirit of Christmas Present
Bernard Bresslaw	Bob Cratchit, Frankenstein's Monster, Spirit of Christmas Future, Convent Girl, Town Crier, Policeman
Peter Butterworth	Dracula, Beggar, Convent Girl, Haggie
Frankie Howerd	Robert Browning, Fairy Godmother

CREW:

Screenplay	Talbot Rothwell
Comedy Consultant	Gerald Thomas
Choir routine	Ralph Tobert
Designer	Roger Allen
Producer	Peter Eton
Director	Ronnie Baxter

By arrangement with Peter Rogers, Creator and Producer of the Carry On series

STORY:

The first Carry On Christmas is a loosely structured spoof of Dickens' immortal "A Christmas Carol", with Sid James leading the cast in the role of Scrooge. On Christmas Eve, the old humbug is haunted by three ghosts who reveal to him, through the power of sauciness and innuendo, the error of his miserly ways.

Charles Hawtrey is the Ghost of Christmas Well-Past and takes Scrooge to see what happened to poor Doctor Frankenstein when he was refused money for some vital research. Frankenstein has created woman but this insatiable sexpot needs a man and without Scrooge's loan, his masterpiece will never be complete.

Barbara Windsor is the best Ghost of Christmas Present Scrooge has ever had and just as he is about to unwrap her he is interrupted by Robert Browning, begging for a loan so he can take his lover, Elizabeth Barrett, to Vienna. Scrooge sends the poet on his way but the ghost shows him the tragic effect his refusal will have on the young lovers.

Bernard Bresslaw's Spirit of Christmas Yet to Come reveals the misery of one of Scrooge's poorest tenants. Cinderella's ugly sisters are off to the Ball, leaving the desperate waif to clean the kitchen floor. But when Cinderella's fairy godmother arrives, it looks like Cinders' lot is about to get better. Scrooge, on the other hand, has a more serious problem.

REVIEW:

Carry On Christmas is a unique piece of television history. In what Philip Jones, Head of Light Entertainment at Thames Television called "the most expensive TV comedy spectacular ever mounted in this country" most of the big name Carry On stars appear together for the first time on the small screen, forming the centrepiece of ITV's Christmas schedule. It was the most watched programme over Christmas 1969 with 8.1 million viewers tuning in.

In translating the Carry On teams' antics to the small screen, Peter Eton was keen not to dwell too much on Dickens' original tale, which is not best known for its comedy trappings. Instead, the loose idea of three ghosts was given a pantomime touch and the result is a relentlessly hilarious and thoroughly anarchic hour of festive silliness.

The cast slip in and out of character, wisecracking to the audience, to each other and in Hawtrey's case to the stage hands. Much of the joy of Carry On Christmas is in watching the team clearly having so much fun. There are several moments when they are unable to control their laughter at the on-screen idiocy. But as magnificent as it all is, every other act pales in comparison to a jaw-dropping performance from Frankie Howerd. His turn as Robert Browning and later as the Fairy Godmother are the definite highlights of a truly spectacular event.

Carry On Christmas is as perfect a bit of festive tomfoolery today as it was all those years ago and sits among the very best of the Carry On team's work on the small screen.

AVAILABILITY
DVD:

Carry On Christmas
Fremantle Home Entertainment, 2006
PAL, Region 2 (Europe, Middle East & Japan), Black & White, Colour

FILM NIGHT SPECIAL –
CARRY ON FOREVER

12/04/1970, 11.30pm
BBC2
30 minutes

Frankie Howerd	Sid James	Joan Sims
Charles Hawtrey	Terry Scott	Bernard Bresslaw
Kenneth Connor	Jacki Piper	Gerald Thomas

CREW:

Film Editor	Colin Jones
Cameraman	Michael Boultbee
Sound	John Purchese

Producer..Barry Brown
Director...Barry Brown
Executive Producer ....Rowan Ayers

In 1970, the long running BBC "Film Night" series dedicated a 30 minute special to the Carry On films. Filmed during the making of Carry On up the Jungle and featuring behind-the-scenes footage and interviews with the cast, Carry On Forever is a unique look at the popularity of the films made at a time when their popularity was at its height.

Gerald Thomas is joined by Joan Sims, Frankie Howerd, Charles Hawtrey, Sid James, Kenneth Connor, Bernard Bresslaw, Terry Scott and Jacki Piper for a series of interviews, talking about their roles in the up-coming Carry On up the Jungle and briefly, although not always entirely seriously, about why the Carry Ons mean so much to them and to audiences around the world.

By modern standards, the content is extremely lightweight, but the ability to see the Carry On team talking so affectionately about the films and why they enjoy such lasting appeal is a genuine treat.

CARRY ON AGAIN CHRISTMAS (OR CARRY ON LONG JOHN)

24/12/1970, 9.10pm
A Thames Television Production for ITV
50 minutes

Sid James .... Long John Silver
Terry Scott .... Squire Treyhornay
Charles Hawtrey .... Old Blind Pew, Night Watchman, Nipper the Flipper
Kenneth Connor .... Dr Livershake
Barbara Windsor.......................... Jim Hawkins
Bernard Bresslaw .... Rollicky Bill
Bob Todd.................................... Ben Gun, Shipmate
Wendy Richard .... Kate

CREW:

Screenplay...Sid Colin & Dave Freeman
Comedy Consultant ....Gerald Thomas
Designer..Roger Allen
Executive Producer ....Peter Eton
Producer..Alan Tarrant
Director...Alan Tarrant

By arrangement with Peter Rogers, Creator and Producer of the Carry On series

STORY:

Drawing on the successful formula of the 1969 Carry On Christmas special, executive producer Peter Eton decided that another masterpiece of classic literature was ripe for the pantomime treatment. This time, Robert Louis Stevenson's "Treasure Island" was the victim of a decidedly liberal interpretation by the Carry On team.

Talbot Rothwell had turned down the opportunity to pen a second festive special and with replacement Sid Colin taken ill shortly after joining the team, Dave Freeman was brought in to hastily finish the script.

The hunt for Treasure Island begins with the tale of a map, or rather a map tattooed on a certain young lady's tail end. Long John Silver and his crew of cut-throats set sail in search of fortune but when the pirate tries and fails to cheat his shipmates, they leave him stranded on the island while they return to England with the booty. There, they celebrate their good fortune and laugh at the terrible fate of the stranded pirate. Meanwhile, back on the island the old sea dog has discovered an altogether more valuable treasure and spends Christmas in the arms of a bevy of beautiful maidens.

REVIEW:

Carry On Long John is an innuendo-packed but surprisingly faithful re-telling of Treasure Island, albeit a highly truncated and shamelessly saucy one. Sexual innuendo is very much the driving force this year and while there's little of the kind of innocent playfulness that made the first Christmas special so much fun, the change to a more traditional narrative style gives the cast a set of characters they can really get their teeth into.

But the biggest difference between the first two Christmas specials in is their appearance. Shortly before Carry On Again Christmas went into production, ITV technicians began industrial action in protest over the changes to working conditions brought about by the move to colour broadcasting. So, along with the rest of Thames' Christmas schedule that year, Carry On Again Christmas was filmed in black & white.

After so many sumptuous colour Carry Ons, it's disappointing to watch the team in monochrome, particularly when it looks as though a great deal of money and effort went into the sets and costumes. However, while it's not as visually playful as the 1969 special, Carry On Again Christmas is an excellent production. It's unique in being the only Carry On special with a proper story and it tells that story in a raucous, slightly more adult way, despite its technical failings.

AVAILABILITY
DVD:

Carry On Christmas
Fremantle Home Entertainment, 2006
PAL, Region 2 (Europe, Middle East & Japan), Black & White, Colour

CARRY ON CHRISTMAS: CARRY ON STUFFING

20/12/1972, 8pm
A Thames Television Production for ITV
50 minutes

Hattie Jacques .... Fiona Clodhopper, Miss Molly Coddle, Miss Harriet, The Good Fairy
Joan Sims .... Lady Clodhopper, Mother, Miss Esmeralda, Princess YoYo

Kenneth Connor .... Chairman, General Clodhopper, Lt Bangham,
Inspector Knicker, Hanky Poo
Barbara Windsor......................... Eve, Miss Clodhopper, Milk Maid, Aladdin
Peter Butterworth   Sir Francis Fiddler, Captain Dripping, Lieutenant
Trembler, Widow Holeinone
Jack Douglas .... Mr Perkin, Adam, Tomkins, Ringworm, Charles Burke,
The Demon King
Norman Rossington .... Valet, Dinner Guest, Genie of the Lamp
Brian Oulton .... Oriental Orator
Billy Cornelius .... Waiter
Valerie Leon............................... Serving Wench
Valerie Stanton .... Demon King's Vision

CREW

Screenplay .... Talbot Rothwell & Dave Freeman
Costumes .... Frank Van Raay
Designer .... Tony Borer
Producer.. Gerald Thomas
Executive Producer .... Peter Rogers
Director.. Ronald Fouracre

By arrangement with Peter Rogers, Creator and Producer of the Carry On series

STORY:

Following a two year absence, in which at least some of the team brought us "All this and Christmas Too", the Carry On Christmas tradition was revived once more in 1972 with Carry On Stuffing.

It's Christmas Eve at the Turnit Inn, where the members of the Pudding Club meet every year to eat, drink and indulge in some festive frivolity. Between courses, they pass the time by sharing tall tales of Christmas past:

In the Garden of Eden Adam wants Eve to give him something very special for Christmas while at the Last Outpost a group of British Colonials enjoy a final meal, maintaining the stiffest of upper lips while war rages outside.

In the Musician's Story the Carry On team sing a pair of Elizabethan madrigals..."Take up your Poles" and "How King Henry got his Hampton Court". In the Sailor's Story two spinsters sit taking tea in their home. To Harriet's distaste, Esmeralda has invited Lieutenants Banghem and Trembler to stay for Christmas. But the house has a dark secret. Finally, in Aladdin the traditional Christmas pantomime is given a Carry On twist.

REVIEW:

Independent Television was criticised by the Independent Broadcasting Authority in 1972 for what it called a "frivolous" collection of planned festive offerings. While the broadcasters revised their Christmas schedules, adding a more religious and arts content, the highlight of their programming remained the Carry On team's return to the small screen.

Audiences of the day were delighted by the gang's return, but with hindsight there is awkwardness to the 1972 special which is at least partly informed by the last minute changes to the script and cast. Having played further down the bill in previous years to Sid James and Terry Scott, Charles Hawtrey demanded top billing when he learned they were not appearing that year. Peter Rogers insisted that Hattie Jacques would be leading the 1972 cast, so just two days before filming began, Hawtrey walked off the project. Gerald Thomas tracked Hawtrey down to the Dorchester and gave him an ultimatum. He could have a second billing or none at all. Hawtrey refused and with that he left Carry On Christmas and the Carry On team forever.

The script was hastily rewritten and Hawtrey's lines were shared among other cast members but the timing of the dispute threw the project into disarray. Hawtrey's departure happened too late for the TV Times to change their planned feature on the programme, so despite his absence from our screens, Hawtrey featured prominently in the magazine's Christmas preview.

Carry On Stuffing opens on a flat note with a deliberately clumsy version of Good King Wenceslas. Meanwhile, the decision to shoot the episode on location certainly gives the Inn atmosphere but it's a strangely hollow one which only serves to keep the audience at arm's length. The studio sequences work better, but on the whole it's a lacklustre attempt at capturing the Christmas – and the Carry On – spirit. Hawtrey's absence is brought home when host Kenneth Connor asks one of the guests for a story and we discover that the guest in question is Connor himself, in heavy make-up. It's an immediate, if unintentional, reminder of the team being short-handed. Elsewhere, Jack Douglas' business with the dinner gong is barely funny the first time round, so by the time you've seen it half a dozen times the Christmas spirit has long since evaporated.

The dinner party sketch is a reworking of past Carry On glories, with lines and even an Oozlum bird lifted straight out of Carry On up the Jungle and dropped into the closing scenes of Carry On up the Khyber. While all this was genuinely funny on the big screen, the re-working of old gags just adds to the overall sense that this year's Carry On is anything but special. Finishing with the gag about a ritual suicide really is the final straw. There are a few glimmers here and there but The Sailor's Story and Aladdin mostly fall flat. The first is dark, rather than funny and the second has a rape joke mere minutes in.

The only real saving grace of the programme is in another piece of recycled material; the wonderful Elizabethan madrigals which were originally intended for inclusion in Carry On Henry. Clever strokes like this make the programme worth watching, but with a finger never too far from the "skip" button. There is just too much in Carry On Stuffing that is clumsy and just plain un-funny.

AVAILABILITY
DVD:

Carry On Christmas
Fremantle Home Entertainment, 2006
PAL, Region 2 (Europe, Middle East & Japan), Black & White, Colour

VHS:

Carry On Christmas
Cinema Club, 1996
PAL, Colour

WHAT A CARRY ON

4/10/1973, 9pm
A Thames Television Production for ITV
50 minutes

Sid James	Barbara Windsor	Kenneth Connor
Peter Butterworth	Bernard Bresslaw	Jack Douglas

Introduced by..Shaw Taylor

CREW:

Programme Associate..Tony Hawes
Producer...Alan Tarrant
Director...Alan Tarrant

To celebrate the Capital's premiere of Carry On London, Shaw Taylor presented a special one hour programme live from the opening night. There he met the principal cast members and talked to them about the Carry Ons and what audiences flocking to the stage revue could expect from the team's first theatrical outing. The programme also featured a number of excerpts from the show's initial three week run at the Birmingham Hippodrome.

Taking up residence in the Victoria Palace's foyer, Taylor interviewed not just the cast of the show but eminent patrons attending the gala first night. Some UK newspapers questioned ITV's devoting an hour of its prime-time schedule to little more than a free advert but the Times, somewhat uncharacteristically, complained that a show as enticing as What a Carry On should be scheduled opposite a Diana Ross TV special on the BBC.

CARRY ON CHRISTMAS

24/12/1973, 9pm
A Thames Television Production for ITV
50 minutes

Sid James	Sid Belcher, Seed Pod, Sir Henry, Sergeant Ball, Robin Hood
Joan Sims	Mother, Senna Pod, Bishop's Wife, Adelle, Salvation Army Lady, Maid Marian, Traffic Warden
Barbara Windsor	Virginia, Crompet, Lady Frances, Fifi, Lady Fanny, Ballet Dancer
Kenneth Connor	Mr Sibley the Shop Manager, Anthro Pod, The Bishop, Private Parkin, Will Scarlet, Ballet Dancer
Peter Butterworth	Carol Singer (2001 BC), Ancient Gent, Darts Player, 2nd German Soldier, Friar Tuck, Ballet Dancer
Bernard Bresslaw	Bean Podkin, Darts Player, Captain Ffing-Burgh, Much, Police Officer, Ballet Dancer
Jack Douglas	Carol Singer (2001 BC), Crapper, 1st German Soldier, Alan A'Dale, Ballet Dancer

Julian Holloway............................Captain Rose
Laraine Humphrys.......................Bed Customer

CREW:

Screenplay...Talbot Rothwell
Choreographer..Terry Gilbert
Music Associate ....Norman Stevens
Designer..Allan Cameron
Producer..Gerald Thomas
Executive Producer ....Peter Rogers
Director...Ronald Fouracre

STORY:

Sid Belcher, a somewhat reluctant department store Father Christmas, tires of how commercial and cynical Christmas has become. Everyone he meets seems to have forgotten the true meaning of Christmas, leading Sid to reflect on how their ancestors must have celebrated the holidays in happier times:

2001 BC – The Pod family are getting ready for Christmas dinner. Father of the cave, Seed Pod brings home a Christmas present for his son, Bean – the lovely Crompet.

1759 – A group of aristocrats relax contentedly after Christmas dinner. Before bed, they decide to play a few festive party games - starting with postman's knock.

1917 – Christmas Eve in the trenches. Spirits are low until a couple of French ladies pay a visit followed closely by two German soldiers.

Carry On ballet – The team don their tutus for a gala performance of (inevitably) the Nutcracker Suite.

1172 – Sherwood Forest. Christmas for Robin Hood looks to be a miserable affair. The merry men have abandoned him and even Marian has gone home to her mother but things do start to look up when the Lady Frances appears.

REVIEW:

Unlike the previous year's somewhat stilted celebration, this final Carry On Christmas is a welcome return to form. Sid's department store Santa is the perfect framing device for a series of sketches which take a humorous look at Christmases past.

The 1973 special is a tremendously polished affair. The sets, created for sketches lasting just a few minutes each are sumptuously realised. The script bears all the trademark wit of Talbot Rothwell at his best with a heady mixture of comedic styles from Sid's leering at a worryingly young Barbara, through a few truly groan-inducing jokes and plenty of Rothwell's more sophisticated playfulness with language. After a couple of years of diminishing returns, the team really cracked the Christmas pantomime spirit with the last of their festive outings.

The style, in keeping with the Carry On films of the period, is far more raucous and saucy than earlier instalments but it still has all the charm and wit of the Carry Ons at their very best. The unlikely sketches are delivered with tremendous gusto; the whole team playing up to their ridiculous characters and the cheesiest of jokes.

The special ends with the team breaking character and wishing the audience in the studio – and at home – a happy Christmas. It's a lovely twist which rounds off a perfect festive treat.

AVAILABILITY

DVD:

Carry On Christmas
Fremantle Home Entertainment, 2006
PAL, Region 2 (Europe, Middle East & Japan), Black & White, Colour

VHS:

Carry On Christmas Capers
Cinema Club, 1996
PAL, Colour

CARRY ON LAUGHING

The Prisoner of Spenda
4/01/1975, 6.20pm
21 minutes
An ATV Networks Production for ITV

Sid James ....Prince Rupert & Arnold Basket
Barbara Windsor...Vera Basket
Joan Sims ....Madame Olga
Jack Douglas..Colonel Yackoff
Kenneth Connor ....Nickoff
Peter Butterworth..Count Yerackers
David Lodge ....Duke Boris
Diane Langton ....Tzana
Rupert Evans ....Major
Ronnie Brody...Waiter

CREW:

Screenplay ....Dave Freeman
Music...John Marshall & Richie Tattersall
Graphics...George Wallder
Animator...Len Lewis
Designer ....Stanley Mills
Executive Producer ....Peter Rogers
Producer...Gerald Thomas
Director..Alan Tarrant

STORY:

The Crown Price of Pluritania has gone missing and, if he is not found in time for his coronation, the evil Duke Boris will seize the throne. Count Yerackers and Colonel Yackoff plan to save the monarchy with a doppelganger of the missing prince, but all the lookalikes are safely in Duke Boris' dungeon, along with the prince himself. When newlyweds Arnold and Vera Basket arrive in Pluritania on their honeymoon Count Yerackers' luck changes because Arnold bears a striking resemblance to the missing prince. But the Count must get to him before the Duke does.

REVIEW:

As the title implies, Spenda is a lightweight pastiche of "The Prisoner of Zenda". The cast do their best to breathe life into the script but the whole production falls apart thanks to some terribly shoddy direction from no less than Alan Tarrant, the man behind countless comedy gems from Hancock to Gurney Slade. One can only assume that Tarrant had a bad run of off-days in the weeks that followed because, aside from a few moments of brilliance, Carry On Laughing is often uncomfortable to watch.

The studio audience barely manage an embarrassed titter once their initial appreciation for such a star cast has been replaced with a collective sense of "uh-oh". Before you know it, Barbara's cackling and Jack's going "whay!" They're familiar Carry On tricks but they are thrown into the script solely for that reason. The script has enough humour and a strong enough excuse for a story, but the direction is loose and unfocused. Opportunities for laughs are missed because the camera is rarely quite where it should be, or because the audience's occasional laughter has muffled a particularly choice line.

Sid James is particularly ill-served, playing a meek, even boring character which is far removed from his usual Carry On persona. Kenneth Connor doesn't really get to do much of anything and Barbara spends most of the episode in a full-on slapper mode. Of the regulars, only Jack Douglas, Peter Butterworth and Joan Sims emerge with their dignity intact but that's largely because they're restricted to playing their tried and tested archetypes from the films

Barbara says it best: "I wish somebody would explain what's happening".

AVAILABILITY
DVD:

Carry On Don't Lose your Head
ITV Studios Home Entertainment, 2003
PAL, Region 2 (Europe, Middle East & Japan), Colour
Special Features: Commentary (Jim Dale), Stills, Trivia, Trailer, Carry On Laughing – The Prisoner of Spenda

DeAgostini Carry On Collection – Carry On Laughing 4
DeAgostini/Carlton, 2003
PAL, Region 2

Carry On Laughing
A&E Home Video, 2004
NTSC, Region 1 (USA & Canada), Colour

VHS:

Carry On – The Prisoner of Spenda (w/ The Nine Old Cobblers, The Case of the Laughing Parrot)
ITC Entertainment, 1992
PAL, Colour

THE BARON OUTLOOK

11/01/1975, 6.20pm
ATV Networks Production for ITV
24 minutes

Sid James	Baron Hubert
Barbara Windsor	Marie
Joan Sims	Lady Isobel
Kenneth Connor	Sir Williams
Peter Butterworth	Friar Roger
David Lodge	Sir Simon de Montfort
Brian Osborne	Gaston
Diane Langton	Griselda
John Carlin	Ethelbert
Linda Hooks	Rosie
Anthony Trent	Herald
John Levene	Soldier

CREW:

Screenplay	Dave Freeman
Music	John Marshall & Richie Tattersall
Graphics	George Wallder
Animator	Len Lewis
Designer	Ray White
Executive Producer	Peter Rogers
Producer	Gerald Thomas
Director	Alan Tarrant

STORY:

The English have invaded France, but Sir Gaston de Lyon manages to escape by exchanging clothes with his busty page, Marie. Marie is captured and brought back to England, to be held prisoner at the Tower of Cleethorpes, under the protection of Baron Hubert FitzBovine. There, she will spend the rest of her days as a prisoner; at least until Baron Hubert discovers that she's really a woman.

REVIEW:

The moment John Levene appears and dead-pans the camera into submission, you know exactly what's in store for the next 25 minutes. I can't tell whether he was acting aloof or simply couldn't deliver the line, but it kills the entire episode dead before it's even had a chance to start. But while Levene is a sucking void of anti-sitcom, Barbara Windsor is in full-on pantomime mode, sticking out her chest and punctuating every line with that bloody laugh.

The pairing of Joan Sims and Sid James, this time in a more active leading role, works well and together, with the other more capable members of the cast, there is a lot of fun to be had in watching the old team. When Joan, Sid, Peter Butterworth and Kenneth Connor are together, it is a joy to watch – a momentary glimpse of greatness.

The comedy rendition of Greensleeves is a definite highlight but by the time we get around to Sid's hoofing version the joke has worn thin and becomes painfully obvious that they are just padding out a poorly written script.

Diane Langton, a graduate of the "big eyes, bust out" school of acting, hits her mark too early and has to stand there, absolutely still, waiting for Kenneth Connor to goose her, despite the fact that he's got at least a couple more lines to get through before he does.

The episode rounds off with Babs cackling like a demented harpy as she flaps her frontage in David Lodge's face. That sort of thing was never particularly funny in the films and that it's the "climax" of this TV episode goes to demonstrate how misjudged Carry On Laughing can be.

AVAILABILITY
DVD:

Carry On Doctor
ITV Studios Home Entertainment, 2003
PAL, Region 2 (Europe, Middle East & Japan), Colour
Special Features: Commentary (Jim Dale), Stills, Trivia, Trailer, Carry On Laughing – Baron Outlook

DeAgostini Carry On Collection – Carry On Laughing 4
DeAgostini/Carlton, 2003
PAL, Region 2

Carry On Laughing
A&E Home Video, 2004
NTSC, Region 1 (USA & Canada), Colour

VHS:

Carry On – The Screaming Winkles (The Baron Outlook, Lamp-Posts of the Empire, Short Knight, Long Daze)
ITC Entertainment, 1992
PAL, Colour

THE SOBBING CAVALIER

18/01/1975, 6.20pm
An ATV Networks Production for ITV
23 minutes

Sid James	Lovelace
Barbara Windsor	Sarah
Joan Sims	Lady Kate
Jack Douglas	Sir Jethro
Peter Butterworth	Oliver Cromwell
David Lodge	Colonel
Bernard Holley	Captain
Brian Osborne	Cavalier

CREW:

Screenplay ....Dave Freeman
Music ....John Marshall & Richie Tattersall
Graphics...George Wallder
Animator...Len Lewis
Designer ....Richard Lake
Executive Producer ....Peter Rogers
Producer...Gerald Thomas
Director...Alan Tarrant

STORY:

England is in the grip of Civil War and Oliver Cromwell is seizing the chattels of anyone who supports the monarchy. Unfortunately for the royalist, Sir Jethro, King Charles has similar plans for anyone supporting Cromwell.

REVIEW:

If your only exposure to the comedy world of Jack Douglas is Alf Ippititimus, then you're in for a pleasant surprise. Jack is magnificent when given a role in which he can act instead of just throwing shapes and shouting at the air.

Equally welcome are the old Carry On favourites as the episode opens with the heart-warming sight of Sid chasing Barbara around a table with some proper double entendre. It is brilliant; in fact, from the opening scenes it looks as though we could be in for a treat.

Sadly, any early promise of comedy gold is soon erased as the remainder of the episode is spent searching the house for Sid in an increasingly leaden romp. This is no Ray Cooney but it does serve to highlight the single most annoying thing about Carry On Laughing. The series has a cast of genuine 1970s superstars. They are all capable of delivering so much more if they are only given the right material which is where The Sobbing Cavalier fails in depressingly spectacular fashion. There simply isn't enough in the script to last the distance. It's repetitive and dull and a waste of the very talented people who made it.

AVAILABILITY
DVD:

Carry On up the Khyber
ITV Studios Home Entertainment, 2003
PAL, Region 2 (Europe, Middle East & Japan), Colour
Special Features: Commentary (Peter Rogers), Stills, Trivia, Trailer, Carry On Laughing – The Sobbing Cavalier

DeAgostini Carry On Collection – Carry On Laughing 4
DeAgostini/Carlton, 2003
PAL, Region 2

Carry On Laughing
A&E Home Video, 2004
NTSC, Region 1 (USA & Canada), Colour

VHS:

Carry On Kitchener (Who Needs Kitchener?, The Sobbing Cavalier, One in the Eye for Harold)
ITC Entertainment, 1992
PAL, Colour

ORGY AND BESS

25/01/1975, 6.20pm
An ATV Networks Production for ITV
24 minutes

Sid James	Sir Francis Drake
Hattie Jacques	Queen Elizabeth
Barbara Windsor	Lady Miranda
Jack Douglas	Master of the Rolls, Lord Essex
Kenneth Connor	King Philip
John Carlin	Sir Walter Raleigh
Norman Chappell	Lord Burleigh
Victor Maddern	Todd
McDonald Hobley	Quaker Reporter
Simon Callow	1st Crew Member
Brian Osborne	2nd Crew Member

CREW:

Screenplay	Barry Cryer and Dick Vosburgh
Music	John Marshall & Richie Tattersall
Graphics	George Wallder
Animator	Len Lewis
Designer	Richard Lake
Executive Producer	Peter Rogers
Producer	Gerald Thomas
Director	Alan Tarrant

STORY:

England is on the eve of war with Spain. Determined to avoid conflict, Good Queen Bess sends for the only man who can help: Sir Francis Drake.

REVIEW:

What's this? Barry Cryer and Dick Vosburgh? That is encouraging.

Suddenly, everything changes. Cryer and Vosburgh's script is a masterpiece that's absolutely jam-packed with gags, twists of language and innuendo. It's a real shock to the system after the last few episodes and you would be forgiven for thinking that ITV had stuck on a repeat of a Carry On film instead.

Then, to top it all, there's Hattie Jacques, who is just magnificent as Queen Elizabeth. Sid, as Drake, is firing all on all cannons, but the two of them together on the small screen with a script of this calibre is a sheer delight. From Sid's skipping up to the queen and greeting her with the words, "Getting any?" it is a relentless barrage of gags and there isn't a single dud among them.

Orgy & Bess is better than all the other Carry On Laughing episodes laid end-to-end and covered in chocolate. Hell, it's better than some of the films – a rare gem that almost, but not quite, makes the whole sorry effort of Carry On Laughing worthwhile.

AVAILABILITY
DVD:

Carry On up the Khyber
ITV Studios Home Entertainment, 2003
PAL, Region 2 (Europe, Middle East & Japan), Colour
Special Features: Commentary (Dilys Laye, Sandra Caron), Stills, Trivia, Trailer, Carry On Laughing – Orgy & Bess

DeAgostini Carry On Collection – Carry On Laughing 2
DeAgostini/Carlton, 2003
PAL, Region 2

Carry On Laughing
A&E Home Video, 2004
NTSC, Region 1 (USA & Canada), Colour

VHS:

Carry On – Orgy & Bess (w/ And In My Lady's Chamber, Under the Round Table)
ITC Entertainment, 1992
PAL, Colour

ONE IN THE EYE FOR HAROLD

1/02/1975, 6.20pm
An ATV Networks Production for ITV
24 minutes

Jack Douglas	Ethelred
Joan Sims	Else
Kenneth Connor	Athelstan
David Lodge	William the Conqueror
Norman Chappell	King Harold
John Carlin	Egbert
Diane Langton	Isolde
Patsy Smart	Old Hag
Brian Osborne	Herald - Knight
Paul Jesson	Messenger

Jerold Wells ....Black Cowl
Linda Hooks ....Nellie
Billy Cornelius ....Pikeman
Nosher Powell...Pikeman

CREW:

Screenplay ....Lew Schwarz
Music...John Marshall & Richie Tattersall
Graphics...George Wallder
Animator...Len Lewis
Designer..Ray White
Executive Producer ....Peter Rogers
Producer..Gerald Thomas
Director...Alan Tarrant

STORY:

It's 1066, and William the Conqueror is getting his troops ready to invade England. With the enemy on the shore, King Harold sends for his secret weapon.

REVIEW:

The less celebrated stars of the Carry On films get a tremendous chance to shine in Carry On Laughing. David Lodge's voice-over and asides to camera get the episode off to a cracking start and Norman Chappell delivers another great performance. John Carlin is also back, but sadly as a slightly less tiresome version of the camp stereotype that was the only sour note in Orgy & Bess.

One in the Eye for Harold is nowhere near as good as its predecessor but it is a cut above most of the other episodes. Sadly, once more the script runs out of ideas before the halfway mark and the remainder consists largely of Diane Langton sticking her chest so far out that she actually defies gravity.

The best part of the episode is when Joan Sims, wearing an alarmingly low-cut top, is trying to seduce Kenneth Connor with the aid of a medieval Mickey Finn. Otherwise the jokes are depressingly thin on the ground.

AVAILABILITY
DVD:

Carry On Again Doctor
ITV Studios Home Entertainment, 2003
PAL, Region 2 (Europe, Middle East & Japan), Colour
Special Features: Commentary (Jim Dale), Stills, Trivia, Trailer, Carry On Laughing – One in the Eye for Harold

DeAgostini Carry On Collection – Carry On Laughing 4
DeAgostini/Carlton, 2003
PAL, Region 2

Carry On Laughing

A&E Home Video, 2004
NTSC, Region 1 (USA & Canada), Colour

VHS:

Carry On Kitchener (Who Needs Kitchener?, The Sobbing Cavalier, One in the Eye for Harold)
ITC Entertainment, 1992
PAL, Colour

THE NINE OLD COBBLERS

8/02/1975, 6.20pm
An ATV Networks Production for ITV
24 minutes

Jack Douglas	Lord Peter Flimsy
Joan Sims	Amelia Forbush
Kenneth Connor	Punter
David Lodge	Inspector Bungler
John Carlin	Vicar
Victor Maddern	Charlie
Patsy Rowlands	Miss Dawkins
Barbara Windsor	Maisie

CREW:

Screenplay	Dave Freeman
Music	John Marshall & Richie Tattersall
Graphics	George Wallder
Animator	Len Lewis
Designer	Richard Lake
Camera	Jack Atchelor
Executive Producer	Peter Rogers
Producer	Gerald Thomas
Director	Alan Tarrant

STORY:

With just one day until the village show, the acts simply aren't ready. To make matters worse, Mr Longhammer dies on stage – literally. There is only one man who can solve the case – Lord Peter Flimsy.

REVIEW:

Joan Sims banging away on a drum kit and a welcome appearance of the lovely Patsy Rowlands are early signs that in the first of Carry On Laughing's Lord Peter Flimsy stories, things might be looking up. The Carry On team always excelled when it came to pastiches of other genres and their take on Dorothy L Sayers' famous detective is brilliantly observed. Jack Douglas and Kenneth Connor are a perfect double act as Lord Peter and his faithful manservant, Punter.

Much of the action takes place at the Jolly Woodman pub from Carry On Dick, where Barbara Windsor has been aged-up to play the elderly landlady. Barbara's great when performing a role that's not all breasts and giggles, so it's a welcome surprise to see her doing something new.

The Nine Old Cobblers is a very different production when compared to previous episodes. The setting is more modern, the pace more gentle and the comedy less forced. Dave Freeman's script is clever and amusing if not outright hilarious. It is certainly a cut above most of the Carry On Laughing episodes. The first series of Carry On Laughing ends on an unexpected high.

AVAILABILITY
DVD:

Carry On up the Jungle
ITV Studios Home Entertainment, 2003
PAL, Region 2 (Europe, Middle East & Japan), Colour
Special Features: Commentary (Jacki Piper, Valerie Leon), Stills, Trivia, Trailer, Carry On Laughing – The Nine Old Cobblers

DeAgostini Carry On Collection – Carry On Laughing 1
DeAgostini/Carlton, 2003
PAL, Region 2

Carry On Laughing
A&E Home Video, 2004
NTSC, Region 1 (USA & Canada), Colour

VHS:

Carry On – The Prisoner of Spenda (w/ The Nine Old Cobblers, The Case of the Laughing Parrot)
ITC Entertainment, 1992
PAL, Colour

UNDER THE ROUND TABLE

26/10/1975, 7.25pm
An ATV Networks Production for ITV
25 minutes

Joan Sims	Lady Guinevere
Bernard Bresslaw	Sir Pureheart
Jack Douglas	Sir Gay
Kenneth Connor	King Arthur
Peter Butterworth	Merlin

Oscar James .... Black Knight
Victor Maddern .... Sir Osis
Norman Chappell .... Sir William
Desmond McNamara.. Minstrel
Valerie Walsh.. Lady Ermintrude
Ronnie Brody.. Shortest Knight
Billy Cornelius .... Man-at-arms
Brian Osborne... Knight
Brian Capron .... Trumpeter

CREW:

Screenplay .... Lew Schwarz
Music.. John Marshall & Richie Tattersall
Graphics.. George Wallder
Animator.. Len Lewis
Designer .... Lewis Logan
Camera .... Mike Whitcutt
Sound.. Len Penfold
Wardrobe... James Dark
Make-Up... Sheila Mann
Lighting.. Pete Dyson
Vision Control .... Gerry Taylor
Vision Mixer.. Felicity Maton
VTR Editor .... Peter Charles
Executive Producer .... Peter Rogers
Producer.. Gerald Thomas
Director... Alan Tarrant

STORY:

Sir Pureheart bravely rescues King Arthur from the dreaded Black Knight and is rewarded with the leadership of the Knights of the Round Table. But Sir Pureheart's insistence on a vow of chastity causes unrest among the other knights and they hatch a plot to trick him into a night of passion.

REVIEW:

From the very first line, this one is a duffer. The script is devoid of anything which could remotely be described as comedy. Instead, it's simply a long string of tried, tested and tired double-entendres cast into a plot so wafer thin that by the end of the first scene you know this is going to be one of the longest half hours of your life. It goes nowhere and does nothing.

Bernard Bresslaw shouts so much that by the end of the first act you wish he had forgotten to turn up that day and poor old Joan Sims is forced to make arch asides to camera every time someone says a line which could possibly be misconstrued as a sexual reference. The situation isn't funny, the comedy is forced and the cast are, frankly, abused. It's horrible.

AVAILABILITY
DVD:

Carry On Loving
ITV Studios Home Entertainment, 2003
PAL, Region 2 (Europe, Middle East & Japan), Colour
Special Features: Commentary (Jacki Piper, Richard O'Callaghan), Stills, Trivia, Trailer,
Carry On Laughing – Under the Round Table

DeAgostini Carry On Collection – Carry On Laughing 2
DeAgostini/Carlton, 2003
PAL, Region 2

Carry On Laughing
A&E Home Video, 2004
NTSC, Region 1 (USA & Canada), Colour

VHS:

Carry On – Orgy & Bess (w/ And In My Lady's Chamber, Under the Round Table)
ITC Entertainment, 1992
PAL, Colour

THE CASE OF THE
SCREAMING WINKLES

2/11/1975, 7.25pm
An ATV Networks Production for ITV
24 minutes

Jack Douglas	Lord Peter Flimsy
Kenneth Connor	Punter
Joan Sims	Mrs MacFlute
Peter Butterworth	Admiral Clanger
David Lodge	Inspector Bungler
Sherrie Hewson	Nurse Millie Teazel
Norman Chappell	Potter
Marianne Stone	Madame Petra
Melvyn Hayes	Charwallah Charlie
John Carlin	Major Merridick
Michael Nightingale	Colonel Postwick

CREW:

Screenplay	Dave Freeman
Music	John Marshall & Richie Tattersall
Graphics	George Wallder
Animator	Len Lewis

Designer ....Lewis Logan
Camera ....Mike Whitcutt
Sound...Len Penfold
Wardrobe...James Dark
Make-Up...Sheila Mann
Lighting...Pete Dyson
Vision Control ....Gerry Taylor
Vision Mixer...Felicity Maton
VTR Editor ....Peter Charles
Executive Producer ....Peter Rogers
Producer...Gerald Thomas
Director...Alan Tarrant

STORY:

A luxurious country hotel is thrown into panic after a guest dies when he mistakenly eats the Admiral's dinner. It's up to master detective Lord Peter Flimsy to crack the case.

REVIEW:

Dave Freeman excels in the Peter Flimsy stories and we are treated to a further half hour of deliciously saucy word play, misdirection and fun. Not a single line is wasted and Freeman throws in plenty of linguistic googlies for the cast to get their teeth into; at times it's almost as if he's trying to catch them out. There's plenty of broader comedy, too and the Benny Hill-like final scenes in the haunted house are as out of place as they are funny.

AVAILABILITY
DVD:

Carry On Henry
ITV Studios Home Entertainment, 2003
PAL, Region 2 (Europe, Middle East & Japan), Colour
Special Features: Commentary (Jacki Piper, Richard O'Callaghan), Stills, Trivia, Trailer, Carry On Laughing – The Case of the Screaming Winkles

DeAgostini Carry On Collection – Carry On Laughing 1
DeAgostini/Carlton, 2003
PAL, Region 2

Carry On Laughing
A&E Home Video, 2004
NTSC, Region 1 (USA & Canada), Colour

VHS:

Carry On – The Screaming Winkles (w/ The Baron Outlook, Lamp-Posts of the Empire, Short Knight, Long Daze)
ITC Entertainment, 1992
PAL, Colour

AND IN MY LADY'S CHAMBER

9/11/1975, 7.25pm
An ATV Networks Production for ITV
25 minutes

Kenneth Connor	Sir Harry
Barbara Windsor	Lottie
Joan Sims	Mrs Breeches
Jack Douglas	Clodson
Bernard Bresslaw	Starkers
Andrew Ray	Willie
Peter Butterworth	Silas
Carol Hawkins	Lilly
Sherrie Hewson	Virginia
Vivienne Johnson	Teeny

CREW:

Screenplay	Lew Schwarz
Music	John Marshall, Richie Tattersall & Max Harris
Graphics	George Wallder
Animator	Len Lewis
Designer	Brian Holgate
Camera	Mike Whitcutt
Sound	Len Penfold
Wardrobe	James Dark
Make-Up	Sheila Mann
Lighting	Pete Dyson
Vision Control	Jim Reeves
Vision Mixer	Caroline Legg
Executive Producer	Peter Rogers
Producer	Gerald Thomas
Director	Alan Tarrant

STORY:

Willy Bulger-Plunger has returned from the Amazon and his father, Sir Harry, plans a lavish dinner in celebration. But Willy hasn't come alone.

REVIEW:

Another much-loved series gets the Carry On treatment in this sideways glance at "Upstairs Downstairs". Schwarz' typically lumpy dialogue and an enormous dollop of unnecessary exposition set the scene for a domestic play of a stranger arriving from a strange land and the comedy of errors that inevitably ensues.

Except that there is nothing inevitable about the comedy in this episode. As Mrs Britches and Clodson, Joan Sims and Jack Douglas do their best, but faced with a script so bluntly monotonous you wouldn't blame them for just shrugging their shoulders and walking off camera. Barbara Windsor is back in full shriek as the Baroness von Titzenhausen but she's far from the worst thing about this shockingly delivered episode. From the endless jibes about the name "TItzenhausen" (there aren't as many as you might think but Lew Schwarz would beg to differ) to the constant verbal confusion of Amazon/St Albans, this is just another shouting, awkward mess.

AVAILABILITY
DVD:

Carry On Matron
ITV Studios Home Entertainment, 2003
PAL, Region 2 (Europe, Middle East & Japan), Colour
Special Features: Commentary (Jacki Piper, Valerie Leon, Patsy Rowlands), Stills, Trivia, Trailer, Carry On Laughing – And in my Lady's Chamber

DeAgostini Carry On Collection – Carry On Laughing 3
DeAgostini/Carlton, 2003
PAL, Region 2

Carry On Laughing
A&E Home Video, 2004
NTSC, Region 1 (USA & Canada), Colour

VHS:

Carry On – Orgy & Bess (w/ And In My Lady's Chamber, Under the Round Table)
ITC Entertainment, 1992
PAL, Colour

SHORT KNIGHT, LONG DAZE

16/11/1975, 7.25pm
An ATV Networks Production for ITV
25 minutes

Joan Sims	Lady Guinevere
Bernard Bresslaw	Sir Lancelot
Jack Douglas	Sir Gay
Kenneth Connor	King Arthur
Peter Butterworth	Merlin
Norman Chappell	Sir William
Brian Osborne	Herald - Knight
Desmond McNamara	Minstrel
Susan Skipper	Mabel
Billy Cornelius	Man-at-arms
Brian Capron	Trumpeter

CREW:

Screenplay ....Lew Schwarz
Music ....John Marshall, Richie Tattersall
& Max Harris
Graphics ....George Wallder
Animator ....Len Lewis
Designer ....Brian Holgate
Camera ....Mike Whitcutt
Sound ....Len Penfold
Wardrobe ....James Dark
Make-Up ....Sheila Mann
Lighting ....Pete Dyson
Vision Control ....Jim Reeves
Vision Mixer ....Caroline Legg
Designer ....Brian Holgate
Camera ....Mike Whitcutt
Sound ....Len Penfold
Wardrobe ....James Dark
Make-Up ....Sheila Mann
Lighting ....Pete Dyson
Vision Control ....Jim Reeves
Vision Mixer ....Caroline Legg
VTR Editor ....Peter Charles
Executive Producer ....Peter Rogers
Producer ....Gerald Thomas
Director ....Alan Tarrant

STORY:

King Arthur is penniless. His coffers are empty and he desperately needs to raise funds. Lady Guinevere comes over all queer and prophesies that a mysterious stranger will come to Camelot and transform the King's fortunes.

COMMENTS:

We return once more to the court of King Arthur for a blatant re-tread of Under the Round Table. You can't help but feel sorry for Jack Douglas, who is forced to sling on a pair of yellow tights and camp it up again, misconstruing every line that comes his way in the hope of squeezing a laugh out of Schwarz's dismal attempts at humour.

Many of the gags come from plays on the word "Knight": You know, "night"? You can almost hear old Lew chuckling away at that one. Joan Sims delivers every line with a wicked sparkle in her eye but the rest of the cast don't appear to be particularly bothered and, honestly, neither should you.

AVAILABILITY
DVD:

Carry On Abroad
ITV Studios Home Entertainment, 2003
PAL, Region 2 (Europe, Middle East & Japan), Colour
Special Features: Commentary (John Clive, Sally Geeson, Carol Hawkins, David Kernan), Stills, Trivia, Trailer, Carry On Laughing – Short Knight, Long Daze

DeAgostini Carry On Collection – Carry On Laughing 2
DeAgostini/Carlton, 2003
PAL, Region 2

Carry On Laughing
A&E Home Video, 2004
NTSC, Region 1 (USA & Canada), Colour

VHS:

Carry On – The Screaming Winkles (w/ The Baron Outlook, Lamp-Posts of the Empire, Short Knight, Long Daze)
ITC Entertainment, 1992
PAL, Colour

THE CASE OF THE COUGHING PARROT

23/11/1975, 7.25pm
An ATV Networks Production for ITV
24 minutes

Jack Douglas	Lord Peter Flimsy
Kenneth Connor	Punter
Joan Sims	Dr Janis Crunbitt
David Lodge	Inspector Bungler
Peter Butterworth	Lost Property Attendant
Sherrie Hewson	Irma Klein
Vivienne Johnson	Freda Filey
Norman Chappell	Ambulance Driver
Brian Osborne	Harry
Johnny Briggs	Norman

CREW:

Screenplay	Dave Freeman
Music	John Marshall, Richie Tattersall & Max Harris
Designer	Anthony Waller
Graphics	George Wallder
Animator	Len Lewis
Camera	Mike Whitcutt
Sound	Len Penfold

Wardrobe .... James Dark
Make-Up .... Sheila Mann
Lighting .... Pete Dyson
Vision Control .... Jim Reeves
Vision Mixer .... Mary Forrest
VTR Editor .... Peter Charles
Executive Producer .... Peter Rogers
Producer .... Gerald Thomas
Director .... Alan Tarrant

STORY:

Dr Janis Crunbitt takes delivery of the mummy of King Ramitupem but when she opens the casket she discovers a murdered body inside. Meanwhile, Lord Peter Flimsy and his faithful retainer, Punter, stumble across a mummified body in the London fog and decide to investigate.

REVIEW:

Lew Schwarz forgets to set his alarm clock and we welcome back Dave Freeman, Lord Peter Flimsy and Punter in another pastiche of Dorothy L Sayers' aristocratic detective.

Once again Freeman's gentler style of writing provides plenty of opportunities for humour in a script which delivers both an engaging story and enough giggles, if not outright laughs, to keep you interested for the full 24 minutes. Building on the lyrical terrorism of Freeman's previous Lord Peter episodes, this time the writer exercises his love of limericks, with some deliciously naughty rhymes. It's a long-overdue respite from the dross of so many of the other episodes.

AVAILABILITY

DVD:

Carry On Dick
ITV Studios Home Entertainment, 2003
PAL, Region 2 (Europe, Middle East & Japan), Colour
Special Features: Commentary (Jack Douglas), Stills, Trivia, Trailer, Carry On Laughing – The Case of the Coughing Parrot

DeAgostini Carry On Collection – Carry On Laughing 1
DeAgostini/Carlton, 2003
PAL, Region 2

Carry On Laughing
A&E Home Video, 2004
NTSC, Region 1 (USA & Canada), Colour

VHS:

Carry On – The Prisoner of Spenda (w/ The Nine Old Cobblers, The Case of the Laughing Parrot)
ITC Entertainment, 1992
PAL, Colour

WHO NEEDS KITCHENER?

30/11/1975, 7.25pm
An ATV Networks Production for ITV
25 minutes

Kenneth Connor ....Sir Harry
Barbara Windsor..Lottie
Joan Sims ....Mrs Breeches
Jack Douglas...Clodson
Bernard Bresslaw ....Klanger
Andrew Ray..Willie
Sherrie Hewson...Virginia
Carol Hawkins...Lilly
Vivienne Johnson ....Teeny
Brian Osborne...Newsboy

CREW:

Screenplay..Lew Schwarz
Music...John Marshall & Richie Tattersall
Graphics...George Wallder
Animator...Len Lewis
Designer..Anthony Waller
Camera ....Mike Whitcutt
Sound...Len Penfold
Wardrobe..James Dark
Make-Up..Sheila Mann
Lighting..Pete Dyson
Vision Control ....Jim Reeves
Vision Mixer...Marry Forrest
VTR Editor ....Peter Charles
Executive Producer ....Peter Rogers
Producer...Gerald Thomas
Director...Alan Tarrant

STORY:

It is the eve of the First World War and the new General of the Bootlaces, Sir Harry, is determined to do his bit for King and Country. But there's something not quite right about his new butler. Meanwhile, the womenfolk have a war of their own to fight as they campaign for equal rights.

REVIEW:

We are back in the world of Upstairs Downstairs once more for an almost identical story to the last time we visited. This week Bernard Bresslaw is playing the stranger in a strange land and his thinly disguised German spy is the sole glimmer of fun in an episode which goes nowhere and delivers nothing of any value, comedic or otherwise.

If you want to know what the episode is like, read the review of And in my Lady's Chamber because it is identical in almost every way. As wonderful as Bresslaw is, it's simply not worth sitting through this rubbish solely for the odd moment when he lifts the episode out of the gutter.

AVAILABILITY
DVD:

Carry On Behind
ITV Studios Home Entertainment, 2003
PAL, Region 2 (Europe, Middle East & Japan), Colour
Special Features: Commentary (Larry Dann, Jack Douglas, Dave Freeman, Patsy Rowlands), Stills, Trivia, Trailer, Carry On Laughing – Who Needs Kitchener?

DeAgostini Carry On Collection – Carry On Laughing 3
DeAgostini/Carlton, 2003
PAL, Region 2

Carry On Laughing
A&E Home Video, 2004
NTSC, Region 1 (USA & Canada), Colour

VHS:

Carry On Kitchener (Who Needs Kitchener?, The Sobbing Cavalier, One in the Eye for Harold)
ITC Entertainment, 1992
PAL, Colour

LAMP POSTS OF THE EMPIRE

7/12/1975, 7.25pm
An ATV Networks Production for ITV
24 minutes

Barbara Windsor	Lady Mary
Kenneth Connor	Stanley
Jack Douglas	Dick Darcy
Bernard Bresslaw	Doctor Pavingstone
Peter Butterworth	Lord Gropefinger
Oscar James	Witchdoctor
Norman Chappell	Businessman
John Carlin	Old Man
Michael Nightingale	Neighbour
Reuben Martin	Mabel
Wayne Browne	Native

CREW:

Screenplay	Lew Schwarz
Music	John Marshall & Richie Tattersall

Graphics	George Wallder
Animator	Len Lewis
Designer	Anthony Waller
Camera	Mike Whitcutt
Sound	Len Penfold
Wardrobe	James Dark
Make-Up	Sheila Mann
Lighting	Pete Dyson
Vision Control	Jim Reeves
Vision Mixer	Marry Forrest
VTR Editor	Peter Charles
Executive Producer	Peter Rogers
Producer	Gerald Thomas
Director	Alan Tarrant

STORY:

The Bermondsey Universal Geographical Society (BUGS) has launched an expedition to rescue Dr Pavingstone, who disappeared while on an expedition to the jungle. But the natives aren't exactly friendly and they have quite a few nasty tricks up their sleeve.

REVIEW:

Things get off to a decorous start with the starched upper lips of Butterworth, Connor and even Barbara holding down the fort until Jack Douglas destroys all the goodwill he has built up over previous episodes by literally crashing in as Alf.

Lew Schwarz appears to have recently watched Carry On up the Jungle and tries to deliver his own take on the film, but Lamp Posts rapidly disappears up its own oozlum. It's not as screechy as his previous episodes but it does share the same paucity of gags and it's more than a tiny bit racist. Lamp Posts of the Empire is offensive in every conceivable way and, like the rest of Schwarz' episodes, it's better to pretend that it simply didn't happen.

AVAILABILITY

DVD:

That's Carry On
ITV Studios Home Entertainment, 2003
PAL, Region 2 (Europe, Middle East & Japan), Colour
Special Features: Commentary (Peter Rogers), Stills, Trivia, Trailer, Carry On Laughing – Lamp Posts of the Empire

DeAgostini Carry On Collection – Carry On Laughing 3
DeAgostini/Carlton, 2003
PAL, Region 2

Carry On Laughing
A&E Home Video, 2004
NTSC, Region 1 (USA & Canada), Colour

VHS:

Carry On – The Screaming Winkles (w/ The Baron Outlook, Lamp-Posts of the Empire, Short Knight, Long Daze)
ITC Entertainment, 1992
PAL, Colour

ELECTRIC THEATRE SHOW – CARRY ON ENGLAND

10/1976 (Regional variations)
Grampian Television
25 minutes

Gerald Thomas	Kenneth Connor	Windsor Davies
Jack Douglas	Patrick Mower	Judy Geeson
Joan Sims	Melvyn Hayes	

CREW:

Writer ....John Doran
Producer..John Doran

    A selection of classic Carry On clips bookend this unique insight into the filming of Carry On England. Gerald Thomas, Kenneth Connor, Windsor Davies, Jack Douglas and Joan Sims talk enthusiastically about their time in the Carry On films while other cast members drift in and out of shot, causing mischief. The team are in high spirits as they lark about behind the scenes and while it's not a particularly revealing documentary the charm is in seeing our beloved team out of character.

CARRY ON COMPILATIONS

With no Carry On films in the pipeline following the box office disappointments of Carry On England and Carry On Emmannuelle, Peter Rogers' idea of emulating EMI's "That's Entertainment" had a dual effect. Not only did it remind cinemagoers that over the past 20 or more years the Carry Ons enjoyed box office glory and earned the love of generations, it also put the thought into cinema-goers' heads that the films were a thing of the past. People stopped asking when the next Carry On film was coming out and as a going concern, the franchise went quiet.

But the frequent and regular repeats of the films on television were gaining the Carry Ons a whole new audience and while there was little prospect of a new Carry On film being made any time in the near future, That's Carry On and the viewing figures earned by the films on TV clearly showed that audiences were just as happy, if not more so, watching the old classics again and again.

CARRY ON LAUGHING

31/12/1981
Peter Rogers Productions for Thames Television
13x25 minutes

Editor...Gerald Thomas
Producer..Peter Rogers
Director...Gerald Thomas

A Carry On clip show was a cheap way of selling the films back to audiences all over again, but compiling such a project would take time. Gerald Thomas spent months locked away in the Pinewood vaults selecting the best clips from the films and packaged them up as a series of thirteen 25 minute episodes.

Financial concerns meant that Carry On Laughing would only draw from the Rank Carry Ons, but that didn't matter to television audiences. One early episode was watched by over 14 million viewers and as much as two years later, repeats of Carry On Laughing compilations were still regularly getting over 10 million viewers.

AVAILABILITY
VHS:

Carry On Laughing-Medical Madness
Cinema Club, 1991
PAL, Colour, 93 minutes

Carry On Laughing – Hysterical History
Cinema Club, 1991
PAL, Colour, 92 minutes

Carry On Laughing – Hilarious Holidays
Cinema Club, 1991
PAL, Colour, 90 minutes

CARRY ON LAUGHING'S CHRISTMAS CLASSICS

22 December 1983, 7.30pm
A Thames Television Production for ITV
24 minutes

Kenneth Williams   Barbara Windsor

CREW:

Original Material .... Talbot Rothwell, Dave Freeman
Editor.. Jack Gardner
Production Designer.. Bill Laslett
Production Assistant .... Caroline Hahn
Producer.. Gerald Thomas
Director.. David Clark

The repeats of the films and the Carry On Laughing compilations were, even in 1983, event television. The compilation shown on 9th May 1983 was the ninth most watched programme on TV that week. When building its Christmas schedules for 1983, ITV approached Peter Rogers with the idea of a special episode of Carry On Laughing; one which would feature at least some new material. Kenneth Williams and Barbara Windsor were lured into the studio to present the links between the clips while reminiscing about the films in much the same way as they had in That's Carry On.

WHAT A CARRY ON!

9/11/1984
Peter Rogers Productions for BBC1
13x25 minutes

CREW:

Editor... Gerald Thomas
Producer.. Peter Rogers
Director.. Gerald Thomas

A second series of classic Carry On clips was made, this time for the BBC. Premiering in November 1984, the format of What a Carry On! was identical to the ITV series, and it went on to enjoy similar success. Together, these two compilations became a regular fixture on TV during the 1980s, first as prime-time viewing and later, as the decade wore on, seemingly as random schedule-fillers.

LAUGH WITH THE CARRY ONS

23/05/1993
Peter Rogers Productions for Central Independent Television
13x25 minutes

CREW:

Editor...Gerald Thomas
Producer...Peter Rogers
Director..Gerald Thomas

The box office success of Carry On Columbus in 1992 was a reminder to broadcasters that the Carry Ons were still very much the people's favourite comedy series. A third Carry On clip show was produced by Central Television in 1993, drawing on both the Rank and Anglo-Amalgamated films. Laugh with the Carry Ons was broadcast between May and August 1993 and, like its predecessors, was a regular schedule-filler long after its initial airing.

NORBERT SMITH: A LIFE

3/11/1989, 10.30pm
Hat Trick Productions for Channel 4
50 minutes

Harry Enfield...Norbert Smith
Melvyn Bragg...Himself
Kenneth Connor ....Greenham Officer
Jack Douglas...Greenham Guard
Barbara Windsor...Greenham Women's Leader

CREW:

Writer ....Harry Enfield, Geoffrey Perkins
Production Design...Graeme Story
Original Music..David Firman
Executive Producer ....Denise O'Donoghue
Producer...Geoffrey Perkins
Director..Geoff Posner

Harry Enfield's spoof documentary traces the life and career of the legendary and entirely fictitious actor, Sir Norbert Smith (Harry Enfield). The programme is presented in the style of the now-defunct ITV arts programme, The South Bank Show, with presenter Melvyn Bragg interviewing Sir Norbert at his home and chronicling a career which encompasses every genre of British film.

Sir Norbert's reminiscences are accompanied by spoofs of a number of great films including the works of Will Hay (Oh, Mr Bankrobber), Hamlet (as told by Noel Coward), Brief Encounter (actually an advert for soap powder) and, of course, the Carry On films.

Carry On Banging lasts just over two minutes but in that time it manages to perfectly recapture the old Carry On magic in a beautifully observed sketch which is both an affectionate tribute to the films and a pretty accurate recreation of what made them so special in the first place.

Barbara Windsor is the leader of a group of protestors camped outside Greenham Common air base and comes face to face with a less than competent bunch of soldiers guarding the entrance to the camp, played by Enfield, Jack Douglas and Kenneth Connor.

AVAILABILITY
VHS:

Norbert Smith: A Life
Polygram, 1991
PAL, Colour

CHANNEL 4 CARRY ON WEEKEND

29/08/1998 - 31/08/1998
Channel 4

The Carry Ons celebrated their 40th anniversary in 1998. By then, the likelihood of a new Carry On film ever being made was next to nothing and, while the public looked back on the films with affection, there was a definite sense that Carry On Columbus had put paid to any idea of them ever returning to cinema screens.

The nostalgia TV industry was getting into its stride by the late '90s and, almost 40 years to the day that Carry On Sergeant was released in the cinemas, Channel 4 hosted a weekend of Carry On films and newly commissioned documentaries to celebrate (or so we were led to believe) Britain's favourite comedy team.

A PERFECT CARRY ON

30/08/98, 9pm
A Tiger Aspect Production for Channel 4
51 minutes

Introduced by..Barbara Windsor
Producer...Rory Sheehan
Director..Rory Sheehan
Executive Producer ....Clive Tulloh

What makes a perfect Carry On? That's the question behind this hour-long romp through the Carry On archive as Barbara Windsor and a bevy of luvvies try to define the formula that made the Carry On films such an important part of the British comedy landscape. Overall, it's a lightweight attempt at a Carry On tribute and while the talking heads offer nothing insightful, they are accompanied by a great selection of clips.

CARRY ON SNOGGING

30/08/1998, 10pm
A Yorkshire Television Production for Channel 4
25 minutes

Producer...Gabrielle Osrin
Director..Gabrielle Osrin
Executive Producer ....Chris Bryer

It's impossible to talk about Carry On Snogging without first mentioning the BBC television series, "The Rock & Roll Years", where old newsreels from a particular year were spliced together accompanied by a soundtrack of that year's most popular hits. Carry On Snogging takes the same idea and presents the news and events of the times when the Carry Ons were delighting audiences for the first time. It is an entertaining glimpse at the way the films reflected our changing culture, but it is told from the inside out and offers no real insight into the films or how they were made.

CARRY ON DARKLY

31/08/1998, 9pm
A Blackwatch Production for Channel 4
51 minutes

Producer...Nicola Black
Director..Paul Gallagher

Carry On Darkly was billed as a frank and occasionally shocking look at the private lives of four of the Carry On films' main contributors.

The programme opens with:

"The four men most associated with the Carry Ons were Kenneth Williams, Charles Hawtrey, Sid James and Frankie Howerd - four men whose deficiencies included promiscuity, wife beating, compulsive gambling and chronic alcoholism; four men whose dark and troubled lives informed their characters."

From there on it's steadily downhill. Carry On Darkly is the antithesis of the celebrated "Heroes of Comedy" documentaries of the time and focuses exclusively on the negative press that the Carry On team garnered during their career. A collection of famous fans tell their favourite anecdotes about the celebrities while archive footage and a general sense of mean-spiritedness demonstrate how wrong they are and that the team are, in fact, philanderers, repressed homosexuals and wife-abusers.

WHAT'S A CARRY ON?

29/12/1998, 10.35pm
A British Film Corporation production for Carlton
51 minutes

Producers ....John Bishop & Chris Skinner
Director:..John Highlander

While earlier celebrations of the Carry Ons' 40th anniversary ended on a sour note, What's a Carry On? is a welcome reminder that behind all the scandal the Carry Ons themselves had lost none of their shine.

What's A Carry On? is a breakneck tour of the films together with interviews of the surviving team members and fans, a visit to some of the series' most memorable locations and an affectionate, un-sensationalised look at why we love the films and the people who made them.

AVAILABILITY

DVD:

Carry On Emmannuelle
ITV Studios Home Entertainment, 2003
PAL, Region 2 (Europe, Middle East & Japan), Colour
Special Features: Commentary (Larry Dann, Jack Douglas), Stills, Trivia, Trailer, What's a Carry On? (50m version)

VHS:

What's a Carry On?
Carlton, 2000
PAL, Colour, 51m

ON LOCATION: THE CARRY ONS

2000
Carlton Cinema
25 minutes

Originally shown on the digital channel Carlton Cinema and now available on the special edition DVD of "Carry On Girls", On Location offers a surprisingly detailed look at some of the locations used in the making of the Carry On films. June Whitfield is our host and as she strolls around some familiar sites, she reminisces about her co-stars and the films they made together. Key locations in the documentary include Waddesdon Manor (Don't Lose your Head), Brighton (At your Convenience, Girls) and a variety of locations in and around Pinewood.

AVAILABILITY
DVD:

Carry On Girls
ITV Studios Home Entertainment, 2003
PAL, Region 2 (Europe, Middle East & Japan), Colour
Special Features: Commentary (Jack Douglas, Patsy Rowlands, June Whitfield), Stills, Trivia, Trailer, On Location – the Carry Ons

COR BLIMEY!

2/04/2000, 9pm
ITV Networks
95 minutes

Geoffrey Hutchings	Sid
Adam Godley	Kenneth
Samantha Spiro	Babs
Jacqueline Defferary	Sally
Kenneth MacDonald	Eddie
Barbara Windsor	Herself
Chrissie Cotteril	Joan Sims
Steve Spiers	Bernard Bresslaw
Hugh Walters	Charles Hawtrey
Derek Howard	Kenneth Connor
David McAlister	Gerald Thomas
Hetty Baynes	Maggie
Louise Delamere	Imogen
Alan Barnes	First AD
Peter Yapp	Cameraman
Maria Charles	Charlie's Mum
Richard Vanstone	Alf
Claire Cathcart	Matron
Abigail McKern	Olga
Barbara Kirby	June
Kellie Bright	Viola
Alan Cox	Orsino
Windsor Davies	Sir Tony Belch
Alice Bailey Johnson	Alice

CREW:

Producer	Margaret Mitchell
Executive Producers	Charlie Pattinson, George Faber, Suzan Harrison
Written & directed by	Terry Johnson

STORY:

Terry Johnson's 1998 play, "Cleo, Camping, Emmanuelle & Dick" was a critical and commercial hit. It told an intimate tale of an ageing lead who tries for one last fling. This remarkably sensitive story managed to pay tribute to its subjects in an entirely unexpected way - in the style of the Carry On films themselves. The play went on to win the 1999 Olivier Award for Best New Comedy and continues to tour provincial theatres to this day.

Cor Blimey! premiered on the ITV network on Monday 24 April, 2000. Like its theatrical predecessor, Cor Blimey! is a charming (but even more speculative) drama about the lives and loves of the Carry On stars.

The film opens at Pinewood studios during the filming of Carry On Cleo as the cast and crew take a well-earned lunch break. Young Barbara is the latest starlet to join the Carry On team and the moment he claps eyes on her, Sid falls hopelessly in love. Over the course of the next few years and several Carry Ons, we explore the relationships between Sid, Barbara and Kenneth as they grow older, wiser and ever more aware that there's never a better moment than right now to try and grab some happiness in life. Sid's infatuation with Barbara becomes an obsession in the intervening years and finally, during the filming of Carry On Girls, Barbara decides she cannot fend off his advances any longer. The pair fall into each other's arms and they begin a torrid affair which will ultimately threaten to destroy both their lives.

REVIEW:

Ten years on and I'm still not sure what to make of Cor Blimey! It's beautifully made, treating the films with the same fondness its audience has for them and even at its most scandalous the film remains sympathetic to the actors upon whom the main characters are based. It also boasts a truly astounding set of performances from a cast who bring the Carry On team to life with impersonations ranging from the brilliant to the downright eerie.

But Cor Blimey! takes the basic idea of its theatrical predecessor and pushes the story even further. It is an extremely biased, even sensationalised view of the relationships between Sid, Kenneth and Barbara; a view which places the actress at the centre of both men's lives. Her relationship with Sid is one of tragic obsession while her friendship with Kenneth becomes the emotional crutch that supports the actor through the final years of his life. I'm not saying any of these things are untrue, but in places they contradict accounts from other Carry On team members and indeed, Barbara Windsor's first autobiography "The Laughter and Tears of a Cockney Sparrow". Barbara is the heart of the film; a fact brought so clumsily home by having the real Barbara Windsor appear at the end, playing herself as she looks back, doe-eyed at her former life and loves.

In making Barbara the central figure in the lives of the Carry On team we are presented with a story which significantly re-writes the biographies of some of its most beloved members. Sid and Kenneth are not the only victims in this piece. Kenneth Connor is shown to be a sad, almost perverse little loner and yet those who knew him tell a very different story of the Kenneth Connor who was a happy and generous family man. Most damning of all, Hattie Jacques is ignored completely. There is something vital missing from this Carry On film – its biggest female star. Only the most cynical person would suggest that there is an obvious reason for that.

As a fiction, which is the only level it can ever truly be judged, Cor Blimey! is a bittersweet portrayal of love in its many forms and how it can both save and destroy lives. As a lasting account of what went on behind the scenes of our favourite films, it's something else entirely.

AVAILABILITY
DVD:

Cor Blimey!
BFS Entertainment, 2001
PAL, Region 0 (Only available in Canada), Colour

CAN WE CARRY ON GIRLS?

5/09/2001, 9pm
A Blackwatch Production for Channel 4
50 minutes

Producer..Nicola Black
Director...Paul Gallagher

The production team behind this mud-slinging 1998 spite-umentary "Carry On Darkly" returned to Pinewood with a documentary looking at the way women were portrayed in the Carry Ons. Were they all just tarts, battle-axes and bimbos? According to the female commentators of Can we Carry On Girls? the women in the Carry Ons were anything but.

They were certainly sex objects but they were also the films' most powerful characters. Contributors reminisce about seeing characters like Barbara on screen and realising that that was what "sexy" meant and about how they were inspired to enter show-business by the strong female characters in the Carry On films. The topic of sexism in the Carry Ons had never been seriously talked about before and Can we Carry On Girls? takes a refreshingly open approach to a fascinating subject.

CARRY ON IN RUDE HEALTH

3/05/2009, 5.55pm
BBC2
5 minutes

Narrator...Jessica Hynes
Producer..Robin Keam

Carry On in Rude Health is an all-too-brief look at the how the Carry On films contributed to the general level of rudeness in Britain. In 2007, the BBC produced a multi-part documentary series on British cinema called "British Film Forever". One episode of that series focused on British comedies and of course the Carry Ons featured heavily. Carry On in Rude Health is a collection of the choicest morsels from the Carry On interviews featured in "British Film Forever" packaged into a delightful five minute summation of what makes the films so special.

GREATEST EVER CARRY ON FILMS

27/12/2011, 10.05pm
An ITV Studios production for Channel 5
50 minutes

Producer...Richard Mortimer
Director..Richard Mortimer

Channel 5's Christmas 2011 Carry On night featured repeats of the 1969 Carry On Christmas and Cor Blimey! Sandwiched between the two was a new documentary which highlighted 10 of the best Carry On films. Former stars, fans and the author of this very book talked affectionately about their favourite Carry On moments. Quite how the top 10 films were chosen remains something of a mystery but the programme cannot be faulted for the affection and enthusiasm with which the films are discussed.

CARRY ON RADIO
CARRY ON UP YER CINDERS

22/12/1990
BBC Radio
29 minutes

Julian Clary	Kenneth Williams as Cinderella
Jonathan Ross	Frankie Howerd as an Ugly Sister
Frankie Howerd	Frankie Howerd as the other Ugly Sister
Claire Rayner	Hattie Jacques as the Fairy Godmother
Arthur Smith	Sid James as Prince Charming
Barbara Windsor	Jim Dale as Buttons
Ned Sherrin	Himself
Rory Bremner	Everyone else

Loose Ends' festive celebration in 1990 was a star-studded retelling of Cinderella with a Carry On twist. In keeping with Loose Ends' usual format, the pantomime was deliberately low-budget and broad, with piped-in audience participation (invariably scathing about the programme and those in it). It's hard to be too cynical about what is intended as a bit of fun, but it's a dreadfully unfunny programme. While it's easy enough to tell the real Frankie Howerd from the Jonathan Ross impersonation, the two talk over each other so much that it's hard to keep up with the banter. Barbara is simply there to cackle whenever there's a lull in the action and the rest of the cast spend far too much time enjoying themselves with their excruciating impersonations to worry about what the audience might make of it all.

CARRY ON CARRYING ON

29/08/1994
BBC Radio 2
60 minutes

Narrator	Fenella Fielding
Researched & Written by	Ross Smith
Production Assistant	Janet Littlechild
Producer	Barry Littlechild

In 1994, Fenella Fielding presented an hour long tribute to the long running Carry On series, joined by Peter Rogers and surviving members of the Carry On team, including Barbara Windsor and Jack Douglas, with archive contributions from the rest of the gang. The programme took a chronological journey through the Carry On films, highlighting key moments from every film from Sergeant to Columbus. Carry On Carrying On was dedicated to Gerald Thomas, who died during the making of the programme.

THE CARRY ON CLAN

Or

WE STARTED AT THE BOTTOM AND STAYED THERE

Or

NO NUDES IS BAD NEWS

Or

THIS IS A STORY WITH A BEGINNING, MIDDLE AND AN END. AND THE END DOESN'T COME SOON ENOUGH

7/04/1996
A Flying Dutchman production for BBC Radio 2
120 minutes

Barbara Windsor...Narrator
Writer ....Robert Rigby
Producer..Robert Rigby

The April 7th 1996 edition of the Radio 2 Arts Programme took a leisurely stroll through the archives in a two-hour programme presented by Barbara Windsor. Featuring extensive interviews with Peter Rogers and other cast members, The Carry On Clan presented a potted biography of every key member of the Carry On team, liberally sprinkled with clips from the films, archive interviews and examples of the cast's other work in film, television and radio.

CARRY ON FOREVER

19/07/2010, 20/07/2010
A Made in Manchester Production for BBC Radio
2x60 minutes

Narrator...Leslie Phillips
Additional Voices...David Benson
Written & Produced by ....Phil Collinge
Executive Producer ....Ashley Burns

This two hour history of the development of the Carry On series was presented by Leslie Philips. Examining the films' enduring popularity and their effect on British comedy today, surviving cast members, including Jacki Piper, Kenneth Cope and Shirley Eaton reminisced about their time on the films. Other cast members appeared in a selection of archive material, including interviews with Kenneth Williams, Sid James, Charles Hawtrey, Hattie Jacques and Joan Sims.

CARRY ON STAGE

The success of the Carry On films was showing no signs of fatigue by 1973, when producer Peter Rogers was approached about the possibility of transferring the team's hugely popular format to the stage.

The Carry On humour has its roots in live theatre and nowhere more so than in the music hall that dominated British popular entertainment from the mid-19th century until well into the 20th. Many of Britain's biggest stars first exercised their talents on the stage before going on to bigger, if not always necessarily better things.

That the Carry On team should return to their spiritual home of variety, and on the very stage where the Crazy Gang catapulted to stardom, was only fitting.

CARRY ON LONDON!

14 September 1973 - 29 September 1973: Birmingham Hippodrome
4 October 1973 – 12 October 1974: Victoria Palace, London

Sid James	Barbara Windsor	Kenneth Connor
Peter Butterworth	Bernard Bresslaw	Jack Douglas
The New Dollys	Les Silhouettes	Lynn Rogers
Les Quatre Rosetti		

CREW:

Executive Producer ....Albert J Knight
Written by...Talbot Rothwell, Dave Freeman
& Eric Merriman
Additional Material ....Ian Grant
Orchestra Director ....Richard Holmes
Manager & Stage Director ....Alan West
Choreography ....Tommy Shaw
Assistant Choreographer...Lynette Leisham
Comedy Director ....Bill Roberton
Choreographer ....Tommy Shaw
Wardrobe...Eve Barnes
Costumes ....R St. John Roper
Designer...Tod Kingman
Special Properties...Peter Pullen

Hospital sketch, Camping sketch, Cleopatra sketch by Talbot Rothwell
What a Carry On, Principal boys' number and other material by Eric Merriman
Elizabethan Madrigals by Dave Freeman

THE PROGRAMME

Round-About Victoria!
The Dancing Girls & Boys

Sidney James, Barbara Windsor, Kenneth Connor, Bernard Bresslaw, Jack Douglas, Peter Butterworth *take up residence!*

What a Carry On!
with Sidney, Barbara, Kenneth, Bernard, Jack & Peter assisted by George Truzzi & Billy Tasker

Carry On Girls
with Trudi van Doorn, The Carry On Showgirls, The Dancing Girls & Boys, introducing Les Quatre Rosetti

Elizabethan Madrigals
with Sidney, Barbara, Kenneth, Bernard & Peter

Deauville 1900
The Showgirls, The Dancing Girls & Boys

The Silhouettes

...and now The Maestro
Sidney James

London Night Out
The Showgirls & Boys

Curtain Time at the Royal Standard Music Hall
Miss Lottie Collins...Trudi Van Doorn
Our Worthy Manager ....Jack Douglas
Barbara Windsor
The Glamazons
Our Patriotic Tableaux...The British Empire - A tribute to our gallant soldiers

Intermission

Carry On Loving!
with Trudi Van Doorn, The Dancing Girls & Boys, The Showgirls

Be Prepared!
The Scoutmaster ....Sidney James
Scout Babcock..Bernard Bresslaw
Scout Muggeridge ....Jack Douglas
Scout Pennimore ....Kenneth Connor
Barbara ....Barbara Windsor
Ethel..Peter Butterworth
Barbara's friends ....Alexandra Dane & Lynne Taylor

The Boys & Girls introduce Singing Star
Lynn Rogers

Cleopatra's Palace on the Nile
The Dancing Girls & Boys, The Showgirls

Cleopatra's Boudoir
Cleopatra (Queen of the Nile).......................................Barbara Windsor
Abdul (a Hefty, Dusky Eunuch)....................................Bernard Bresslaw
Grabatiti (High Priest) ....Peter Butterworth
Mark Antony (Lend me your Ears)................................Kenneth Connor

Caesar (Rome's Godfather)..Sidney James
Titus Atticus (Captain of the Guard) ....Jack Douglas
Smile
with Sidney, Barbara, Kenneth, Bernard, Jack, Peter and the Company

During the production of Carry On Girls wheels were set in motion for a Carry On stage show featuring the cream of the Carry On cast doing what they do best before a live audience. With the Carry On films still doing great business at the box-office, the prospect of a gala Carry On stage production was big news and the show, which was budgeted at £150,000 (£50,000 of which was reportedly earmarked for the costumes alone) was headline news during the summer of 1973. Inevitably, much of that press coverage was concentrated on the dancing girls who would grace the Carry On stage.

In the best music hall tradition, a tradition which many of the Carry On regulars, and of course the humour of the films themselves were steeped in, Carry On London! would take the form of a revue.

Wary of another well-publicised failure like Lionel Bart's 1965/66 box-office disaster, Twang!, Barbara Windsor had decided that the kind of audience Carry On London! was aiming for was not for her. However, Sid James intervened and persuaded Barbara to sign up. A number of other Carry On regulars who had been approached including Joan Sims, would not appear in the eventual production.

The format for Carry On London! was originally envisaged as a return to the style of the knockabout antics the Crazy Gang had become so famous for during their hugely successful "Crazy Week" shows at the Victoria Palace. The concept centred around the Carry On team performing a series of sketches based on some of the films' more classic moments and supplemented by spectacular turns from the cream of the revue circuit.

The show opened at Birmingham's Hippodrome on 14th September 1973 for a limited run to give the team a chance to try out the material and iron out any kinks before taking up residence at London's prestigious Victoria Palace theatre. Initially, the team were less than enthusiastic about the shape the show had taken during the writing process. Talbot Rothwell was taken ill in the early stages and while Eric Merriman and Dave Freeman were brought in to complete the script, there was a general feeling among the cast that they were little more than glorified compères to the cabaret acts which would dominated the planned bill.

Some hasty rewriting and fine tuning during the Birmingham run led to a revised script with significantly more for the Carry On team to sink their teeth into. By the time the show's three week try-out was complete, they had a solid couple of hours of entertainment, balancing Carry On sketches with a number of elements designed to appeal to more traditional music hall fans. One key feature of the show would be an extended segment entitled "Curtain Time at the Royal Standard Music Hall"; a tribute to the long-running venue that had once stood on the very spot occupied by the Victoria Palace theatre.

Sid James' leering Henry VIII and wife-to-be "Anne of Cleavage" led a saucy madrigal telling the story of how the King got his Hampton Court (which originally appeared in the previous year's Carry On Christmas TV special). Bernard Bresslaw donned the Matron's outfit for a hospital sketch where Jack Douglas was forced to endure a series of botched operations and Sid and Barbara were Mark Antony and Cleopatra in a sketch adapted from Carry On Cleo.

The opening night of the show's transfer to the Victoria Theatre was celebrated on ITV with a one hour TV special, "What A Carry On", presented by Shaw Taylor. Selected highlights of the production's Birmingham run were scattered throughout to give audiences at home a taste of the fun on offer.

While some reviewers were less than impressed with the show's more traditional roots and lamented the lack of anything new and ground-breaking from the Carry On team, the public got exactly what they wanted and the show played twice nightly to packed houses for the next year.

In the words of Jack Douglas, "How lovely to come to the West End and crack the subtle stuff."

CARRY ON LAUGHING (WITH THE SLIMMING FACTORY)

16th June - September 1976: The Royal Opera House, Scarborough

Jack Douglas..Jack Hardy
Kenneth Connor ....Major Chambers
Peter Butterworth...Willie Strokes
Liz Fraser ....Milly
Anne Aston ....Candy Maple
Beau Daniels ....Mrs Babbington
Danny O'Dea...Albert Waterman
Barbara Sumner ....Alice Pringle
Linda Hooks ....Hilde

CREW:

Written by...Sam Cree
Designer...Saxon Lucas
Wardrobe..Judi Tillotson
Theatre & General Manager...John Palmer
Company & Stage Manager ....Tommy Layton
Deputy Stage Manager...Sue Smith
Director..Bill Roberton

Act 1
Monday Morning
Wednesday Morning

Interval

Act 2
Thursday Afternoon
Thursday Night

Two years after the roaring success of Carry On London!, the team returned to the stage with an altogether different kind of show for the 1976 summer season. For the summer holidays, Scarborough's Royal Opera House was transformed into the Slimming Factory as holidaymakers were invited to check in and Carry On Laughing.

Unlike its theatrical predecessor, Carry On Laughing with the Slimming Factory was a traditional farce based around a single on-going story. Sam Cree's original script was entitled "Carry On Slimming" but the title was changed to reflect the recent popularity of the Carry On Laughing television series. The production was directed by former comedy director on Carry On London and brother of Jack Douglas, Bill Roberton.

Jack Douglas, Peter Butterworth and Kenneth Connor were ably assisted by former Carry On starlet Liz Fraser and former Golden Shot star, Anne Aston. Despite misgivings from the cast over a script which, according to Gerald Thomas, was "very thin material" and the spectre of Sid James' recent death, the show played to packed houses and enjoyed popular, if not always critical, success.

WOT A CARRY ON IN BLACKPOOL

22 May - 27 June 1992
26 July - 25 October 1992 (Sundays Only)
North Pier, Blackpool

Leading Man	Bernard Bresslaw
Leading Lady	Barbara Windsor
Juvenile Lead	Andrew Grainger
Light Comedy Relief	Richard Gauntlett
The Merry Maids	Jaqueline Dunnley, Rachel Woolrich, Melanie Holloway, Natalie Holtom
The Jolly Juveniles	Jonathan Blazer, Julian Essex Spurrier

CREW:

Written by	Barry Cryer & Dick Vosburgh
Orchestra Director	Tim Parkin
Choreographer	Paul Robinson
Wardrobe Mistress	Heidi Wynter
Costumes	Kathryn Waters
Music Associate	Phil Phillips
Set Design	Gareth Bowen
Sound Design	Clement Rawling
Stage Manager	Sharon Curtis
Company Stage Manager	James Skeggs
Director	Tudor Davies

Act 1

Arrival:
"Youv'e Got to Carry On"
"Phone Home"
"At the Digs"

Rehearsals:
"T'aint Nobody's Business if I do"

"Specialty"
"Tricky Business"

Out of Town:
"Old Fashioned Girl"
"Slippin' Around the Corner"
"Blackpool's own Darby & Joan"
"Slippin' Around the Corner to the Rose & Crown"

Act 2

It's Show Time:
"Get Happy"
"Out of their Minds"

London Medley:
"Vultures for Culture"
"Chelsea Party"
"Convent Garden"
"Speciality"

Just go to the Movies:
"Charlie Chaplin"
"Frankenstein's Monster"
"Betty Grable"
"Wot a Carry On"
"Mum Interrupts"

Finale:
"One Step"

The third theatrical Carry On was a proper end of the pier show; a summer season on Blackpool's North Pier.

In keeping with the traditional seaside setting, the show was a mixture of songs and sketches all based loosely around a 1940s revue company performing a seaside show for holidaymakers. Bernard Bresslaw and Barbara Windsor were the only members of the Carry On team to tread the boards in a show directed by Tudor Davies, who had worked extensively in theatre with Barbara before, during her "Carry On Barbara" one-woman show.

According to her autobiography "All of Me", Barbara was taken somewhat by surprise on arriving in Blackpool to discover that she'd been given second billing to Bernard Bresslaw. The show, as it had been described to her, was to have been a traditional revue with little or no Carry On material. In fact, at the time she signed her contract, Barbara maintains she had no idea the Carry On name would even be used.

Wot a Carry On in Blackpool received less than enthusiastic reviews but managed to pack them in for the duration of its limited run and continued with once-weekly Sunday shows throughout the summer until late October.

While the Carry On team didn't go on to produce any further stage extravaganzas there was one notable stage production which tells the story (or at least a story) of what went on behind the scenes of the Carry Ons. Terry Johnson's "Cleo, Camping, Emmanuelle & Dick" was an affectionate take on the backstage antics of Sid, Barbara and Kenneth, and went on to spawn the television film, "Cor Blimey!"

CLEO, CAMPING, EMMANUELLE & DICK

21st September 1998 – 16th January 1999
Lyttleton Theatre, South Bank, London

Geoffrey Hutchings..Sid
Gina Bellman ....Imogen
Jacqueline Defferary..Sally
Adam Godley..Kenneth
Kenneth MacDonald..Eddie
Samantha Spiro..Barbara

CREW:

Written & Directed by ....Terry Johnson
Music...Barrington Pheloung
Set Designer ....William Dudley
Lighting Designer ....Simon Corder
Costumer Designer ....Nettie Edwards

COMMENTS:

Cleo, Camping, Emmanuelle & Dick were originally billed as an examination of the way relationships developed between the Carry On films' leading stars, Sid, Kenneth and Barbara. The story unfolded via a series of visits to the Carry On set during the making of the eponymous films.

From its Eric Rogers-inspired opening theme, Cleo, Camping, Emmanuelle & Dick told the story of the Carry Ons in the language of the films themselves, using a collection of familiar gags including highly suggestive fruit, pinging bras and familiar catchphrases. But the high-spirits of the team in their early days are replaced with an increasingly bittersweet tone as we revisit them over the years.

The complex, conflicting and ultimately destructive relationship between Sid James and Barbara Windsor is dealt with sensitively, focusing on the real people behind the stories rather than the salacious gossip that has formed the backbone of so many other examinations of the Carry Ons.

Most surprising of all, though, is that the play managed to balance the off-screen tragedy of the Carry On stars with genuinely funny moments which could have come straight out of the films, such as Barbara's driver lying in wait for Sid outside his caravan or Sid's continual innuendo-laden references to passion fruit.

The three stars of Cleo, Camping, Emmanuelle & Dick; Samantha Spiro, Adam Godley and Geoffrey Hutchings, delivered hauntingly familiar portrayals of the Carry On stars in a production which trod a delicate line between fact and fiction, all wrapped up in the trappings of the films whose story the play set out to tell.

The show was a breakaway success winning for author and director Terry Johnson the 1999 Olivier Award for Best New Comedy along with two further Olivier nominations for Adam Godley in the role of Kenneth, and for William Dudley's set design.

NOT A CARRY ON
THE LOST CARRY ONS

Peter Rogers registered a great many Carry On names over the years with titles such as "Carry On Charlie", a planned comedy retelling of the story of the Bonnie Prince. While many of them were simply vague ideas for future projects, several came significantly closer to reaching cinema screens.

WHAT A CARRY ON (1958). In November 1958, with Carry On Sergeant doing record business in cinemas and Carry On Nurse close to completion, Peter Rogers announced to the press his plan for an on-going series of films under the "Carry On" banner. He went so far as to announce the names of the next four Carry On films. They would be Carry On Teacher, Carry On Constable, Carry On Regardless and What a Carry On.

Surviving records reveal no details about What a Carry On, but Norman Hudis had been working on an idea about an amateur dramatics society staging a production of Romeo and Juliette. That particular idea found its way onto cinema screens as the climax of Carry On Teacher.

CARRY ON SMOKING (1961). Everyday professions were the order of the day in Norman Hudis' Carry On scripts such as the Army, the NHS and the police force. So, a natural next step was, of course, the Fire Brigade. The original outline for Carry On Smoking features a fire station which takes on four well-intentioned idiots. Ultimately, Peter Rogers passed on the idea, concerned that a real-life disaster would make the film's subject too sensitive for comedy.

CARRY ON FLYING (1962). Michael Pertwee approached Peter Rogers with an idea for another profession to undergo the Carry On treatment. Pertwee's original concept was given to Norman Hudis to develop, and Hudis built a story around his own wartime experiences in the Royal Air Force. Jim Dale was initially considered as the dashing young pilot leading the film. The idea was eventually dropped due to a combination of budgetary concerns and the same caution that had scuppered Carry On Smoking.

CARRY ON SPACEMAN (1962). Bob Monkhouse originally developed the outline for a proposed Carry On film which took a humorous look at the British space programme, starring Sid James as an enthusiastic amateur who builds a rocket in his back garden. The idea was deemed too ambitious for Peter Rogers' more modest productions.

CARRY ON ESCAPING. Talbot Rothwell served in the Royal Air Force during World War 2. Shot down over German-occupied Norway, he served out much of the war in an internment camp (the same camp where Peter Butterworth was imprisoned). There, he turned to writing, developing spirited revues to raise the morale of fellow prisoners. Carry On Escaping was based on Rothwell's formative years as a writer, with the camp entertainments being staged to raise both the spirits of the inmates and, more importantly, to disguise the noises of prisoners tunnelling underneath the fence.

Availability: Carry On Escaping script available in "The Complete A-Z of Everything Carry On" by Richard Webber, Harper Collins, 2005 (ISBN: 0007182236)

CARRY ON AGAIN NURSE (1979). The Carry On films were targeting a more mature audience by the late 1970s and George Layton and Jonathan Lynn's script for Carry On Again Nurse would have taken the films even more firmly down that path. When Carry On England was still in production, Peter Rogers was confident that an "AA" rating wouldn't harm the film's success but the subsequent hasty cutting of material to secure an "A" and the film's re-release proved a sobering experience. Excluding large segments of the potential audience was having a damaging effect on sales while Carry On Emmanuelle paved the way to full "AA" status. It is inconceivable that the films would have taken the sexual content further in pursuit of an "X" certificate. Thus, Layton and Lynn's script was ultimately shelved when the Carry Ons were rested following the ever diminishing box office returns of England and Emmannuelle.

CARRY ON DALLAS / CARRY ON TEXAS (1987). Throughout the 1980s, Dallas was the most famous series on television. The machinations of the Ewing clan in their pursuit of oil, sex and revenge were the perfect target for some Carry On fun. Vince Powell's script told the everyday tale of the Screwing family, with Kenneth Williams playing the lead, RU Screwing. Jack Douglas was his brother Bobby and Barbara Windsor would have been the "poison dwarf", Lucy. Unsurprisingly, the family name raised a few eyebrows and was toned down during the early stages of pre-production to Ramming.

In May 1987, Bernard Bresslaw, Jack Douglas, Terry Scott and Barbara Windsor appeared on the TVam sofa to talk about plans for the new £2m Carry On film, which was scheduled to begin shooting that autumn at Pinewood. Gerald Thomas, in an interview with the Daily Express that same month said that the Rammings would be a wealthy English family settling in the heart of cattle country where they would clean up in the sewage business.

Thomas informed Lorimar, the production company in charge of Dallas, of their intention to film a pastiche. Lorimar consented to the project, but the royalty for re-use of their original concept was so prohibitively expensive that, for now, the Rammings were consigned to the shelf.

CARRY ON AGAIN NURSE / CARRY ON NURSING (1987). Taking a fresh look at the future of the Carry Ons, Peter Rogers invited Norman Hudis for a meeting to talk about reviving the tried and tested medical Carry On theme once again. Hudis flew to the UK to meet with Rogers and drafted an outline for what was to have become Carry On Nurse. Hudis' story centred on a hospital which faced crippling NHS cuts and the medical team's attempts to keep the place open.

In December 1987, Gerald Thomas, Bernard Bresslaw and Jack Douglas appeared on the BBC's Breakfast Time programme to talk about the Carry On team's planned return to the screen for their 30th anniversary in Carry On Nursing. Thomas joked that in terms of content, the new film would feature rather more "bums than tits" as they had learned from audiences in the 1970s that the secret of the Carry Ons' success was in their appeal to a broad family audience. Any new Carry On film would have to appeal to wider demographic than the last couple of entries in the series.

While Hudis, who was by now living in the USA, completed the script, Peter Rogers tried to reach an agreement with the Writer's Guild of America which would have allowed the script to go into production without incurring their prohibitively high fees for transatlantic deals. In the end, an agreement could not be reached which would make the film's £1.5m budget cost effective and the idea was shelved.

Availability: Norman Hudis' script for Carry On Again Nurse is published in "The Lost Carry Ons" by Morris Bright & Robert Ross, Boxtree, 2000 (ISBN: 1852279907)

CARRY ON DOWN UNDER (1988).

With the earlier Carry On Texas proving too costly to produce, Vince Powell heavily re-worked his original script and, thanks to an unexpected source of funding from Australia, moved the action to the outback where the Ramming family would become sheep farmers.

Gerald Thomas visited Australia and met with the financier to agree a deal and begin scouting locations but shortly after his return to England, the team received notice that the finance had fallen through. Unable to salvage the project for financial reasons, it too was abandoned.

CARRY ON LONDON (2003, 2006 and 2008).

In 2003, a gala launch at the House of Commons proclaimed that Peter Rogers had signed an agreement with producer James Black to bring the Carry Ons into the new millennium.

Carry On London told the story of a low-budget limousine company, Lenny's Limos, who had managed to secure the contract for transporting celebrities to and from the prestigious Herbert Film Awards in London.

Ex-EastEnders star Shaun Williamson was signed up to play the chauffeur, Dickie Ticker. Daniella Westbrook, another ex- (and at the time of writing current once more) EastEnders star was contracted to play the sexy young bombshell and appeared in tabloids dressed in Barbara Windsor's revealing "Goldie Locks" costume from Carry On Again Doctor. After an initial flurry of activity, Williamson eventually walked away from the proposed film in 2004; shortly after producer James Black left the project.

Carry On London was re-launched again in 2006 at that year's Cannes Film Festival, with new backer Intandem Films introducing the press to their newest stars, Shane Ritchie as the owner of Lenny's Limos, former Miss Sweden, Victoria Silvstedt as starlet Penny Pink and Vinnie Jones as nightclub owner (and not-so-secret gangster) Tony le Berc, aka "Two Fingers" Tony. Shady magazine publisher Sir Desmond Uppingham Knightly and Hollywood movie producer IP Freely would soon be cast in the story of how Britain's most prestigious film awards became embroiled in the world of gangsters, divas and saucy Carryings On.

The film, which was budgeted at £6.4m, was initially to have been directed by Comic Strip co-creator and Carry On Columbus star Peter Richardson, but later that same year, former Red Dwarf director Ed Bye was announced as the new director.

A script was finally signed off by all parties in March 2008 and the film went into pre-production at Pinewood Studios. Executive Producer Peter Rogers, at the 50th Anniversary Carry On celebration went on to confirm that more Carry Ons would follow if London was a success.

By 2009, filming had progressed no further and the script had gained a new name. According to Carry On London Ltd.'s Brian Baker, Carry On to the Next Round, as it was now known would be directed by Charlie Higson and feature a new, younger cast including Justin Lee Collins, Jennifer Ellison and James Dreyfuss.

With the death of Peter Rogers in April 2009, it appeared that Carry On London, and indeed the Carry On franchise as a whole, was history. Carry On London ceased pre-production and in February 2010, the company went into liquidation.

WHAT A CARRY ON

The Carry On films were made at breakneck speed. On average, it took just six weeks to film each instalment. In their down time, and to give exhibitors a chance to satisfy audiences who couldn't get enough of the Carry On style of humour, the team made a succession of other films which would feature the same cast and crew. The comedies of Peter Rogers and Gerald Thomas were a growing cottage industry which would turn out up to four films a year.

Deciding which films would bear the "Carry On" name was often a last minute affair. Carry On Cabby was known as "Call me a Cab" until shortly before it hit the cinemas. Original ideas for Carry On Constable became the later Rogers/Thomas comedy "The Big Job" and the play, "Ring for Catty" which inspired Carry On Nurse was later filmed as "Twice Round the Daffodils".

If you love the Carry Ons films, there's a lesser known collection of features made by and starring the same team which are Carry Ons in all but name. That they are not better remembered is, perhaps, simply due to a quirk of naming.

PLEASE TURN OVER

1959

Screenplay by Norman Hudis
Based on "Book of the Month" by Basil Thomas
Music Composed & Conducted by Bruce Montgomery

CAST   CHARACTER

CAST	CHARACTER
Ted Ray	Edward Halliday
Jean Kent	Janet Halliday
Leslie Phillips	Dr Henry Manners
Joan Sims	Beryl
Julia Lockwood	Jo Halliday
Tim Seely	Robert Hughes
Charles Hawtrey	Jeweller
Dilys Laye	Millicent Jones
Lionel Jeffries	Ian Howard
June Jago	Gladys Worth
Colin Gordon	Maurice
Joan Hickson	Saleswoman
Victor Maddern	Manager
Ronald Adam	Mr Appleton
Cyril Chamberlain	Mr Jones
Myrtle Reed	Mrs Moore
Marianne Stone	Mrs Waring
Leigh Madison	Cashier
Anthony Sagar	Barman
Lucy Griffiths	Gossip
George Street	Removal Man

Noel Dyson...Mrs Brent
Paul Cole ....Newspaper boy
Celia Hewitt...Young woman
George Howell..Butcher's boy

CREW

Director of Photography ....Edward Scaife
Camera Operator..Alan Hume
Editor..John Shirley
Sound Recordists ....Robert T MacPhee
& Gordon K McCallum
Art Direction...Carmen Dillon
Production Manager ....Frank Bevis
Make-up ....Alex Garfath
Hairdresser...Frieda Steiger
Assistant Director ....Peter Manley
Set Dresser ....Robert Cartwright
Producer...Peter Rogers
Director..Gerald Thomas

Duration: 86 minutes
Black & White

STORY

Jo Halliday (Julia Lockwood) lives a quiet life, working as a hairdresser and living at home with her nagging mother (Jean Kent) and stuffy father (Ted Ray). When the local newspaper reveals that Jo is in fact the author of The Naked Truth, a scandalous bestseller about a young girl who flees her family to become a prostitute in London, the Hallidays' friends and neighbours believe the book is based on their real lives. At work, Jo's father is suspected of theft and at home her mother is accused of being a harlot who's been leading a secret affair with a retired Army officer for the past 20 years.

Jo returns from London with her fiancée (Tim Seely), who plans to turn the book into a play only to discover the whole town in outrage amid accusations of infidelity, fraud and deceit.

AVAILABILITY
DVD:

Please Turn Over
Optimum Home Entertainment, 2011
PAL, Region 2 (Europe, Middle East & Japan), Black & White

Comic Icons – The Leslie Phillips Collection (Please Turn Over, No Kidding, Crooks Anonymous, Watch your Stern)
Optimum Home Releasing, 2007
PAL, Region 2 (Europe, Middle East & Japan), Black & White

WATCH YOUR STERN

1960

Screenplay by Alan Hackney & Vivian A Cox
Based on "Something about a Sailor" by Earle Couttie
Music Composed & Conducted by Bruce Montgomery

CAST   CHARACTER

CAST	CHARACTER
Kenneth Connor	Ordinary Seaman Blissworth
Eric Barker	Captain David Foster
Leslie Phillips	Lt Cmdr Bill Fanshawe
Joan Sims	Ann Foster
Noel Purcell	Admiral Sir Humphrey Pettigrew
Hattie Jacques	Agatha Potter
Spike Milligan	Civilian Electrician 1
Eric Sykes	Civilian Electrician 2
Sid James	CPO Mundy
David Lodge	Security Sergeant
Victor Maddern	Sailor fishing for bike
Ed Devereaux	Commander Phillips
Robin Ray	Flag Lieutenant
George Street	Security Guard
Peter Howell	Admiral's Secretary
Arch Taylor	Coxswain
Michael Brennan	Security Guard
Leila Williams	WREN driver
Richard Bennett	Officer of the Day
Carl Conway	Sailor
Rory MacDermot	Security Guard
Eric Corrie	Engineer
Sailors:	Hedley Colson, Walter Cavan, Raf Jover, Jack Smethurst, Dickie Owen, John Mathews, Bill Cartwright, Peter Byrne, Ivor Danvers, Charles Vance, Michael Nightingale, Michael Julian

CREW

Director of Photography	Edward Scaife
Camera Operator	Alan Hume
Sound Recordists	Robert T MacPhee & Bill Daniels
Editor	John Shirley
Art Director	Carmen Dillon
Assistant Director	Jack Causey

Production Manager ....Frank Bevis
Casting..Betty White
Marjorie Lavelly ....Continuity
Costumes ....Joan Ellacott
Make-up ....Biddy Chrystal
Hairdresser...Alex Garfath
Set Dresser ....Peter Lamont
Wardrobe...Ben Foster
Naval Advisor..Lieut. Com. Peter Peake RN (Rtd)
Producer...Peter Rogers
Director..Gerald Thomas

Duration: 85 minutes
Black & White

STORY

Captain Foster (Eric Barker) entrusts the plans for important modifications to a top secret Navy torpedo with bungling Ordinary Seaman Blissworth (Kenneth Connor). Blissworth manages to lose the plans and he and Foster attempt to cover up their mistake by substituting the missing blueprints with those of the ship's refrigeration system. But when an inspector calls to carry out tests on the modified torpedo, Blissworth and the crew find themselves in an awkward spot.

AVAILABILITY

DVD:

Watch your Stern
Optimum Home Releasing, 2011, 2004
PAL, Region 2 (Europe, Middle East & Japan), Black & White

Comic Icons – The Leslie Phillips Collecton (Please Turn Over, No Kidding, Crooks Anonymous, Watch your Stern)
Optimum Home Releasing, 2007
PAL, Region 2 (Europe, Middle East & Japan), Black & White

VHS:

The Big Job / Watch your Stern
Warner Home Video, 1994
PAL, Black & White

RAISING THE WIND

1961

Screenplay by Bruce Montgomery
Music Composed & Conducted by Bruce Montgomery

CAST

CHARACTER

CAST	CHARACTER
James Robertson Justice	Sir Benjamin Boyd
Leslie Phillips	Mervyn Hughes
Paul Massie	Malcolm Stuart
Kenneth Williams	Harold Chesney
Liz Fraser	Miranda Kennaway
Eric Barker	Dr Morgan Rutherford
Jennifer Jayne	Jill Clemons
Jimmy Thompson	Alex Spendlove
Sid James	Sid
Esma Cannon	Mrs Deevens
Geoffrey Keen	Sir John
Jill Ireland	Janet
Victor Maddern	Removal Man
Lance Percival	Harry
Joan Hickson	Mrs Bostwick
David Lodge	Taxi Driver
Ambrosine Phillpotts	Mrs Featherstone
Brian Oulton	Concert Agent
Douglas Ives	Street Musician
Bernard Hunter	1st Flute
Peter Howell	Professor Lumb
George Woodbridge	Yorkshire Orchestra Leader
Cyril Chamberlain	LAMA Porter
Peter Byrne	1st Horn
Peter Burton	1st Viola
Eric Chitty	Elderly Man at Concert
Jim Dale	Bass Trombone
Henry Davies	Carpenter
Nigel Arkwright	4th Cellist
John Antrobus	Street Musician
Tom Clegg	Street Musician
Frank Forsyth	Professor Gerald Abrahams
Terence Holland	1st Trombone
Oliver Johnston	Professor Parkin
Dorinda Stevens	Doris
Michael Nightingale	Investigator
Ian Wilson	Drummer
Michael Miller	Barman Mike

CREW

Director of Photography .... Alan Hume
Camera Operator .... Dudley Lovell
Editor .... John Shirley
Assistant Director .... Jack Causey
Continuity .... Sue Dyson
Production Manager .... Bill Hill
Art Director .... Carmen Dillon
Sound Recordists .... Robert T MacPhee & Bill Daniels
Casting Director .... Betty White
Wardrobe .... Joan Ellacott
Make-up .... George Blackler
Hairdresser .... Biddy Chrystal
Title Sketches .... Gerald Hoffnung
Producer .... Peter Rogers
Director .... Gerald Thomas

Duration: 87 minutes
Colour

STORY

Students at a prestigious music school decide to share the cost of finding somewhere to live and practice their playing by sharing a flat together. When student Malcolm Stuart (Paul Massie) risks losing his scholarship by selling a jingle to an advertising agency his friends rally round to raise enough funds to buy back the rights.

AVAILABILITY

DVD:

Raising the Wind
Optimum Home Releasing, 2010
PAL, Region 2 (Europe, Middle East & Japan), Colour

VHS:

Raising the Wind
Warner Home Video, 1990
PAL, Colour

TWICE ROUND THE DAFFODILS

1962

Screenplay by Norman Hudis
Based on "Ring for Catty" by Patrick Cargill & Jack Beale
Music Composed & Conducted by Bruce Montgomery

CAST — CHARACTER

CAST	CHARACTER
Juliet Mills	Catty
Donald Sinden	Ian Richards
Donald Houston	John Rhodes
Kenneth Williams	Henry Halfpenny
Ronald Lewis	Bob White
Andrew Ray	Chris Walker
Joan Sims	Harriet Halfpenny
Jill Ireland	Janet
Lance Percival	George Logg
Sheila Hancock	Dora
Nanette Newman	Joyce
Renee Houston	Matron
Amanda Reiss	Dorothy
Mary Powell	Mrs Rhodes
Barbara Roscoe	Mary
Frank Forsyth	Dorothy's Father
Olwen Brookes	Dorothy's Mother
Peter Jesson	Joyce's Young Man
Nora Gordon	Cleaner

CREW

Director of Photography	Alan Hume
Editor	John Shirley
Art Director	Carmen Dillon
Assistant Director	Anthony Waye
Sound Recordists	Robert T MacPhee & Bill Daniels
Continuity	Penny Daniels
Production Manager	Bill Hill
Casting	Betty White
Wardrobe	Joan Ellacott
Make-up	George Blackler
Hairdresser	Biddy Chrystal
Producer	Peter Rogers
Director	Gerald Thomas

Duration: 87 minutes
Black & White

STORY

Four new patients in a hospital tuberculosis ward all take a shine to their nurse, Catty (Juliet Mills). There's love all around on the ward as the male patients pursue the pretty young nurses while they do their best to get through the day unmolested.

AVAILABILITY

VHS:

Twice Round the Daffodils
Warner Home Video, 1990
PAL, Colour

Twice Round the Daffodils / Nurse on Wheels
Warner Home Video, 1994
PAL, Colour

THE BIG JOB

1965

Screenplay by John Antrobus, Talbot Rothwell
Music Composed & Conducted by Eric Rogers

CAST   CHARACTER

CAST	CHARACTER
Sid James	George "the Brain"
Sylvia Sims	Myrtle Robbins
Dick Emery	Frederick "Booky" Binns
Joan Sims	Mildred Gamely
Lance Percival	Timothy "Dipper" Day
Jim Dale	Harold
Deryck Guyler	Police Sergeant
Edina Ronay	Sally Gamely
Reginald Beckwith	Registry Office Official
Michael Ward	Undertaker
Brian Rawlinson	Henry Blobbitt
David Horne	Judge
Frank Forsyth	Bank Cashier
Frank Thornton	Bank Official
Wanda Ventham	Dot Franklin
Peter Jesson	Ernest
Michael Graham	Boy on bench
Penelope Lee	Girl on bench
Fred Griffiths	Dustman
Gertan Klauber	Milkman
Patrick Allen	Narrator

CREW

Director of Photography	Alan Hume
Associate Producer	Frank Bevis
Camera Operator	Geoffrey Godar
Editor	Rod Nelson-Keys
Assistant Director	Peter Bolton
Sound Recordists	C LeMesuirier, CC Stevens
Sound Mixer	Dudley Messenger
Production Manager	Ron Jackson
Art Direction	Bert Davey
Costumes	Yvonne Caffin
Penny Daniels	Continuity
Make-up	Stella Rivers & Geoffrey Rodway
Producer	Peter Rogers
Director	Gerald Thomas

Duration: 85 minutes
Colour

STORY:

A gang of bank robbers are caught and imprisoned by the police, but not before their leader George "the Brain" (Sid James) secretes their £50,000 loot in the trunk of a hollow tree.

The robbers are released 15 years later and head straight for the spot where the loot was hidden, only to discover that the tree now sits in the garden of the recently-built police station. George and his gang rent a room in a house overlooking the station and set to work trying to recover their stolen loot.

AVAILABILITY

DVD:

The Big Job
Optimum Home Entertainment, 2011
PAL, Region 2 (Europe, Middle East & Japan), Black & White

VHS:

The Big Job / Watch your Stern
Warner Home Video, 1994
PAL, Black & White

The Big Job
Warner Home Video, 2000
PAL, Black & White

NURSE ON WHEELS

1963

Screenplay by Norman Hudis, based on "Nurse is a Neighbour" by John Burke
Original music composed & conducted by Eric Rogers

CAST   CHARACTER

Juliet Mills	Joanna Jones
Ronald Lewis	Henry Edwards
Joan Sims	Deborah Wallcott
Noel Purcell	Abel Worthy
Esma Cannon	Mrs Jones
Raymond Huntley	Vicar
Athene Seyler	Miss Farthingale
Norman Rossington	George Judd
Ronald Howard	Dr Harold Golfrey
Joan Hickson	Mrs Wood
Renee Houston	Mrs Beacon
Jim Dale	Tim Taylor
George Woodbridge	Mr Beacon
David Horne	Dr Golfrey Senior
Deryck Guyler	Driving Examiner
Barbara Everest	Nurse Merrick
Brian Rawlinson	Policeman
Amanda Reiss	Ann Taylor
Peter Jesson	Mr Top
Virginia Vernon	Miss Maitland
Anthony Buckingham	Small boy

CREW

Director of Photography	Alan Hume
Associate Producer	Frank Bevis
Editor	Archie Ludski
Camera Operator	James Bawden
Assistant Director	Anthony Waye
Sound Recordists	C Le Mesurier & Robert T MacPhee
Continuity	Gladys Goldsmith
Art Director	Lionel Couch
Costume	Joan Ellacott
Make-up	George Blackler & Alex Garfath
Hairdresser	Stella Rivers
Producer	Peter Rogers
Director	Gerald Thomas

Duration: 82 minutes
Black & White

STORY:

Joanna Jones (Juliet Mills) moves with her elderly mother (Esma Cannon) to a quiet rural village to take up a job as District Nurse. At first, the locals are suspicious of the young nurse, but she soon wins them over and falls in love with local farmer, Henry Edwards (Ronald Lewis). But Joanna and Henry's relationship hits trouble when he evicts a caravan belonging to an expectant couple from his land.

AVAILABILITY

DVD:

Nurse on Wheels
Optimum Home Entertainment, 2007
PAL, Region 2 (Europe, Middle East & Japan), Colour

VHS:

Nurse on Wheels
Warner Home Video, 1990
PAL, Colour

BLESS THIS HOUSE

1972

Screenplay by Dave Freeman
Music Composed & Conducted by Eric Rogers

CAST

CHARACTER

Sid James	Sid Abbott
Diana Coupland	Jean Abbott
Sally Geeson	Sally Abbott
Peter Butterworth	Trevor Lewis
Terry Scott	Ronald Baines
June Whitfield	Vera Baines
Robin Askwith	Mike Abbott
Carol Hawkins	Kate Baines
Patsy Rowlands	Betty Lewis
George A Cooper	Mr Wilson
Bill Maynard	Oldham
Marianne Stone	Muriel
Janet Brown	Annie Hobbs
Julian Orchard	Tom Hobbs
Tommy Godfrey	Alf Murray
Wendy Richard	Carol
Patricia Franklin	Mary
Molly Weir	Mary's Mother
Ed Devereaux	Jim
Johnny Briggs	Open Truck Driver
Frank Thornton	Mr Jones
Norman Mitchell	Police Sergeant
Brian Osborne	Removal Van Driver
Margie Lawrence	Alma
Lindsay Marsh	Myra
Myrtle Reed	Lady Customer
Margaret Lacey	Vicar's Wife
Michael Howe	Wilfred
Georgina Moon	Moira
David Rowlands	Photographer
Billy Cornelius	Police Constable
Michael Nightingale	Vicar
Maggie Wright	Daphne

CREW

Director of Photography	Alan Hume
Editor	Alfred Roome
Camera Operator	Godfrey Godar

Art Director ....Lionel Couch
Sound Recordists ....Ken Barker & Bill Daniels
Continuity...Joy Mercer
Production Manager ....Roy Goddard
Assistant Director ....David Bracknell
Wardrobe...Courtenay Elliott
Make-up ....Geoffrey Rodway
Hairdresser...Stella Rivers
Set Dresser ....John Jarvis
Producer...Peter Rogers
Director...Gerald Thomas

Duration: 87 minutes
Colour

STORY:

Sid Abbott (Sid James) and his friend Trevor (Peter Butterworth) escape the stresses of family life by distilling their own whisky in the garden shed. When customs officer Ronald Baines (Terry Scott) and his wife (June Whitfield) move in next door, illegal spirits are just the start of Sid's troubles; his son Mike (Robin Asquith) has also taken a shine to the Baines' daughter (Carol Hawkins).

AVAILABILITY
DVD:

Bless this House
ITV Studios, 2003
PAL, Region 2 (Europe, Middle East & Japan), Colour

Bless this House
Network, 2008
PAL, Region 2 (Europe, Middle East & Japan), Colour

VHS:

Bless this House
Cinema Club, 1986
PAL, Colour

Bless this House
Carlton Home Entertainment, 2003
PAL, Colour

CARRY ON COLLECTIBLES
COLLECTIBLES & EPHEMERA:

BEER MATS & POSTERS

KP Nuts, 1995

In 1995, KP Nuts launched a "Carry On Nibbling" advertising campaign. Promotional posters and beer mats were widely available, featuring Sid James, Kenneth Williams and Charles Hawtrey, each accompanied by a saucy slogan:

Sid: "Keep your hands off my nuts!"

Kenneth: "Nuts! Ooh, matron!"

Charles: "I say, my nuts are chilli"

Museum of the Moving Image, 1998

From December 1998 through to May 1999, London's Museum of the Moving Image (MOMI) was home to a celebration of 40 years of the Carry Ons. Original props, costumes and production material went on display to the public in a specially constructed Carry On exhibition in London's National Film Theatre. A trio of Carry On beer mats, featuring Sid James, Kenneth Williams and Barbara Windsor were among the commemorative items on sale at the event.

OFFICIAL CARRY ON CALENDAR

Slow Dazzle, 1996 – 2009

Global, 2010

Flame Tree Art Calendars, 2011

Licence holders may have changed over the years but the calendar concept remains reassuringly similar. From 2011, the Carry On calendar is available in two formats: the standard 12" square or a thinner desk-format. Each variant contains a different collection of stills from the Carry On films, including some from scenes cut from the final prints.

CARRY ON YO-YO

Museum of the Moving Image, 1998

Another promotional item available at the MOMI Carry On 40th anniversary exhibition, this is one of the more esoteric official items of Carry On memorabilia; a wooden yo-yo proudly emblazoned with the Carry On logo.

MENSWEAR

Burtons, 1998

Burtons, the menswear retailer, released a range of Carry On branded clothing in 1998 featuring Sid James, Kenneth Williams and Barbara Windsor. The faces of the stars were emblazoned on T-shirts, boxer shorts and socks just in time for the Christmas market.

FRUIT MACHINE

Maygay, 1998

Priced at a shade under £3000, the Carry On fruit machine was designed to grace the more discerning drinking establishments of our fair isle. One even turned up in the Queen Vic pub on EastEnders in 1999, which must have amused Barbara Windsor no end.

POSTCARDS
London Postcard Company, 1998

A set of 32 postcards that featured Carry On UK poster art from every film from Sergeant to Emmannuelle. Fans of Cabby and Cleo were spoiled rotten by the inclusion of two separate designs for each film.

BOOKMARKS
London Postcard Company, 1998

The wide-ranging potential of card-based collectibles was not lost to the people at the London Postcard Company. The same year, they released a set of 4 Carry On 40th anniversary bookmarks, each featuring two of the Carry On poster images from Carry On Cruising, Carry On Don't Lose your Head, Carry On Follow that Camel, Carry On Doctor, Carry On up the Khyber, Carry On Matron, Carry On Girls and Carry On Behind.

DIE-CAST VEHICLES
Lledo, 1998

Scale model specialist Lledo released a set of six 1:60 scale Carry On themed vehicles in 1998 as part of their "Days Gone" range. While the vehicles themselves weren't specifically based on anything seen in the Carry On films, each was emblazoned with the Carry On logo and, where there was enough space, a replica of the UK poster art for the film they represented. The range included:
• Carry On Sergeant: Army truck (Incorrectly labelled "Heathercroft National Service Depot")
• Carry On Teacher: School coach
• Carry On Constable: Police van
• Carry On Cabby: Taxi
• Carry On Camping: VW camper
• Carry On Matron: Ambulance

BIRTHDAY CARDS
Cartel International, 1998

A set of 14 birthday cards, featuring stills from Carry On Doctor, Carry On Camping, Carry On Again Doctor, Carry On up the Jungle, Carry On Abroad and Carry On Girls. Each card came with an appropriately saucy slogan.

BUSTS
British Comedy Society, 1998

For the Carry On 40th anniversary reunion at Pinewood, the British Comedy Society commissioned pewter busts of Kenneth Williams, Sid James, Charles Hawtrey and Hattie Jacques. Following the event, a limited number of resin replicas were made available by the Society, priced at £65 each.

STAMPS
Benham, 1999

Benham issued a series of souvenir postage stamps featuring stills from the Carry On films together with a beautiful first day cover of a painting entitled "Carry On Forever" by artist Keith Turley. A second edition was released the same year in aid of the Variety Club of Great Britain.

TOBY JUGS
Royal Doulton, 2001
Royal Doulton released two pairs of Carry On Toby Jugs, each limited to 1000 copies and commemorating a classic entry in the series. The first set featured Hattie Jacques as Matron and Kenneth Williams as Dr Tinkle from Carry On Doctor. The second featured Sid James as Sir Sidney-Ruff Diamond and Charles Hawtrey as Private Widdle from Carry On Up the Khyber.

TRADING CARDS
Cards Inc, 2003
A series of eight promotional trading cards were released by Cards Inc in 2003, heralding the launch of a full set of cards based on the Carry On films, featuring classic images and trivia. The preview set featured images from Carry On Doctor, Carry On up the Khyber, Carry On Camping, Carry On Again Doctor, Carry On up the Jungle, Carry On Abroad and Carry On Dick. The full set of trading cards was ultimately cancelled.

PHONE CARDS
Swift Telecom, 2001
A set of three pre-paid phone cards featuring the UK Quad poster artwork for Carry On Jack, Carry On Cleo and Carry On Screaming.

JOAN SIMS TRIBUTE COLLECTION TRADING CARDS
Cards Inc / Carlton, 2004
A limited edition set of 18 cards featuring stills from Joan Sims' film career. The set was produced in association with the British Comedy Society to commemorate the unveiling of a memorial plaque to Joan at Pinewood Studios.

BOBBIN' HEADS
Cards Inc, 2005
Cards Inc released two series of bobble-headed Carry On figures. The first, based on Carry On up the Khyber, included Private Widdle, Bunghit Din, Sir Sidney Ruff-Diamond and The Khasi of Kalabar. A second set, based on Carry On Camping, included Sid Boggle, Dr Soaper and Barbara.

ACTION FIGURES
Product Enterprise, 2005
Product Enterprise released a number of limited edition action figures based on popular franchises including Doctor Who, The Avengers and the Gerry Anderson series. Their first entry into the world of Carry On was a 12" Kenneth Williams figure, dressed in his costume from Carry On Cleo. The figure came on a Carry On branded base which shrieked a series of familiar catchphrases from the film.

A series of further figures were planned to include a Barbara Windsor nurse (incorrectly labelled as being from Carry On Again Doctor – the character was dressed as Carry On Doctor's Nurse May). From Carry On up the Khyber, a figure of Sid James as Sir Sidney was planned, as was a Charlie Muggins from Carry On Camping. All three figures were due for release in 2006 but were ultimately cancelled when Product Enterprise consolidated their range to focus on high end collectibles.

CARRY ON IN YOUR POCKET
Underground Toys, 2006
Novelty keychain which, when pressed, would emit one of six classic lines from the Carry On films:
- Leslie Philips: "Ding Dong, Carry On"
- Kenneth Williams: "Well don't just stand there man, get it out. Get it out!"
- Kenneth Williams: "Matron, take them away!"
- Kenneth Williams: "Oooh, I do feel queer"
- Kenneth Williams: "Ere, stop messin' about"
- Sid James' laugh

CARRY ON POSTER MUGS
Ethos, 2007
Released individually or in two collectors' sets, the Ethos Carry On mugs feature the original UK Quad poster artwork for the Rank Carry On films from Don't Lose your Head through to Carry On England.

CARRY ON SOUND BITE MUGS
Ethos, 2007
Ethos also released a set of four mugs featuring the likenesses of Sid James, Barbara Windsor, Kenneth Williams and Charles Hawtrey. A sound chip was embedded into the base of each mug which would emit a selection of each star's classic lines whenever it was picked up. Batteries were included, but rarely replaced.

CARRY ON COLOUR CHANGE MUGS
Ethos, 2007
Cornering the market in Carry On crockery, Ethos released a set of four colour changing mugs featuring images from the Carry On films which, when filled with heated liquid, would unveil a saucy surprise. The first two sported stills from Carry On Again Doctor; one of Dr Stoppidge helping Ellen with her corsets and another of Dr Nookey examining Goldie Locks. A third featured a still of Sid James in Esme Crowfoot's bed, taken from Carry On Loving and the fourth was an image of Kenneth Williams as Stuart Farquhar in Abroad with his trousers down.

CARRY ON PICNIC SET
Ethos, 2007
Having exhausted the possibilities of porcelain Carry On ephemera, in 2007, Ethos fired up its moulds and produced a 16 piece Carry On Camping picnic set, comprising bowls, saucers, plates and beakers all emblazoned with Carry On Camping stills. Available as a

set or individually, the line-up was completed by a commemorative Carry On Camping tray bearing the film's UK Quad poster artwork and a serving spoon and fork emblazoned with the Carry On Camping logo.

CARRY ON POKER CHIPS

CollectablesMania, 2007

By far the most pointless Carry On collectible produced to date was a series of five packs of poker chips with a Carry On theme. Each pack represented a particular film and lucky candidates included Carry On Doctor, Carry On Up the Khyber, Carry On Camping, Carry On Henry and Carry On Matron. They came in glossy presentation packs, complete with trivia notes and six individual plastic chips emblazoned with stills from the film they represented.

ROYAL MAIL CARRY ON FIRST DAY COVERS

Royal Mail, 2008

The Royal Mail's celebration of classic Carry On and Hammer Films in 2008 gave way to a series of philatelic collectibles, including stamps, postcards and presentation packs featuring UK Quad posters for Carry On Sergeant, Carry On Cleo and Carry On Screaming! From the Hammer stable, Dracula, the Mummy and the Curse of Frankenstein were represented.

CARRY ON "CIGARETTE" CARDS

Sporting Profiles, 2010

Speciality card manufacturer Sporting Profiles released a series of 20 Carry On portrait "cigarette" cards, featuring specially commissioned drawings of the Carry On team.

JIGSAWS

Falcon Deluxe, 2010

Falcon Deluxe released two Carry On jigsaws in 2010, both featuring a selection of Carry On UK poster artwork. The jigsaws came in 1000 and 250 piece sets, each with a different arrangement of Carry On artwork.

Wasgij, 2011

Wasgij specialises in jigsaws with a difference. Each release was accompanied by a visual mystery that could only be solved by completing the jigsaw. In 2011, the company commissioned an original Carry On painting from artist Graham Thompson that depicted a classic moment from the Carry On films' history and posed the question..."What is the elephant surprised by?" (answers on a postcard.)

BOOKS
FICTION:

POPCULT!
David Barnett
Pendragon Press, 2011
ISBN: 1906864241
When cultural historian Stuart Balfour hears of a surviving copy of the fabled "lost" film, Carry On you Old Devil, he is swept into the mysterious underground organisation known as popCULT!

RING FOR CATTY: A PLAY IN THREE PARTS
Patrick Cargill & Jack Beale
S French, 1956
ISBN: B0000CJKFB
Script of Cargill & Beale's play that was the original inspiration for Carry On Nurse and went on to be filmed as Twice Round the Daffodils.

CARRY ON DOCTOR – THE WICKEDLY FUNNY STORY THAT STARTS WHERE THE FILM ENDS
Norman Giller
Andre Deutsch Ltd, 1996
ISBN: 0233990275
Doctors Kilmore and Tinkle take on the corrupt Mayor and the dreaded Matron in a war for the future of Haven Hospital.

CARRY ON UP THE KHYBER – THE WICKEDLY FUNNY STORY THAT STARTS WHERE THE FILM ENDS
Norman Giller
Andre Deutsch Ltd, 1996
ISBN: 0233990305
With the Raj once more under British Command, Sir Sidney and Lady Joan tackle the Khasi's latest nefarious scheme: The Great Curry Powder Plot.

CARRY ON LOVING – THE WICKEDLY FUNNY STORY THAT STARTS WHERE THE FILM ENDS
Norman Giller
Andre Deutsch Ltd, 1996
ISBN: 0233990291
The Wedded Bliss Agency runs into financial difficulties, due to all the free love that's going on around them. Sid has a brainwave and launches an Undating Agency, to help men break away from their troubled relationships.

CARRY ON HENRY – THE WICKEDLY FUNNY STORY THAT STARTS WHERE THE FILM ENDS

Norman Giller
Andre Deutsch Ltd, 1996
ISBN: 0233990321
King Henry VIII needs to improve his public image and hires Will the Quill to write his biography. But when the randy king sets his sights on wife number seven, his image is the last thing on his mind.

CARRY ON ABROAD – THE WICKEDLY FUNNY STORY THAT STARTS WHERE THE FILM ENDS
Norman Giller
Andre Deutsch Ltd, 1996
ISBN: 0233990313
Stuart Farquhar leads another coach-load of tourists on a package tour of the Costa Packet but their hosts Pepe and Floella have learned from their mistakes and are out for every penny they can get.

CARRY ON ENGLAND – THE WICKEDLY FUNNY STORY THAT STARTS WHERE THE FILM ENDS
Norman Giller
Andre Deutsch Ltd, 1996
ISBN: 0233990283
Captain Melly and Sergeant-Major Bloomer lead the search for a Nazi spy who is on a mission to assassinate Winston Churchill.

CLEO, CAMPING, EMMANUELLE & DICK
Terry Johnson
Methuen, 1998
ISBN: 0413735001
Script of Terry Johnson's hugely successful play which premiered at the Lyttleton Theatre in 1998.

CARRY ON EMMANNUELLE
Lance Peters
Arrow Books, 1978
ISBN: 0099182203
Novel based on Lance Peters' original script for Carry On Emmannuelle. Concerned over the original story's adult content, Peter Rogers insisted that the book feature no stills or logo which could associate the content with the Carry On series of films.

NON-FICTION:

CARRY ON UNCENSORED
Morris Bright & Robert Ross
Boxtree, 1999
ISBN: 0752217984

THE LOST CARRY ONS
Morris Bright & Robert Ross
Boxtree, 2000
ISBN: 1852279907

POCKET ESSENTIALS: THE CARRY ON FILMS
Mark Campbell
Pocket Essentials, 2003
ISBN: 190404803X

THE OFFICIAL CARRY ON QUIZ BOOK
Chris Cowlin & Paul Burton
Apex Publishing, 2007
ISBN: 9781904444978

THE CARRY ON BOOK
Kenneth Eastaugh
David & Charles, 1978
ISBN: 0715374036

WHAT A CARRY ON! THE OFFICIAL STORY OF THE CARRY ON FILMS
Sally & Nina Hibbin
Hamlyn, 1988
ISBN: 0600558193

CARRY ON LAUGHING
Adrian Rigglesford
Virgin, 1996
ISBN: 075350006X

CARRY ON ACTORS
Andrew Ross
Apex Publishing, 2011
ISBN: 1906358958

THE CARRY ON COMPANION
Robert Ross
Batsford, 1996
ISBN: 0752217984

THE CARRY ON STORY
Robert Ross
Reynolds & Hearn, 2005
ISBN: 190311196X

THE OFFICIAL BOOK OF CARRY ON FACTS, FIGURES & STATISTICS
Kevin Snelgrove

Apex Publishing, 2008
ISBN: 9781906358099

THE COMPLETE A-Z OF EVERYTHING CARRY ON
Richard Webber
Harper Collins, 2005
ISBN: 0007182236

FIFTY YEARS OF CARRY ON
Richard Webber
Century, 2008
ISBN: 1844138437

BIOGRAPHY:

IT'S NOT A REHEARSAL
Amanda Barrie
Headline, 2003
ISBN: 075531123X

A TWITCH IN TIME: JACK DOUGLAS' LIFE STORY
Sue Benwell with Jack Douglas
Able, 2002
ISBN: 1903607248

MR CARRY ON, THE BIOGRAPHY OF PETER ROGERS
Morris Bright & Robert Ross
BBC, 2000
ISBN: 0563551836

KENNETH WILLIAMS UNSEEN
Wes Butters & Russell Davies
Harper Collins, 2008
ISBN: 0007280858

WHATSHISNAME: THE LIFE & DEATH OF CHARLES HAWTREY
Wes Butters
Tomahawk Press, 2010
ISBN: 0955767075

A WRITE CARRY ON: THE STORY OF A MAN IN THE SHADOWS
Mike Cobley
Wholepoint Productions, 2012
ISBN: N/A

ROSE IN THE BUD: EARLY DAYS IN THE MUSIC HALL WITH FRANKIE HOWERD
Gladys Critchell

Self-published, 1994
ISBN: N/A

KENNETH WILLIAMS: A BIOGRAPHY
Michael Freedland
Weidenfeld & Nicolson, 1990
ISBN: 0297797018

TITTER YE NOT! THE LIFE OF FRANKIE HOWERD
William Hall
HarperCollins, 1992
ISBN: 0586217738

ON THE WAY I LOST IT
Frankie Howerd
Star, 1977
ISBN: 035239594X

SID JAMES
Cliff Goodwin
Century, 1995
ISBN: 0712675868

NO LAUGHING MATTER: HOW I CARRIED ON
Norman Hudis
Apex Publishing, 2008
ISBN: 9781906358150

TUESDAY'S CHILD: THE LIFE & DEATH OF IMOGEN HASSALL
Dan Leissner
Midnight Marquee, 2002
ISBN: 1887664475

CHARLES HAWTREY: THE MAN WHO WAS PRIVATE WIDDLE
Roger Lewis
Faber & Faber, 2002
ISBN: 0571210899

FRANKIE HOWERD: STAND UP COMEDIAN
Graham McCann
Fourth Estate, 2004
ISBN: 1841153109

HATTIE JACQUES, THE AUTHORISED BIOGRAPHY
Andrew Merriman
Aurum, 2007
ISBN: 9781845132576

FRANKIE HOWERD: THE ILLUSTRATED BIOGRAPHY
Mick Middles
Headline, 2000
ISBN: 0747239436

HELLO
Leslie Phillips
Orion, 2006
ISBN: 0752868896
Audio CD (abridged):
Orion, 2006
ISBN: 0752873865

THE COMPLETE SID JAMES
Robert Ross
Reynolds & Hearn, 2000
ISBN: 1903111943

THE COMPLETE FRANKIE HOWERD
Robert Ross
Reynolds & Hearn, 2001
ISBN: 1903111080

SID JAMES, COCKNEY REBEL
Robert Ross
JR Books 2009
SBN: 190677935X

HIGH SPIRITS
Joan Sims
Partridge, 2000
ISBN: 1852252804

KENNETH WILLIAMS: BORN BRILLIANT
Christopher Stevens
John Murray, 2010
ISBN: 1848541953

STAR TURNS: THE LIFE & TIMES OF BENNY HILL & FRANKIE HOWERD
Barry Took
Weidenfeld & Nicolson, 1992
ISBN: 0297812971

BLIMEY! IT'S THE SID JAMES BOOK
Gary Wharton
Lushington Publishing, 2007
ISBN: 0954218744

AND JUNE WHITFIELD
June Whitfield
Bantam, 2000
ISBN: 0593045823

AT A GLANCE: AN ABSOLUTELY FABULOUS LIFE
June Whitfield
Wiedenfeld & Nicolson, 2009
ISBN: 029785562X

BRUCE MONTGOMERY: A LIFE IN MUSIC & BOOKS
David Whittle
Ashgate, 2007
ISBN: 0754634434

JUST WILLIAMS: AN AUTOBIOGRAPHY
Kenneth Williams
HarperCollins, 1986
ISBN: 0006370829
Audio Cassette:
BBC Radio Collection, 1998
ISBN: 0563225971

THE KENNETH WILLIAMS DIARIES
Kenneth Williams (editor, Russell Davies)
HarperCollins, 1993
ISBN: 0006380905

THE KENNETH WILLIAMS LETTERS
Kenneth Williams (editor, Russell Davies)
HarperCollins, 1995
ISBN: 0006380921

BARBARA: THE LAUGHTER & TEARS OF A COCKNEY SPARROW
Barbara Windsor
Arrow, 1991
ISBN: 0099721104

ALL OF ME: MY EXTRAORDINARY LIFE
Barbara Windsor
Headline, 2000
ISBN: 0747266441
Audio Cassette:
Hodder & Stoughton, 2000
ISBN: 1840323779

MISCELLANEOUS:

THE WU-HEY TO BETTER COOKING
Jack Douglas
Golden Eagle Press, 1975
ISBN: 0901482234

TRUMPS
Frankie Howerd
Dent, 1982
ISBN: 0460045504

HOWERD'S HOWLERS
Frankie Howerd
Octopus, 1985
ISBN: 0862735103

ACID DROPS
Kenneth Williams
Dent, 1980
ISBN: 0460044826

BACK DROPS
Kenneth Williams
Futura, 1984
ISBN: 0708824641

I ONLY HAVE TO CLOSE MY EYES
Kenneth Williams & Beverlie Manson
Dent, 1986
ISBN: 0460061755

THE COMPLETE ACID DROPS
Kenneth Williams
Orion, 2000
ISBN: 0752837257

BARBARA WINDSOR'S BOOK OF BOOBS
Barbara Windsor
Hamlyn, 1979
ISBN: 0600315630

CDS, RECORDS & CASSETTES:
7"/CD SINGLES:

Carry On Screaming
Boz Burrell
Columbia, 1966
Cat: DB 7972

Our House/She's Gone (Carry On London!)
Sid James
Pye, 1973
Cat: 7N45281

Smile, Smile, Smile (Carry On London!)
Kenny Ball
Pye, 1973
Cat: 7N45275

Love Crazy / Since I've Been Away from my Love
Masterplan
Satril, 1978
Cat: SAT 136

Carry On Columbus
Fantastic Planet (Malcolm McLaren)
A&M Records, 1992
CD: Cat: AMCD065
12": Cat: AMY0065
2x12": Cat: AMY0065DJ

Am I Right / Carry On Clangers / Let it Flow / Waiting for Sex
Erasure
Mute, 1992
7": Cat: Mute134
12": Cat: 12Mute134
CD: Cat: CDMute134

What A Carry On
O'Leary & Bragg
Storehouse, 2000
CD: STORECD0217

LP/CD/CASSETTE

Oh! What a Carry On
Various Artists
Music for Pleasure (EMI), 1971
Cat: MFP1416UK
Comedy songs from the Carry On team

A Slice of Pye: Collected London Cast Recordings
Various Artists

Pye, 1973
Cat: DRG13114 (CD)
A collection of songs from contemporary productions. Includes "Our House" and "Smile, Smile, Smile" from Carry On London!

Carrying On – Entertainment from the Carry On Team
Various Artists
EMI, 1993
Cat: ECC282
A compilation of songs & sketches from the Carry On team

Carry On Up the Jungle / Carry On Up the Khyber
Various Artists
EMI, 1995
Cat: GAGDMC051
Original film soundtrack with additional narration by Patrick Allen. Also available individually.

Carry On Doctor / Carry On Follow that Camel
Various Artists
EMI, 1995
Cat: GAGDMC052
Original film soundtrack with additional narration by Peter Gilmore & Patrick Allen. Also available individually.

Carry On Camping / Carry On Don't Lose your Head
Various Artists
EMI, 1995
Cat: GAGDMC053
Original film soundtrack with additional narration by Joan Sims & Patrick Allen. Also available individually.

Oh! What a Carry On
Various Artists
EMI Gold, 2005
Cat: 8668682
Re-release of the original 1971 compilation with additional tracks.

Carry On – 20 Years of the Carry On films
Various Artists
Silva Screen, 2005
Cat: SILCD1168
Themes, cues and dialog taken from the original film soundtracks.

The Carry On Album, Music from the Films
Gavin Sutherland & the Prague Philharmonic Orchestra
ASV, 1999
Cat: CD CDWHL2I 19
Newly performed renditions of classic Carry On themes.

What a Carry On
Gavin Sutherland and the Royal Sinfonia
Dutton Vocalion, 2005
Cat: CDSA 6810

Newly performed renditions of classic Carry On themes.

HOME VIDEO

DVD

(for individual releases, see Carry On Films, Carry On TV)

Carry On Sergeant – Carry On Screaming!
Warner Home Video, 2001
PAL, Region 2 (Europe, Middle East & Japan)
Colour, Black & White
Standard editions with no special features.

Carry On Don't Lose your Head – Carry On Emmannuelle
Cinema Club, 2001
PAL, Region 2 (Europe, Middle East & Japan)
Colour
Standard editions with no special features

DeAgostini Carry On DVD partwork: Carry On Sergeant – Carry On Emmannuelle
DeAgostini/Carlton, 2003
PAL, Region 2 (Europe, Middle East & Japan), Colour, Black & White
Standard editions with no special features. A further four volumes were released containing the Carry On Laughing TV series

Ultimate Edition releases: Carry On Sergeant – Carry On Emmannuelle
ITV Studios Home Entertainment, 2006, 2008
PAL, Region 2 (Europe, Middle East & Japan)
Colour, Black & White
For special features, see individual film releases

Carry On Quizzing
ITV Studios Home Entertainment, 2006
PAL, Region 2 (Europe, Middle East & Japan)
Colour, Black & White
Interactive DVD game

VHS

(for individual releases, see Carry On Films, Carry On TV)

Carry On Nurse
EMI, 1979
PAL, Black & White

Carry On Cleo
Thorn EMI, 1980
PAL, Colour

Carry On Matron, Carry On Abroad, That's Carry On
Rank Video Library, 1980
PAL, Colour

Carry On Cowboy

EMI, 1981, 1983
PAL, Colour

Carry On up the Khyber, Carry On up the Jungle, Carry On Camping, Carry On Henry, Carry On at your Convenience, Carry On Girls, Carry On Behind, Carry On England
Rank Video Library, 1981
PAL, Colour

Carry On Emmannuelle
CBS/Fox, 1981
PAL, Colour

Carry On Follow that Camel, Carry On Doctor, Carry On Again Doctor, Carry On Loving, Carry On Dick
Rank Video Library, 1984
PAL, Colour

Carry On Cruising
Warner Home Video, 1986
PAL, Colour

Carry On Camping
Rank Video Library 1986
PAL, Colour

Carry On Sergeant – Carry On Screaming!
Warner Home Video, 1988, 1995
PAL, Colour, Black & White

Carry On Don't Lose your Head – Carry On Emmannuelle
Cinema Club, 1986-1988, 1992, 1999
PAL, Colour

Carry On Camping
Pickwick Video Ltd, 1990
PAL, Colour

That's Carry On
Weintraub, 1991
PAL, Colour

Carry On Camping
Rank Classics, 1992
PAL, Colour

Carry On Sergeant – Carry On Screaming! (Double pack releases)
Warner Home Video, 1993, 2001
PAL, Colour, Black & White

Carry On Columbus
Warner Home Video, 1993, 1999
PAL, Colour

Carry On - Don't Lose your Head – Carry On Emmannuelle (Double pack releases)

Cinema Club, 2000
PAL, Colour

Carry On Don't Lose your Head – Carry On Emmannuelle
Carlton Visual Entertainment, 2003
PAL, Colour

DeAgostini Carry On VHS partwork: Carry On Sergeant – Carry On Emmannuelle (plus fact file magazine)
DeAgostini/Carlton, 2003
PAL, Colour, Black & White

BETAMAX:

Carry On Nurse
EMI, 1979
PAL, Black & White

Carry On Cleo
Thorn EMI, 1980
PAL, Colour

Carry On Abroad, That's Carry On
Rank Video Library, 1980
PAL, Colour

Carry On up the Khyber, Carry On Camping, Carry On up the Jungle, Carry On Henry, Carry On at your Convenience, Carry On Girls, Carry On Behind, Carry On England
Rank Video Library, 1981
PAL, Colour

Carry On Emmannuelle
CBS/Fox, 1981
PAL, Colour

Carry On Cowboy
EMI, 1981, 1983
PAL, Colour

Carry On Follow that Camel, Carry On Doctor, Carry On Again Doctor, Carry On Dick
Rank Video Library, 1984
PAL, Colour

BEHIND THE SCENES DIRECTORY OF CAST

A

Adams, Jill: WPC Harrison (Constable)
Aird, Holly: Maria (Columbus)
Ajibadi, Yemi: Witch Doctor (Up the Jungle)
Alexander, Terence: Trevor Trelawney (Regardless)
Allen, Andrea: Minnie (Cowboy)
Allen, Keith: Pepi the Poisoner (Columbus)
Allen, Patrick: Narrator (Don't Lose your Head, Doctor, Up the Khyber)
Allison, Bart: Granddad (Doctor), Grandpa Grubb (Loving)
Antrobus, John: 5th Citizen (Constable), Manservant (Columbus)
Arden, Mark: Mark (Columbus)
Arnall, Julia: Trudi Trelawney (Regardless)
Askwith, Robin: Larry (Girls)
Aston, Anne: Candy Maple (Carry On Laughing with "The Slimming Factory" (stage))
Aubrey, Diane: Honoria (Constable)

B

Baden-Semper, Nina: Nosha (Up the Jungle)
Bailey, Andrew: Genghis (Columbus)
Bailey, Anthony: Rider (Dick)
Baird, Anthony: 1st Guard (Spying)
Baksh, Shakira: Scrubba (Again Doctor)
Balfour, Michael: Matt (Constable)
Ball, Vincent: Jenkins (Cruising), Ship's Officer (Follow that Camel)
Ballet Montparnasse, the: Dancing Girls (Cowboy)
Banks, Peter: Gunner Thomas (England)
Barker, Eric: Captain Potts (Sergeant), Inspector Mills (Constable), The Chief (Spying), Ancient General (Emmannuelle)
Baron, Lynda: Meg (Columbus)
Barrie, Amanda: Anthea (Cabby), Cleopatra (Cleo)
Barry, Hilda: Grandma Grubb (Loving)
Bartlett, Richard: Gunner Drury (England)
Bayntun, Amelia: Mrs Fussey (Camping), Corset Lady (Loving), Mrs Spragg (At your Convenience), Mrs Jenkins (Matron), Mrs Tuttle (Abroad)
Beaumont, Susan: Frances James (Nurse)
Beck, James: Mr Roxby (Loving - *Scene Cut*)
Beevers, Diana: Penny Lee (Teacher)
Benham, Joan: Cynical Lady (Emmannuelle)
Bennett, Peter: Passer-by (Constable)
Berens, Harold: Cecil the Torturer (Columbus)
Best, Gloria: Funhouse Girl (Spying), Handmaiden (Cleo), Bridget (Cowboy)
Binning, Tanya: Virginia (Cleo)

Bisset, Donald: Patient (Again Doctor)
Blain, Josephine: Hospitality Girl (Up the Khyber)
Blake, Denis: Rubbatiti (Screaming!)
Blazer, Jonathan: Jolly Juvenile (Wot a Carry On in Blackpool (stage))
Bluthal, John: Head Waiter (Spying), Corporal Clotski (Follow that Camel), Royal Tailor (Henry)
Boa, Bruce: US Ambassador (Emmannuelle)
Boddey, Martin: 6th Specialist (Sergeant), Perkins (Nurse)
Boon, Eric: Shorty (Constable), Second (Regardless)
Boyce, David: Customer with Ear (Columbus)
Bradley, Josie: Pianist (Loving)
Brambell, Wilfrid: Mr Pullen (Again Doctor)
Brayshaw, Deborah: French Buxom Blonde (Emmannuelle)
Bregonzi, Alec: 1st Storeman (Sergeant), Photographer (At your Convenience - *Scene cut*)

BRESSLAW, BERNARD

Born: 25th February 1934, Stepney, London, UK
Died: 11th June 1993, Enfield, London, UK
First Film Appearance: Men of Sherwood Forest (1954)
First Carry On Appearance: Carry On Nurse (1959) - body double for Terence Longdon
First Starring Carry On Appearance: Carry On Cowboy (1965)
Final Film Appearance: Leon the Pig Farmer (1992)

Carry On Appearances: Little Heap (Cowboy), Sockett (Screaming!), Sheikh Abdul Abulbul (Follow that Camel), Ken Biddle (Doctor), Bunghit Din (Up the Khyber), Bernie Lugg (Camping), Upsidaisi (Up the Jungle), Gripper Burke (Loving), Bernie Hulke (At your Convenience), Ernie Bragg (Matron), Brother Bernard (Abroad), Peter Potter (Girls), Sir Roger Daley (Dick), Arthur Upmore (Behind), Bob Cratchit/Frankenstein's Monster/ Spirit of Christmas Future/Convent Girl/Town Crier/Policeman (Carry On Christmas 1969 (TV)), Rollicky Bill (Carry On Again Christmas (TV)), Bean Podkin/Capting Ffing-Burgh/ Dart Player/Much/Police Officer/Ballet Dancer (Carry On Christmas 1973 (TV)), Performer (What a Carry On! (TV)), Sir Pureheart (Carry On Laughing - Under the Round Table (TV)), Sir Lancelot (Carry On Laughing - Short Knight, Long Daze (TV)), Starkers (Carry On Laughing - And in My Lady's Chamber (TV)), Klanger (Carry On Laughing - Who Needs Kitchener? (TV)), Dr Pavingstone (Carry On Laughing - Lamp Posts of the Empire (TV)), Carry On London! (stage), Leading Man (Wot a Carry On in Blackpool (stage))

Other Notable Appearances: The Army Game (Associated Television, 1957-1958), I Only Arsked (Film, 1958), Meet the Champ (BBC Television, 1960), Our House (ABC Television, 1961-1962), Doctor Who - The Ice Warriors (BBC Television, 1967), Clochemerle (BBC Television, 1972), Krull (Film, 1983), Mann's Best Friends (Channel 4, 1985)

Finest Hour (and a bit):
Carry On Follow that Camel. Bernie's most famous Carry On persona is the lovable idiot, usually in thrall to whatever seedy character Sid's playing at the time. While these characters are always fun, light and, of course funny, Bernie really gets a chance to show just how great an actor he was when playing against this type. As Sheikh Abdul Abulbul,

he chews his way through Follow that Camel, a boggle eyed scheming maniac intent on destroying the incompetent infidels under Commandant Burger. It's a beautiful role and Bernie really gives it everything he's got in a brilliant, mesmerising performance. In our more enlightened climate, seeing Bernie (and occasionally the other team members, but for some reason, usually Bernie) blacked up is a little jarring but the intent was pure enough at the time and if there is any racism on display, it's directed more at the archetypal stiff upper-lips of Bo and Simpkins.

One to Forget:
Carry On Loving. It's hardly his fault, but Bernie's role in Carry On Loving gives him little to do other than shout and throw people around various rooms. The jealous boyfriend character is a necessary one, given the nature of the relationship between Esme Crowfoot and Sid, but it's a terribly under-written role. What's particularly galling is that the character detracts from the otherwise stellar quality of one of the finest Carry Ons in the series.

Seen & Heard:
Film Night Special - Carry On Forever (BBC2, 12/04/1970)
What a Carry On (Thames Television, 4/10/1973)
Bernard Bresslaw - Comedy's Gentle Giant (BBC Radio, 1/01/1994)

Briggs, Johnny: Sporran Soldier (up the Khyber), Plasterer (Behind), Melly's Driver (England), Norman (Carry On Laughing - The Case of the Coughing Parrot (TV))
Brinton, Tim: BBC Newscaster (Emmannuelle)
Brody, Ronnie: Little Man (Don't Lose your Head), Henry (Loving), Waiter (Carry On Laughing - The Prisoner of Spenda (TV)), Shortest Knight (Carry On Laughing - Under the Round Table (TV))
Bromley, Sydney: Sam Houston (Cowboy)
Brooking, John: 3rd Sea Lord (Jack)
Brooks, Ray: Giorgio (Abroad)
Browne, Wayne: Native (Carry On Laughing - Lamp Posts of the Empire (TV))
Bryan, Dora: Norah (Sergeant)
Burton, Louise: Private Evans (England), Girl at Zoo (Emmannuelle)
Burton, Peter: Hotel Manager (At your Convenience)

BUTTERWORTH, PETER

Born: 4th February 1919, Bramhall, Stockport, UK
Died: 16th January 1979, Coventry, UK

First Film Appearance: William Comes to Town (1948)
First Carry On Appearance: Carry On Cowboy (1965)
Final Film Appearance: The First Great Train Robbery (1979)

Carry On Appearances: Doc (Cowboy), Detective Constable Slobotham (Screaming!), Citizen Bidet (Don't Lose your Head), Simpson (Follow that Camel), Mr Smith (Doctor), Brother Belcher (Up the Khyber), Josh Fiddler (Camping), Shuffling Patient (Again Doctor), Sinister Client (Loving), Charles, Earl of Bristol (Henry), Pepe (Abroad), Admiral (Girls),

Tom (Dick), Henry Barnes (Behind), Major Carstairs (England), Richmond (Emmannuelle), Dracula/Street Beggar/Convent Girl/Haggie the Ugly Sister (Carry On Christmas 1969 (TV)), Captain Alistair Dripping/Sir Francis Fiddler/Admiral Rene/Widow Holinone (Carry On Christmas 1972 (TV)), Caveman Carol Singer/Ancient Gent/Darts Player/German Soldier/Friar Tuck/Ballet Dancer (Carry On Christmas 1973 (TV)), Performer (What a Carry On! (TV)), Count Yerackers (Carry On Laughing - The Prisoner of Spenda (TV)), Friar Roger (Carry On Laughing - The Baron Outlook (TV)), Oliver Cromwell (Carry On Laughing - The Sobbing Cavalier (TV)), Admiral Clanger (Carry On Laughing - The Case of the Screaming Winkles (TV)), Lost Property Attendant (Carry On Laughing - The Case of the Coughing Parrot (TV)), Merlin (Carry On Laughing - Under the Round Table (TV)), Merlin (Carry On Laughing - Short Knight, Long Daze (TV)), Silas (Carry On Laughing - And in My Lady's Chamber (TV)), Lord Gropefinger (Carry On Laughing - Lamp Posts of the Empire (TV)), Carry On London! (stage), Willie Strokes (Carry On Laughing with "The Slimming Factory" (stage))

Other Notable Appearances: Old Mother Riley's Jungle Treasure (1951), Those Kids (ABC Weekend Television, 1956), Meet the Champ (BBC Television, 1960), Doctor Who - The Time Meddler (BBC Television, 1965), Doctor Who - The Daleks' Masterplan (BBC Television, 1966), Catweazle (London Weekend Television, 1970-1971), A Class by Himself (Harlech Television, 1971), Odd Man Out (Thames Television, 1977)

Finest Hour (and a bit):
Carry On up the Khyber. Finding an outstanding performance from Peter Butterworth is no easy feat. Butterworth is simply brilliant in all of his roles. There's not a bad portrayal among them but in Carry On up the Khyber, we get to see Butterworth deliver a performance that takes in all the best characteristics from his many Carry On roles. From the selfish, deceitful sex maniac at the start of the film to the gibbering nervous wreck at the end, Butterworth's performance in Carry On up the Khyber is one of the finest by any member of the Carry On gang. The final dinner scene is one of the highlights of the entire Carry On series, but there's nobody finer at that table than Butterworth, slowly descending into madness as Sir Sidney and the others maintain their characteristic stiff upper lip.

One to Forget:
Carry On Loving. There are a few films where Butterworth makes little more than a cameo appearance and there's absolutely nothing not to love about them apart from their brevity. As wonderful as Butterworth's scene is in the Wedded Bliss Agency, it is all too brief.

Seen & Heard:
What a Carry On (Thames Television, 4/10/1973)
This is your Life: Peter Butterworth (Thames Television, 5/03/1975)

Byrne, Peter: Bridegroom (Cabby)

C

Cain, Simon: Short (Cowboy), Riff (Follow that Camel), Tea Orderly (Doctor), Bagpipe Soldier (Up the Khyber), X-Ray Man (Again Doctor), Barman (At your Convenience)
Callow, Simon: 1st Crew Member (Carry On Laughing - Orgy & Bess (TV))

Campion, Gerald: Andy Galloway (Sergeant)

Cannon, Esma: Deaf Old Lady (Constable), Miss Cooling (Regardless), Bridget Madderley (Cruising), Flo Sims (Cabby)

Capron, Brian: Trumpeter (Carry On Laughing - Under the Round Table (TV)), Trumpeter (Carry On Laughing - Short Knight, Long Daze (TV))

Cardew, Jane: Henry's 2nd Wife (Henry - *Scene cut*)

Cargill, Patrick: Raffish Customer (Regardless), Spanish Governor (Jack) - *See also Crew*

Carlin, John: Officer (England), French Parson (Emmannuelle), Ethelbert (Carry On Laughing - The Baron Outlook (TV)), Sir Walter Raleigh (Carry On Laughing - Orgy & Bess (TV)), Egbert (Carry On Laughing - One in the Eye for Harold (TV)), Vicar (Carry On Laughing - The Nine Old Cobblers (TV)), Major Merridick (Carry On Laughing – the Case of the Screaming Winkles (TV)), Old Man (Carry On Laughing - Lamp Posts of the Empire (TV))

Caron, Sandra: Fanny (Camping)

Carroll, Edwina: Nerda (Up the Jungle)

Casley, Alan: Kindly Seaman (Cruising)

Castle, Roy: Captain Keene (Up the Khyber)

Chamberlain, Cyril: Gun Sergeant (Sergeant), Bert Able (Nurse), Alf (Teacher), Thurston (Constable), Policeman (Regardless), Tom Tree (Cruising), Sarge (Cabby)

Chappell, Norman: Allbright (Cabby), 1st Plotter (Henry), Mr Thrush (Loving - *Scene cut*), Lord Burleigh (Carry On Laughing - Orgy & Bess (TV)), King Harold (Carry On Laughing - One in the Eye for Harold (TV)), Potter (Carry On Laughing - The Case of the Screaming Winkles (TV)), Ambulance Driver (Carry On Laughing - The Case of the Coughing Parrot (TV)), Sir William (Carry On Laughing - Under the Round Table (TV)), Sir William (Carry On Laughing - Short Knight, Long Daze (TV)), Businessman (Carry On Laughing - Lamp Posts of the Empire (TV))

Clarke, Ronald: 6th Storeman (Sergeant)

Clary, Julian: Don Juan Diego (Columbus)

Clegg, Tom: Massive Micky McGee (Regardless), Doorman (Spying), Sosages (Cleo), Blacksmith (Cowboy), Oddbodd (Screaming!), Trainer (Loving)

Clunes, Martin: Martin (Columbus)

Clifton, Philip: Injured Footballer (Emmannuelle)

Clifton, Zena: Au Pair Girl (Matron), Susan Brooks (Girls)

Clifford, Peggy Ann: Willa Claudia (Cleo)

Clive, John: Dandy (Henry - *Scene cut*), Robin Tweet (Abroad), Isaak the Tailor (Dick)

Clulow, Jennifer: 1st Lady (Don't Lose your Head)

Coburn, Brian: Trapper (Cowboy), Highwayman (Dick)

Cockburn, Peter: Commentator (Camping)

Cole, Paul: Atkins (Teacher)

Colleano, Gary: Slim (Cowboy)

Collings, Jeannie: Private Edwards (England)

Collins, Laura: Nurse (Matron)

Collins, Marian: Bride (Cruising), Bride (Cabby), Girl at Dirty Dick's (Jack), Amazon Guard (Spying)

Connor, Jeremy: Jeremy Bishop (Nurse), Willy (Constable), Footpad (Dick), Student with Ice Cream (Behind), Gunner Hiscocks (England)

CONNOR, KENNETH

Born: 6th June 1918, Islington, London
Died: 28th November 1993, London, UK

First Film Appearance: Poison Pen (1939)
First Carry On Appearance: Carry On Sergeant (1958)
Final Film Appearance: Carry On Emmannuelle (1978)

Carry On Appearances: Horace Strong (Sergeant), Bernie Bishop (Nurse), Gregory Adams (Teacher), Constable Charlie Constable (Constable), Sam Twist (Regardless), Dr Arthur Binn (Cruising), Ted Watson (Cabby), Hengist Pod (Cleo), Claude Chumley (Up the Jungle), Lord Hampton of Wick (Henry), Mr Tidey (Matron), Stanley Blunt (Abroad), Mayor Frederick Bumble (Girls), Constable (Dick), Major Leep (Behind), Captain S Melly (England), Leyland (Emmannuelle), Dr Livershake (Carry On Again Christmas (TV)), Club Chairman, Lt Bangham, Inspector Knicker, General Clodhopper, Hanky Poo (Carry On Christmas 1972 (TV)), Mr Sibley, the Store Manager/Bishop/Anthro Pod/Private Parkin/Will Scarlet/Ballet Dancer (Carry On Christmas 1973 (TV)), Performer (What a Carry On! (TV)), Nickoff (Carry On Laughing - The Prisoner of Spenda (TV)), Sir William (Carry On Laughing - The Baron Outlook (TV)), King Philip (Carry On Laughing - Orgy & Bess (TV)), Athelstan (Carry On Laughing - One in the Eye for Harold (TV)), Punter (Carry On Laughing - The Nine Old Cobblers (TV)), Punter (Carry On Laughing - The Case of the Screaming Winkles (TV)), King Arthur (Carry On Laughing - Under the Round Table (TV)), King Arthur (Carry On Laughing - Short Knight, Long Daze (TV)), Sir Harry Bulger-Plunger (Carry On Laughing - And in My Lady's Chamber (TV)), Sir Harry Bulger-Plunger (Carry On Laughing - Who Needs Kitchener? (TV)), Stanley (Carry On Laughing - Lamp Posts of the Empire (TV)), Carry On London! (stage), Major Chambers (Carry On Laughing with "The Slimming Factory" (stage))

Other Notable Appearances: A Show Called Fred (Associated Rediffusion Television, 1956), Dentist in the Chair (1960), Four Feather Falls (Granada Television, 1960), Watch your Stern! (1961), What a Carve Up! (1961), On the House (Yorkshire Television, 1970-1971), All this and Christmas Too! (Thames Television, 1971), Blackadder the Third (BBC Television, 1987), Hi-de-Hi (BBC Television, 1986-1988), Allo Allo (BBC Television, 1984-1992), Norbert Smith – A Life (Channel 4, 1989)

Finest Hour (and a bit):
Carry On Abroad. Kenneth Connor was typically cast in the early Carry Ons as the comedy romantic lead: a sympathetic character who ultimately gets the girl but goes through more than his fair share of pratfalls along the way. After a six year absence from the Carry On team, a time in which the role of male comedy lead had been filled with comedic aplomb by Jim Dale, Kenneth had to find a new niche. Stanley Blunt in Carry On Abroad is the perfect example of the sort of character Kenneth would do so well in the later films. Blunt is an uptight blusterer who eventually learns to let it all hang out and give in to the madness that descends around him. Hoping to get away for a weekend of sun and sauce with his repressed, waspish wife, Blunt is locked in a frenzy of sexual tension. By the end of the film, he and his wife are romping with wild abandon in bed in front of their fellow holidaymakers as the hotel collapses around their ears. Kenneth's come a long way since the whimsical, sentiment-heavy types he played in the earlier films, but if you prefer your Carry Ons high on naughtiness and low on mawkish romance, then

Abroad is the perfect film to see Kenneth at his very best.

One to Forget:
Carry On England. Kenneth's double act with co-star Windsor Davies is the highlight of a relentlessly dull and heartless Carry On. Between the battery's best efforts to overthrow their superior officers and Captain Melly's attempts to knock them into shape, there's little room for the generous, fun-filled comedy for which the Carry Ons are so loved. With that in mind, the nature of Kenneth's performance is irrelevant – he's playing a character who is fundamentally - and in no way comedically - flawed. Melly is a petty, bitter, incompetent little man and the humour in the film revolves around how miserable his life can become.

Seen & Heard:
Desert Island Discs (BBC Radio, 22/06/1964)
Film Night Special - Carry On Forever (BBC 2, 12/04/1970)
What a Carry On (Thames Television, 4/10/1973)
The Electric Theatre Show – Carry On England (Grampian, 1976)
Movie Memories (Anglia Television, 17/03/1982)
The Kenneth Connor Story (BBC Radio, 1989)

Coombs, Pat: Patient (Doctor), New Matron (Again Doctor)
Cooper, June: Girl (Don't Lose your Head), Hospitality Girl (Up the Khyber)
Cope, Kenneth: Vic Spanner (At your Convenience), Cyril Carter (Matron)
Corbett, Harry H: Detective Sergeant Sidney Bung (Screaming!)
Cordell, Shane: Attractive Nurse (Nurse)
Corduner, Allan: Sam (Columbus)
Cornelius, Billy: Oddbodd Junior (Screaming!), Soldier (Don't Lose your Head), Patient in Plaster (Again Doctor), Guard (Henry), Constable (Girls), Tough Man (Dick), Man with Salad (Behind), Waiter (Carry On Christmas 1972 (TV)), Pikeman (Carry On Laughing - One in the Eye for Harold (TV)), Man-at-Arms (Carry On Laughing - Under the Round Table (TV)), Man-at-Arms (Carry On Laughing - Short Knight, Long Daze (TV))
Cornelius, Joe: Second Maitre d'Hotel (Loving)
Corrie, Eric: 3rd Citizen (Constable)
Counsell, Jenny: Night Nurse (Again Doctor)
Cowling, Brenda: Matron (Girls), Wife (Behind)
Cox, Jenny: Veronica (Behind)
Cribbins, Bernard: Midshipman Albert Poop-Decker (Jack), Harold Crump (Spying), Mordecai Mendoza (Columbus)
Cross, Larry: Perkins (Cowboy)
Crowe, Sara: Fatima (Columbus)
Cummings, Bill: 2nd Thug (Spying)
Curry, Ian: Eric (Constable), Leonard Beamish (Regardless)
Curtis, Alan: Conte di Pisa (Henry), Police Chief (Abroad)

D

DALE, JIM

Real Name: James Smith
Born: 19th August 1935, Rothwell, UK

First Film Appearance: Raising the Wind (1961)
First Carry On Appearance: Carry On Cabby (1963)

Carry On Appearances: Expectant Father (Cabby), Carrier (Jack), Carstairs (Spying), Horsa (Cleo), Marshall P Knutt (Cowboy), Albert Potter (Screaming!), Lord Darcy de Pue (Don't Lose your Head), Bertram Oliphant West (Follow that Camel), Dr Jim Kilmore (Doctor), Dr James Nookey (Again Doctor), Christopher Columbus (Columbus)

Other Notable Appearances: Six-Five Special (BBC Television, 1957-1958), The Plank (1967), Join Jim Dale (Associated Television, 1969), Rogues Gallery (Granada Television, 1969), Digby, The Biggest Dog in the World (1973), Pete's Dragon (1977), The Spacemen & King Arthur (1979), Pushing Daisies (ABC Television, 2007-2009)

Finest Hour (and a bit):
Carry On Cowboy. Throughout his 10 year tenure with the Carry Ons, Jim Dale specialised in the young, romantic idiot role. Jim is a master of slapstick and his willingness (and that of the insurers) to do his own stunts led to some amazing physical comedy. In Carry On Cowboy, Marshall P. Knutt manages to defeat the bad guys and get the girl through sheer luck. His relationship with Annie is a slapstick farce delivered with perfect comic timing and wide eyed gormlessness. That it's all done within the confines of one of the most lavish and comedically sparkling films in the series makes Cowboy the perfect example of Jim's particular brand of Carry On humour.

One to forget:
Carry On Jack. Carry On Jack is far from a typical Carry On film in that it's more of a funny historical drama than an all-out romp. Jim has one of the best roles in the film, in terms of comedy, but with just a few lines he's sadly under-used in a film which, more than most, desperately needed every laugh it could get.

Seen & Heard:
This is Your Life: Jim Dale (Thames Television, 21/11/73)
British Film Forever (BBC Television, 2007)
The Greatest Ever Carry On Films (Channel 5, 27/12/11)

Dale, Toby: Inquisitor (Columbus)
Dane, Alexandra: Female Instructor (Doctor), Busti (Up the Khyber), Stout Woman (Again Doctor), Emily (Loving), Uncredited role (At your Convenience - *Scene cut*), Lady in Low-Cut Dress (Behind)
Danielle, Suzanne: Emmannuelle Prevert (Emmannuelle)
Daniels, Danny: Nosha Chief (Up the Jungle)
Daniels, Beau: Mrs Babbington (Carry On Laughing with "The Slimming Factory" (stage))
Dann, Larry: Boy (Teacher), Clive (Behind), Gunner Shaw (England), Theodore Valentine (Emmannuelle)

Darvey, Diana: Maureen (Behind)

Davenport, Claire: Blonde in Pub (Emmannuelle)

Davenport, David: Bilius (Cleo), Sergeant (Don't Lose your Head), Major-Domo (Henry)

David, Evan: Bridegroom (Cruising)

Davies, Windsor: Fred Ramsden (Behind), Sergeant Major "Tiger" Bloomer (England)

De Wolff, Francis: Agrippa (Cleo)

Dempster, Jeremy: Recruit (Sergeant)

Dene, Carmen: Mexican Girl (Cowboy), Hospitality Girl (Up the Khyber)

Desmonde, Jerry: Martin Paul (Regardless)

Devereaux, Ed: Sergeant Russell (Sergeant), Alec Lawrence (Nurse), Mr Panting (Regardless), Young Officer (Cruising), Hook (Jack)

Diamond, Arnold: 5th Specialist (Sergeant)

Dickenson, Terry: Recruit (Sergeant)

Dietrich, Monica: Girl (Don't Lose your Head), Katherine Howard (Henry)

Dignam, Basil: 3rd Specialist (Sergeant)

Don, Dominique: Girl at Dirty Dick's (Jack), Harem Girl (Follow that Camel), Belcher's Indian Girl (Up the Khyber)

Dorning, Robert: Prime Minister (Emmannuelle)

Douglas, Angela: Annie Oakley (Cowboy), Doris Mann (Screaming!), Lady Jane Ponsonby (Follow that Camel), Princess Jelhi (Up the Khyber)

DOUGLAS, JACK

Real Name: Jack Roberton

Born: 26th April 1929, Newcastle Upon Tyne, UK

Died: 18th December 2008, Isle of Wight, UK

First Film Appearance: Carry On Matron (1972)

First Carry On Appearance: Carry On Matron (1972)

Final Film Appearance: Carry On Columbus (1972)

Carry On Appearances: Twitching Father (Matron), Harry (Abroad), William (Girls), Sergeant Jock Strapp (Dick), Ernie Bragg (Behind), Bombardier Ready (England), Lyons (Emmannuelle), Marco the Cereal Killer (Columbus), Mr Firkin/Adam/Ringworm the Butler/Charles Burke/The Demon King (Carry On Christmas 1972 (TV)), Performer (What a Carry On! (TV)), Caveman Carol Singer/Crapper/German Soldier/Alan A'Dale/Ballet Dancer (Carry On Christmas 1973 (TV)), Colonel Yackoff (Carry On Laughing - The Prisoner of Spenda (TV)), Sir Jethro Houndsbotham (Carry On Laughing - The Sobbing Cavalier (TV)), Master of the Rolls/Lord Essex (Carry On Laughing - Orgy & Bess (TV)), Ethelred (Carry On Laughing - One in the Eye for Harold (TV)), Lord Peter Flimsy (Carry On Laughing - The Nine Old Cobblers (TV)), Lord Peter Flimsy (Carry On Laughing - The Case of the Screaming Winkles (TV)), Lord Peter Flimsy (Carry On Laughing - The Case of the Coughing Parrot (TV)), Sir Gay (Carry On Laughing - Under the Round Table (TV)), Sir Gay (Carry On Laughing - Short Knight, Long Daze (TV)), Clodson (Carry On Laughing - And in My Lady's Chamber (TV)), Clodson (Carry On Laughing - Who Needs Kitchener? (TV)), "Elephant" Dick Darcy (Carry On Laughing - Lamp Posts of the Empire (TV)), Carry On London! (stage), Alf Hardy (Carry On Laughing with "The Slimming Factory" (stage))

Other Notable Appearances: Dave's Kingdom (Associated Television, 1964), Not on Your Nellie (London Weekend Television, 1975), The Shillingbury Blowers (ATV, 1980), Shillingbury Tales (ATV, 1981), Norbert Smith – A Life (Channel 4, 1989)

Finest Hour (and a bit):
Carry On Emmannuelle. On film, Jack Douglas' Carry On career consisted mainly of characters based on his Alf Ippititimus stage persona - the twitching idiot who never did learn not to stand next to someone with a full tray of drinks. It was a two-dimensional character which hid the fact that when he was allowed to act in a role, Jack was magnificent. As Lyons, in Carry On Emmannuelle, Jack is superb as the softly spoken, discrete butler who has to struggle with the most indiscreet mistress in the world.

One to Forget:
Carry On Columbus. There's a great deal worth forgetting about Carry On Columbus, but Jack's role is so tiny, so inconsequential, that he may as well have not been in the film at all. As laudable as it was to bring back the old Carry On gang, the juxtaposition between old and new generations of comic performers was, with very few exceptions, disastrous. In hindsight, Jack got off lightly, but it's a shame to see one of the Carry Ons' most loyal players reduced to little more than a walk-on role.

Seen & Heard:
What a Carry On (Thames Television, 4/10/1973)
Look Who's Talking (Border Television, 1975)
The Electric Theatre Show – Carry On England (Grampian, 1976)
This is Your Life: Jack Douglas (BBC1, 17/04/1985)
Carry On Jack Douglas (SoundTV, 2005)
That Reminds Me; Jack Douglas (BBC Radio, 11/12/2001)

Further Reading:
The "Wu-hey" to Better Cooking by Jack Douglas, Golden Eagle Publishing, 1975 (ISBN: 0901482234)
A Twitch in Time: Jack Douglas' Life Story - 60 Years in Showbusiness by Jack Douglas & Sue Benwell, Able Publishing, 2002 (ISBN: 1903607248)

Douglas, Sally: Girl at Dirty Dick's (Jack), Amazon Guard (Spying), Antony's Dusky Maiden (Cleo), Kitkata (Cowboy), Girl (Screaming!), Harem Girl (Follow that Camel)
Douglas, Su: Countess Joanna (Columbus)
Duff, Duncan: Inquisitor (Columbus)
Duff, Lesley: Norma (Camping)
Dunnley, Jacqueline: Merry Maid (Wot a Carry On in Blackpool (stage))
Durkin, Patrick: Recruit (Sergeant), Jackson (Nurse), 2nd Guard (Spying), William (Dick)
Dyson, Noel: Vague Woman (Constable), District Nurse (Cabby)

E

Eagles, Leon: Recruit (Sergeant)
East, Suzanna: Colette (Emmannuelle)
Eaton, Shirley: Mary Sage (Sergeant), Nurse Dorothy Denton (Nurse), Sally Barry (Constable)

Eden, Eve: 11th Wife (Up the Khyber)
Edwards, Ray: Man with Soapy Water (Behind)
Ellison, Angela: Cloakroom Girl (Spying)
Emmanuel, Heather: Plump Native Girl (Again Doctor), Pregnant Lubi (Up the Jungle)
Emmett, EVH: Narrator (Cleo)
Essex, David: Page Boy (Henry - *Scene cut*)
Evans, Barbara: 13th Wife (Up the Khyber)
Evans, Rupert: Stunt Orderly (Again Doctor), Major (Carry On Laughing - The Prisoner of Spenda (TV))

F

Fabrizi, Mario: Cook (Cruising)
Fagan, James: Concorde Steward (Emmannuelle)
Farrar, Sonny: Violinist (Loving)
Faulkner, James: Torquemada (Columbus)
Faulkner, Max: Highwayman (Dick)
Feeney, Pat: 4th Storeman (Sergeant)
Fenemore, Hilda: Rhoda Bray (Nurse), Agitated Woman (Constable)
Fielding, Fenella: Penny Panting (Regardless), Virula Watt (Screaming!)
Firbank, Ann: Helen Lloyd (Nurse)
Fleischer, Charles: Pontiac (Columbus)
Ford, Helen: Ward Cleaner (Doctor)
Ford, Joanna: Vestal Virgin (Cleo)
Forsyth, Frank: 2nd Specialist (Sergeant), John Gray (Nurse), 4th Citizen (Constable), Chauffeur (Cabby), 2nd Sea Lord (Jack), Professor Stark (Spying), Desk Sergeant (Screaming!)

FREEMAN, DAVE

Born: 22nd August 1922, London, UK
Died: 28th March 1995, London, UK

First Film: The Magnificent Seven Deadly Sins (Screenplay, 1971)
First Carry On: Carry On Behind (Screenplay, 1975)
Final Film: Carry On Columbus (Screenplay, 1992)

Carry On Appearances: Inquisitor (Columbus) - *See also Crew*

Other Notable Productions: Great Scott, It's Maynard (Writer, BBC Television, 1955), The Avengers: The Rotters (Teleplay, ABC Weekend Television, 1968), Bless this House (Thames Television, 1971-1976), Bless this House (Screenplay, 1972), Bernie (Writer, Thames Television, 1978), Terry & June (Writer, BBC Television, 1980-1982), Keep it in the Family (Writer, Thames Television, 1983)

Francis, Derek: Sir Edmund Burke (Doctor), Farmer (Camping), Bishop (Loving), Farmer (Henry), Arthur (Matron), Brother Martin (Abroad)
Franklin, Patricia: Farmer's Daughter (Camping), Mrs Dreery (Loving), Rosemary (Girls),

Vera Bragg (Behind), Corporal Cook (England)

Fraser, Liz: Delia King (Regardless), Glad Trimble (Cruising), Sally (Cabby), Sylvia Ramsden (Behind), Milly (Carry On Laughing with "The Slimming Factory" (stage))

Furse, Judith: Formidable Lady (Regardless), Battleaxe (Cabby), Dr Crow (Spying)

Futcher, Hugh: Scrawny Native (Spying), Guard (Don't Lose your Head), Cab Driver (Again Doctor), Ernie (At your Convenience), 2nd Policeman (Abroad), 2nd Citizen (Girls), Painter (Behind)

Fyson, Mavise: Francis Cake (Girls)

Galili, Hal: Cowhand (Cowboy)

Garlick, Stephen: Small Boy (Doctor)

Gatrell, John: 4th Specialist (Sergeant)

Gauntlett, Richard: Light Comedy Relief (Wot a Carry On in Blackpool (stage))

Geeson, Judy: Sergeant Tilly Willing (England)

Geeson, Sally: Lily (Abroad), Debra (Girls)

Gianelli, Gina: Harem Girl (Follow that Camel)

Gifford, Alan: Commissioner (Cowboy)

Gill, Tom: 1st Citizen (Constable)

Gilmore, Peter: Dancy (Cabby), Patch (Jack), Galley Master (Cleo), Curly (Cowboy), Robespierre (Don't Lose your Head), Captain Bagshaw (Follow that Camel), Henry (Doctor), Private Ginger Hale (Up the Khyber), Henry (Again Doctor), Francis, King of France (Henry), Governor of the Canaries (Columbus)

Glover, David: Hotel Manager (Follow that Camel)

Goddard, Willoughby: Very Fat Man (Cruising)

Gold, Liz: 2nd Wife (Up the Khyber)

Gordeno, Peter: Shaman (Columbus)

Gordon, Norah: Elderley Woman (Spying)

Gosney, Barrie: Coach Driver (Jack)

Goss, Helen: Mary's Mum (Sergeant)

Gould, Graydon: Recruit (Sergeant)

Grady, Mike: Boy Lover (Loving)

Grainger, Andrew: Juvenile Lead (Wot a Carry On in Blackpool (stage))

Grainger, Gail: Moira Plunkett (Abroad)

Grant, Angela: Harem Girl (Follow that Camel), Hospitality Girl (Up the Khyber), Miss Bangor (Girls)

Grant, Gilly: Sally G-String (Camping), Nurse in Bath (Matron)

Grant, Peter: Cardinal (Columbus)

Greene, Leon: Malabonce (Don't Lose your Head), Torturer (Henry), Chef (At your Convenience)

Griffiths, Fred: 2nd Ambulance Driver (Nurse), Taxi Driver (Regardless), Taxi Driver (Loving)

Griffiths, Lucy: Trolley Lady (Nurse), Miss Horton (Constable), Auntie (Regardless), Patient (Doctor), Old Lady in Headphones (Again Doctor), Woman (Loving - *Scene cut*), Woman with Hat (Behind)

Guyler, Deryck; Surgeon Hardcastle (Doctor)

Grainger, Gail: Moira Plunkett (Abroad)

H

Hallam, John: Burpa on Rooftop (Up the Khyber)
Hallett, John: Substitute Football Player (Emmannuelle)
Hamilton, Jean; Girl at Dirty Dick's (Jack), Nosha (Up the Jungle)
Hampshire, Barbara: Private Carter (England)
Hancock, Sheila: Senna Pod (Cleo)
Handl, Irene: Madge Hickson (Nurse), Distraught Woman (Constable)
Hardy, Mark: Guard at Caesar's Palace (Cleo)
Harmer, Juliet: Mrs Bentley (Matron - *Cut scene*)
Harrington, Joy: Lady (Dick)
Harris, Alexander: 3rd Storeman (Sergeant)
Harris, Anita: Corktip (Follow that Camel), Nurse Clarke (Doctor)
Hart, David: Customs Officer (Emmannuelle - *Scene cut*)
Hartnell, William: Sergeant Grimshaw (Sergeant)
Hassall, Imogen: Jenny Grubb (Loving)
Hawkins, Carol: Marge (Abroad), Sandra (Behind), Lilly (Carry On Laughing - And in My Lady's Chamber (TV)), Lilly (Carry On Laughing - Who Needs Kitchener? (TV))

HAWTREY, CHARLES

Real Name: George Frederick Joffe Hartree
Born: 30th November 1914, Hounslow, UK
Died: 27th October 1988, Deal, UK
First Film Appearance: Tell Your Children (1922)
First Carry On Appearance: Carry On Sergeant (1958)
Final Film Appearance: Carry On Abroad (1972)

Carry On Appearances: Peter Golightly (Sergeant), Humphrey Hinton (Nurse), Michael Bean (Teacher), PC Timothy Gorse (Constable), Gabriel Dimple (Regardless), Terry "Pint Pot" Tankard (Cabby), Walter Sweetley (Jack), Charlie Bind (Spying), Seneca (Cleo), Big Heap (Cowboy), Dan Dann (Screaming!), Duc de Pommfrit (Don't Lose your Head), Captain Le Pice (Follow that Camel), Mr Barron (Doctor), Private Jimmy Widdle (Up the Khyber), Charlie Muggins (Camping), Dr Ernest Stoppidge (Again Doctor), Walter Bagley/King Tonka (Up the Jungle), James Bedsop (Loving), Sir Roger de Lodgerley (Henry), Charles Coote (At your Convenience), Dr Francis A Goode (Matron), Eustace Tuttle (Abroad), Spirit of Christmas Past/Angel/Convent Girl/Buttons (Carry On Christmas 1969 (TV)), Old Blind Pew/Nightwatchman/Nipper the Flipper (Carry On Again Christmas (TV))

Other Notable Appearances: Boys Will be Boys (1935), Good Morning Boys (1937), Where's that Fire? (1940), Passport to Pimlico (1949), The Army Game (Associated Television, 1957-1958), I Only Arsked (1958), Please Turn Over (1960), Dentist on the Job (1961), Our House (ABC Television, 1961-1962), Best of Friends (ABC Television, 1963), Zeta One (1969), Grasshopper Island (Southern TV, 1971), Supergran (Tyne-Tees Television, 1987)

Finest Hour (and a bit):
Carry On at your Convenience. Charles Hawtrey's Carry On persona was pretty much set in stone from the very beginning, in Carry On Sergeant. The effete, saucer-eyed fool

who brings chaos crashing down around him, oblivious to the consequences of his never-less-than well-meaning actions is a beautiful creation. But there was so much more to Hawtrey's characters than a cheap laugh about his (lack of) stature or his weakness for the bottle. In Carry On at your Convenience, Hawtrey is a powerful figure - an expert in his field, as high-spirited and fey as always but with a darker sexual undercurrent. If you can bear it, consider his relationship with Agatha Spanner; decorum and fine dining on the surface, but with a darker sexuality just below the surface. Convenience is his greatest film, not just because it shows another side of Hawtrey's usual character but that it does so in a completely no-holds-barred way. The scenes on Brighton's Palace Pier as the team get increasingly sauced are a joy to watch.

One to Forget:
Carry On Screaming. Like so many of his contemporaries, Hawtrey seemed incapable of giving a bad performance, at least when it came to the Carry Ons. Picking a role where he's anything less than perfect is impossible, so once again it comes down to a film where he is so under-used he may as well not have bothered. In early drafts of Carry On Screaming, Hawtrey wasn't included in the cast. When one newspaper preview commented that a Carry On without Hawtrey wasn't quite the same, a role was written especially for him. Dan Dann's a vital character, in that he holds the key to the mystery of the grisly carryings on in the woods, but it's a disappointingly small role.

Seen & Heard:
Film Night Special - Carry On Forever (BBC2, 12/04/1970)
Movie Memories (Anglia Television, 28/01/1981)
Carry On Darkly (Channel 4, 30/09/1998)
Cor Blimey! (ITV, 25/04/2000)

Further Reading:
Charles Hawtrey 1914-1988: The Man who was Private Widdle by Roger Lewis, Faber & Faber, 2001 (ISBN 0571210899)
Whatshisname: The Life & Death of Charles Hawtrey by Wes Butters, Tomahawk Press, 2010 (ISBN: 0955767075)

Hayes, Melvyn: Gunner Shorthouse (England), Charwallah Charlie (Carry On Laughing - The Case of the Screaming Winkles (TV))
Hayes, Patricia: Mrs Beasley (Again Doctor)
Hempel, Anouska: New Canteen Girl (At your Convenience)
Henderson, Don: Bosun (Columbus)
Herbert, Percy: Mr Angel the Bosun (Jack), Charlie (Cowboy)
Herbert, Philip: Ginger (Columbus)
Hewlett, Donald: Dean (Behind)
Hewson, Sherrie: Carol (Behind), Nurse Millie Teazel (Carry On Laughing - The Case of the Screaming Winkles (TV)), Irma Klein (Carry On Laughing - The Case of the Coughing Parrot (TV)), Virginia (Carry On Laughing - And in My Lady's Chamber (TV))
Hickson, Joan: Sister (Nurse), Mrs May (Constable), Matron (Regardless), Mrs Grubb (Loving), Mrs Dukes (Girls)
Hill, Jennifer: Girl at Dirty Dick's (Jack)
Hines, Roy: Harry Bird (Teacher)

Hobbs, Michael: Inquisitor (Columbus)

Hobley, McDonald: Quaker Reporter (Carry On Laughing - Orgy & Bess (TV))

Holden, Katherina: 5th Wife (Up the Khyber)

Holland, Terence: Handsome Passer-by (Cruising)

Holley, Bernard: Captain (Carry On Laughing - The Sobbing Cavalier (TV))

Holloway, Julian: Ticket Collector (Follow that Camel), Simmons (Doctor), Major Shorthouse (Up the Khyber), Jim Tanner (Camping), Adrian (Loving), Sir Thomas (Henry), Major Butcher (England), Captain Rhodes (Carry On Christmas 1973 (TV))

Holtom, Natalie: Merry Maid (Wot a Carry On in Blackpool (stage))

Hooks, Linda: Bird of Paradise (Dick), Nurse (Behind), Army Nurse (England), Rosie (Carry On Laughing - The Baron Outlook (TV)), Nellie (Carry On Laughing - One in the Eye for Harold (TV)), Hilde (Carry On Laughing with "The Slimming Factory" (stage))

Horsley, John: Anaesthetist (Nurse - *Scene cut*)

Horton, Marian: Glamcab Driver (Cabby)

Houston, Donald: 1st Officer Jonathan Howett (Jack)

Houston, Renée: Molly (Cabby), Madame (Spying), Agatha Spanner (At your Convenience)

Howell, George: Billy Haig (Teacher)

Howerd, Frankie: Francis Bigger (Doctor), Professor Inigo Tinkle (Up the Jungle), Robert Browning/Fairy Godmother (Carry On Christmas 1969 (TV))

Hughes, Geoffrey: Willie (At your Convenience)

Humphrys, Laraine: Eileen Denby (Girls), Bird of Paradise (Dick), Bed Customer (Carry On Christmas 1973 (TV))

Hunt, Michael: Recruit (Sergeant)

Hunter, Bernard: Wine Waiter (Regardless)

Hunter, Robin: Mr Darling (Matron)

Hurndell, William: Riff (Follow that Camel)

Hutchinson, Bill: 1st Reporter (Emmannuelle)

Hyde-White, Wilfrid: The Colonel (Nurse)

I

Ingram, Joan: Bald-Headed Dowager (Don't Lose your Head)

Ireland, Jill: Jill Thompson (Nurse)

Irving, Penny: Bird of Paradise (Dick)

Ives, Douglas: Fanatic Patient (Regardless)

J

Jackson, Brian: Recruit (Sergeant)

Jacobson, Helli Louise: Nudist (Behind)

JACQUES, HATTIE

Real Name: Josephine Edwina Jacques

Born: 7th February 1922, Sandgate, Kent, UK

Died: 6th October 1980, Kensington, London, UK

First Film Appearance: Green for Danger (1946)

First Carry On Appearance: Carry On Sergeant (1958)
Final Film Appearance: Three for All (1975)

Carry On Appearances: Captain Clark (Sergeant), Matron (Nurse), Grace Short (Teacher), Sergeant Laura Moon (Constable), Sister (Regardless), Peggy Hawkins (Cabby), Matron (Doctor), Miss Haggerd (Camping), Matron (Again Doctor), Sophie Bliss (Loving), Beattie Plummer (At your Convenience), Matron (Matron), Floella (Abroad), Martha Hoggett (Dick), Elizabeth Barrett/Nun/Passer-By (Carry On Christmas 1969 (TV)), Fiona Clodhopper/Miss Harriet/Miss Molly Coddles/Fairy Godmother (Carry On Christmas 1972 (TV)), Queen Elizabeth I (Carry On Laughing - Orgy & Bess (TV))

Other Notable Appearances: Oliver Twist (1948), Scrooge (1951), Mother Riley Meets the Vampire (1952), Hancock's Half Hour (BBC Radio 1956-1958), Hancock's Half Hour (BBC Television 1957), The Square Peg (1959), Follow a Star (1959), Make Mine Mink (Film 1960), Our House (ABC Television 1961-1962), Miss Adventure (ABC Television 1964), Sykes (BBC Television 1960-1979)

Finest Hour (and a bit):
Carry On Cabby. While Hattie Jacques will forever be remembered as the fearsome Matron she played so often, without doubt her finest Carry On film is Carry On Cabby. Cabby was made in the days when Hattie's name wasn't yet synonymous with hospital comedy. She was a much sought after young star and perfectly suited to the role of the romantic female lead. As Peggy Hawkins, Hattie is the doting wife, put upon by her workaholic husband Charlie until she can take no more. As her alter-ego, Mrs Glam, Hattie is a seductress; a husky voiced madam controlling her empire of curvaceous cabbies. As dual roles go, Hattie plays both to utter perfection. She's magnificent.

One to Forget:
Carry On Dick. In Carry On terms, nobody was particularly well-served by Carry On Dick, a film which marks the end of the "classic" Carry On era. That it was Hattie's last film makes her role as Martha Hoggett all the more ignominious - she's a downtrodden, snooping housekeeper. Her scant presence in the film is barely felt, but when she is on screen she's invariably nagging, niggling or just generally getting in the way. It's a terribly underwritten part for one of the longest serving and best-loved Carry On stars.

Seen & Heard:
Desert Island Discs (BBC Radio, 16/10/1961)
This is your Life: Hattie Jacques (BBC1, 12/02/1963)
The Comediennes – Hattie Jacques (BBC Radio, 26/01/1995)
The Unforgettable Hattie Jacques (ITV, 21/01/2000)
Radio Roots – Hattie Jacques (BBC Radio, 17/10/2000)
Legends – Hattie Jacques (ITV, 31/07/2001)
Heroes of Comedy – Hattie Jacques (Channel 4, 9/03/2002)
Hattie (BBC Four, 17/05/2010)
Barbara Windsor's Funny Girls – Hattie Jacques (BBC Radio, 12/07/2011)

Further Reading:
A Jobbing Actor by John Le Mesurier, Elm Tree Books, 1984 (ISBN: 1845135830)
Dear John by Joan Le Mesurier, Sidgwick & Jackson, 2001 (ISBN: 0283063726)
Hattie: The Authorised biography of Hattie Jacques by Andy Merriman, Aurum Press,

2007 (ISBN: 1845132572)
Do You think that's Wise?...The Life of John Le Mesurier by Graham McCann, Aurum Press, 2010 (ISBN: 1845135830)

Jago, June: Sister (Regardless), Sister Hoggett (Doctor)
James, Oscar: Black Knight (Carry On Laughing - Under the Round Table (TV)), Witchdoctor (Carry On Laughing - Lamp Posts of the Empire (TV))

JAMES, SID

Real Name: Solomon Joel Coen
Born: 8th May 1913, Johannesburg, South Africa
Died: 26th April 1976, Sunderland, UK

First Film Appearance: Black Memory (1947)
First Carry On Appearance: Carry On Constable (1960)
Final Film Appearance: Carry On Dick (1974)

Carry On Appearances:
Sergeant Frank Wilkins (Constable), Bert Handy (Regardless), Captain Wellington Crowther (Cruising), Charlie Hawkins (Cabby), Mark Antony (Cleo), Johnny Finger/The Rumpo Kid (Cowboy), Sir Rodney Ffing/The Black Fingernail (Don't Lose your Head), Charlie Roper (Doctor), Sir Sidney Ruff-Diamond (Up the Khyber), Sid Boggle (Camping), Gladstone Screwer (Again Doctor), Bill Boosey (Up the Jungle), Sidney Bliss (Loving), King Henry VIII (Henry), Sid Plummer (At your Convenience), Sid Carter (Matron), Vic Flange (Abroad), Sidney Fiddler (Girls), Dick Turpin/The Reverend Flasher (Dick), Ebeneezer Scrooge (Carry On Christmas, 1969 (TV)), Long John Silver (Carry On Again Christmas (TV)), Mr Belcher/Santa Claus/Seed Pod/Sir Henry/Sergeant Ball/Robin Hood (Carry On Christmas 1973 (TV)), Performer (What a Carry On! (TV)), Prince Rupert/Arnold Basket (Carry On Laughing - The Prisoner of Spenda (TV)), Baron Hubert (Carry On Laughing - The Baron Outlook (TV)), Lovelace (Carry On Laughing - The Sobbing Cavalier (TV)), Sir Francis Drake (Carry On Laughing - Orgy & Bess (TV)), Carry On London! (stage)

Other Notable Appearances: Hancock's Half Hour (BBC Radio 1954-1959), Hancock's Half Hour (BBC Television 1956-1960), Citizen James (BBC Television 1960-1962), Taxi! (BBC Television 1963-1964), George & the Dragon (Associated Television 1966-1968), Two in Clover (Thames Television 1969-1970), Bless This House (Thames Television 1971-1976), Bless This House (1972)

Finest Hour (and a bit):
Carry On at your Convenience. Carry On at your Convenience gives Sid many of his most memorable moments. His sudden good luck at the betting shop is a hilarious theme running through the film, but when the Carry On gang set out for Brighton on the annual works' outing, Sid really gets a chance to shine. In particular, his conversation with Joan over the garden wall at the end of their boozy day out is one of the most genuinely touching moments in the Carry Ons. There's a different kind of innuendo as the pair hint at having more than a night cap and resign themselves to domestic fidelity. It's a beautiful, affectionate scene and a refreshing reminder that Sid was more than just the dirty old man of the Carry On team.

One to Forget:
Carry On Dick. Sid's performance in Carry On Dick is as strong as you'd expect from a consummate old pro, but he's far too old to be chasing after nubile fillies. There's a lot to love about Carry On Dick, particularly Sid's role as the softly spoken Reverend Flasher, but the backroom antics with Barbara Windsor are a step too far and make for less than comfortable viewing.

Seen & Heard:
Film Night Special - Carry On Forever (BBC2, 12/04/1970)
What a Carry On (Thames Television, 4/10/1973)
Sid James (BBC Radio, 16/06/1976)
Without Walls – Seriously Seeking Sid (Channel 4, 1/01/1993)
Carry On Darkly (Channel 4, 30/09/1998)
The Unforgettable Sid James (ITV, 4/12/2000)
Heroes of Comedy – Sid James (Channel 4, 23/02/2002)
Cor Blimey! (ITV, 25/04/2000)
The Many Faces of Sid James (BBC2, 6/04/2013)
Sid James: Not Just a Dirty Laugh (BBC Radio 4, 29/04/2013)

Further Reading:
Sid James by Clifford Goodwin, Arrow, 1995 (ISBN: 0753505541)
Cleo, Camping, Emmanuelle & Dick by Terry Johnson, Methuen, 1998 (ISBN: 0413735001)
The Complete Sid James by Robert Ross, Reynolds & Hearn, 2000 (ISBN: 1903111943)
Blimey! It's the Sid James Book by Gary Wharton, Lushington Publishing, 2007 (ISBN: 0954218744)
Sid James – Cockney Rebel by Robert Ross, JR Books, 2009 (ISBN: 190677935X)

Jesson, Paul: Messenger (Carry On Laughing - One in the Eye for Harold (TV))
Jesson, Peter: Car Salesman (Cabby), Companion (Cleo), Lawrence (Follow that Camel - *Scene cut*)
Johns, Malcolm: Sentry (Emmannuelle)
Johnson, Gloria: Vestal Virgin (Cleo)
Johnson, Judi: Funhouse Girl (Spying), Gloria's Bridesmaid (Cleo)
Johnson, Sidney: Man in Glasses (Behind)
Johnson, Vivienne: Freda (England), Freda Filey (Carry On Laughing - The Case of the Coughing Parrot (TV)), Teeny (Carry On Laughing - And in My Lady's Chamber (TV)), Teeny (Carry On Laughing - Who Needs Kitchener? (TV))
Jonah, Willie: Nosha (Up the Jungle)
Jones, Helga: Harem Girl (Follow that Camel)
Jones, Peter: Chaplain (Doctor), Brigadier (England)
Judd, Edward: 5th Storeman (Sergeant)
Julian, Charles: Old Man in Ruby Room (Regardless)

K

Karen, Anna: Hefty Girl (Camping), Wife (Loving)
Kasket, Harold: Hotel Gentleman (Follow that Camel)
Kavann, Darryl: Punchy (Cabby)

Kay, Bernard: Injured Recruit (Sergeant)
Kaye, Davy: Josh the Undertaker (Cowboy), Benny (At your Convenience)
Keen, Penny: Girl (Don't Lose your Head)
Keith, Penelope: Plain Nurse (Doctor - *Scene cut*)
Kelly, Sam: Sir Roger's Coachman (Dick), Projectionist (Behind)
Kemp, Sally: Girl with Cow (Camping)
Kennedy, Ken: Wall-eyed Man (Constable)
Kent, Faith: Berkeley Matron (Again Doctor)
Kenwright, Bill: Reporter (Matron)
Kernan, David: Nicholas Phipps (Abroad)
Kerr, Fraser: Houseman
Klauber, Gertan: Code Clerk (Spying), Marcus (Cleo), Spiv (Follow that Camel - *Scene cut*), Wash Orderly (Doctor), Bidet (Henry), Postcard Seller (Abroad), German Soldier (Emmannuelle)
Knight, Elizabeth: Jane (Camping), Nurse Willing (Again Doctor)
Knight, Rosalind: Nurse Nightingale (Nurse), Felicity Wheeler (Teacher)
Konyils, Chris: Nosha (Up the Jungle)
Koumani, Maya: Amazon Guard (Spying)
Kwouk, Burt: Wang (Columbus)

L

Lacey, Rebecca: Chiquita (Columbus)
Lake, Janetta: Girl with Dog (Constable)
Lancaster, Ann: Miss Armitage (Again Doctor)
Langham, Chris: Hubba (Columbus)
Langton, Diane: Private Alice Easy (England), Tzana (Carry On Laughing - The Prisoner of Spenda (TV)), Griselda (Carry On Laughing - The Baron Outlook (TV)), Isolde (Carry On Laughing - One in the Eye for Harold (TV))
Lavender, Ian: Joe Baxter (Behind)
Law, Mary: 1st Shop Assistant (Constable)
Lawrence, Marjie: Serving Maid (Henry)
Laye, Dilys: Flo Castle (Cruising), Lila (Spying), Mavis (Doctor), Anthea Meeks (Camping)
Layton, George: Doctor (Behind)
Leon, Valerie: Harem Girl (Up the Khyber), Store Assistant (Camping), Deirdre (Again Doctor), Leda (Up the Jungle), Jane Darling (Matron), Paula Perkins (Girls), Serving Wench (Carry On Christmas 1972 (TV))
Levene, John: Soldier (Carry On Laughing - The Baron Outlook (TV))
Lewis, Jacqueline: Pat Gordon (Teacher)
Lipman, Maureen: Countess Esmeralda (Columbus)
Livings, Henry: Recruit (Sergeant)
Lloyd, Vivien: Verna (Camping)
Locke, Harry: Mick (Nurse), Sam (Doctor), Porter (Again Doctor)
Lodge, David: Connoisseur (Regardless), Police Inspector (Girls), Bullock (Dick), Landlord (Behind), Captain Bull (England), Duke Boris (Carry On Laughing - The Prisoner of Spenda (TV)), Sir Simon de Montfort (Carry On Laughing - The Baron Outlook (TV)), Colonel (Carry On Laughing - The Sobbing Cavalier (TV)), William the Conqueror (Carry

On Laughing - One in the Eye for Harold (TV)), Inspector Bungler (Carry On Laughing - The Nine Old Cobblers (TV)), Inspector Bungler (Carry On Laughing - The Case of the Screaming Winkles (TV)), Inspector Bungler (Carry On Laughing - The Case of the Coughing Parrot (TV))

Logan, Jimmy: Bert Conway (Abroad), Cecil Gaybody (Girls)

Longdon, Terence: Miles Heywood (Sergeant), Ted York (Nurse), Herbert Hall (Constable), Montgomery Infield-Hopping (Regardless)

Lovegrove, Arthur: Old Cowhand (Cowboy)

Low, Michael: Lusty Youth (Camping)

Lowe, Ken: Maître d'Hotel (Loving)

Lowe, Olga: Madame Fifi (Abroad)

Lucas, Mike: Lusty Youth (Camping)

Lumb, Jane: Amazon Guard (Spying), Vestal Virgin (Cleo)

Lupino Lane, Lauri: Husband (Loving)

Lynch, Kenny: Bus Conductor (Loving) - *See also Crew*

Lynn, Jack: Admiral of the Fleet (Emmannuelle)

M

MacDonald, Tamsin: 10th Wife (Up the Khyber)

MacKenzie, Verna Lucille: Gong Lubi (Up the Jungle)

MacLean, Don: Inquisitor with Sandwiches (Columbus)

MacNamara, Diana: Princess Stephanie (Don't Lose your Head)

McCord, Cal: Mex (Cowboy)

McCorkindale, Don: Recruit (Sergeant), Tubby (Cabby)

McGeagh, Stanley: Short-Sighted Man (Behind), Journalist (Emmannuelle)

McGee, Henry: Harold Hump (Emmannuelle)

McGuirk, William: Flunky (Henry)

McNamara, Desmond: Minstrel (Carry On Laughing - Under the Round Table (TV)), Minstrel (Carry On Laughing - Short Knight, Long Daze (TV))

Maddern, Victor: Criminal Type (Constable), 1st Sinister Passenger (Regardless), Milchmann (Spying), Sergeant Major (Cleo), Man in Launderette (Emmannuelle), Todd (Carry On Laughing - Orgy & Bess (TV)), Charlie (Carry On Laughing - The Nine Old Cobblers (TV)), Sir Osis (Carry On Laughing - Under the Round Table (TV))

Madison, Leigh: Sheila (Sergeant), Miss Winn (Nurse)

Mahoney, Janet: Gay (Loving)

Manger, Melita: Woman with Salad (Behind)

Manley, Rosemary: Girl at Dirty Dick's (Jack)

March, Cathi: Lubi Lieutenant (Up the Jungle)

March, Elspeth: Lady Binder (Don't Lose your Head), Hospital Board Member (Again Doctor)

March, Lindsay: Shapely Nurse (Matron), Air Hostess (Abroad - *Scene Cut)*

Marion-Crawford, Howard: Wine Organiser (Regardless)

Marsden, Betty: Mata Hari (Regardless), Harriet Potter (Camping)

Martin, Reed: Poco Hontas (Columbus)

Martin, Reuben: Gorilla (Up the Jungle), Gorilla (Emmannuelle), Gorilla (Carry On Laughing - Lamp Posts of the Empire (TV))

Martinus, Derek: Recruit (Sergeant)

Martyn, Larry: Rifle Range Owner (At your Convenience), Electrician (Behind)

Maskell, Marianne: Hospital Nurse (Emmannuelle)

Matthews, John: Sergeant Matthews (Sergeant), Tom Mayhew (Nurse)

Mayall, Rik: The Sultan (Columbus)

Maynard, Bill: Mr Dreery (Loving), Guy Fawkes (Henry), Fred Moore (At your Convenience), Freddy (Matron), Mr Fiddler (Abroad - *Scene cut*), Bodkin (Dick)

Maxine, Margot: Harem Girl (Follow that Camel)

Medwin, Michael: Ginger (Nurse)

Mellinger, Michael: Chindi (Up the Khyber)

Meredith, Jill Mai: Shapely Miss (Cruising), Cigarette Girl (Spying)

Mervyn, William: Sir Cyril Ponsonby (Follow that Camel), Lord Paragon (Again Doctor), Physician (Henry)

Miller, Larry: Big Chief (Columbus)

Mills, Freddie: Crook (Constable), Lefty (Regardless)

Mills, Juliet: Sally (Jack)

Mitchell, Billy J: Gunner Childs (England)

Mitchell, Norman: Bespectacled Businessman (Cabby), Native Policeman (Spying), Heckler (Cleo), Cabby (Screaming!), Drunken Husband (Emmannuelle)

Mitchell, Warren: Spencius (Cleo)

Molineaux, Cheryl: Women's Ward Nurse (Doctor)

Monkhouse, Bob: Charlie Sage (Sergeant)

Montez, Richard: Riff at Abdul's Tent (Follow that Camel)

Moon, George: Scrawny Man (Camping), Mr Giles (Dick)

Moon, Georgina: Joy (Camping), Sally (Behind)

Moore, Maureen: Pretty Probationer (Regardless)

Moore, Valerie: Lubi Lieutenant (Up the Jungle)

Moses, Albert: Doctor (Emmannuelle)

Mossman, George: Stagecoach Driver (Dick)

Mower, Patrick: Sergeant Len Able (England)

Munt, Peter: Henry's Courtier (Henry)

Murden, Vicki: Hospitality Girl (Up the Khyber)

Murdoch, Jane: Nurse (Doctor)

Murton, Lionel: Clerk (Cowboy)

Muzurus, Jan: Spanish Captain (Jack)

N

Nelson, Howard: Harry Hernia (Emmannuelle)

New Dollys, The: (Carry On London! (stage))

Newby, Tricia: Private Murray (England), Nurse in Surgery (Emmannuelle)

Nichols, Dandy: Mrs Roper (Doctor)

Nightingale, Michael: Wine Bystander (Regardless), Businessman (Cabby), Town Crier (Jack), Caveman (Cleo), Bank Manager (Cowboy), "What Locket" Man (Don't Lose your Head), Butler (Follow that Camel), Man in Cinema (Camping), Pearson (Matron), City Type (Girls), Squire Trelawney (Dick), Officer (England), Police Commissioner (Emmannuelle), Colonel Postwick (Carry On Laughing - The Case of the Screaming

Winkles (TV)), Neighbour (Carry On Laughing - Lamp Posts of the Empire (TV))

Noble, Lisa: 8th Wife (Up the Khyber)

Noble, Trisha: Sally (Camping)

Nolan, Margaret: Miss Jones (Cowboy), Buxom Lass (Henry), Popsy (At your Convenience), Mrs Tucker (Matron), Dawn Brakes (Girls), Lady Daley (Dick)

Norman, Jane: 3rd Reporter (Emmannuelle)

O

O'Brien, Richard: Rider (Cowboy)

O'Callaghan, Richard: Bertrum Muffett (Loving), Lewis Boggs (At your Convenience)

O'Dea, Danny: Albert Waterman (Carry On Laughing with "The Slimming Factory" (stage))

Olley, Richard: Gunner Parker (England)

Orchard, Julian: Rake (Don't Lose your Head), Doctor (Follow that Camel), Fred (Doctor), Duc de Poncenay (Henry)

O'Shea, Milo: Len (Cabby)

O'Sullivan, Richard: Robin Stevens (Teacher)

Osborne, Brian: Ambulance Driver (Matron), Stallholder (Abroad), 1st Citizen (Girls), Browning (Dick), Bob (Behind), Gunner Owen (England), Gaston (Carry On Laughing - The Baron Outlook (TV)), Cavalier (Carry On Laughing - The Sobbing Cavalier (TV)), 2nd Crew Member (Carry On Laughing - Orgy & Bess (TV)), Herald-Knight (Carry On Laughing - One in the Eye for Harold (TV)), Harry (Carry On Laughing - The Case of the Coughing Parrot (TV)), Knight (Carry On Laughing - Under the Round Table (TV)), Herald-Knight (Carry On Laughing - Short Knight, Long Daze (TV)), Newsboy (Carry On Laughing - Who Needs Kitchener? (TV))

Osborne, Zorenah: Harem Girl (Follow that Camel)

Oulton, Brian: Henry Bray (Nurse), Store Manager (Constable), Brutus (Cleo), Store Manager (Camping), Oriental Orator (Carry On Christmas 1972 (TV))

Owen, Bill: Corporal Bill Copping (Sergeant), Percy Hickson (Nurse), Mike Weston (Regardless), Smiley Sims (Cabby)

Ozanne, Christine: Fat Maid (Nurse)

P

Palmer, Edward: Elderly Resident (Girls)

Parker, Cecil: 1st Sea Lord (Jack)

Parsons, Nicholas: Wolf (Regardless)

Pavlovic, Drina: Courting Girl (Behind)

Peacock, Danny: Tonto the Torch (Columbus)

Pearce, Jaqueline: 3rd Lady (Don't Lose your Head)

Peart, Pauline: Gloria Winch (Girls)

Pegge, Edmund: Bowler (Follow that Camel)

Percival, Lance: Wilfred Haines (Cruising)

Pertwee, Bill: Barman (Loving), Manager (At your Convenience – *scene* cut), Fire Chief (Girls)

Pertwee, James: Inquisitor (Columbus)

Pertwee, Jon: Soothsayer (Cleo), Sheriff Albert Earp (Cowboy), Dr Fettle (Screaming!),

Duke of Costa Brava (Columbus)
Phillips, Dorothea: Aunt Beatrice Grubb (Loving)
Phillips, Leslie: Jack Bell (Nurse), Alistiar Grigg (Teacher), Constable Tom Potter (Constable), King of Spain (Columbus)
Phillpotts, Ambrosine: Yoki's Owner (Regardless), Aristocratic Lady (Cabby)
Piper, Jacki: June (Up the Jungle), Sally Martin (Loving), Myrtle Plummer (At your Convenience), Sister (Matron)
Planer, Nigel: The Wazir (Columbus)
Plytas, Steve: Arabian Official (Emmannuelle)
Pohlmann, Eric: Sinister Man (Regardless), The Fat Man (Spying)
Poole, Jackie: Betty (Camping)
Posta, Adrienne: Norma Baxter (Behind)
Powell, Nosher: Footpad (Dick), Pikeman (Carry On Laughing - One in the Eye for Harold (TV))
Prowse, Dave: Torturer (Henry)
Pryor, Christine: Girl (Don't Lose your Head)
Pyle, Jennifer: Hilda (Camping)

Q

Quatre Rosetti, Les: (Carry On London! (stage))
Quince, Peter: Gunner Sharpe (England)

R

Rawlinson, Brian: Steward (Cruising), Hessian Driver (Cleo), Stagecoach Guard (Cowboy)
Ray, Andrew: Willie (Carry On Laughing - And in my Lady's Chamber (TV)), Willie (Carry On Laughing - Who Needs Kitchener? (TV))
Ray, Robin: Assistant Manager (Constable)
Ray, Ted: William Wakefield (Teacher)
Raymond, Cyril: Army Officer (Regardless)
Reed, Gavin: Window Dresser (Loving)
Rees, Llewellyn: Lord Chief Justice (Emmannuelle)
Reeves, Kynaston: Testy Old Man (Regardless)
Regan, Linda: Private Taylor (England)
Reid, Beryl: Mrs Valentine (Emmannuelle)
Reuber-Staier, Eva: Bird of Paradise (Dick)
Richard, Wendy: Miss Willing (Matron), Ida Downe (Girls), Kate (Carry On Again Christmas (TV))
Richardson, Gordon: Uncle Ernest Grubb (Loving)
Richardson, Peter: Bart Columbus (Columbus)
Ridley, Arnold: Alderman Pratt (Girls)
Ridley, Douglas: 2nd Plotter (Henry)
Rigby, Peter: Henry's Courtier (Henry)
Roberts, Nancy: Old Lady (Regardless)
Roberts, Trevor: Henry's Courtier (Henry)
Robin, Dany: Jacqueline (Don't Lose your Head)
Robinson, Cardew: Fakir (Up the Khyber)

Robinson, Joe: Dynamite Dan (Regardless)
Roderick, George: Waiter (Again Doctor)
Rodgers, Anton: Young Man (Cruising), Hardy (Jack)
Rodgers, Christine: Amazon Guard (Spying), Handmaiden (Cleo)

ROGERS, ERIC

Born: 25th September 1921, Halifax, UK
Died: 9th April 1981, Buckinghamshire, UK

First Film: The Wedding of Lilli Marlene (1953)
First Carry On: Carry On Cabby (1963)
Final Film: Carry On Emmannuelle (1978)

Carry On Appearances: Pianist (Cowboy), Bandleader (Again Doctor) - *See also Crew*

Other Notable Productions: Dr. No (Conductor, 1962), Nurse on Wheels (Composer, 1963), The Big Job (Composer, 1965), Three Hats for Lisa (Composer, 1966), Doctor in Trouble (Composer, 1970), Bless this House (Composer, 1972), No Sex Please we're British (Composer, 1975)

Seen & Heard:
BBC Proms – Music from Great British Films (BBC Television, 28/07/2007)

Rogers, Lynn: (Carry On London! (stage))
Rollings, Gordon: Night Porter (Doctor)
Ronay, Edina: Dolores (Cowboy)
Rosenblat, Barbara: ATS Girl (England)
Rossington, Norman: Herbert Brown (Sergeant), Norm (Nurse), Referee (Regardless), Valet/Tardy/Dinner Guest/Genie of the Lamp (Carry On Christmas 1972 (TV))
Rossini, Jan: Hoopla Girl (At your Convenience - *Scene cut*)

ROWLANDS, PATSY

Born: 19th January 1931, Palmer's Green, London, UK
Died: 22nd January 2005, Hove, East Sussex, UK

First Film Appearance: Over the Odds (1961)
First Carry On Appearance: Carry On Again Doctor (1969)
Final Film Appearance: Crimestrike (1990)

Carry On Appearances: Miss Fosdick (Again Doctor), Miss Dempsey (Loving), Queen (Henry), Hortence Withering (At your Convenience), Evelyn Banks (Matron), Miss Dobbs (Abroad), Mildred Bumble (Girls), Mrs Giles (Dick), Linda Upmore (Behind), Miss Dawkins (Carry On Laughing - The Nine Old Cobblers (TV))

Other Notable Appearances: Gert & Daisy (Associated-Rediffusion Television, 1959), Inside George Webley (Yorkshire Television, 1968-1970), Bless this House (Thames Television, 1971-1976), Tottering Towers (Thames Television, 1971-1972), Bless this House (1972),

Follow that Dog (Southern Television, 1974), The Squirrels (Associated Television, 1974-1977), The Nesbitts are Coming (Yorkshire Television, 1980), Kinvig (London Weekend Television, 1981), In Loving Memory (Yorkshire Television, 1982-1986), Hallelujah! (Yorkshire Television, 1983-1984), The Setbacks (Thames Television, 1985-1986), Rainbow (Thames Television, 1987-1992), The Cazalets (BBC Television, 2001)

Finest Hour (and a bit):
Carry On Loving. Patsy's first Carry On appearance sets the tone for her character through the rest of her time with the series. As the put-upon Miss Dempsey, Patsy plays a thoroughly downtrodden drudge who knows what she wants but struggles to articulate it. What she usually wants is a man and the way she puts it over is through a campaign of failed attempts to appear coquettish. She is a pent-up mess of sexual frustration who spends most the film getting ever closer to bursting point.

One to Forget:
Carry On Dick: Carry On Dick is not best known for its imaginative use of characters and Patsy is the least best served of all the regular team. Calling her fleeting presence in the film a cameo would be overly generous as she pops up to speak a line or two near the end of the film and then vanishes into obscurity. Patsy has played briefer roles, such as the short-lived queen at the start of Carry On Henry, but her presence sets the film up and provides a short but hilarious gag. In Carry On Dick, she might as well not be there at all.

Russell, Robert: Policeman (Loving)

S

Sagar, Anthony: Stores Sergeant (Sergeant), 1st Ambulance Driver (Nurse), 2nd Citizen (Constable), Bus Conductor (Regardless), Cook (Cruising), Policeman (Screaming!), Heckler (Henry – *Scene cut*), Man in Hospital (Loving)
Saleh, Nejdet: Fayid (Columbus)
Sayle, Alexei: Achmed (Columbus)
Schiller, Stephanie: New Nurse (Nurse)
Scott, Anne: Harem Girl (Follow that Camel), 4th Wife (Up the Khyber)
Scott, Steven: Burpa Guard (Up the Khyber)

SCOTT, TERRY

Real Name: Owen John Scott
Born: 4th May 1927, Watford, UK
Died: 26th July 1994, Godalming, UK

First Film Appearance: Blue Murder at St Trinian's (1957)
First Carry On Appearance: Carry On Sergeant (1958)
Final Film Appearance: Carry On Matron (1972)

Carry On Appearances: Sergeant Paddy O'Brien (Sergeant), Sergeatn Major MacNutt (Up the Khyber), Peter Potter (Camping), Cecil/Jungle Boy (Up the Jungle), Terence Philpot (Loving), Cardinal Wolsey, Henry), Dr Prodd (Matron), Mr Allcock (At your Convenience - *Scene cut*), Dr Frank N Stein/Convent Girl/Mr Barrett/Baggie the Ugly Sister (Carry On Christmas 1969 (TV)), Squire Trelawney (Carry On Again Christmas (TV))

Other Notable Appearances: Scott Free (BBC Television, 1957), Too Many Crooks (1959), I'm All Right Jack (1959), Double Bunk (1961), What a Whopper (1961), Hugh & I (BBC Television, 1962-1967), Hugh & I Spy (BBC Television, 1968), Scott On... (BBC Television, 1964-1974), Bless this House (1972), Happy Ever After (BBC Television, 1974-1979), Terry & June (BBC Television, 1979-1987), Danger Mouse (Thames Television, 1981-1992)

Finest Hour (and a bit):
Carry On Loving. Surly sexual predator, Terence Philpot, is the sort of character you really shouldn't like. He's deeply untrustworthy and driven by one single thought – getting his leg over. In the hands of Terry Scott, Philpot becomes a mischievous rogue, funny and charming, but hopelessly awkward. From the innocent oaf Jungle Boy in Carry On up the Jungle to the thoroughly hacked-off Peter Potter in Carry On Camping, Terry Scott could play any character. My personal favourite is the chap who turns his back on a mousey, Victorian values girl only to throw everything he has at her when he realises she might be a bit of a goer. Like Dr Prodd in Carry On Matron, he could simply be a one-dimensional sex fiend but instead he is remarkably endearing.

One to Forget:
Carry On Sergeant: Scott played a rather minor character in Carry On Sergeant, a relatively straight role which helped to set up the theme of Grimshaw's bet. He had just a few lines and none of them were particularly funny. While Carry On Sergeant is a lovely film, Terry Scott's part in it is very much as a supporting character so if you're looking for an archetypal Carry On performance, you would be better off looking elsewhere.

Seen & Heard:
Film Night Special - Carry On Forever (BBC2, 12/04/1970)
This is Your Life: Terry Scott (Thames Television, 22/11/1978)
The Unforgettable Terry Scott (ITV, 22/09/2010)

Shacklock, Harry: Lavatory Attendant (Loving)
Shafeek, Dino: Immigration Officer (Emmannuelle)
Shaw, Denis: 2nd Sinister Passenger (Regardless)
Shaw, Richard: Captain of Soldiers (Don't Lose your Head)
Shaw, Susan: Jane Bishop (Nurse)
Shelley, Carol: Helen Delling (Regardless), Dumb Driver (Cabby)
Shute, Valerie: Pat (Camping), Nurse (Again Doctor), Girl Lover (Loving), Maid (Henry - *Scene cut*), Miss Smethurst (Matron)
Silhouettes, Les: (Carry On London! (stage))
Silvers, Phil: Sergeant Ernie Nocker (Follow that Camel)
Simpson, Georgina: Men's Ward Nurse (Again Doctor)

SIMS, JOAN

Real Name: Irene Joan Marian Sims
Born: 9th May 1930, Laindon, Essex, UK
Died: 28th June 2001, Chelsea, UK

First Film Appearance: The Square Ring (1953)

First Carry On Appearance: Carry On Nurse (1959)
Final Film Appearance: The Fool (1990)

Carry On Appearances: Nurse Stella Dawson (Nurse), Sarah Allcock (Teacher), WPC Gloria Passworthy (Constable), Lily Duveen (Regardless), Calpurnia (Cleo), Belle (Cowboy), Emily Bung (Screaming!), Desiree Dubarry (Don't Lose your Head), Zig-Zig (Follow that Camel), Chloe Gibson (Doctor), Lady Joan Ruff-Diamond (Up the Khyber), Joan Fussey (Camping), Mrs Ellen Moore (Again Doctor), Lady Evelyn Bagley (Up the Jungle), Esme Crowfoot (Loving), Queen Marie of Normandy (Henry), Chloe Moore (At your Convenience), Mrs Tidey (Matron), Cora Flange (Abroad), Connie Philpotts (Girls), Madame Desiree (Dick), Daphne Barnes (Behind), Private Jennifer Ffoukes-Sharpe (England), Mrs Dangle (Emmannuelle), Lady Rhoda Cockhorse/Miss Esmerelda/Princess Yo-Yo/Clodhopper's Mother-in-Law (Carry On Christmas 1972 (TV)), Bishop's Wife/ Adele/Virginia's Mum/Salvation Army Lady/Traffic Warden/Maid Marian/Ballet Dancer/ Senna Pod (Carry On Christmas 1973 (TV)), Madame Olga (Carry On Laughing - The Prisoner of Spenda (TV)), Lady Isobel (Carry On Laughing - The Baron Outlook (TV)), Lady Kate Houndsbotham (Carry On Laughing - The Sobbing Cavalier (TV)), Else (Carry On Laughing - One in the Eye for Harold (TV)), Mrs MacFlute (Carry On Laughing - The Case of the Screaming Winkles (TV)), Dr Janis Crunbitt (Carry On Laughing - The Case of the Coughing Parrot (TV)), Lady Guinevere (Carry On Laughing - Under the Round Table (TV)), Lady Guinevere (Carry On Laughing - Short Knight, Long Daze (TV)), Mrs Breeches (Carry On Laughing - And in My Lady's Chamber (TV)), Mrs Breeches (Carry On Laughing - Who Needs Kitchener? (TV))

Other Notable Appearances: Trouble in Store (1953), Doctor in the House (1954), The Belles of St Trinian's (1954), Doctor at Sea (1955), The Naked Truth (1957), Carry On Admiral (1957), Just My Luck (1957), Doctor in Love (1960), Please Turn Over (1960), Our House (ABC Weekend Television, 1960), Watch your Stern (1961), Twice Round the Daffodils (1962), The Big Job (1965), Doctor in Clover (1966), Stop Messing About (BBC Radio, 1969-1970), Doctor in Trouble (1970), One of our Dinosaurs is Missing (1975), Til Death Us Do Part (BBC Television, 1974), The Howerd Confessions (Thames Television, 1976), Lord Tramp (Southern Television, 1977), Worzel Gummidge (Southern Television, 1979-1980), Born & Bred (Thames Television, 1978-1980), Doctor Who – Trial of a Time Lord (BBC Television, 1986), Farrington of the FO (Yorkshire Television, 1986-1987), Simon & the Witch (BBC Television, 1987-1988), On the Up (BBC Television, 1990-1992), Martin Chuzzlewit (BBC Television, 1994), As Time Goes By (BBC Television, 1994-1998), Last of the Blonde Bombshells (BBC Television, 2000)

Finest Hour (and a bit):
Carry On at your Convenience. Joan's Carry On persona changed dramatically over the course of her career with this series. From the pretty young Nurse Dawson she went on to play the fading beauty in films like Cowboy or Cleo before moving into entirely less pleasant characters in Screaming. Joan played every character brilliantly, but given a character who lets her hair down, she's utterly infectious. Joan Sims' laughter is enough to brighten any film and she rarely laughs louder or more heartily than in Carry On at your Convenience. Her trading of innuendo in the works canteen is one of the all-out funniest scenes in any Carry On, especially when she later goes on to that beautiful, sensitive moment with Sid at near the end of the film. Delightful.

One to Forget:
Carry On Dick. Another Carry On regular who was badly served by the strained writing of Carry On Dick. Joan's not really in the film long enough to warrant any kind of fleshing out of her character. As the "madam" of Les Oiseaux des Paradis, she gets to show off her flirtatious side, with the odd glimpse of her less glamorous roots slipping through, but it's a role which goes nowhere other than to fuel an on-going gag.

Seen & Heard:
Film Night Special - Carry On Forever (BBC2, 12/04/1970)
The Electric Theatre Show – Carry On England (Grampian, 1976)
Movie Memories (Anglia Television, 4/07/1985)
What's a Carry On? (ITV, 29/12/1998)
The Unforgettable Joan Sims (ITV, 21/05/2002)

Further Reading:
High Spirits by Joan Sims, Partridge Press, 2000 (ISBN: 1852252804)

Sinden, Marc: Captain Perez
Singuineau, Frank: Riff at Abdul's Tent (Follow that Camel), Porter (Again Doctor)
Skipper, Susan: Mabel (Carry On Laughing - Short Knight, Long Daze (TV))
Slattery, Tony: Baba the Messenger (Columbus)
Sloan, Carol: Harem Girl (Follow that Camel)
Smart, Patsy: Old Hag (Carry On Laughing - One in the Eye for Harold (TV))
Smethurst, Jack: Recruit (Sergeant)
Smith, Madeline: Mrs Pullitt (Matron)
Smith, Vicki: Amazon Guard (Spying), Vestal Virgin (Cleo), Polly (Cowboy)
Snell, Patsy: Harem Girl (Follow that Camel)
Solomon, Prudence: Ha Ha (Columbus)
Sommer, Elke: Professor Anna Vooshka (Behind)
Spenser, David: Servant (Up the Khyber)
Spurrier, Julian Essex: Jolly Juvenile (Wot a Carry On in Blackpool (stage))
St Clair, Jean: Mrs Smith (Doctor)
Stanley, Charles: Porter (Nurse), Geoff (Cabby)
Stanley, Norman: Drunk (Cowboy)
Stanton, Marita: Rose Harper (Nurse)
Stanton, Valerie: Demon King's Vision (Carry On Christmas 1972 (TV))
Stelfox, Shirley: Bunny Waitress (At your Convenience)
Stensgaard, Yutte: Trolley Nurse (Again Doctor), Mrs Roxby (Loving - *Scene cut*)
Stephen, Susan: Nurse Georgie Axwell (Nurse)
Stevens, Dorinda: Young Woman (Constable), 2nd Woman at Dirty Dick's (Jack)
Stevens, Julie: Gloria (Cleo)
Stevens, Ronnie: Drunk (Cruising)
Stewart, Graham: 2nd Storeman (Sergeant), George Field (Nurse)
Stewart, Roy: Nosha (Up the Jungle)
Stockbridge, Sara: Nina the Model (Columbus)

Stoll, David: Distraught Manager (Regardless)

Stone, Marianne: Alice Able (Nurse), 1st Woman at Dirty Dick's (Jack), Mrs Parker (Screaming!), Landlady (Don't Lose your Head), Mother (Doctor), Maud (At your Convenience), Miss Putzova (Matron – *Scene Cut*), Miss Drew (Girls), Maggie (Dick), Mrs Rowan (Behind), Madame Petra (Carry On Laughing - The Case of the Screaming Winkles (TV))

Stone, Philip: Robinson (Loving), Mr Bulstrode (At your Convenience - *Scene cut*)

Street, George: Club Reception Man (Regardless)

Summerfield, Eleanor: Mrs Riley (Regardless – *scene cut*)

Sumner, Barbara: Alice Pringle (Carry On Laughing with "The Slimming Factory" (stage))

Sydney, Derek: Algerian Gent (Spying), Major-Domo (Up the Khyber)

T

Tafler, Jonathan: Inquisitor (Columbus)

Tafler, Sydney: Strip Club Manager (Regardless)

Tanner, Gordon: 1st Specialist (Sergeant)

Tarr, Ron: Bearded Man in Audience (Girls)

Tasker, Billy: (Carry On London! (stage))

Taylor, Jack: Cliff (Constable), MC/1st Railway Policeman (Regardless), 1st Thug (Spying)

Taylor, Larry: Riff (Follow that Camel), Burpa at Door-Grille (Up the Khyber), Tough Man (Dick)

Taylor, Thelma: Seneca's Servant (Cleo)

Taylor, Shaw: Presenter (What a Carry On! (TV))

Thau, Leon: Stinghi (Up the Khyber)

THOMAS, GERALD

Born: 10th Decermber 1920, Hull, UK
Died: 9th November 1993, Buckinghamshire, UK

First Film: The Twenty Questions Murder Mystery (Editor, 1950)
First Carry On: Carry On Sergeant (1958)
Final Film: Carry On Columbus (1992)

Carry On Appearances (Actor): Voice of Oddbodd Jr (Screaming!), Voice of Mynah Bird (Behind) - *See also Crew*

Other Notable Productions: Doctor in the House (Editor, 1954), Above Us the Waves (Editor, 1955), Circus Friends (Director, 1956), Time Lock (Director, 1957), Please Turn Over (Director, 1960), Watch your Stern (Director, 1961), Raising the Wind (Director, 1961), Twice Round the Daffodils (Director, 1962), Nurse on Wheels (Director, 1963), The Big Job (Director, 1965), Bless This House (Director, 1972), Carry On Laughing (Director, Thames Television, 1981), What a Carry On (Director, BBC Television, 1984), Laugh with the Carry Ons (Director / Editor, Central Television, 1993)

Seen & Heard:
Film Night Special - Carry On Forever (BBC 2, 12/04/1970)
The Electric Theatre Show – Carry On England (Grampian, 1976)

Thomas, Lisa: Sally (Cowboy)

Thompson, Jimmy: Mr Delling (Regardless), Sam Turner (Cruising), Nelson (Jack)

Thornton, Frank: Mr Jones (Screaming!)

Tobias, Silvestre: Abdullah (Columbus)

Todd, Bob: Pump Patient (Again Doctor), Ben Gunn/Shipmate (Carry On Again Christmas (TV))

Toothill, Paul: Gunner Gale (England)

Towb, Harry: Doctor in Film (At your Convenience)

Trent, Anthony: Herald (Carry On Laughing - The Baron Outlook (TV))

Truzzi, George: (Carry On London! (stage))

Tyler, Virginia: Funhouse Girl (Spying), Handmaiden (Cleo)

U

Unwin, Stanley: Landlord (Regardless)

V

Van der Zyl, Nikki: Messenger (Don't Lose your Head)

Van Doorn, Trudi: (Carry On London! (stage))

Van Eyssen, John: Mr Stephens (Nurse)

Van Ost, Valerie: Glamcab Driver (Cabby), 2nd Lady (Don't Lose your Head), Nurse Parkin (Doctor), Out-Patients Sister (Again Doctor)

Vancao, Colin: Cousin Wilberforce Grubb (Loving)

Vaughan, Sue: Hospitality Girl (Up the Khyber)

Ventham, Wanda: Pretty Bidder (Cleo), 1st Wife (Up the Khyber)

Ventura, Vivianne: Spanish Secretary (Jack)

Villiers, James: Recruit (Sergeant)

W

Waller, Kenneth: Barman (Behind)

Walsh, Valerie: Lady Ermintrude (Carry On Laughing - Under the Round Table (TV))

Ward, Guy: Dandy (Emmannuelle)

Ward, Haydn: Recruit (Sergeant)

Ward, Michael: Photographer (Regardless), Man in Tweeds (Cabby), Archimedes (Cleo), Vivian (Screaming!), Henri (Don't Lose your Head)

Ware, Neville: 2nd Reporter (Emmannuelle)

Warwick, Gina: Harem Girl (Follow that Camel)

Wattis, Richard: Cobley (Spying)

Watts, Gwendolyn: Mrs Barron (Doctor), Night Sister (Again Doctor), Frances Kemp (Matron)

Way, Ann: Aunt Victoria Grubb (Loving)

Webb, Lincoln: Nosha with Girl (Up the Jungle)

Webster, Malcolm: Recruit (Sergeant)

Weir, Molly: Bird Owner (Regardless)

Wells, Jerold: Black Cowl (Carry On Laughing - One in the Eye for Harold (TV))

Westwood, Patrick: Burpa in Crowd (Up the Khyber)

Whitaker, Caroline: Mary Parker (Girls), Student (Behind)

White, Carol: Sheila Dale (Teacher)
White, Donna: Vestal Virgin (Cleo), Jenny (Cowboy)
White, Jane: Irene (Teacher)
White, Jenny: Nurse in Bath (Doctor)
White, Nick: Sent-Off Footballer (Emmannuelle)
Whitfield, June: Meg (Nurse), Evelyn Blunt (Abroad), Augusta Prodworthy (Girls), Queen Isabella of Spain (Columbus)
Whittaker, Ian: Medical Corporal (Sergeant), Shop Assistant (Regardless)
Wilde, Brian: Man from Cox & Carter (Doctor), 2nd Warder (Henry)
Williams, David: 7th Storeman (Sergeant), Andrew Newman (Nurse)

WILLIAMS, KENNETH

Born: 22nd February 1926, Islington, UK
Died: 15th April 1988, Camden, UK

First Film Appearance: Valley of Song (1953)
First Carry On Appearance: Carry On Sergeant (1958)
Final Film Appearance: Carry On Emmannuelle (1978)

Carry On Appearances: James Bailey (Sergeant), Oliver Reckitt (Nurse), Edwin Milton (Teacher), PC Stanley Benson (Constable), Francis Courtenay (Regardless), Leonard Marjoribanks (Cruising), Captain Fearless (Jack), Desmond Simkins (Spying), Julius Caesar (Cleo), Judge Burke (Cowboy), Doctor Olando Watt (Screaming!), Citizen Camembert (Don't Lose your Head), Commandant Burger (Follow that Camel), Dr Kenneth Tinkle (Doctor), The Khasi of Kalabar (Up the Khyber), Dr Kenneth Soaper (Camping), Dr Frederick Carver (Again Doctor), Percival Snooper (Loving), Thomas Cromwell (Henry), WC Boggs (At your Convenience), Sir Bernard Cutting (Matron), Stuart Farquhar (Abroad), Captain Desmond Fancey (Dick), Professor Roland Crump (Behind), Himself (That's Carry On), Emile Prevert (Emmannuelle), Performer (Carry On Laughing's Christmas Classics (TV))

Other Notable Appearances: Hancock's Half Hour (BBC Radio, 1955-1959), Beyond our Ken (BBC Radio, 1958-1964), Make Mine Mink (1960), Raising the Wind (1961), Twice Round the Daffodils (1962), Diary of a Madman (BBC Radio, 1963), Round the Horne (BBC Radio, 1965-1968), International Cabaret (BBC Television, 1966-1974), Just a Minute (BBC Radio, 1968-1988), Stop Messing About (BBC Radio, 1969-1970), The Secret Life of Kenneth Williams (BBC Radio, 1971, 1973, 1975), Kenneth Williams Playhouse (BBC Radio, 1975), Agaton Sax (1976), Oh Get on with It! (BBC Radio, 1976), The Hound of the Baskervilles (1978), The Whizz-Kids' Guide (Southern Television, 1981), Willo the Wisp (BBC Television, 1981), An Audience with Kenneth Williams (London Weekend Television, 1983), Galloping Galaxies (BBC Television, 1985), Wogan (BBC Television, 1987)

Finest Hour (and a bit):
Carry On at your Convenience. I have to admit that I am a complete sucker for Carry On at your Convenience. Much of my love for the film is the simple story, delivered with such panache. However, I also believe that in this film we see the very best of so many of the Carry On regulars playing the archetypal characters for which they are best known.

As WC Boggs, Kenneth is mercurial, repressed, frustrated, boozed up and finally, thanks to some much needed care from Miss Withering, a seemingly normal, happy individual. It is a tremendously varied performance which doesn't once fall back on the tried and tested "Snide" character.

One to Forget:
Carry On Spying. Kenneth's early fame on radio is due in no small measure to his broader characters like the dreaded "Snide" but in Carry On Spying he plays a barely toned-down version of that nasal nuisance. That's all very well if you happen to like "Snide", but other than that, there's precious little to love in Kenneth's performance, that is, apart from the scene in the bathroom which still gets me every time.

Seen & Heard:
Good Afternoon – Is it Fun Being Funny? (Thames Television, 1/07/1974)
Comic Roots – Kenneth Williams (BBC2, 2/09/1983)
Look Who's Talking (Border Television, 1983)
An Audience with Kenneth Williams (London Weekend Television, 23/12/1983)
Desert Island Discs (BBC Radio, 26/07/1987)
Radio Lives – Kenneth Williams (BBC Radio, 9/06/1994)
The South Bank Show – Kenneth Williams (ITV, 18/09/1994)
Radio Lives – I Am yer Actual Quality (BBC Radio, 27/12/1994)
Turns of the Century – Kenneth Williams (BBC Radio, 8/12/1995)
Reputations – Kenneth Williams (BBC2, 24/05/1998, 25/05/1998)
Kenneth Williams – A Life on the Box (BBC1, 28/08/1998)
Kenneth Williams – The Parkinson Interviews (BBC1, 1998)
Carry On Darkly (Channel 4, 30/09/1998)
Cor Blimey! (ITV, 25/04/2000)
Legends – Kenneth Williams (ITV, 17/08/2000)
Heroes of Comedy – Kenneth Williams (Channel 4, 7/10/2000)
The Unforgettable Kenneth Williams (ITV, 23/09/2001)
The Private World of Kenneth Williams (BBC Radio, 4/11/2003)
Kenneth Williams – In his Own Words (BBC Four, 13/03/2006)
Fantabulosa (BBC Four, 13/03/2006)

Further Reading:
Acid Drops by Kenneth Williams, Dent, 1980 (ISBN: 0460044826)
Back Drops by Kenneth Williams, Futura, 1984 (ISBN: 0708824641)
Just Williams – An Autobiography, Harper Collins, 1986 (ISBN: 0006370829)
I Only have to Close my Eyes by Kenneth Williams, Dent, 1986 (ISBN: 0460061755)
Kenneth Williams – A Biography by Michael Friedland, Weidenfeld & Nicholson, 1990 (ISBN: 0297797018)
The Kenneth Williams Diaries edited by Russell Davies, Harper Collins, 1993 (ISBN: 0006380905)
The Kenneth Williams Letters edited by Russell Davies, Harper Collins, 1995 (ISBN: 0006380921)
The Complete Acid Drops by Kenneth Williams, Orion, 2000 (ISBN: 0752837257)
Kenneth Williams: Unseen by Wes Butters & Russell Davies, Harper Collins, 2008 (ISBN: 0007280858)
Born Brilliant – The Life of Kenneth Williams by Christopher Stevens, John Murray, 2011 (ISBN: 184854197X)

Willoughby, Anna: Girl (Don't Lose your Head)
Wilson, Audrey: Amazon Guard (Spying), Jane (Cowboy)
Wilson, Ian: Advertising Man (Regardless), Clerk (Cabby), Ancient Carrier (Jack), Messenger (Cleo)
Wilson, Richard: Don Juan Felipe (Columbus)

WINDSOR, BARBARA

Real Name: Barbara Ann Deeks
Born: 6th August 1937, Shoreditch, UK

First Film Appearance: Make Mine a Million (1959)
First Carry On Appearance Carry On Spying (1964)

Carry On Appearances: Daphne Honeybutt (Spying), Nurse Sandra May (Doctor), Babs (Camping), Goldie Locks (Again Doctor), Bettina (Henry), Nurse Susan Ball (Matron), Miss Sadie Tompkins (Abroad), Hope Springs (Girls), Harriet (Dick), Herself (That's Carry On), Cinderella/Fanny/Sprit of Christmas Present (Carry On Christmas 1969 (TV)), Jim Hawkins (Carry On Again Christmas (TV)), Milk Maiden/Eve/Maid?Miss Clodhopper/Aladdin (Carry On Christmas 1972), Virginia/Crompet the Pit Cavegirl/Fifi/Lady Fanny/Ballet Dancer/Lady Frances of Bristol (Carry On Christmas 1973 (TV)), Performer (What a Carry On! (TV)), Vera Basket (Carry On Laughing - The Prisoner of Spenda (TV)), Marie (Carry On Laughing - The Baron Outlook (TV)), Sarah (Carry On Laughing - The Sobbing Cavalier (TV)), Lady Miranda (Carry On Laughing - Orgy & Bess (TV)), Maisie (Carry On Laughing - The Nine Old Cobblers (TV)), Baroness Lottie Von Titsenhausen (Carry On Laughing - And in My Lady's Chamber (TV)), Baroness Lottie Von Titsenhausen (Carry On Laughing - Who Needs Kitchener? (TV)), Lady Mary Airey-Fairey (Carry On Laughing - Lamp Posts of the Empire (TV)), Performer (Carry On Laughing's Christmas Classics (TV)), Carry On London! (stage), Leading Lady (Wot a Carry On in Blackpool (stage))

Other Notable Appearances: The Rag Trade (BBC Television, 1961-1963), Sparrows Can't Sing (1963), Crooks in Cloisters (1964), A Study in Terror (1965), Wild, Wild Women (BBC Television, 1969), Not Now Darling (1973), Worzel Gummidge (Southern Television, 1980), Filthy, Rich & Catflap (BBC Television, 1987), Norbert Smith – A Life (Channel 4, 1989), Bluebirds (BBC Television, 1989), EastEnders (BBC Television, 1994-2010)

Finest Hour (and a bit):
Carry On Henry: There's not a great deal to love about Carry On Henry. It's a tale of deceit and betrayal where everyone gets a knife in their back apart from young Bettina. Barbara Windsor is best known as the blonde bombshell who wasn't afraid of flashing her boobs, but in Carry On Henry, she plays a more restrained character; the most chaste and innocent in the film. While she is certainly saucy, Bettina remains the untouched object of affection and much of the best comedy in the film comes from there. Barbara's performance in Carry On Henry is one of the highlights of an otherwise lacklustre film.

One to Forget:
Carry On Matron. Barbara is surplus to requirements in Carry On Matron. Susan Ball serves no purpose in the film other than to "out" Kenneth Cope but, given that he was about to call off the whole caper at the time she discovers him, the film could have just as

376 CARRY ON CONFIDENTIAL / CARRY ON BEHIND THE SCENES

easily have reached its conclusion without her. Barbara doesn't really get much to work with outside of her scenes with Cope, tending to compound the sense that her presence in the film is simply unnecessary.

Seen & Heard:
What a Carry On (Thames Television, 4/10/1973)
Look Who's Talking (Border Television, 24/03/1975)
Desert Island Discs (BBC Radio, 23/09/1990)
This is your Life: Barbara Windsor (BBC1, 30/09/1992)
The Obituary Show – Barbara Windsor (Channel 4, 15/11/1994)
An Invitation to Remember (ITV, 8/01/1995)
The Best of British – Barbara Windsor (BBC1, 4/11/1998)
Cor Blimey! (ITV, 25/04/2000)
BBC Hall of Fame (BBC Television, 7/05/2000)
You Only Live Once (BBC Television, 30/10/2001)
Gloria's Greats (Biography Channel, 12/02/2005)
Channel 4 Comedy Roast – Barbara Windsor (Channel 4, 5/01/2011)
Barbara Windsor's Funny Girls (BBC Radio, 2011)

Further Reading:
Barbara Windsor's Book of Boobs, Hamlyn, 1979 (ISBN: 0600315630)
Barbara: The Laughter & Tears of a Cockney Sparrow by Barbara Windsor, Arrow, 1991 (ISBN: 0099721104)
All of Me: My Extraordinary Life by Barbara Windsor, Headline, 2000 (ISBN: 0747266441)

Winsor, Elsie: Cloakroom Attendant (Girls)
Wise, Barbara: Julia Oates (Girls)
Woodall, Corbet: ITN Newscaster (Emmannuelle)
Woodbridge, George: Ned (Jack)
Woolf, Vicki: 3rd Wife (Up the Khyber)
Wyldeck, Martin: Mr Sage (Sergeant)
Wyler, Carol: Maureen Darcy (Girls)
Wyllie, Bruce: Football Referee (Emmannuelle)

Y
Yang, Madame: Chinese Lady (Regardless)
Young, Joan: Suspect (Constable)
Young, Karen: Girl (Don't Lose your Head), Harem Girl (Follow that Camel), Hospitality Girl (Up the Khyber)

DIRECTORY OF CREW

A

Alexander, William: Assistant Art Director (Loving, Henry, At Your Convenience, Matron)

Allen, Roger: Designer (Carry On Christmas 1969 (TV), Carry On Christmas 1970 (TV))

Alstone, Alex: Co-Composer "Too Late" w/Geoffrey Parsons (Spying)

Ambrose, Edward: Assistant Art Director (Columbus)

Angelinetta, Olga: Hairdresser (Teacher, Jack)

Antrobus, John: Additional Script (Sergeant, Columbus)

Arnell, Jane: Casting (Columbus)

Atchelor, Jack: Camera (Carry On Laughing - The Prisoner of Spenda (TV), Carry On Laughing - The Baron Outlook (TV), Carry On Laughing - The Sobbing Cavalier (TV), Carry On Laughing - Orgy & Bess (TV), Carry On Laughing - One in the Eye for Harold (TV), Carry On Laughing - The Nine Old Cobblers (TV))

B

Bailey, Michael: Designer (Carry On Laughing - Lamp Posts of the Empire (TV))

Bamber, Terry: Assistant Director (Columbus)

Baker, Natalie: 2nd Assistant Editor (Columbus)

Barker, Ken: Sound Recordist (Cowboy, Screaming!, Don't Lose your Head, Follow that Camel, Doctor, Up the Khyber, Camping, Again Doctor, Up the Jungle, Loving, Henry, At your Convenience, Matron, Abroad, Girls, Dick, Behind, That's Carry On)

Barley, Ken: Chargehand Plasterer (Columbus)

Barnes, Eve: Wardrobe Mistress (Carry On London! (stage))

Batt, Bert: Assistant Director (Teacher, Matron)

Baverstock, Brian: Unit Driver (Columbus)

Bawden, James: Camera Operator (Doctor, Up the Khyber, Camping, Again Doctor, Up the Jungle, Loving, At your Convenience, Matron)

Baxter, Ronnie: Director (Carry On Christmas 1969 (TV))

Beale, Jack: Original Story w/Patrick Cargill (Nurse)

Beaver, Les: Chargehand Rigger (Columbus)

Bennison, Bill: Assistant Art Director (Abroad)

Best, Peter: Dubbing Editor (Matron, Abroad, Dick, Emmannuelle)

Bevis, Frank: Production Manager (Sergeant, Nurse, Teacher, Constable, Cabby, Jack, Spying, Cleo, Cowboy), Associate Producer (Screaming!)

Binney, Neil: Camera Operator (Up the Khyber, Behind)

Bishop, Charles: Set Dresser (Dick, Behind)

Blackler, George: Make-Up Designer (Nurse, Teacher, Constable, Regardless, Cruising)

Blezard, John: Art Director (Again Doctor)

Blues, Bob: Accounts (Columbus)

Blunden, Chris: Editor (Columbus)

Boita, Peter: Editor (Sergeant, Emmannuelle)

Bolton, Peter: Assistant Director (Cabby, Spying, Cleo, Cowboy, Screaming!)

Bone, Alan: Assistant Stage Manager (Carry On Laughing with "The Slimming Factory" (stage))

Bonnichon, Lisa: Assistant to John Goldstone (Columbus)

Borer, Tony: Designer (Carry On Christmas 1972 (TV))

Bowen, Gareth: Set Design (Wot a Carry On in Blackpool (stage))

Bracknell, David: Assistant Director (Follow that Camel, Loving, Henry, At your Convenience, Abroad, Dick)

Bray, Ken: Stills Cameraman (England, Emmannuelle)

Brock, Denis: Gaffer Electrician (Columbus)

Brook, Olga: Continuity (Cleo)

Browne, Derek: Camera Operator (Henry)

Buck, Jane: Continuity (Dick)

C

Cadman, Tom: Stills Cameraman (Dick)

Caffin, Yvonne: Costume Designer (Constable, Spying, Doctor, Camping)

Cameron, Allan: Designer (Carry On Christmas 1973 (TV))

Campling, David: Dubbing Editor (Doctor)

Cargill, Patrick: Original Story w/Jack Beale (Nurse) - *See also Cast*

Carter, Michael: Dubbing Mixer (Columbus)

Causey, Jack: Assistant Director (Regardless, Cruising, Don't Lose your Head, Camping, Up the Jungle, Girls, England)

Charles, Peter: VTR Editor (Carry On Laughing - The Case of the Screaming Winkles (TV), Carry On Laughing - The Case of the Coughing Parrot (TV), Carry On Laughing - Under the Roudn Table (TV), Carry On Laughing - Short Knight, Long Daze (TV), Carry On Laughing - And in My Lady's Chamber (TV), Carry On Laughing - Who Needs Kitchener? (TV))

Cherrill, Roger: Sound Editor (Nurse)

Childs, Peter: Art Director (Columbus)

Church, Tony: Screenplay (That's Carry On)

Chrystal, Biddy: Hairdresser (Regardless, Cruising, Cabby, Spying)

Clark, David: Director (Carry On Laughing's Christmas Classics (TV))

Clegg, Terry: Location Manager (Follow that Camel), Assistant Director (Doctor)

Colin, Sid: Co-Writer (Spying), Script (Carry On Christmas 1970 (TV))

Collins, Jayne: Performer, Theme "Carry On Columbus" (Columbus)

Connor, Sean: Clapper Loader (Columbus)

Couch, Lionel: Art Director (Teacher, Regardless, Don't Lose your Head, Camping, Loving, Henry, At your Convenience, Matron, Abroad, Dick, Behind, England)

Coulter, Phil: Co-Writer "Don't Lose your Head" Theme w/Bill Martin (Don't Lose your Head)

Cox, Ian: Technical Advisor (Jack)

Crane, John: Vision Control (Carry On Laughing - Lamp Posts of the Empire (TV))

Cree, Sam: Script (Carry On Laughing with "The Slimming Factory" (stage))

Crouch, Ken: Wardrobe (Columbus)

Cryer, Barry: Script (Wot a Carry On in Blackpool (stage)), Script (Carry On Laughing - Orgy & Bess (TV))

Curtis, Sharon: Stage Manager (Wot a Carry On in Blackpool (stage))

D

Daniel, Danny: Sound Recordist (Loving, Henry, At your Convenience, Matron, Dick, Behind, England, That's Carry On, Emmannuelle)

Daniels, Bill: Sound Recordist (Nurse, Constable, Cruising, Cabby, Jack, Spying, Cleo, Camping, Again Doctor)

Daniels, Penny: Continuity (Nurse, Cruising, Cabby, Jack, Spying, Screaming!)

Dark, Gregory: Assistant Director (Emmannuelle)

Dark, James: Wardrobe (Carry On Laughing - The Case of the Screaming Winkles (TV), Carry On Laughing - The Case of the Coughing Parrot (TV), Carry On Laughing - Under the Round Table (TV), Carry On Laughing - Short Knight, Long Daze (TV), Carry On Laughing - And in My Lady's Chamber (TV), Carry On Laughing - Who Needs Kitchener? (TV), Carry On Laughing - Lamp Posts of the Empire (TV))

Davey, Bert: Art Director (Cleo, Cowboy, Screaming!)

Davies, Tudor: Director (Wot a Carry On in Blackpool (stage))

Davis, Gordon: Accounts (Columbus)

Davis, Joan: Continuity (Sergeant, Constable)

Davison, Rita: Continuity (Don't Lose your Head, Henry, At your Convenience)

Dawe, Cedric: Art Director (Doctor)

Day, Tilly: Continuity (Teacher)

De Gaye, Phoebe: Costumer Designer (Columbus)

Dernley, Doreen: Continuity (Camping)

Devis, Jimmy: Camera Operator (Don't Lose your Head, Abroad, Girls, Dick)

Dick, Ted: Co-Writer "Carry On Screaming!" Theme w/Myles Rudge (Screaming!)

Dillon, Carmen: Art Director (Constable, Cruising)

Dixon, Vernon: Set Dresser (Constable)

Du Prez, John: Composer (Columbus)

Durham, Marcel: Dubbing Editor (Loving)

Duse, Anna: Costume Designer (Again Doctor)

Dyson, Pete: Lighting (Carry On Laughing - The Case of the Screaming Winkles (TV), Carry On Laughing - The Case of the Coughing Parrot (TV), Carry On Laughing - Under the Round Table (TV), Carry On Laughing - Short Knight, Long Daze (TV), Carry On Laughing - And in My Lady's Chamber (TV), Carry On Laughing - Who Needs Kitchener? (TV), Carry On Laughing - Lamp Posts of the Empire (TV))

E

Ellacott, Joan: Costume Designer (Sergeant, Nurse, Regardless, Cruising, Cabby, Jack)

Elliott, Courtenay: Costume Designer (Up the Jungle, Loving, Henry, At your Convenience, Matron, Abroad, Girls, Dick, Behind, England, Emmannuelle)

Eton, Peter: Producer (Carry On Christmas 1969 (TV)), Executive Producer (Carry On Christmas 1970 (TV))

Evans, George: Co-Author, Original Treatment (Dick)

Exshaw, Denise: Set Decorator (Columbus)

F

Fennell, Lorraine: Production Co-Ordinator (Columbus)

Fordyce, Ann: Hairdresser (Cleo)

Forrest, Mary: Vision Mixer (Carry On Laughing - And in My Lady's Chamber (TV), Carry On Laughing - Who Needs Kitchener? (TV), Carry On Laughing - Lamp Posts of the Empire (TV))
Foster, Patrick: Dubbing Editor (Girls, Behind, England)
Fouracre, Ronald: Director (Carry On Christmas 1972 (TV), Carry On Christmas 1973 (TV))
Francis, Peter: Art Department Assistant (Columbus)

FREEMAN, DAVE

Born: 22nd August 1922, London, UK
Died: 28th March 1995, London, UK

First Film: The Magnificent Seven Deadly Sins (Screenplay, 1971)
First Carry On: Carry On Behind (Screenplay, 1975)
Final Film: Carry On Columbus (Screenplay, 1992)

Carry Ons: Screenplay (Behind, Columbus), Script (Carry On Christmas 1970 (TV), Carry On Christmas 1972 (TV), Carry On Laughing - The Prisoner of Spenda (TV), Carry On Laughing - The Baron Outlook (TV), Carry On Laughing - The Sobbing Cavalier (TV), Carry On Laughing - The Nine Old Cobblers (TV), Carry On Laughing - The Case of the Screaming Winkles (TV), Carry On Laughing - The Case of the Coughing Parrot (TV)), Original Material (Carry On Laughing's Christmas Classics (TV)), Script (Carry On London! (stage)) - *See also Cast*

Other Notable Productions: Great Scott, It's Maynard (Writer, BBC Television, 1955), The Avengers: The Rotters (Teleplay, ABC Weekend Television, 1968), Bless this House (Thames Television, 1971-1976), Bless this House (Screenplay, 1972), Bernie (Writer, Thames Television, 1978), Terry & June (Writer, BBC Television, 1980-1982), Keep it in the Family (Writer, Thames Television, 1983)

G

Gamley, Douglas: Co-composer (Cruising)
Gardner, Jack: Assistant Editor (Cowboy, Follow that Camel, Doctor, Up the Khyber, Camping, Again Doctor, Up the Jungle, Loving, Henry, At your Convenience, Matron, Abroad, Girls, Dick, Behind, England, Emmannuelle), Editor (That's Carry On), Editor (Carry On Laughing's Christmas Classics (TV))
Gilbert, Terry: Choreographer (Don't Lose your Head), Choreographer (Carry On Christmas 1973 (TV))
Gladstone, Natasha: Floor Runner (Columbus)
Gladstone, Stuart: Production Runner (Columbus)
Godar, Godfrey: Camera Operator (Cabby, Jack, Spying, Cleo, Cowboy, Screaming!, England, Emmannuelle)
Goddard, Roy: Production Manager (Girls, Dick, Behind, England, That's Carry On, Emmannuelle)
Goldsmith, Gladys: Continuity (Regardless, Cowboy)
Goldstone, John: Producer (Columbus)

Gordeno, Peter: Dance Staging (Columbus)

Gorman, Lee: Co-Writer, Theme "Carry On Columbus" (Columbus)

Grant, Ian: Additional material (Carry On London! (stage))

Grantham, Robin: Make-Up Designer (Emmannuelle)

Gregory, Nicky: Unit Nurse (Columbus)

Groom, Jim: Sound Editor (Cowboy)

Gunner, Michael: Chargehand Painter (Columbus)

H

Hahn, Caroline: Production Accountant (Carry On Laughing's Christmas Classics (TV))

Haine, Geoffrey: Assistant Director (Sergeant)

Haines, Taffy: Sound Recordist (Abroad)

Hall, Alan: Camera Operator (Follow that Camel)

Hamshire, Keith: Stillsman (Columbus)

Harris, Becky: Assistant Director (Columbus)

Harris, Julie: Costume Designer (Cleo)

Harris, Max: Composer & Conductor (England), Music (Carry On Laughing - Under the Round Table (TV), Carry On Laughing - Short Knight, Long Daze (TV), Carry On Laughing - And in My Lady's Chamber (TV))

Hawes, Tony: Programme Associate (What a Carry On! (TV))

Hawkins, John: VTR Editor (Carry On Laughing - Lamp Posts of the Empire (TV))

Hearn, Bill: Chargehand Carpenter (Columbus)

Hennessy, Peter: Director of Photography (Sergeant)

Herlihy, Joyce: Production Supervisor (Columbus)

Higgins, Mike: Assistant Director (Emmannuelle)

Hill, Bill: Production Manager (Cruising)

Hiscott, Richard: Footsteps Editor (Columbus)

Hobbs, Nick: Stunt Double (Girls)

Hoesli, John: Set Dresser (Emmannuelle)

Holding, Jacky: Accounts (Columbus)

Holgate, Brian: Designer (Carry On Laughing - Under the Round Table (TV), Carry On Laughing - Short Knight, Long Daze (TV))

Holland, Brian: Dubbing Editor (Henry, At your Convenience)

Holmes, Debbie: Performer, Theme "Carry On Columbus" (Columbus)

Holmes, Richard: Orchestra Director (Carry On London! (stage))

Honeyborne, Sue: Wardrobe (Columbus)

Horrocks, Peter: Dubbing Editor (Columbus)

Horsley, Keith: Unit Driver (Columbus)

Hosgood, Stanley: Assistant Director (Nurse)

Howitt, Peter: Set Dresser (Loving, Henry, At your Convenience)

HUDIS, NORMAN

Born: 27th July 1923, Stepney, UK

First Film: Breakaway (Screenplay, 1955)

First Carry On: Carry On Sergeant (Screenplay, 1958)

Carry Ons: Screenplay (Sergeant, Nurse, Teacher, Constable, Regardless, Cruising)

Other Notable Productions: Twice Round the Daffodils (Screenplay, 1962), Our House (Creator, Writer, ABC Weekend Television, 1960-1962), Nurse on Wheels (Screenplay, 1963), The Karate Killers (Screenplay, 1967), The Man from UNCLE (1967-1968), A Monkey's Tale (1999)

Seen & Heard:
What's a Carry On? (ITV, 29/12/1998)

Further Reading:
No Laughing Matter: How I Carried On by Norman Hudis, Apex, 2008 (ISBN: 190635815X)

Hume, Alan: Camera Operator (Sergeant, Nurse, Teacher, Constable), Director of Photography (Regardless, Cruising, Cabby, Jack, Spying, Cleo, Cowboy, Screaming!, Don't Lose your Head, Follow that Camel, Doctor, Henry, Abroad, Girls, Emmannuelle, Columbus)
Hume, Martin: Camera Operator (Columbus)
Hume, Simon: Camera Focus (Columbus)
Humphrey, Gordon: Standby Rigger (Columbus)
Hydes, Jim: Make-Up Artist (Cabby, Jack)

I
Imi, Tony: Director of Photography (That's Carry On)

J
Jackson, Ron: Unit Manager (Cowboy, Screaming!)
Jay, Gina: Casting Assistant (Columbus)
Jennings, Paul: Stunt Double (Columbus)
Jones, Robert: Art Director (Girls)

K
Keys, Basil: Associate Producer (Regardless)
Keys, Rod: Editor (Cowboy, Screaming!, Don't Lose your Head)
Kingman, Tod: Designer (Carry On London! (stage))
Knight, Albert J: Executive Producer (Carry On London! (stage))
Knight, Amanda: Make-Up (Columbus)
Knowles, Josephine: Continuity (Up the Jungle, Loving)
Korer, Jo: Wardrobe (Columbus)

L
Lake, Richard: Designer (Carry On Laughing - The Sobbing Cavalier (TV), Carry On Laughing - Orgy & Bess (TV), Carry On Laughing - The Nine Old Cobblers (TV))
Lamont, Peter: Assistant Art Director (Matron)
Lancaster, Christopher: Sound Editor (Jack, Spying, Cleo), Dubbing Editor (That's Carry On)
Langdon, Donald: Executive Producer for Cleves Investment Ltd (Emmannuelle)

Larry: Title sketches for Doctor, Up the Khyber, Camping, Girls

Laslett, Bill: Designer (Carry On Laughing's Christmas Classics (TV))

Lavelly, Marjorie: Continuity (Girls, Behind, England, Emmannuelle)

Layton, Tommy: Company & Stage Manager (Carry On Laughing with "The Slimming Factory" (stage))

Legg, Carole: Vision Mixer (Carry On Laughing - Under the Round Table (TV), Carry On Laughing - Short Knight, Long Daze (TV))

Leisham, Lynette: Assistant Choreographer (Carry On London! (stage))

Lemare, Paul: Sound Recordist (Girls)

Lewin, Margaret: Wardrobe Mistress (Matron, Dick, Emmannuelle)

Lewis, Jane: Wardrobe (Columbus)

Lewis, Len: Animator (Carry On Laughing (TV) - all)

Logan, Lewis: Designer (Carry On Laughing - The Case of the Screaming Winkles (TV), Carry On Laughing - The Case of the Coughing Parrot (TV))

Logie, Seymour: Sound Editor (Sergeant)

Love, Sarah: Hairdresser (Columbus)

Love, Sue: Hairdresser (Columbus)

Lovell, Dudley: Camera Operator (Regardless, Cruising)

Lucas, Saxon: Designer (Carry On Laughing with "The Slimming Factory" (stage))

Ludski, Archie: Sound Editor (Cruising), Editor (Cabby, Jack, Spying, Cleo)

Lynch, Kenny: Wrote "Love Crazy" - the theme for Emmannuelle *(see also Cast)*

M

MacPhee, Robert T: Sound Recordist (Sergeant, Nurse, Teacher, Constable, Regardless, Cruising, Cowboy, Up the Khyber, Up the Jungle)

McCallum, Gordon K: Sound Recordist (Sergeant, Teacher, Regardless, Cabby, Cleo, England)

McCallum Tait, Kenneth: Set Dresser (Girls)

McDonald, Philip: Standby Props (Columbus)

McLaren, Malcolm: Co-Writer, Theme "Carry On Columbus" (Columbus)

Maguire, Steve: Assistant Editor (Columbus)

Manley, Peter: Assistant Director (Constable)

Mann, Sheila: Make Up (Carry On Laughing - The Case of the Screaming Winkles (TV), Carry On Laughing - The Case of the Coughing Parrot (TV), Carry On Laughing - Under the Round Table (TV), Carry On Laughing - Short Knight, Long Daze (TV), Carry On Laughing - And in My Lady's Chamber (TV), Carry On Laughing - Who Needs Kitchener? (TV), Carry On Laughing - Lamp Posts of the Empire (TV))

Manning, Colin: Camera Grip (Columbus)

Marden, Richard: Editor (England)

Marshall, John: Music (Carry On Laughing (TV) - all)

Martin, Bill: Co-Writer "Don't Lose your Head" Theme w/Phil Coulter (Don't Lose your Head)

Masterplan: Performed "Love Crazy" (Emmannuelle)

Maton, Felicity: Vision Mixer (Carry On Laughing - The Case of the Screaming Winkles (TV), Carry On Laughing - The Case of the Coughing Parrot (TV))

Melhuish, Andrew: Assistant Dialogue Editor (Columbus)

Mercer, Joy: Continuity (Follow that Camel, Doctor, Matron, Abroad)
Merriman, Eric: Script (Carry On London! (stage))
Merry, Susanna: Continuity (Again Doctor)
Messenger, Dudley: Sound Recordist (Don't Lose your Head, Follow that Camel, Doctor)
Michael Sammes Singers: Sang theme to "Don't Lose your Head"
Michell, Ted: Scenic Artist (Columbus)
Miller, Colin: Dubbing Editor (Up the Khyber, Camping, Again Doctor, Up the Jungle)
Mills, Stanley: Designer (Carry On Laughing - The Prisoner of Spenda (TV))

MONTGOMERY, BRUCE

Real Name: Robert Bruce Montgomery
Other Names: Edmund Crispin (Author)

Born: 2nd October 1921, Buckinghamshire, UK
Died: 15th September 1978, Devon, UK

First Film: Which Will ye Have? (1949)
First Carry On: Carry On Sergeant (1958)
Final Film: The Brides of Fu Manchu (1966)

Carry Ons: Composer & Musical Director (Sergeant, Nurse, Teacher, Constable, Regardless, Cruising)

Other Notable Productions: Doctor in the House (Original Music, 1954), Doctor in Love (Original Music, 1960), Please Turn Over (Original Music, 1960), Watch your Stern (Original Music, 1961), Raising the Wind (Screenplay, Original Music, 1961), Twice Round the Daffodils (Original Music, 1962), Detective – The Moving Toyshop (Original Story, BBC Television, 30/03/1964), The Brides of Fu Manchu (Original Music, 1966)

Further Reading:
The Case of the Gilded Fly by Edmund Crispin, Gollancz, 1944
The Moving Toyshop by Edmund Crispin, Gollancz, 1946
Love Lies Bleeding by Edmund Crispin, Gollancz, 1948
Buried for Pleasure by Edmund Crispin, Gollancz, 1948
The Long Divorce by Edmund Crispin, Gollancz, 1951
Beware of the Trains by Edmund Crispin, Gollancz, 1953
Fen Country by Edmund Crispin, Littlehampton, 1979 (ISBN: 0575027177)
Bruce Montgomery: A Life in Music & Books by David Whittle, Ashgate, 2007 (ISBN: 0754634434)

Monzani, Sarah: Make-Up (Columbus)
Morgan, Terence: Set Dresser (Teacher)
Mothersill, Don: Wardrobe (England)
Mounsey, Peter: Standby Painter (Columbus)
Munro, Chris: Sound Recordist (Columbus)
Murray, Vi: Wardrobe (Matron, Dick, England)
Murton, Peter: Set Dresser (Sergeant)

N

Nelson, Wally: Sound Editor (Don't Lose your Head), Dubbing Editor (Follow that Camel)
Newell, Christine: Assistant Dubbing Editor (Columbus)
Nieder, Graham: Sound Maintenance (Columbus)

O

Orton, Pearl: Hairdresser (Nurse)
Owen, John: Casting Director (Dick, England)

P

Paley, Alan: Dialogue Editor (Columbus)
Palmer, John: Theatre & General Manager (Carry On Laughing with "The Slimming Factory" (stage))
Parkin, Tim: Orchestra Director (Wot a Carry On in Blackpool (stage))
Parsons, Geoffrey: Co-Composer "Too Late" w/Alex Alstone (Spying)
Partleton, WT: Make-Up Designer (Spying)
Pattenden, Ken: Construction Manager (Columbus)
Penfold, Len: Sound (Carry On Laughing - The Case of the Screaming Winkles (TV), Carry On Laughing - The Case of the Coughing Parrot (TV), Carry On Laughing - Under the Round Table (TV), Carry On Laughing - Short Knight, Long Daze (TV), Carry On Laughing - And in My Lady's Chamber (TV), Carry On Laughing - Who Needs Kitchener? (TV), Carry On Laughing - Lamp Posts of the Empire (TV))
Peters, Lance: Screenplay (Emmannuelle)
Phillips, Phil: Music Associate (Wot a Carry On in Blackpool (stage))
Picton, Don: Set Dresser (Abroad, England)
Poccetty, Billy: Best Boy (Columbus)
Potter, Gillie: Title Design (Columbus)
Pottle, Harry: Production Designer (Columbus)
Powell, Ivor: Assistant Director (Again Doctor)
Pullen, Peter: Special Properties (Carry On London! (stage))
Pursall, David: Co-Author, Screenplay (England)

R

Raine, David: Boat Consultant (Columbus)
Rawling, Clement: Sound Design (Wot a Carry On in Blackpool (stage))
Reardon, Ray: Performer, "Carry On Screaming!" Theme (Screaming!)
Reeves, Jim: Vision Control (Carry On Laughing - Under the Round Table (TV), Carry On Laughing - Short Knight, Long Daze (TV), Carry On Laughing - And in My Lady's Chamber (TV), Carry On Laughing - Who Needs Kitchener? (TV))
Richards, Yvonne: Continuity (Up the Khyber)
Ridout, Arthur: Sound Editor (Regardless, Cruising, Cabby, Screaming!)
Rivers, Stella: Hairdresser (Sergeant, Constable, Cowboy, Screaming!, Don't Lose your Head, Follow that Camel, Doctor, Up the Khyber, Camping, Again Doctor, Up the Jungle, Loving, Henry, At your Convenience, Matron, Abroad, Girls, Dick, Behind, England)
Roberton, Bill: Comedy Director (Carry On London! (stage)), Director (Carry On Laughing with "The Slimming Factory" (stage))
Robinson, Paul: Choreographer (Wot a Carry On in Blackpool (stage))
Rodway, Geoffrey: Make-Up Designer (Sergeant, Cruising, Cabby, Jack, Cleo, Cowboy,

Screaming!, Don't lose your Head, Follow that Camel, Doctor, Up the Khyber, Camping, Again Doctor, Up the Jungle, Loving, Henry, At your Convenience, Matron, Abroad, Girls, Dick, Behind, England)

Rogers, Alan: Lyrics, "Carry On Cowboy", "This is the Night for Love" (Cowboy)

ROGERS, ERIC

Born: 25th September 1921, Halifax, UK
Died: 9th April 1981, Buckinghamshire, UK

First Film: The Wedding of Lilli Marlene (1953)
First Carry On: Carry On Cabby (1963)
Final Film: Carry On Emmannuelle (1978)

Carry Ons: Composer & Musical Director (Cabby, Jack, Spying, Cleo, Cowboy, Screaming!, Don't Lose your Head, Follow that Camel, Doctor, Up the Khyber, Camping, Again Doctor, Up the Jungle, Loving, Henry, At your Convenience, Abroad, Girls, Dick, Behind, That's Carry On, Emmannuelle), Original Music (Carry On Laughing's Christmas Classics (TV)) - *See also Cast*

Other Notable Productions: Dr. No (Conductor, 1962), Nurse on Wheels (Composer, 1963), The Big Job (Composer, 1965), Three Hats for Lisa (Composer, 1966), Doctor in Trouble (Composer, 1970), Bless this House (Composer, 1972), No Sex Please we're British (Composer, 1975)

Seen & Heard:
BBC Proms – Music from Great British Films (BBC Television, 28/07/2007)

ROGERS, PETER

Born: 20/02/1914, Rochester, Kent, UK
Died: 14/04/2009, Buckinghamshire, UK

First Film: Dear Murderer (Screenplay, 1947)
First Carry On: Carry On Sergeant (Producer, 1958)
Final Film: Carry On Columbus (Executive Producer, 1992)

Carry Ons: Producer (Sergeant-Emmannuelle), Executive Producer (Carry On Christmas 1972 (TV), Carry On Christmas 1973 (TV), Carry On Laughing (TV) - all), Producer (Carry On Laughing 1981 (TV), What a Carry On 1984 (TV), Laugh with the Carry Ons 1993 (TV))

Other Notable Productions: Circus Friends (Screenplay, 1956), Time Lock (Screenplay, Producer, 1957), Ivanhoe (Sydney Box Productions for ITV, Executive Producer, 1958), Please Turn Over (Producer, 1960), Watch your Stern (Producer, 1961), Raising the Wind (Producer, 1961), Twice Round the Daffodils (Producer, 1962), Nurse on Wheels (Producer, 1963), The Big Job (Producer, 1965), Bless this House (Producer, 1972)

Seen & Heard:
Film Night Special - Carry On Forever (BBC2, 12/04/1970)

Desert Island Discs (BBC Radio, 20/10/1973)
What's a Carry On? (ITV, 29/12/1998)
British Film Forever (BBC Television, 2007)

Further Reading:
Mr Carry On: The Biography of Peter Rogers by Morris Bright & Robert Ross, BBC
Books, 2000 (ISBN: 0563551836)

Roome, Alfred: Editor (Follow that Camel, Doctor, Up the Khyber, Camping, Again Doctor,
Up the Jungle, Loving, Henry, At your Convenience, Matron, Abroad, Girls, Dick, Behind)

ROTHWELL, TALBOT

Born: 12th November 1916, Bromley, UK
Died: 28th February 1981, Worthing, UK

First Film: Is Your Honeymoon Really Necessary? (Screenplay, 1953)
First Carry On: Carry On Cabby (Screenplay, 1963)
Final Film: Carry On Dick (Screenplay, 1974)

Carry Ons: Screenplay (Cabby, Jack, Spying (w/Sid Colin), Cleo, Cowboy, Screaming!
Don't Lose your Head, Follow that Camel, Doctor, Up the Khyber, Camping, Again
Doctor, Up the Jungle, Loving, Henry, At your Convenience, Matron, Abroad, Girls, Dick),
Script (Carry On Christmas 1969 (TV)), Script (Carry On Christmas 1972 (TV)), Script
(Carry On Christmas 1973 (TV)), Original Material (Carry On Laughing's Christmas
Classics (TV)), Script (Carry On London! (stage))

Other Notable Productions: Make Mine a Million (Screenplay, 1959), The Big Job
(Screenplay, 1965), Three Hats for Lisa (Screenplay, 1966), Up Pompeii (Writer, BBC
Television, 1969-1970, 1975)

Seen & Heard:
This is Your Life: Talbot Rothwell (Thames Television, 9/12/1970)

Further Reading:
Queen Elizabeth Slept Here by Talbot Rothwell, English Theatre Guild, 1951 (ISBN:
B0000CI1VT)

Rudge, Myles: Co-Writer "Carry On Screaming!" Theme w/Ted Dick (Screaming!)

S

St. John Roper, R: Costumes (Carry On London! (stage))
Scaife, Ted: Director of Photography (Constable)
Schwarz, Lew: Script (Carry On Laughing - One in the Eye for Harold (TV), Carry On
Laughing - Under the Round Table (TV), Carry On Laughing - And in My Lady's Chamber
(TV), Carry On Laughing - Short Knight, Long Daze (TV), Carry On Laughing - Who
Needs Kitchener? (TV), Carry On Laughing - Lamp Posts of the Empire (TV))
Seddon, Jack: Co-Author, Screenplay (England)

Selby-Walker, Emma: Costume Designer (Screaming!, Don't Lose your Head, Follow that Camel, Up the Khyber)

Serpant, Leonard: Standby Stagehand (Columbus)

Shampan, Jack: Art Director (Jack, Emmannuelle)

Shaw, Tommy: Choreographer (Carry On London! (stage))

Sherman, Aaron: Prosthetics (Ear) (Columbus)

Sherriff, Betty: Hairdresser (Emmannuelle)

Shirley, John: Editor (Nurse, Teacher, Constable, Regardless, Cruising)

Skeggs, James: Company Stage Manager (Wot a Carry On in Blackpool (stage))

Skinner, Audrey: Assistant to Peter Rogers & Gerald Thomas (Columbus)

Smith, Sue: Deputy Stage Manager (Carry On Laughing with "The Slimming Factory" (stage))

Snel, Otto: Sound Recordist (Emmannuelle), Chief Dubbing Editor (Columbus)

Staffell, Laurell: Dress Designer (Teacher)

Stephens, Jack: Art Director (Cabby)

Stevens, CC: Sound Recordist (Spying, Screaming!)

Stevens, Norman: Music Associate (Carry On Christmas 1973 (TV))

Steward, Ernest: Director of Photography (Up the Khyber, Camping, Again Doctor, Up the Jungle, Loving, At your Convenience, Matron, Dick, Behind, England)

Swinburne, Jack: Production Manager (Don't Lose your Head, Follow that Camel, Doctor, Up the Khyber, Camping, Again Doctor, Up the Jungle, Loving, Henry, At your Convenience, Matron, Abroad)

T

Taksen, Arthur: Set Dresser (Nurse)

Tarrant, Alan: Producer/Director (Carry On Christmas 1970 (TV), What a Carry On! (TV), Carry On Laughing (TV) - all)

Tattersall, Richard: Music (Carry On Laughing (TV) - all)

Tasker, Ann: Unit Publicist (Columbus)

Tandy, Gareth: Assistant Director

Taylor, Gerry: Vision Control (Carry On Laughing - The Case of the Screaming Winkles (TV), Carry On Laughing - The Case of the Coughing Parrot (TV))

Taylor, Jeremy: Master of Horse (Cowboy, Don't Lose your Head)

Taylor, Kevin: Dubbing Mixer (Columbus)

THOMAS, GERALD

Born: 10th December 1920, Hull, UK
Died: 9th November 1993, Buckinghamshire, UK

First Film: The Twenty Questions Murder Mystery (Editor, 1950)
First Carry On: Carry On Sergeant (1958)
Final Film: Carry On Columbus (1992)

Carry Ons: Director (All), Comedy Consultant (Carry On Christmas 1969 (TV), Carry On Christmas 1970 (TV)), Producer (Carry On Christmas 1972 (TV), Carry On Christmas 1973 (TV), Carry On Laughing (TV) - all, Carry On Laughing's Christmas Classics (TV)), *See also Cast*

Other Notable Productions: Doctor in the House (Editor, 1954), Above Us the Waves (Editor, 1955), Circus Friends (Director, 1956), Time Lock (Director, 1957), Please Turn Over (Director, 1960), Watch your Stern (Director, 1961), Raising the Wind (Director, 1961), Twice Round the Daffodils (Director, 1962), Nurse on Wheels (Director, 1963), The Big Job (Director, 1965), Bless This House (Director, 1972), Carry On Laughing (Director, Thames Television, 1981), What a Carry On (Director, BBC Television, 1984), Laugh with the Carry Ons (Director / Editor, Central Television, 1993)

Seen & Heard:
Film Night Special - Carry On Forever (BBC 2, 12/04/1970)
The Electric Theatre Show – Carry On England (Grampian, 1976)

Thomson, HAR: Director of Photography, Locations (Up the Khyber)
Tillotson, Judi: Wardrobe Mistress (Carry On Laughing with "The Slimming Factory" (stage))
Tingey, Cynthia: Costume Designer (Cowboy)
Tobert, Ralph: Choir Routine (Carry On Christmas 1969 (TV))
Toms, Donald: Unit Manager (Cabby, Jack, Spying, Cleo)
Torbett, Charles: Property Master (Columbus)

U
Unsworth, Maggie: Script Supervisor

V
Van Raay, Frank: Costumes (Carry On Christmas 1970 (TV))
Vetchinsky, Alex: Art Director (Sergeant, Nurse, Spying, Follow that Camel, Up the Khyber, Up the Jungle)
Vosburgh, Dick: Script (Wot a Carry On in Blackpool (stage)), Script (Carry On Laughing - Orgy & Bess (TV))

W
Wain, Gerry: Master of Horse (Dick)
Waller, Anthony: Designer (Carry On Laughing - And in My Lady's Chamber (TV), Carry On Laughing - Who Needs Kitchener? (TV))
Wallder, George: Graphics (Carry On Laughing (TV) - all)
Waters, Kathryn: Costume Designer (Wot a Carry On in Blackpool (stage))
Watson, Claude: Unit Manager (Regardless)
Waye, Anthony: Assistant Director (Jack)
Weingreen, Peter: Assistant Director (Up the Khyber)
West, Alan: Manager & Stage Director (Carry On London! (stage))
Whitcutt, Mike: Camera (Carry On Laughing - The Case of the Screaming Winkles (TV), Carry On Laughing - The Case of the Coughing Parrot (TV), Carry On Laughing - Under the Round Table (TV), Carry On Laughing - Short Knight, Long Daze (TV), Carry On Laughing - And in My Lady's Chamber (TV), Carry On Laughing - Who Needs Kitchener? (TV), Carry On Laughing - Lamp Posts of the Empire (TV))
White, Betty: Casting Director (Sergeant, Nurse, Teacher, Constable, Regardless, Cruising)
White, Jason: Stunt Arranger (Columbus)

White, Ray: Designer (Carry On Laughing - The Baron Outlook (TV), Carry On Laughing - One in the Eye for Harold (TV))
Wiggins, Leslie: Sound Editor (Teacher, Constable)
Williams, Brock: Original Concept (Constable)
Williams, David: Standby Carpenter (Columbus)
Winterborn, Brian: Production Buyer (Columbus)
Wyer, Reginald: Director of Photography (Nurse, Teacher), Co-Author, Original Treatment (Dick)

ACKNOWLEDGEMENTS

The book you hold in your hands is the product of years of research, not just by myself but also a lively and extremely generous community of Carry On fans around the world. In particular, I would like to thank the readers of Carry On Line and The Whippit Inn for their support and enthusiasm.

Special thanks to Brett Tremble and Graeme Johnston for taking on the daunting task of checking my scribblings for accuracy and to Peter West for casting his professional eye over the manuscript. The efforts of these three gents mean the following pages are devoid of words I've made up, dates I've serially failed to remember and numerous other errors and cock-ups.

Thanks also to thank Matt West and Robert Hammond for supporting the book from day one, to Jess Pillings for packaging it in my very own Carry On film poster and to Mark Frost for taking on the mammoth task of translating what I thought a book should look like into something altogether more entertaining.

Finally, and most importantly, thanks to Peter Rogers, Gerald Thomas and the cast and crew of the Carry Ons for giving us so many laughs over the years. May their legend live forever.

JAUNT

AN UNOFFICIAL GUIDE TO
THE TOMORROW PEOPLE

by Andy Davidson

Shape-changing robots, military masterminds, ITV technicians – it's a deadly universe out there, but the Tomorrow People are here to help.

The Tomorrow People are man's next step up the evolutionary ladder: Homo superior. From their secret base deep below the streets of London, they offer hope of a better future for the human race as members of the all-powerful Galactic Federation.

Jaunt follows **The Tomorrow People** from its origins in the creative melting-pot of 1970s children's television to a worldwide hit. It revisits them in the 1990s for some light-hearted **Avengers**-style action and returns a decade later for a series of bold, challenging audio plays.

Homo superior has been with us for forty years, and **Jaunt** chronicles the phenomenon that is again preparing to return to our screens in a big-budget US adaptation.

Jaunt includes exclusive interviews with series creator Roger Price, producer Ruth Boswell and the Tomorrow People themselves – Nicholas Young, Peter Vaughan Clarke, Elizabeth Adare, Mike Holoway and Misako Koba.

With an introduction from Roger Price, **Jaunt** also features the complete script of the unmade ninth series adventure *Mystery Moon*.

ISBN 978-1-908630-23-0

A is for Avon, Z is for Xenon Base

MAXIMUM POWER!

THE COMPLETE, UNAUTHORISED GUIDE TO ALL 64 EPISODES OF BLAKE'S 7!

by Matthew West, Andrew Orton, Chris Orton, Phil Ware, Andy Davidson & Robert Hammond

Maximum Power! is a new **Blake's 7** programme guide telling the full untold story (aside from all the other books), most of which we made up, about this fantastic, ridiculous, fun and silly BBC TV hit series.

What you can't learn from this book you could fit in a matchbox. Spray it silver. Stick a ping pong ball on it. Some staples. The nozzle from a glue bottle. Tie a bit of string to the top, dangle it from a light fitting and call it a Zeta Class Pursuit Ship.

With a foreword from second Federation trooper on the left (uncredited), Harry 'Aitch' Fielder, this book is set to break new sales records for **Blake's 7** merchandise – we might just shift more than twenty of them.

100% of authors' proceeds from this book will be equally divided between three charities – Great Ormond Street Hospital, Great North Air Ambulance and Asthma UK.

ISBN 978-1-908630-00-1

JN-T

THE LIFE & SCANDALOUS TIMES OF

by Richard Marson

For more than a decade, John Nathan-Turner, or 'JN-T' as he was often known, was in charge of every major artistic and practical decision affecting the world's longest-running science fiction programme, **Doctor Who**. Richard Marson brings his dramatic, farcical, sometimes scandalous and often moving story to life with the benefit of his own inside knowledge and the fruits of over 100 revealing interviews with key friends and colleagues, those John loved and those from whom he became estranged. The author has also had access to all of Nathan-Turner's surviving archive of paperwork and photos, many of which appear here for the very first time.

"Extraordinary. A great piece of work. I read it in two days' flat, I couldn't stop. I've never seen a biographer enter the story like that, it was brilliant and invigorating. It really is a major piece of **Doctor Who** history and the history of an entire industry. An entire age, really. In the end, I think the book is clear - we have to forgive JN-T. That ending - he didn't deserve that. And I think by writing about it, you have made something elegant and even beautiful out of such a wretched mess. And I think that's very kind of you indeed. This book says a lot about JN-T but it says a lot about your good and kind heart too."

Russell T.Davies (Writer/Producer)

ISBN 978-1-908630-13-1

JUSTYCE SERVED

A SMALL START WITH A BIG FINISH
AN ALTERNATIVE DOCTOR WHO AUDIO UNIVERSE

by Alun Harris and Matthew West

In 1984 a group of **Doctor Who** fans began a project which would continue for another decade and eventually lead to much greater things.

Audio Visuals: Audio Adventures in Time & Space were a non-profit, fan endeavour creating full-cast audio **Doctor Who** drama. 27 plays later the majority of the creative team would go on to be involved with Big Finish, an officially licensed range of **Doctor Who** audio dramas.

For many fans Audio Visuals seem almost canon. Nicholas Briggs was our Doctor. We remember the Daleks' destruction of Gallifrey before it even happened on TV. We supported our Doctor through drug addiction, companion-loss and the horror of Justyce.

This book is a guide to those days.

With contributions from Nicholas Briggs, Gary Russell, Nigel Fairs, John Ainsworth, John Wadmore, Alistair Lock, Patricia Merrick, Richard Marson, Jim Mortimore, Andy Lane, Chris M Corney and many others, all wrapped up in a new cover by Tim Keable.

Celebrate **Doctor Who** fan creativity at its very best.

100% OF THE THE AUTHORS' PROFITS FROM THIS BOOK WILL BE DONATED TO INVEST IN M.E and AMNESTY INTERNATIONAL UK.

ISBN 978-1-908630-03-2

← Turn Left

An Unofficial & Unauthorised Guide to Doctor Who Road Signs

'When I first heard about this book, I had a feeling that I might like it, that it might appeal to my own, slightly left-field, sense of humour. I was wrong. **Turn Left** exceeds every expectation I had. I absolutely adore it. **10 out of 10.**'

Starburst Magazine

by Andy X. Cable

Many *Doctor Who* fans love to collect things whether it's old episodes, books, scripts, replica costumes or used underwear; they'll collect it to the very end. Andy Cable used to have a website which drew well over two million hits in just a week and his love for **Doctor Who** couldn't have been stronger, but when his collection was cruelly taken away he bounced back and started a new collection.

Armed only with his little black book and a small blue pen he'd got from Argos he began listing and cataloguing **Doctor Who** related road signs and now his collection, which he's spent very nearly seven months working on, is presented here in what he hopes will be the first of several volumes. His passion will become your passion in this genuine and thrilling fanatical page-turner.

ISBN 978-1-908630-14-8

YOU AND WHO

CONTACT HAS BEEN MADE
VOLUMES ONE & TWO

Edited by J.R. Southall and Christopher Bryant

As it enters its anniversary year, **Doctor Who** is more popular than ever before. This wholly original blend of science fiction concepts and magical storytelling, updated for the 21st century, is delighting a whole new generation of fans, alongside those of us who waited patiently for the inevitable regeneration.

You and Who: Contact Has Been Made Volume One is a record of how that relationship began, covering the 26 'classic' years of the series, as written by the show's own fans.

You and Who: Contact Has Been Made Volume Two continues from Volume 1, following the show going from strength to strength in the 21st century, as written by the show's own fans.

THESE BOOKS ARE PRODUCED IN AID OF CHILDREN IN NEED.

ISBN 978-1-908630-36-0 / ISBN 978-1-908630-37-7

COMING SOON FROM MIWK PUBLISHING

MAC
THE LIFE AND WORK OF MALCOLM HULKE

by John Williams

Malcolm Hulke wrote some of the best-loved *Doctor Who* stories and novelizations and his work continues to be influential long after his premature death in 1979. All the various manifestations of *Doctor Who* since then, including the Big Finish audio adventures and the 2005 series have returned regularly to his creations, particularly the Silurians and Sea Devils, but also to his abiding ideas and themes.

Despite this enduring influence, little is known about the man himself aside from his background as a member of the Communist Party of Great Britain and the bare facts of his career as a writer. That career involved writing for some landmark television series including **Armchair Theatre**, **Pathfinders in Space**, **The Avengers**, **Crossroads** and, of course, **Doctor Who**.

Hulke was the writers' writer. He was always professional, never missed a deadline and would take pride in turning his hand to anything. Although engaged in an intensely solitary profession he constantly forged alliances either with other writers such as Eric Paice and Terrance Dicks, or enthusiastically engaged with socially significant group endeavours such as Unity Theatre or the Writers' Guild. All these aspects of his life will be explored in depth and add to the picture of a complex and paradoxical individual.

ISBN 978-1-908630-09-4

NOW WHAT?

An Unofficial & Unauthorised Guide to Luther

by Robert Hammond

Detective Chief Inspector John Luther is a near-genius obsessed by the violent cases and their perpetrators in his work for the Serious Crime Unit – an obsession that has a profound effect on him, those he works with, and those he loves.

A masked killer, violent diamond thieves, a former squaddy executing police officers, a traitor within the ranks of his own staff... all part of the daily grind for Luther, with its accompanying darkness that threatens to corrupt his morals and methods, and push him further toward the dirtier end of policing.

Luther – a worldwide television hit that won leading man Idris Elba the Golden Globe award for best miniseries actor in 2011.

Now What? is a comprehensive handbook to all three critically-acclaimed series. It includes previously unseen script extracts, facts, location information, new interviews, a complete episode guide, plus a foreword and exclusive contributions from the series creator and writer, Neil Cross.

ISBN 978-1-908630-67-4

COMING SOON FROM MIWK PUBLISHING

THE QUEST FOR PEDLER
THE LIFE AND IDEAS OF DR KIT PEDLER

by Michael Seely

For many people, Kit Pedler is best remembered as the man who created the Cybermen for **Doctor Who**, a real life scientist who was brought in to act as an advisor and bring some science to the fiction. The Cybermen were his ultimate scientific horror: where the very nature of a man was altered by himself, by his own genius for survival, creating a monster. Pedler was that rare animal, a scientist with an imagination. He liked to think 'What if...?'

With two doctorates to his name, and as Head of Anatomy at the Institute of Ophthalmology investigating the nature of the retina, Dr. Kit Pedler began to share the suspicions being voiced in the 1960s towards the role of the scientist in society, who saw research as an end to itself and left the moral dilemmas to the politicians in a world where the people were conditioned to accept an intolerable environment. He was at the beginnings of the 'Soft' or 'Alternative Technology' movement that wanted to develop a sustainable science that would not deplete the world of its natural resources or poison the environment with its pollution.

Before his premature death in 1981, he had just finished a documentary series for ITV called **Mind Over Matter**, which was the first serious look at the world of the paranormal through the eyes of his enquiring and rational, but imaginative mind.

With contributions from his family, friends, colleagues and critics, this book tells the story behind a fascinating, charismatic, complicated, and demanding human being; a natural teacher who didn't just want to pontificate about the problems facing the world in a television or radio studio, but actually do something practical about them.

ISBN 978-1-908630-1-24

www.miwk.com

www.facebook.com/MiwkPublishingLtd

www.twitter.com/#!/MiwkPublishing